Homeland SECURITY
AN INTRODUCTION

Dr. Richard H. WARD
Associate Vice President for Research
Professor of Criminal Justice
Sam Houston State University
Huntsville, Texas

Dr. Kathleen L. KIERNAN
Assistant Director (Ret.)
Bureau of ATF
Adjunct Professor of Criminal Justice
Sam Houston State University
Huntsville, Texas

Dr. Daniel MABREY
Director
Institute for the Study of Violent Groups
Criminal Justice Center
Sam Houston State University
Huntsville, Texas

 LexisNexis®

 anderson publishing
A member of the LexisNexis Group

Homeland Security: An Introduction

Copyright © 2006
> Matthew Bender & Company, Inc., a member of the LexisNexis Group

Phone 877-374-2919
Web Site www.lexisnexis.com/anderson/criminaljustice

Ward, Richard H.
    Homeland security: an introduction -- 1st Ed.
  Richard H. Ward, Kathleen L. Kiernan, Daniel Mabrey
      Includes bibliographical references and index.
      ISBN 1-59345-304-3 (paperback)

Front cover illustration by Kamil Vojnar
Cover design by Tin Box Studio, Inc./Cincinnati, Ohio

EDITOR Janice Eccleston
ACQUISITIONS EDITOR Michael C. Braswell

Dedication

Dr. Ward dedicates this book to his wife, Michelle, his children Jeanne Marie, Jonathan Berkeley and Michelle Sophia, and grandchildren, Declan and Keeley.

Dr. Kiernan dedicates this book to her husband Joseph and family and to law enforcement colleagues who have been involved in homeland security for generations.

Dr. Mabrey dedicates this book to his parents, Joel and Nancy Mabrey, and to his brother Clint.

Acknowledgments

We are especially indebted to Ginny Wilson, Jane Buckwalter, Julia Maddox, Melissa Mugno, and Cali Luco, without whom this book would not have been possible, for their many contributions. Debra McCall, for her invaluable assistance as executive administrative assistant to Dr. Ward; and Amanda Burris, all at Sam Houston State University.

A great many individuals have contributed to this book and, at the risk of omitting someone, the authors would like to express their appreciation to:

Sam Houston State University
Harriet Brewster
Dr. James Dozier
Chris Fisher
Megan Good
Dr. John Miller
Joseph Serio
Martha Whatley
Dr. Steve Young

Taiwan National Police
Wen Chih "Billy" Huang
Shih-ya "Connie" Kuo

Chinese People's Public Security University
Dr. Jianming Mei

Montgomery County Sheriff's Office
Corporal Jermaine Jenkins
Deputy Mike Plata

Law Enforcement Management Institute of Texas (LEMIT)
Josh Lyons
Jay Stahle
Rita Watkins
David Webb

Institute for the Study of Violent Groups (ISVG)
Sameer Abdelmottlep
Patrick Alexander

Sajeewa Amaradasa
Hasan Arslan
Megan Crank
Michael Coates
Phillip Davis
Stephen Dufour
Gabriel Eid
Tarik Eser (Turkish National Police)
Joseph French
Victor Ghanie (Botswana National Police)
Dr. Chris Hale
Jeff Handy
Phillip Hensley
Josh Hill
John Hitzeman
Austin Huckabee
David Kahn
Seksan Khruakham (Royal Thai Police)
Tony Leal
Wanhee Lee
Andrew Link
Vesna Markovic
Duncan McCallum
Jairo Patino
Prapon Sahapattana (Royal Thai Police)
Erick Swickheimer
Minwoo Yun

Individuals
Joseph Booth, LTC—Louisiana State Police Department
Dr. Hakan Can—Pennsylvania State University–Harrisburg
William Casey—Deputy Superintendent, Boston Police Department
Bill Dyson, (FBI, Ret.)—Institute for Intergovernmental Research
Dennis Fasioni—Bureau of Alcohol, Tobacco, Firearms, and Explosives
Dr. Robert Hanser—Kaplan University and University of Louisiana at Monroe
Dr. Cindy Hill—Mahina Group
Dr. Sean Hill—Mahina Group
Dr. Sean Malinowski—Los Angeles Police Department
Roger Massey—National Security Agency
Shaun McKey
Dr. Nathan Moran—Midwestern State University
David Peters—University of Illinois at Chicago Police Department
Timothy R. Sample—President, Intelligence and National Security Alliance
Lt. Julio Sanchez—U.S. Army
Dr. Gene Scaramella—Kaplan University

Robert Schmidt—President, Infragard NMA
Frank Sleeter—Chief, Sun Prairie Police Department, Wisconsin
Tim Stone—FBI

We are indebted also to our editor at LexisNexis, Janice Eccleston, whose skilled hand helped bring together the writing of three contributors from very different points of reference.

A great many others made suggestions and provided assistance, and we apologize to those who we may have failed to list here.

Finally, and certainly not least, we would like to thank our families for their support over the years.

Preface

This book is designed to serve as a primary text for those interested in Homeland Security, and will also serve as an ancillary text in introductory criminal justice or terrorism-related courses.

The authors of this book bring more than 65 years of experience in the broad field of criminal justice, and a wealth of knowledge about the subject of terrorism and organizational theory. They have taught, visited, or served as consultants in more than 75 countries, frequently working with law enforcement and military personnel in those regions where terrorism has a long history.

Dr. Richard H. Ward, a former New York City detective, has served in executive administrative positions at John Jay College of Criminal Justice, the University of Illinois at Chicago, and most recently as Associate Vice President for Research and Special Programs, following seven years as Dean and Director of the College and Criminal Justice Center at Sam Houston State University (SHSU). He has served as a consultant or advisor to numerous countries throughout the world on counterterrorism and international organized crime, and as an advisor to police departments throughout the United States. He holds his doctorate from the University of California at Berkeley.

Dr. Kathleen L. Kiernan retired as Assistant Director of the Bureau of Alcohol, Tobacco and Firearms Office of Strategic Intelligence and Information after 29 years of government service. Currently the CEO of an international consulting firm specializing in law enforcement and intelligence, she holds her doctorate from Northern Illinois University.

Dr. Daniel Mabrey currently serves as Director of the Institute for the Study of Violent Groups at Sam Houston State University. He is a certified State and Local Anti-Terrorism Trainer (SLATT) and has lectured throughout the world on terrorism-related issues. He completed his Ph.D. at the College of Criminal Justice (SHSU).

Table of Contents

Part III
Homeland Security Strategies and Initiatives   137

Chapter 7
Critical Infrastructure Protection   139

Chapter 8
Transportation Infrastructure in the U.S.   159

List of Figures and Tables

Threats Against the United States and the Creation of Homeland Security

The Department of Homeland Security (DHS) was created in the aftermath of the September 11, 2001 attacks on the World Trade Center in New York City, the Pentagon in Washington DC, and the downing of United Flight 93 in Shanksville, Pennsylvania. The creation of DHS represented the single greatest reorganization of government since the creation of the Department of Defense after World War II. Under DHS, 22 federal agencies and more than 180,000 federal workers were consolidated into a single department for the sole purpose of ensuring the security of the United States within its continental borders.

Part I of this text attempts to place the creation of DHS within a historical context of the threats that have faced the United States in recent history as well as chronicle the reforms and restructuring of the various law enforcement and intelligence agencies, the military, and private sector changes in the past 50 years. From the left-wing threats of the 1960s and 1970s to the rise of the right wing and the militia movement in the late 1980s and 1990s, it is important to realize that the threats to homeland security predate the 9/11 attacks and many of these threats remain. That said, the 9/11 attacks were the sole impetus behind creating the Department of Homeland Security, and the resulting global war on terrorism will be ongoing for the foreseeable future.

The rapidly changing global jihadist threat, although existing since the early 1990s, became real to America's policymakers and general public when the 19 hijackers crashed four airliners into targets on American soil in 2001. The details of this attack are chronicled in this book because this represented the starting point for crafting America's homeland security strategy. These attacks exposed the vulnerable underbelly of America's homeland defense apparatus, and the first three years of DHS' existence have been directed at preventing another 9/11-type attack.

In the immediate aftermath of the 9/11 attacks, U.S. lawmakers and the Bush Administration convened a special commission to investigate the 9/11 attacks and the weaknesses in U.S. national security that prevented the identification and interdiction of the terrorist plot. This commission, known as the 9/11 Commission, produced one of the most widely read and highly acclaimed government reports in the history of the United States detailing the 9/11 plot, the weaknesses and vulnerabilities in the national security system, and made recommendations about how to improve national security to prevent attacks like 9/11 from ever happening again. In terms of homeland security, the 9/11 Commission Report is one of the most important documents because it lays out the areas within homeland security that require the most resources and attention. The details of the 9/11 Commission and its 567-page report are detailed in this text because of their importance in guiding the homeland security mission of the United States.

Finally, Part I addresses the creation of the Department of Homeland Security and outlines some of its early efforts to shore up the existing homeland mechanisms within the U.S. law enforcement and intelligence agencies and the military.

Chapter 1

Protecting the Homeland

INTRODUCTION

Prior to the September 11, 2001, air attacks on the World Trade Center and the Pentagon, few Americans were aware of or familiar with the concept known today as homeland security. Not since World War II has there been such a collective response to threats aimed at the United States. There has been a massive reorganization of government at the federal, state, and local level. There have been major changes in our legal systems, the private sector, and the everyday lives of citizens at work and at leisure. Homeland security is now more than an idea developed by government planners: it is a new aspect of our society that encompasses physical security, law enforcement, the judiciary, laws, and the political system, as well as food and agricultural production. Health care, travel, immigration, and the quality of life in a democratic environment have been impacted by the concept of homeland security.

THE BEGINNING

To understand this phenomenal change in American life, it is worthwhile to examine the historical and political components of mass violence, terrorism, large scale domestic threats, and world events that set the stage for a complete transformation and rethinking of America's security, and the place of the United States in the world.

Violence and terrorism are not alien to American culture. One of the earliest violent groups that engendered broad appeal, mostly in the South, was the Ku Klux Klan, which flourished even after the Civil War. There are other groups which threaten everything from racial and religious freedom to the freedom of ideas. The impact of globalism, a corporate culture, increasing federalism and the slow decline of an emphasis on states' rights has also changed the way Americans live.

Figure 1.1 Immigration by Region and Selected Country of Last Residence

	Immigration by Region and Selected Country of Last Residence													
	1820–1840	1841–1860	1861–1880	1881–1900	1901–1910	1911–1920	1921–1930	1931–1950	1951–1970	1971–1990	1991–2002	2003	2004	Total 183 Years 1820–2004
Total Number of Immigrants to USA	750,949	4,311,465	5,127,015	8,934,177	8,795,386	5,735,811	4,107,209	1,563,470	5,837,156	11,831,376	11,223,467	705,827	946,142	69,869,450
Europe	602,168	4,050,019	4,337,066	8,290,836	8,056,040	4,321,887	2,463,194	968,713	2,449,219	1,561,918	1,715,222	102,843	130,151	39,049,276
Austria-Hungary	—	—	80,769	946,426	2,145,266	836,342	63,548	39,753	129,765	40,913	31,216	2,181	3,683	4,319,862
Austria	—	—	70,133	460,119	668,209	453,649	32,868	28,423	87,727	27,818	19,161	1,163	2,442	1,851,712
Hungary	—	—	10,444	308,969	808,511	442,693	30,680	11,330	42,038	13,095	12,055	1,018	1,241	1,682,074
Belgium	50	9,812	13,955	38,344	41,635	33,746	15,846	17,006	27,767	12,395	8,934	518	746	220,754
Czechoslovakia	—	—	—	—	—	3,426	102,194	22,740	4,191	13,250	13,599	1,474	1,870	162,744
Denmark	1,252	4,288	48,865	138,363	65,285	41,983	32,430	7,952	20,185	9,809	7,475	436	568	378,891
France	54,443	153,620	108,192	81,234	73,379	61,897	49,610	51,432	96,358	57,422	45,847	2,933	4,209	840,576
Germany	160,183	1,386,293	1,505,650	1,958,122	341,498	143,945	412,202	340,636	668,561	166,375	135,757	8,102	10,270	7,237,594
Greece	69	47	282	18,287	167,519	184,201	51,084	18,092	133,577	130,746	30,241	914	1,213	736,272
Ireland	261,719	1,694,838	872,649	1,043,898	339,065	146,181	211,234	30,762	81,328	43,459	59,919	1,010	1,518	4,787,580
Italy	2,692	11,101	67,484	959,202	2,045,877	1,109,524	455,315	125,689	399,602	196,622	68,936	1,904	2,495	5,446,443
Netherlands	2,539	19,040	25,643	80,459	48,262	43,718	26,948	22,010	82,883	22,730	17,508	1,329	1,713	394,782
Norway-Sweden	1,295	34,834	320,543	889,643	440,039	161,469	165,780	29,465	77,232	25,654	22,551	1,520	2,011	2,172,036
Norway	—	—	95,323	271,601	190,505	66,395	68,531	14,840	38,419	8,105	6,230	386	457	760,792
Sweden	—	—	115,922	618,042	249,534	95,074	97,249	14,625	38,813	17,549	16,321	1,134	1,554	1,265,817
Poland	390	1,269	14,997	148,526	69,149	4,813	277,734	24,597	63,524	120,486	189,406	11,016	13,972	870,730
Portugal	1,009	1,605	16,740	44,486	69,149	89,732	29,994	10,752	95,653	142,141	25,890	821	1,062	529,034
Romania	—	—	11	19,098	53,008	13,311	67,646	4,947	3,570	43,250	61,952	3,311	4,064	274,168
Soviet Union	366	1,008	41,796	718,572	1,597,306	921,201	61,742	1,941	3,136	96,638	573,437	33,563	36,646	4,087,352
Spain	4,741	11,507	11,963	13,150	27,935	68,611	28,958	6,156	52,553	59,574	20,649	1,107	1,453	308,357
Switzerland	8,078	29,655	51,579	113,167	34,922	23,091	29,676	16,059	36,128	17,084	15,140	867	1,193	376,639
United Kingdom	103,299	691,018	1,154,939	1,078,895	525,950	341,408	339,570	170,878	416,646	296,547	190,181	11,220	16,680	5,337,231
Yugoslavia	—	—	—	—	—	1,888	49,064	7,411	28,606	49,302	116,594	8,296	13,211	274,372
Other Europe	43	84	1,009	964	39,945	31,400	42,619	20,435	27,954	17,521	79,990	10,321	11,574	283,859
Asia	91	41,679	188,919	144,804	323,543	247,236	112,059	53,623	580,891	4,326,335	3,460,109	236,039	314,489	10,029,817
China	11	41,432	187,502	76,510	20,605	21,278	29,907	21,637	44,421	471,073	525,909	37,395	45,942	1,523,622
Hong Kong	—	—	—	—	—	—	—	—	90,548	211,682	128,038	5,020	5,421	440,709
India	48	79	232	337	4,713	2,082	1,886	2,257	29,162	414,920	495,840	47,157	65,472	1,064,185
Iran	—	—	—	—	—	—	241	1,575	13,727	161,308	84,349	4,709	5,898	271,807
Israel	—	—	—	—	—	—	—	476	55,078	81,986	49,260	3,719	5,206	195,725
Japan	—	—	335	28,212	129,797	83,837	33,462	3,503	86,238	96,860	87,556	6,724	8,652	565,176
Korea	—	—	—	—	—	—	—	107	40,757	601,384	204,213	12,177	19,441	878,079

Figure 1.1, continued

Total Number of Immigrants to USA	1820-1840	1841-1860	1861-1880	1881-1900	1901-1910	1911-1920	1921-1930	1931-1950	1951-1970	1971-1990	1991-2002	2003	2004	Total 183 Years 1820-2004
	750,949	4,311,465	5,127,015	8,934,177	8,795,386	5,735,811	4,107,209	1,563,470	5,837,156	11,831,376	11,223,467	705,827	946,142	69,869,450
Philippines	—	—	—	—	—	—	—	5,219	117,683	903,751	603,489	43,258	54,632	1,728,032
Turkey	28	142	535	34,207	157,369	134,066	33,824	1,863	13,661	36,632	45,623	3,332	4,489	465,771
Vietnam	—	—	—	—	—	—	—	—	4,675	453,602	353,218	21,270	30,064	862,829
Other Asia	4	26	315	5,538	11,059	5,973	12,739	16,986	84,941	893,137	882,614	51,278	69,272	2,033,882
America	**45,375**	**137,189**	**570,651**	**465,939**	**361,888**	**1,143,671**	**1,516,716**	**514,841**	**2,713,318**	**5,597,960**	**5,438,934**	**306,793**	**407,471**	**19,220,746**
Canada & Newfoundland	16,110	101,032	537,518	396,615	179,226	742,185	924,515	280,245	791,262	326,877	249,489	16,555	22,437	4,584,066
Mexico	11,417	6,349	7,353	2,884	49,642	219,004	459,287	82,908	753,748	2,296,137	2,671,583	114,984	173,664	6,848,960
Caribbean	16,299	24,188	23,003	62,108	107,548	123,424	74,899	65,227	593,304	1,613,177	1,169,985	67,660	81,893	4,022,715
Cuba	—	—	—	—	—	—	15,901	35,884	287,484	409,441	222,915	8,722	15,385	995,732
Dominican Republic	—	—	—	—	—	—	—	6,777	103,189	400,170	378,981	26,157	30,049	945,323
Haiti	—	—	—	—	—	—	—	1,102	38,941	194,714	221,368	11,942	13,502	481,569
Jamaica	—	—	—	—	—	—	—	—	83,775	345,725	198,893	13,082	13,565	655,040
Other Caribbean	16,299	24,188	23,003	62,108	107,548	123,424	58,998	21,464	79,915	263,127	147,828	7,757	9,392	945,051
Central America	151	817	252	953	8,192	17,159	15,769	27,526	146,081	602,728	666,498	53,435	60,299	1,599,860
El Salvador	—	—	—	—	—	—	—	5,805	20,887	247,975	277,391	27,915	29,285	609,258
Other Central America	151	817	252	953	8,192	17,159	15,769	21,721	125,194	354,753	389,107	25,520	31,014	990,602
South America	1,398	4,803	2,525	3,379	17,280	41,899	42,215	29,634	349,568	757,588	681,335	54,155	69,177	2,054,956
Argentina	—	—	—	—	—	—	—	4,687	69,207	57,224	33,914	3,217	4,672	172,921
Colombia	—	—	—	—	—	—	—	5,081	90,076	200,196	163,320	14,455	17,887	491,015
Ecuador	—	—	—	—	—	—	—	2,754	46,621	106,392	96,850	7,040	8,351	268,008
Other South America	1,398	4,803	2,525	3,379	17,280	41,899	42,215	17,112	143,664	393,776	387,251	29,443	38,267	1,123,012
Other America	—	—	—	—	—	—	31	29,301	79,355	1,453	47	4	1	110,192
Africa	**71**	**265**	**670**	**1,207**	**7,368**	**8,443**	**6,286**	**9,117**	**43,046**	**257,672**	**461,283**	**45,640**	**62,510**	**903,578**
Oceania	**12**	**187**	**11,128**	**16,539**	**13,024**	**13,427**	**8,726**	**17,034**	**38,098**	**86,447**	**69,634**	**5,102**	**6,929**	**286,287**
Not Specified	103,232	82,126	18,581	14,852	33,523	1,147	228	142	12,584	1,044	78,285	9,410	24,592	379,746

Information from U.S. Citizenship and Information Services

As the country emerged from the Great Depression of the 1920s, the social structure was influenced largely by economic growth and an emphasis on individual rights. Throughout the 1920s and 1930s and America's participation in World War I, the country saw great migration from the south and a growth in northern cities. Throughout the early years of immigration to the United States, the largest influx of new immigrants was from Europe. During this time, immigrants from Europe made up more than one-half of the entire immigrant population. (See Figure 1.1) As cities grew, so did political corruption.

The Immigration Act of 1917 put restrictions on immigrants, including an $8 fee per person, a literacy exam, and the exclusion of certain people ("idiots," polygamists, insane people, beggars, and vagrants). The Immigration Act of 1924 added restrictions, including the National Origins Quota System. This system limited immigration of each nationality to no more than two percent of that nationality in the United States' population according to the 1890 census. On June 1, 1927, the system was changed to a limit of 150,000 immigrants per year, with the quota of each nationality determined by the 1920 census.

By this time, the industrial revolution was beginning to overtake the agricultural economic structure. The telephone was rapidly unifying the country on a personal level, and the radio was the primary means of electronic communication. It would be some time before the emergence of air and vehicle travel as we know it today and the largest mass security threat involved infectious diseases such as influenza, pneumonia, and measles.

Prior to World War II, America was not generally viewed as a world power. It was only beginning to expand its global reach, particularly in such countries as the Philippines, Panama, Guam, the Marshall Islands, and American Samoa. America's lengthy borders with Canada and Mexico were not viewed as threatening in any meaningful way. The Mounted Guards (often called Mountain Inspectors), a forerunner of the current U.S. Border Patrol, was authorized by Congress in 1915 to patrol for illegal immigrants at inspection stations along the U.S. borders. Congress passed the Labor Appropriation Act of 1924 which officially sanctioned the U.S. Border Patrol to secure the borders. In 1940, the U.S. Border Patrol had 1,531 officers, whereas today there are more than 18,000. There was no Federal Aviation Commission (created by the Federal Aviation Act of 1958), Transportation Security Administration (created by the Aviation and Transportation Security Act of 2001), or Bureau of Alcohol, Tobacco, Firearms and Explosives (created by the Treasury Department Order No. 120-1 of 1972).

In 1945, President Harry S. Truman's Cabinet consisted of 11 cabinet positions; in 2002 President George W. Bush's had 16 (see Figure 1.2). The Cabinet's purpose, according to Article 11, Section 2 of the Constitution, is to advise the President on any subjects of which he should be knowledgeable. Throughout history, positions have been added and removed, determined by the needs of the times. George Washington created three departments: Foreign Affairs (renamed State in August 1781), Treasury, and

War; his cabinet also included the Attorney General and the Vice President. The Postmaster General was a Cabinet member from 1872 to 1971; the Postmaster General was under the Governor of the Postal Service, which eventually became the U.S. Post Office. In 1947, the Departments of War and the Navy were combined into the Department of Defense. The Department of Transportation was created in 1966; the Department of Energy, in 1977; the Department of Education, in 1980; the Department of Veterans' Affairs, in 1988; and the Department of Homeland Security, in 2002.

Figure 1.2   Presidential Cabinet Positions – 1945 and 2006

1945	2006
Secretary of State (1790-present)	Secretary of State (1790-present)
Secretary of Defense (1947-present)	Secretary of Defense (1947-present)
Attorney General (1789-present)	Attorney General (1789-present)
Secretary of Agriculture (1889-present)	Secretary of Agriculture (1889-present)
Secretary of Commerce (1913-present)	Secretary of Commerce (1913-present)
Secretary of the Interior (1849-present)	Secretary of the Interior (1849-present)
Secretary of Labor (1913-present)	Secretary of Labor (1913-present)
Secretary of Treasury (1789-present)	Secretary of Treasury (1789-present)
Postmaster General (1789-1971)	Secretary of Veterans Affairs (1989-present)
Secretary of the Navy (1798-1849)	Secretary of Education (1979-present)
Secretary of War (1789-1947)	Secretary of Energy (1977-present)
	Secretary of Health and Human Services (1980-present)
	Secretary of Homeland Security (2002-present)
	Secretary of Housing and Urban Development (1966-present)
	Secretary of Transportation (1967-present)
	Vice President (Cabinet-level rank)
	White House Chief of Staff (Cabinet-level rank)
	Administrator of Environmental Protection Agency (Cabinet-level rank)
	Director of the National Drug Control Policy (Cabinet-level rank)
	Director of the Office of Management and Budget (Cabinet-level rank)
	U.S. Trade Representative (Cabinet-level rank)

Information from The White House, www.whitehouse.gov

Following World War II, America's criminal justice system (and one must use the term *system* with care) was primarily local. With the exception of the Federal Bureau of Investigation (FBI) and the Secret Service, there were far fewer federal agencies, and their sizes were considerably smaller (see Figure 1.3). This was a period of relative calm, with national security of lesser concern than what President Dwight Eisenhower referred to as the threat of the "military industrial complex." In 1947 the Office of Strategic Services (OSS), the country's international intelligence arm, was restructured as the Central Intelligence Agency (CIA). This was viewed as a threat by FBI Director J. Edgar Hoover, who had used the FBI to conduct large international espionage operations in South America. The creation of the CIA marked the beginning of decades of hostility and a lack of cooperation between the two agencies. Many believe this situation was a critical failure in our inability to gather effective intelligence prior to 9/11. Indeed, some would argue that the proliferation of "three letter" agencies contributed to a fragmented law enforcement system that virtually guaranteed a lack of coordination and cooperation. As of June 2002, federal law enforcement agencies employed more than 93,000 full time personnel capable of making arrests and carrying firearms. Today, this number exceeds 1 million personnel.

Figure 1.3   Growth of Federal Law Enforcement (All numbers are approximates)

Agency	Date Established	1970	1993	2000	2002	2004
ATF	1972	2,554	1959	1,967	2,335	2,373
U.S. Customs (now Customs and Border Protection)	1789	*	10,120	10,522	11,634	27,705
Drug Enforcement Administration	1972	2,775***	2,813	4,161	4,020	4,400
Federal Bureau of Investigation	1908	8,000****	10,075	11,523	11,248	12,242
USDA Forest Service, Law Enforcement & Investigations	1862	*	732	586	658	600
Immigration and Naturalization Services (now Immigration and Customs Enforcement)	1891	8,000	9,466	17,654	19,101	10,399
Internal Revenue Service (Criminal Investigation Division)	1919	1,457	3,621	2,746	2,855	2,777
U.S. Marshals	1789	*	2,153	2,735	2,646	3,233
U.S. Postal Inspection Services	1880	*	3,587	3,412	3,135	2,976
Secret Service	1865	520**	2,186	4,039	4,256	4,769

* Information not available
** 1963 estimates
*** 1972 estimates
**** late 1970s estimates

Information from agency websites and Bureau of Justice Statistics *Federal Law Enforcement Officers* reports from years 2002, 2000, 1998, 1993. Reports available online at www.ojp.usdoj.gov.

In addition to the lack of coordination among federal agencies, cooperation among the components of the criminal justice triad—police, courts and corrections—has never really been strong, and a series of court decisions served to hamper the information and intelligence efforts of each organization.[1]

FROM THE 1960S TO THE 1990S

Criminal justice reforms began to take shape toward the end of the 1950s and early 1960s, and despite the Korean War (1950-1953), the primary focus on security was an increasing crime problem and the beginning of the civil rights movement. America's involvement in the Vietnam War placed greater emphasis on the need for better information and intelligence. During this period, the FBI and other federal, state, and local agencies were accused of illegal wiretaps, the use of disinformation strategies, and the fabrication of evidence.[2] Widespread civil disorder in major cities was a common occurrence, with police responses being the focus of media attention. Television brought conflict on the streets and the war in Vietnam into the living rooms of Americans.

Groups bent on violence formed, taxing law enforcement's ability to mount an effective strategy to cope with a series of bombings and attacks on police, government facilities, and personnel. Two distinctive groups emerged with revolutionary zeal and the belief that the only way to bring about change was to inflame the public and bring down the government. The Black Panther Party formed in opposition to Dr. Martin Luther King Jr.'s nonviolent approach to civil rights. The Weathermen, an offshoot of the Students for a Democratic Society (SDS) mounted a series of protests. The Weather Underground, a splinter group of the Weathermen, mounted a campaign of violence using bombs as their weapon of choice.

The Black Panther Party

The Black Panther Party was formed in Oakland, California in 1966 to promote black liberation through the use of violence, under the guise of self-defense. The group was strongly influenced by the militant revolutionary Malcolm X; its goals included unity for the international working class and joint action with white revolutionary groups. Central to the party's ideology was the Ten Point Plan outlining the goals of the organization, including full employment, decent housing, and end to police brutality and the murder of black people, and having juries of their peers at court trials. The group struggled with internal problems, as well as the COINTELPRO operations of the FBI. The Church Committee Report detailed ways in which the U.S. government, mainly the FBI, had used COINTELPRO to undermine the Black Panther Party. In the 1970s, some members joined the Black Liberation Army, and others adopted a more peaceful approach to liberation. A current group, calling itself the New Black Panther Party, is not a part of the Black Panther Party described here.

Students for a Democratic Society (SDS)

The Students for a Democratic Society (SDS) was created in 1960 in Ann Arbor, Michigan. It was an outgrowth of a group called the League for Industrial Democracy. SDS's political manifesto, known as the Port Huron statement, criticized the U.S. government for failing to achieve international peace and for overlooking numerous social ills, including racism, militarism, and poverty. Although the group was formed to protest numerous issues, it focused on protesting the Vietnam War and contributed to the formation of a movement called the "New Left." The group initially took a nonviolent approach, but SDS became extremely militant and factions of the group became violently aggressive and confrontational. The group dissolved in 1969 because of internal problems. Many of the more radical members joined other groups, such as the Weathermen. The group was mostly known for its ability to actively organize and involve young people in politics and activism.

The Weathermen

In 1969, the Weathermen, also known as Weather Underground, evolved from the Students for a Democratic Society. Originally known as the Revolutionary Youth Movement, the group broke away from moderate members to form the organization that would later take part in bombings, jailbreaks, and riots. The Weathermen advocated the violent overthrow of the government and the system of capitalism. The first event organized by the Weathermen was in October 1969; 300 members blew up a statue dedicated to the police officers killed in the 1886 Haymarket Riot. After three Weathermen were accidentally killed while preparing a bomb, the group adopted a non-lethal approach. Instead of attacking areas without warning and taking the risk of hurting or killing people, the group began to call in warnings to buildings before an attack. Some of the attacks of the Weathermen include the U.S. Capitol, the Pentagon, police buildings, prisons, and the rebuilt Haymarket Riot statue. By the mid to late 1970s, the group began to dissolve, with some turning themselves into the police or joining other revolutionary groups. The FBI's COINTELPRO operations were focused on the Weathermen, although very few convictions were made against members from these investigations.

Despite widespread turmoil and protests throughout the country, which were focused mainly on the police, these activities were not generally viewed as a threat to domestic security. Nevertheless, a number of state and federal investigations and commissions, including the National Advisory Commission on Civil Disorders (1968), also known as The Kerner Report, and the President's Commission on Law Enforcement and the Administration of Justice (1968) called for major reforms. (See Appendix 1.)

For the most part, these reforms had little impact on federal agencies, with one exception—a restriction on surveillance tactics and the use of electronic surveillance, such as wiretapping and eavesdropping.

In the late 1970s, "right-wing" and single-issue groups developed. Some focused on real and imagined grievances against government entities; others on specific issues, such as abortion, environmental protection, animal rights, and white power. The rise of the white power movement, which centered on racial and religious bigotry, began with the Aryan Nation movement in 1974, led by Pastor Richard Butler (1918-2004). Many other hate groups and movements developed from this group, including the Christian Identity, Creativity Movement (formerly World Church of the Creator), and Nationalist Socialist movements. Racist groups such as Phineas Priesthood, the Order, National Alliance, and Stormfront share many ideologies and beliefs; their members may have dual membership in different groups with similar values.

Following the end of the Vietnam War, with the arrests or indictments of the leadership of the Weather Underground movement and the fall of the Black Panther Party and other "left-wing" groups, the domestic threat shifted toward right wing movements. Primary law enforcement initiatives against these groups became the responsibility of the federal government, and the FBI was vested with the responsibility for investigating domestic terrorism. In 1980, a Joint Terrorism Task Force (JTTF), including federal, state and local law enforcement was established in New York City. JTTFs were developed in other cities, and by the time of the terrorist attacks on September 11, 2001, there were 35 such task forces. There are currently more than 100 JTTFs, in all 56 field offices of the FBI and additional annexes.

In the 1980s and 1990s, incidents against American interests were primarily terrorist attacks on military and embassy buildings and private corporations located outside the United States.

GLOBAL TERRORISM

In 1986 the U.S. Congress gave the FBI jurisdictional authority to investigate attacks against Americans that occur outside the United States. In 1989, it allowed the FBI to arrest foreigners outside the United States without the consent of their home country. This made tracking and detaining terrorists and terrorist allies easier for the FBI, although the lack of information sharing with other agencies made their goals harder to achieve.

In the United States, the FBI's criminal investigation division assumed responsibility for investigating domestic terrorist organizations. Investigations involving international subjects were part of the counter-intelligence unit, which had responsibility for identifying spies and threats associated with other countries. Generally, these units operated independently and because of a variety of policy and legal restrictions, there was little cooperation between them.[3]

Global Terror Attacks

- The October 1983 truck bomb on the Marine Barracks in Lebanon killed 241 U.S. Marines.

- The December 1988 explosion of Pan American flight 103 from London to New York killed 270 people, including 189 Americans.

- The October 1993 firefight in Mogadishu, Somalia where insurgents shot down two black hawk helicopters; 18 U.S. Special Forces killed and 79 injured.

- The November 1995 car bomb outside a Saudi-U.S. joint training facility in Riyadh, Saudi Arabia killed five Americans and two Indian officials.

- The June 1996 truck bomb in the Khobar Towers which housed U.S. Air Force personnel in Dhahran, Saudi Arabia killed 19 U.S. citizens and wounded 515 people, including 372 Americans.

- The February 26, 1996 suicide bombing on a bus in Jerusalem killed 26 people, including three Americans and injured 80 people, including three Americans.

- The August 7, 1998 attack on the U.S. embassies in Nairobi, Kenya and Dar es Salaam, Tanzania killed 301 and injured approximately 5,096 people.

U.S. and Saudi military personnel survey the damage to Khobar Towers caused by the explosion of a fuel truck, on June 25, 1996. There were numerous U.S. casualties and the facility housed U.S. service members and served as the headquarters for the U.S. Air Force's 4404th Wing (Provisional), Southwest Asia. *Photo courtesy of Department of Defense.*

- The October 12, 2000 attack on the USS Cole in the harbor of Aden, Yemen killed 17 and injured 39.

In addition to "successful" attacks against U.S. citizens, there were also some foiled attacks during this period. These include:*

- An attempted assassination attempt on former President George H. Bush on April 14, 1993 by Iraqi agents in Kuwait.

- The 1986 attempted bombings by Black P Stone Nation, under the direction of Libyan leader Moammar Khadafy.

- Failed plots masterminded by Ramzi Ahmad Yousef (responsible for World Trade Center bombings in 1993) and supported by the terror group al Qaeda.

- An attempted assassination of Pope John Paul II during his visit to the Philippines in 1994.

- Planned bombing of U.S. and Israeli embassies in Manila in 1994.

- Planned assassination of President Bill Clinton during his visit to the Philippines in 1995.

- Failed bombing of numerous U.S. trans-Pacific flights in 1995.

---

* Estimates and attack details are reported from the March 31, 2004 Congressional Research Service (CRS) Report.

The number of JTTFs increased with units in most major cities, and they successfully investigated a number of threats and attacks that had an international dimension. Most notable were the arrests of members of a Chicago black street gang called Almighty Black P Stones Nation (Black Stone Rangers). They were to receive $2.5 million from the leader of Libya, Moammar Khadafy, to carry out attacks in the United States, including the bombing of U.S. government buildings and American Airlines. In the final stages of purchasing weapons for the impending attacks, the Black Stone Rangers realized that their weapons dealers were, in fact, federal agents. More than 50 members were arrested and charged with conspiracy to commit terrorist acts against the United States and assorted weapons violations. Some of the members not arrested are believed to be hiding in Africa.

The arrests of Muslim extremists involved in the February 26, 1993 attack on the World Trade Center in New York were helped by the involvement of the city's JTTF. Within a month of the bombing, four suspects had been arrested and their trials began in September 1993. During the six-month trial, more than 200 witnesses and 1,000 pieces of evidence were presented in the case. In March 1994, each of the suspects was convicted on all 83 counts presented against them; they were each given 240 years in prison and fined $250,000. On February 7, 1995, the mastermind of the bombing, Ramzi Yousef, was arrested in Pakistan and handed over to U.S. authorities. On January 8, 1998, Yousef was sentenced to 240 years in prison. Without the help and authority of the JTTF, the investigation into the attack would not have been as thorough and the terrorists would not have been found as easily. The JTTF helped New York City and the country move from a feeling of panic to one of safety and normalcy almost immediately; without their assistance, it might have taken months or years to make that transition.

Following the Gulf War in 1991, there was increasing interest in the U.S. by the intelligence field in the growth of Islamic extremism, and fundraising for radical movements. Nevertheless, the FBI and law enforcement officials viewed right wing, anti-government, or white power groups as the greatest threat to domestic security.[4]

During the 1990s more than 500 domestic violent groups were identified, most of which were affiliated with right wing extremism, or focused on single-issue protests.[5] Law enforcement leaders, facing an increase in violent crime, did not view terrorism as a significant local problem, but rather as one best left to the FBI and other federal agencies. The right-wing extremists comprised many ideologies and groups, including: skinheads, neo-Nazis, militiamen, anti-government, Christian Identity, and anti-abortion. The attacks on the World Trade Center in February 1993 and the Murrah Federal Building in Oklahoma City (by Timothy McVeigh) in April 1995 were viewed as exceptional events, rather than a growing trend of extremist violence that should affect policy and organizational structures. Few police academies and virtually no college or university offered courses on terrorism. Scant attention was being paid to what was rapidly becoming a global threat.

The 1990s were also characterized by terrorists who believed in "leaderless resistance:" by acting alone or in localized cells they tried to ensure that their organizations would not be charged with attacks. A decentralized approach to terror and action was taken by groups like Earth Liberation Front (ELF), Animal Liberation Front (ALF), and White Aryan Resistance (WAR).

There were hundreds of reported terrorist attacks throughout the world in the 1990s, including 150 in 1999 alone. There was no "terrorism" law in the Federal Code, and individuals were charged with the specific crimes they planned or committed. Popular thinking was that a terrorism law would give a defendant a means of claiming that his or her actions were politically motivated, rather than a heinous crime. By charging an individual with a specific crime, such as murder, the government could argue that, regardless of the motivation, it was still a serious crime.

Extremist Attacks on American Soil

- Between 1978 and 1995, Theodore John Kaczynski, also known as the Unabomber, made several homemade bombs that killed three and injured 23 people.

- In 1984, followers of the cult Bagwan Shree Rajneesh sprayed ten salad bars in The Dalles, Oregon with salmonella, causing 751 people to become ill.

- On February 26, 1993 a bomb exploded in an underground garage of the World Trade Center in New York City. The blast killed six people, injured about 1,000, and cost approximately $600 million in damage to the building.

- On April 19, 1995 a bomb was detonated in front of the Alfred P. Murrah Federal Building in Oklahoma City, Oklahoma. The blast killed 166 and injured hundreds of other people. Timothy McVeigh and Terry Nichols were charged and convicted of the attack; McVeigh was executed in 2001 and Nichols is serving a life sentence in prison.

- The July 1996 bombing at Centennial Park during the Atlanta Olympics, which killed one person and injured more than 100

- Summer 1999 shooting spree by lone gunmen targeting minorities in the Chicago and Los Angeles metropolitan areas killed three people.

- In October 2001, five confirmed letters laced with anthrax were sent through the U.S. Postal Service and killed four people and sickened 17. Estimates of the damage caused to the post office in Hamilton, New Jersey that came into contact with all of the letters are upwards of $80-$100 million.

- Between May 3 and May 6, 2002, college student Lucas John Helder constructed 18 pipe bombs which he placed in mailboxes around the Midwest and other parts of the country; six people were injured.

- In October 2002, two men, John Allen Muhammad and Lee Boyd Malvo (age 17 at time of crimes) went on a three week long shooting spree in the Washington DC metro area and surrounding areas. Ten people were killed and three others were critically wounded.

Although terrorism was not high on the radar screens of many law enforcement organizations and the public's consciousness, it would be an error to conclude that all government agencies were unconcerned about the threat. There were some, a few individuals, in the FBI, CIA, State Department, military, and other federal agencies who did perceive terrorism as a threat to America's security.[6] In the FBI's 1998 five-year strategic plan, economic and national security, including terrorism, were the top priorities. Congress and elected officials either did not perceive a major threat or believed the problem was insignificant. One exception at the national level was the threat of weapons of mass destruction: a low level effort began in the 1990s to try to understand this phenomenon. The focus was on the ability of rogue countries, or state sponsored efforts, to create nuclear, biological or chemical weapons.[7]

It was in the mid 1990s that terrorism, or the possibility of a terrorist attack, became the theme of novels, movies, television specials, and other mass media. Still, the reality of a threat here, in the United States, was not a high concern of the public, the political structure, or most law enforcement agencies. It was viewed as something that happened to others in other countries.

Over the four decades leading up to the new millennium the world shifted from the cold war and a series of mutually destructive attacks using guerilla tactics to a new form of violence characterized by terrorism as a method of waging war. According to the U.S. State Department's report *Patterns of Global Terrorism: 2000,* 19 Foreign Terrorist Organizations (FTOs) were designated in the Near East, including al Qaeda, Hizbollah, and Hamas.[8] These groups were involved in some form of political violence, and the Arab-Israel conflict served as a catalyst and training model for conflicts around the world.

Widespread travel, communications, migration, and a global media enterprise had moved the world from a state of isolation. These changes contributed to international relationships and the development of global trade. However, they were also key factors in the growth of terrorism, usually related to foreign conflicts, but also threatening to U.S. interests. The fall of the Soviet Union had made the United States the most powerful country in the world, and a target of hatred for radicals and fanatics. This was especially true for a small but potent group of radical Muslims who began to unite under the banner of al Qaeda, led by Osama bin Laden.

Purges in the CIA had virtually eliminated the use of spies and human intelligence, known as HUMINT, in favor of the use of sophisticated technology and electronic surveillance (signals intelligence), known as SIGINT. Further, the shortage of individuals with language abilities, particularly Arabic and Farsi, made translation of terrorist-related intercepts slow or non-existent.

Within the United States, the FBI's counterintelligence program was also deficient. A shortage of funds and personnel, and a completely inadequate computer-based intelligence system, hampered the ability to analyze and identify the forthcoming threat. Although several of the al Qaeda operatives in the US were known to the FBI prior to the 9/11 attacks, a number of warning signs, such as the pilot training of several attackers, were ignored.

During President Clinton's Administration, billions of dollars were allocated to counterterrorism, including more than $1 billion in the 1996 budget. In his State of the Union address in 1996, President Clinton allocated another $25 billion to defense spending over the following six years. According to the State Department's annual *Patterns of Global Terrorism* report of 1997, Cuba, Iran, Iraq, Libya, North Korea, Sudan, and Syria were listed as state sponsors of terrorism.[9] In 1999, the Clinton Administration allocated $10 billion to counterterrorism efforts, including research on WMDs.

A joint terrorist watchlist between the State Department's Consular Affairs Bureau and the INS was created by INS Commissioner Doris Meissner in response to the 1993 World Trade Center attacks. The list named suspected terrorists and was available to consular officers and border inspectors. By 1998, the list had prevented 97 suspected terrorists from entering the country.

Local police departments were largely unfamiliar with the threat of terrorism. Local intelligence gathering efforts concentrated on drug trafficking and organized crime. And, for more than a decade, police officers were trained to ignore the collection of information on traffic stops (at least three of the 9/11 perpetrators had been stopped by police for traffic violations prior to the attack). The culture of secrecy within intelligence agencies and the focus on domestic terrorist groups further contributed to a breakdown in cooperation.[10] For example, two 9/11 hijackers, Nawaf al Hazmi and Khalid al al-Mihdar, were identified by the CIA as participating in an al Qaeda meeting in Malaysia on January 5-8, 2000. The CIA failed to pass this information on to the FBI or NSA and did not put either man on the terrorist watch list.

As the country approached the millennium, an awareness of the threat of a doomsday attack, or the vulnerability of the technological infrastructure was heightened, and both the public and private sector devoted resources aimed at this problem. When January 1, 2000 passed without incident, concern for this issue became a low priority as the new administration took office.

ENTER THE 21ST CENTURY

The election of President George W. Bush brought significant changes in personnel throughout the government, but the Directors of the CIA and FBI, George Tenet and Louis Freeh, respectively, remained in office, as did one of the major figures familiar with global terrorism, Richard Clarke. Clarke, who served under the first Bush administration and the Clinton administration, would later become a severe critic of administration policies under three presidents.[11]

Several months before the September 11, 2001 terror attack, a briefing to President Bush on national security reportedly mentioned both Osama bin Laden and the al Qaeda movement as threats to national security.[12] According to other reports, the FBI continued to view domestic groups as the greatest terrorist threat in the United States throughout the 1990s and early 2000s.[13]

Country Reports on Terrorism

The State Department is responsible for publishing an annual report detailing the year's world wide terrorist activity and terrorist organizations, as outlined in Title 22, Chapter 38, Section 2656F of the United States Code. This section of the Code requires the annual Report, named *Country Reports on Terrorism* (formerly *Patterns of Global Terrorism*), to include information on countries in which the U.S. "has sought cooperation during the previous five years in the investigation or prosecution of an act of international terrorism against U.S. citizens or interests," including the involvement and willingness of a foreign country in assisting the U.S. government in apprehending, convicting, and punishing those responsible for the terrorist act and in the prevention of future terrorist attacks. *Country Reports on Terrorism* serves to include all significant terrorist events, groups, and state sponsors of terrorism for the previous year. The 2004 report lists 44 groups as foreign terrorist organizations. listing six countries as state sponsors of terrorism. When the CIA developed the Counter Terrorism Center (CTC) in 1986, the State Department became responsible for the Report and renamed it *Patterns of Global Terrorism*. Until 2003, the CTC for the CIA continued to collect and analyze the data with the State Department, who then released the Report to the public. In 2003, the Terrorist Threat Integration Center (TTIC) took over the collection and analysis responsibilities from the CTC. The Patterns of Global Terrorism report was renamed Country Reports on Terrorism in 2004, and listed the following countries as supporters of terrorism: Cuba, Iran, Libya, North Korea, Sudan, and Syria. Libya was removed from the list in 2006.

Foreign Terrorist Organizations
(January 2006)

17-Nov
Abu Nidal Organization (ANO)
Abu Sayyaf Group (ASG)
Al-Aqsa Martyrs Brigade
Ansar al-Islam (AI)
Armed Islamic Group (GIA)
Asbat al-Ansar
Aum Shinrikyo (Aum)
Basque Fatherland and Liberty (ETA)
Communist Party of Philippines/New People's Army (CPP/NPA)
Continuity Irish Republican Army (CIRA)
Gama'a al-Islamiyya (IG)
HAMAS
Harakat ul-Mujahidin (HUM)
Hizballah
Islamic Jihad Group (IJG)
Islamic Movement of Uzbekistan (IMU)
Jaish-e-Mohammed (JEM)
Jama'at al-Tawhid wa'al-Jihad
Jemaah Islamiya Organization (JI)
Al-Jihad (AJ)
Kahane Chai (Kach)
Kongra-Gel (KGK)

Lashkar e-Tayyiba (LT)
Lashkar i Jhangvi (LJ)
Liberation Tigers of Tamil Eelam (LTTE)
Libyan Islamic Fighting Group (LIFG)
Moroccan Islamic Combatant Group (GICM)
Mujahedin-e Khalq Organization (MEK)
National Liberation Army (ELN)
Palestine Liberation Front (PLF)
Palestinian Islamic Jihad (PIJ)
Popular Front for the Liberation of Palestine (PFLP)
Popular Front for the Liberation of Palestine-General Command (PFLP-GC)
Al-Qa'ida
Real IRA (RIRA)
Revolutionary Armed Forces of Colombia (FARC)
Revolutionary Nuclei (RN)
Revolutionary People's Liberation Party/Front (DHKP/C)
Sajid Badat
Salafist Group for Call and Combat (GSPC)
Shining Path (SL)
Tanzim Qa'idat al-Jihad fi Bilad al-Rafidayn (QJBR)
United Self-Defense Forces of Colombia (AUC)

The arrest of Ahmed Ressam by U.S. Customs at the Canadian border with a trunk containing explosives with the intent of blowing up Los Angeles International Airport in December 1999 (see Sidebar) was touted as a major victory against terrorism, but otherwise the new year and new century came and went peacefully, without incident. In his book, *Bush at War*, Washington Post assistant managing editor Bob Woodward noted that, prior to 9/11, the administration's primary international focus included Osama bin Laden and the al Qaeda organization and the increased availability of weapons of mass destruction (WMDs). It also mentioned that the Pentagon had been working on a military plan of action for Iraq.

Ahmed Ressam

On December 14, 1999, Ahmed Ressam, using false Canadian identification papers in the name of Benni Antoine Noris, attempted to enter the United States at Port Angeles, Washington, by ferry. Immigration inspectors found Ressam's story of going to Seattle for a business trip suspicious. After questioning and a name check, and with no evidence to hold Ressam, the inspector allowed the car onto the ferry. In Port Angeles, customs inspectors questioned Ressam and noticed that he exhibited suspicious behavior, and searched his car and found several green bags of white powder, four black boxes, two pill bottles, and two jars of brown liquid in the spare tire compartment beneath the trunk. Ressam ran, entered a busy intersection, and tried to carjack a car before he was captured.

It was later discovered that the brown liquid was a highly unstable relative of nitroglycerin. The Royal Canadian Mounted Police identified Ressam as an Algerian named Ahmed Ressam and confirmed that he had terrorist ties. Further investigation led investigators to two co-conspirators involved in the plot to bomb Los Angeles International Airport on New Year's Day. Ressam was sentenced to between 57 and 130 years in prison, which was cut in half when he agreed to testify against the other conspirators.

America's response to the attacks was shock, but also a renewed sense of patriotism. The public was galvanized by President Bush who declared war on those responsible. Immediately al Qaeda and Osama bin Laden were accused of being behind the attack. The country's military response focused on the Taliban government in Afghanistan, which was accused of harboring and supporting bin Laden and other terrorists.

In the United States, law enforcement agencies began a massive investigative effort, while at the same time developing a defensive strategy in major cities. The nineteen hijackers involved in the attacks were identified within days. The surprise airline hijackings were compared to the attack on Pearl Harbor, where the number of lives lost was actually less than on 9/11.[14]

The administration was faced with what was undeniably the worst terrorism catastrophe in the country's history. The coming months would bring questions, controversy, and confusion. Federal, state, and local agencies scrambled to mount a defensive effort that included police, fire, and medical personnel. However, it quickly became obvious that the country was not well prepared to cope with a crisis of this magnitude. In addition to public safety organizations, there was a need to involve the private sector, infrastructure groups, and the community in developing a protective strategy. Congress was calling for major government reforms, and the bulk of criticism was aimed at the FBI and CIA.

Subsequent investigations and eventually the report of the 9/11 Commission would identify major failures in intelligence sharing, cooperation, and planning. One can argue that the failures were the result of the development of organizational cultures that prohibited cooperation, a lack of interest and support by elected officials, a misguided American public, an ineffective legal system, and a national media that had also overlooked the threat.

Earlier interventions included the development of a Law Enforcement Working Group (LEWG)[15] that brought together key federal officials in a frantic effort to catch-up with the current situation. The term "Homeland Security" emerged as the defining aspect of a major reorganization of the governmental bureaucracy, the implementation of new laws—including the USA PATRIOT Act—and a complete transformation of local law enforcement and the many entities considered likely targets of future attacks.

In the months immediately following 9/11, as the military response began in Afghanistan in October 2001, public support for the Bush administration grew. However, as the media and Congressional critics began to push for an investigation into the terror attacks, and a quick victory in Afghanistan, the administration's focus shifted to military action in Iraq. Much has been written about the decision to invade Iraq, and the apparent intelligence failures that led the administration to believe that Saddam Hussein was stockpiling weapons of mass destruction. The ensuing Congressional debate and a series of U.S. efforts to involve the United Nations in bringing down the Hussein regime ended in a U.S. declaration of war against Iraq on March 20, 2003, which became a serious challenge to the Bush administration.

On September 14, 2001, just three days after the terrorist attacks stunned the nation, Vice President Dick Cheney recommended a new White House position to manage and coordinate all agencies involved in responding to and preventing future attacks. On September 20, 2001, President Bush announced to a joint session of Congress that a new cabinet-level position, the Office of Homeland Security, would be led by Pennsylvania governor Tom Ridge as Homeland Security Advisor. During the same speech, President Bush announced that al Qaeda, under the leadership of Osama bin Laden, was responsible for the terror attacks on September 11, 2001.

The Department of Homeland Security was created by the Homeland Security Act of 2002, on January 23, 2002. The three primary missions of the Department are (1) to prevent terrorist attacks within the United States; (2) to reduce America's vulnerability to terrorism; and (3) to minimize the damage from potential attacks and natural disasters.

In 2001 President George W. Bush announced what was the largest reorganization of government since the Second World War. As he noted:

> Our nation has been put on notice: We are not immune from attack. We will take defensive measures against terrorism to protect Americans. Today, dozens of federal departments and agencies, as well as state and local governments, have responsibilities affecting homeland security. These efforts must be coordinated at the highest level. . . . Many will be involved in this effort, from FBI agents to intelligence operatives to the reservists we have called to active duty. All deserve our thanks, and all have our prayers. (From President Bush's speech at the September 20, 2001 joint session of Congress)

Although the 9/11 catastrophe served as a catalyst for the reorganization, many of the intelligence and operational failures of the criminal justice and intelligence communities were an ongoing source of concern. Intergovernmental rivalries persisted among federal agencies, especially between the FBI and the CIA, as well as among federal, state and local law enforcement groups. The United States, unlike every other country, is characterized by a decentralized and fragmented collection of governmental organizations that includes no fewer than 20,000 police departments, 60 federal agencies with law enforcement powers, and as many as 13 individual intelligence agencies at the national level. Historically, communication and coordination among these organizations has been weak at best and catastrophic at worst. Duplication of effort, overlapping jurisdictional disputes, differing legal systems, and ongoing competition for resources have been obvious for decades. Nevertheless, those with the power to correct such deficiencies, elected officials and national leaders, chose to ignore the problems and give way to political pressures from a variety of sources.

CHANGING GLOBAL PERSPECTIVE

Although the 9/11 attacks led to change, global and domestic events of the past two or three decades should have made it clear that there were emerging threats to the country's security. These threats went far beyond the scope of the intelligence or criminal justice communities, as well as the nation's military. America has never been without some form of terrorism or political violence; however, the capabilities of those who wish to bring death and destruction has increased dramatically. There is a new dimension to the domestic threat because of the availability of more sophisticated weapons and technology. To date, the means of violence have generally remained the same—bombs, assaults, and assassination—but their impact has grown significantly.

Ironically, perhaps the individual who most clearly recognized America's vulnerability was Osama bin Laden, who viewed the soft underbelly of the global economy as a major weakness. Attacks on American interests domestically and abroad have tended to support the idea that by creating fear people will change their habits—stop flying, stop shopping, and avoid potential threats.[16] For years, the airlines have known that the hijacking or downing of an airplane would result in a decrease in customers. The 2001 Anthrax scare and the DC sniper case further support the premise that security involves much more than target hardening and dependence on traditional methods of criminal investigation. Intelligence and better training of local law enforcement have become high priorities.

Following 9/11, "heads will roll" statements and promises of cooperation and communication would be a recurring theme of newly appointed officials. The new model envisioned for domestic security would bring together many disparate elements of government. A new military command, known as U.S. Northern Command (US NORTHCOM) would also be created.[17] Ultimately, the move to establish a Department of Homeland Security would impact more than 180,000 personnel in 22 federal agencies.

The vision of homeland security encompasses virtually every aspect of American life. The following chapters identify and explain the structure, philosophy and legal implications of an unprecedented change in the way citizens of the United States live and work in this new environment.

KEY CONCEPTS

- Realignments and constantly improving agencies in the criminal justice field have been happening since the inception of the U.S. The government and organizations react according to the events and social changes that occur during specific periods.

- America's vulnerability to terror attacks was evident before 9/11 and numerous attacks were committed within the Unite States as well as against American interests abroad.

- Before 9/11, the greatest perceived threat to the country was from domestic terror groups.

- The Department of Homeland Security was created in response to the lack of intelligence sharing, coordination, and cooperation between key federal agencies.

- Many changes among law enforcement took place during the 1960-70s. Three commissions were formed to update the current society: The National Advisory Commission on Civil Disorders (Kerner Commission), The President's Commission on Law Enforcement and Administration of Justice, and the U.S. Senate Select Committee to Study Governmental Operations with Respect to Intelligence Activities Report (Church Committee).

ADDITIONAL READINGS

Aviation and Transportation Security Act of 2001

Federal Aviation Act of 1958

Foreign Intelligence Surveillance Act of 1978 (FISA)

The Homeland Security Act of 2002

The Immigration Act of 1917

The Immigration Act of 1924

Labor Appropriation Act of 1924

National Advisory Commission on Civil Disorders (Kerner Report)

Patterns of Global Terrorism Reports

The President's Commission on Law Enforcement and the Administration of Justice (1968)

United States Senate Select Committee to Study Governmental Operations with Respect to Intelligence Activities Report (Church Committee Report)

Homeland Security Act of 2002

RELATED WEBSITES

Bureau of Alcohol, Tobacco, Firearms, and Explosives www.atf.gov

Central Intelligence Agency www.cia.gov

Citizenship and Immigration Services www.uscis.gov

Customs and Border Protection www.cbp.gov

Department of Homeland Security www.dhs.gov

Federal Aviation Administration www.faa.gov

Federal Bureau of Investigation www.fbi.gov

Northern Command www.northcom.mil

Secret Service www.secretservice.gov

State Department www.state.gov

Transportation Security Administration www.tsa.gov

White House www.whitehouse.gov

The Institute for the Study of Violent Groups www.isvg.org

REFERENCES

Builta, J. (1966). *Extremist Groups: An International Compilation of Terrorist Organizations, Violent Political Groups, and Issue-Oriented Militant Movements,* First Edition. Huntsville, TX: Office of International Criminal Justice.

Cronin, Audrey Kurth (2006). "Terrorist Attacks by al-Qaeda." Memorandum from the Congressional Research Service to the House Government Reform Committee. Available online through the Federation of American Scientists: http://www.fas.org/irp/crs/033104.pdf.

Hill, Sean (2002). *Extremist Groups: An International Compilation of Terrorist Organizations, Violent Political Groups, and Issue-Oriented Militant Movements,* Second Edition. Huntsville, TX: Office of International Criminal Justice.

Institute for the Study of Violent Groups (2006). *Extremist Groups: An International Compilation of Terrorist Organizations, Violent Political Groups, and Issue-Oriented Militant Movements,* Third Edition. Huntsville, TX: Office of International Criminal Justice.

Thompson, Paul (2004). *The Terror Timeline: Year by Year, Day by Day, Minute by Minute: A Comprehensive Chronicle to the Road to 9/11—and America's Response.* New York, NY: Harper Collins Publishers.

U.S. Department of State (2001). *Patterns of Global Terrorism.* Washington, DC: Office of the Coordinator for Counterterrorism.

U.S. Department of State (1998). *Patterns of Global Terrorism.* Washington, DC: Office of the Coordinator for Counterterrorism.

Woodward, Bob (2004). *Plan of Attack.* New York, NY: Simon & Schuster.

Woodward, Bob (2002). *Bush at War.* New York, NY: Simon & Schuster.

NOTES

[1] The three components of the criminal justice system—law enforcement, courts, and corrections—do not really work together as a "system," but rather as individual entities, often working against, instead of with, each other. This is most evident in the Foreign Intelligence Surveillance Act of 1978 (FISA). This Act removed the power of attorney generals to grant surveillance of foreign powers and their agents without any court review. It required court review of proposed surveillance, and was interpreted to require that a search could only be granted if its primary purpose was to obtain foreign intelligence. The Justice Department then interpreted the court's findings to mean that criminal prosecutors could be briefed on information from the Act but could not be involved with its collection. Another limit on effectiveness of cooperation among agencies occurred in 1995 when Attorney General Janet Reno issued formal procedures for the Justice Department prosecutors and FBI regarding the exact methods for sharing between the two agencies. These guidelines were misinterpreted by both agencies with the result that information that was allowed to be shared was not shared. The Office of Intelligence Policy and Review in the Justice Department became the office that completed information sharing with the FBI. Because of rumors, misunderstandings, and other barriers, agents (especially FBI agents) kept relevant information that was retrieved under FISA secret from other agents, even agents that were in the same agency, as well as other agencies.

[2] COINTELPRO was created in 1956 to "neutralize" domestic dissidents. It resulted in the FBI using illegal means and materials to gain arrests and convictions against political dissidents in the 1950s and 1960s. These operations, which included warrantless wiretapping, illegal mail-opening, and the use of electronic surveillance, were deemed

improper by the Church Committee Reports. COINTELPRO programs were used against many political dissidents and activists, the most famous being Dr. Martin Luther King Jr., the Black Panthers, the Ku Klux Klan, and the Students for a Democratic Society (SDS). More than 2,000 COINTELPRO cases were initiated between 1956 and 1971. The programs were officially ended in April 1971.

[3]   Before 9/11, the FBI measured its level of success by different methods, most of which were statistics of arrests, indictments, prosecutions, and convictions. This approach makes the efforts of those working on counterintelligence operations, which are known for producing few quantitative results after lengthy investigations, seem insignificant to those in the FBI world. Also, the FBI has a single office in charge of entire investigations to help deter duplication and conflict among agents working on the same cases. It has been reported that field offices in the U.S. that are not the primary offices for investigations are not quick to help or to provide additional information or manpower to other offices. This ineffectiveness contributes to miscommunication and non-communication within the agency.

[4]   The FBI divided the terrorist threat into two categories: international and domestic. During the 1990s, domestic right wing groups focused on single issue ideologies such as abortion, ecology, animal rights, government, militias, neo-Nazi, and white power were prevalent. These groups generally use public attacks to gain media attention. The FBI considered right wing groups the "most dangerous domestic terror threat to the country."

[5]   The Southern Poverty Law Center identified 537 hate groups and chapters active in the United States in 1999. In the 1996 publication *Extremist Groups: An International Compilation of Terrorist Organizations, Violent Political Groups, and Issue-Oriented Militant Movements* compiled by Jeffrey A. Builta, 33 domestic extremist groups were identified and described in detail. The second edition of *Extremist Groups*, composed by Sean Hill in 2002, included 28 domestic terror groups. According to the Council of Foreign Relations, 335 incidents that were considered suspected or confirmed terrorism by the FBI were reported between 1980 and 2000, of which about 75% were carried out by Americans. The Institute for the Study of Violent Groups, housed at Sam Houston State University, lists 241 domestic terrorist and extremist groups in the United States and an additional 600 international terror and extremist groups (January 2006 estimates).

[6]   The CIA established a Counterterrorism Center in 1986 and President Clinton's National Security Advisor, Richard Clarke, recognized that the subject was important. Louis Freeh was appointed Director of the FBI in 1993 by President Clinton and would stay in that position until June 2001. Freeh recognized terrorism as a major threat and developed more legal attaché offices abroad, focusing on the Middle East. He also created a Counterterrorism Division (similar to the Counterterrorist Center in the CIA) and tried to improve cooperation between the FBI and CIA. A separate Counterintelligence Division was created in 1999. In 2000, Attorney General Janet Reno declared counterterrorism to be the primary priority of the Department of Justice.

[7]   The Defense Against Weapons of Mass Destruction Act of 1996 addressed the availability of weapons of mass destruction (WMD) in many countries, especially countries in the former Soviet Union. The Act identified WMDs as a significant threat to the United States and called for the President to take immediate action to help prevent future attacks. Before the Congressional Committee on National Security, in March 1996, Mark Gebicke's testimony on "Chemical and Biological Defense: Emphasis Remains Insufficient to Resolve Continuing Problems" included details of the vulnerabilities of the United States to biological and chemical attacks. He also noted budgetary deficits, equipment shortages and vaccine shortages. Many reports during this time presented similar concerns. In May 2001 testimony to Congress, it was noted that the FBI investigated 779 WMD-related incidents between 1997 and 2000. Many of the investigations were of individuals or small groups and were determined to be false. Ricin and Anthrax were considered the most prevalent WMD agents.

[8]   As of January 2006, 44 groups are designated as Foreign Terrorist Organizations (FTOs). Six countries are considered state sponsors of terrorism, including Cuba (March 1, 1982), Iran (January 19, 1984), Libya (December 29, 1979), North Korea (January 20, 1988), Sudan (August 12, 1993), and Syria (December 29, 1979).

[9]   The Patterns of Global Terrorism Report of 1996, published by the State Department annually since 1985, included Cuba, Iran, Iraq, Libya, North Korea, Sudan, and Syria as state sponsors of terrorism. Iraq was deleted as a state sponsor of terrorism on October 20, 2004 for the following reasons: dramatic change in the leadership and government of Iraq; Iraq vowed to not support international terrorism; and Iraq provided a guarantee that it would not support acts of terrorism in the future. In May 2006, Libya was also removed from the state sponsors list after agreeing to pay reparations to the Lockerbie bombing victims' families and renouncing their pursuit of weapons of mass destruction.

[10]   Counterterrorism efforts were not completely overlooked and a number of federally funded training programs were in effect to help the police better understand domestic terrorism, and to train first responders in how to handle major crises, including terrorist attacks. One of these programs, SLATT (State and Local Anti-Terrorism Training), works with the FBI to help prevent and investigate acts of terrorism. Since its inception in 1996, the group had developed a three day training program for local police, but the primary thrust was toward the identification of domestic terrorists.

[11]   Clarke, in his book, *Against All Enemies: Inside America's War on Terror*, published in March 2004, and in testimony before the 9/11 Commission claimed that he recommended a more aggressive approach in dealing with the al Qaeda threat following attacks on the USS Cole and the American embassies in Africa.

[12]   According to Bob Woodward's *Plan of Attack*, a national security briefing in January 2001 attended by President Bush, Vice President Cheney, National Security Advisor Condoleezza Rice, CIA Director George Tenet and his deputy for operations James L. Pavitt, the issue of the major threats from al Qaeda and Osama bin Laden were discussed and, according to Tenet and Pavitt, an immediate response was necessary to prevent the threats from coming to fruition.

[13]   According to the FBI's 1996 *Terrorism in the United States* report, the threat of domestic terrorism had increased dramatically and such acts were committed much more frequently than international acts of terror. According to the 1996 report, right wing extremist groups were the most active and greatest threat for domestic terrorism.

[14]   The attack on Pearl Harbor resulted in 2,403 deaths, and more than 1178 injuries, compared with 2,972 deaths as a result of the terrorist attacks of September 11, 2001. Of these deaths, more than 2,000 were killed at the World Trade Center, 125 at the Pentagon, and 44 on Flight 93 that crashed in Pennsylvania.

[15]   The Law Enforcement Working Group was initiated by the Intelligence Community (IC) to bring IC professionals together with representatives of federal law enforcement agencies to increase the knowledge of each other and to expand the dialogue as to information sharing, cross-training opportunities, and overall enhancement of interagency relationships. The effort included (as a pilot program) the provision of top secret security clearances to a small group of chiefs of police to explore the potential access to information between state and local enforcement agencies and the IC. Generally speaking, this was an entirely new experience for both communities and helped to inform the national level debate. The LEWG construct was embraced and showed some measurable results, primarily in the broadening of interagency relationships; however, jurisdictional and legal impediments have to date impeded the construct from being formally adopted by the IC or DHS.

[16]   The 9/11 terror attacks clearly instilled a fear in Americans that transferred to their economic abilities. New York City, the largest city in the United States, was economically crippled for the first few years after the attacks. (See Chapter 2)

[17]   NORTHCOM is made up of approximately 1,200 servicemen and women from all military branches to serve out the Command's mission of homeland defense and civil support. NORTHCOM was created on October 1, 2002 in response to the domestic security issues faced by the United States. The Command's headquarters is in Peterson Air Force Base in Colorado Springs, Colorado and is under the direction of the Defense Department, and is one of the nine U.S. military designations throughout the world, the others being U.S. European Command, U.S. Pacific Command, U.S. Joint Forces Command, U.S. Southern Command, U.S. Central Command, U.S. Special Operations, U.S. Strategic Command, and U.S. Transportation Command.

Chapter 2

The 9/11 Attacks and the Genesis of Homeland Security

INTRODUCTION

On Tuesday, September 11, 2001, a quiet and clear day, at 8:46 A.M. (Eastern Standard Time) a Boeing 767 struck the 93rd to 99th floors of the North Tower of the World Trade Center in lower Manhattan in New York City. Shortly after, a second Boeing 767 struck the South Tower of the World Trade Center between the 77th and 85th floors. In Washington, DC, a Boeing 757 struck the west corridor of the Pentagon. Within minutes, radio and television reports throughout the nation reported the series of attacks, and passengers aboard another aircraft bound for San Francisco International Airport found themselves the victims of a skyjacking; a number of passengers tried to overpower the hijackers and caused the plane to crash in a field in Pennsylvania.

On this fateful day, 2,972 people died: eight pilots, 25 flight attendants, 213 passengers, and 19 hijackers lost their lives on the planes. More than 2,000 civilians, 343 New York Fire Department members, 37 Port Authority Police Department members, and 23 New York Police Department members were killed in New York. At the Pentagon in Washington, DC 70 civilians and 55 military service members died.

New York, NY, September 27, 2001—The remaining section of the World Trade Center became a symbol of defiance. *Photo by Bri Rodriguez/ FEMA News Photo.*

It is believed that a fifth attack had been planned, but was never carried out. The National Commission on Terrorist Attacks upon the United States (commonly referred to as the 9/11 Commission), speculated that the plane that went down in Pennsylvania was targeting the Capitol or the White House in Washington, DC.

In reports from January 2002, victims of the World Trade Center had been born in more than 25 countries, including the United States, Canada, China, Colombia, Cuba, Dominican Republic, Ecuador, Germany, Guyana, Haiti, India, Ireland, Italy, Jamaica, Japan, Korea, Pakistan, Philippines, Poland, Russia, Taiwan, Trinidad and Tobago, Ukraine, United Kingdom, and Yugoslavia among others.[1]

The attacks, which caught the country and the law enforcement and intelligence communities completely by surprise, were orchestrated by Osama bin Laden and a nebulous terrorist organization known as al Qaeda. Both the organization and bin Laden were known to intelligence agencies and government officials, and had been the subject of investigation for more than five years prior to the attack.

Much has been written about the attack, but perhaps the most accurate and comprehensive account is in the 9/11 Commission Report that was made public in 2004. This report, highly critical of the intelligence community, particularly the CIA and the FBI, ultimately resulted in sweeping reforms throughout government, including the establishment of the Office of Homeland Security, and eventually the Department of Homeland Security with a cabinet level position for its Secretary. The concept of homeland security has had a major impact on all levels of government, from local to federal, through efforts to prevent, prepare for, and react to future attacks.

Hundreds of books and thousands of articles have been written regarding the 9/11 terror attacks; most are highly critical of the political, intelligence, and government communities. Many authors have speculated on individual and political decisions made by politicians and agency heads over decades that gave rise to the growth of the fanatical Muslim movement throughout the world. There is a general belief that Middle Eastern terrorism is focused on the Arab-Israeli conflict: in actuality, the reasons are much more complex. An analysis of the 9/11 attacks led to a better understanding of the concept of homeland security in the United States.

PLANNING THE ATTACK

The 9/11 attacks were a surprise to the intelligence community. In hindsight, however, there were clues as to the intention of Osama bin Laden and his inner circle of conspirators. Significantly, he made a series of statements, at least as early as 1992, denouncing the United States and Western influence in the Middle East. He began by espousing the need to cut off the "head of the snake,"[2] referring to the West, and specifically the United States' influence in the Middle East.

It is unclear when bin Laden became a source of concern to the United States. He had fought alongside and supported the Taliban movement against the Russians in the 1980s during the Soviet occupation of Afghanistan (1979-1989). But, by 1992 he had clearly emerged as an enemy of the

United States. To say there were no American intelligence interests in the bin Laden threat would be an error as he and his organization were persons of interest to the global intelligence community. On August 21, 1998, the U.S. State Department listed al-Qaeda[3] as a Foreign Terrorist Organization (FTO). On November 4, 1998, bin Laden and several members of al-Qaeda, including Mohamed Atta and Mohamed Rashid Daoud al-Owhali, were named in an indictment in the Southern District of New York.[4] Bin Laden is believed to be responsible for the October 12, 2000, attacks on the USS Cole in Aden, Yemen, which killed 17 U.S. Navy personnel and nearly sank the ship. He is also reportedly responsible for the attacks on the American embassies in Kenya and Tanzania on August 7, 1998; the Kenya attack killed 12 Americans and 201 others (mostly Kenyans) and destroyed the embassy. The Tanzania attack killed 11 people.

What escaped most intelligence agencies, especially in the western world, was the nature of al Qaeda's organization, and its reach into countries throughout the world. Various agencies in the U.S., as well as other countries, had a great many pieces of the puzzle locked in their files and computers; however, no one had put those pieces together in a way that identified the coming threat. Nor had intelligence agencies discovered the sophistication of this new enemy, the way in which they used the internet as a primary form of communication.

From January 5-8, 2000, a meeting between al Qaeda operatives took place in Kuala Lumpur, Malaysia. The purpose of the meeting was to plan and discuss future attacks and how they should be carried out. Some of the attacks discussed were the 9/11 attack on the World Trade Center and October 2000 bombings on the USS Cole. The meeting was monitored by the Malaysian Secret Police, as requested by the CIA.

Planning for the 9/11 attack is believed to have begun in 1996, following the first attack on the World Trade Center in 1993. This attack, which should have been a warning signal, was deemed a failure, although it killed six people, injured more than 1,000 people, and caused extensive damage, including a half billion dollars in property damage. The FBI, ATF, and other local and federal agencies were successful in arresting the perpetrators, who are currently serving long terms in the federal prison system. This may have created a sense that the attack was an aberration, a single event, not an indication of future attacks.

The 9/11 attackers had distinct roles: those who were an integral part of the planning process and would lead the attacks; and those who would assist in the takeover of the planes, but had little knowledge of the dimensions of the attack. It is still unclear whether all the attackers were aware they were undertaking a suicide mission against the World Trade Center and the Pentagon.

THE FIFTH POSSIBILITY

According to authorities, Zacarias Moussaoui could potentially have been the twentieth hijacker in the 9/11 attack at the World Trade Center, had it not been for the alertness of flight instructors in Minnesota.

A French national of Moroccan descent, Moussaoui was born on May 30, 1968. He was a resident of the United Kingdom, and, according to his indictment, he held a master's degree from Southbank University. In April 1998, he attended the al Qaeda-affiliated Khalden Camp in Afghanistan. Moussaoui arrived in the United States in February 2001, and from that time until May 2001, he attended Airman Flight School in Norman, Oklahoma. After ending the Airman flight program early, Moussaoui attempted to complete his training at Pan Am International Flight Academy in Minneapolis, Minnesota in August 2001. He attracted the attention of instructors with his erratic behavior when he arrived for 747 simulator training without holding a pilot's license.

On August 16, 2001, Moussaoui was taken into custody, initially on immigration charges. When questioned by local and federal agents, Moussaoui denied he was affiliated with al Qaeda. Evidence recovered when he was arrested was regarded suspiciously, and Moussaoui remained in custody. While in custody, the events of September 11, 2001, occurred, and investigators immediately questioned Moussaoui regarding them. Moussaoui steadfastly denied his involvement, but he was charged in December of 2001 with six counts of conspiracy. These charges included conspiracy to commit acts of terrorism transcending national boundaries, conspiracy to commit aircraft piracy, conspiracy to destroy aircraft, conspiracy to use weapons of mass destruction, conspiracy to murder United States employees, and conspiracy to destroy property.

Moussaoui admitted his membership in al Qaeda and confessed his plan to fly a plane into the White House during a later mission. He petitioned the court to represent himself without a lawyer and pled guilty to all counts of the indictment on April 22, 2005. In 2006, Moussaoui was sentenced to six consecutive life terms without the possiblity of parole.

THE ATTACK

On the morning of September 11, 2001, four planes were hijacked almost simultaneously as they left airports in Newark, NJ, Boston, and Washington, DC.

American Airlines flight 11 from Boston's Logan International Airport to Los Angeles International Airport was hijacked shortly after its 7:59 A.M. takeoff; the last communication from the plane to traffic control occurred at 8:41 A.M., and it is believed this is when the plane was hijacked. The airliner carried 92 people, including nine flight attendants and two pilots. The terrorists were Mohamed Atta, Abdul Aziz al Omari, Satam al Suqami, Wail al Shehri, and Waleed al Shehri. The hijackers used knives, pepper spray, and the threat of a bomb to take control of the flight and overcome the cockpit. The plane was diverted to New York City and crashed into the 110-story tall World Trade Center North Tower at 8:46 A.M., killing all 92 people on board and countless people inside the Tower. The building collapsed at 10:28 A.M.

United Airlines flight 175 from Boston's Logan International Airport to Los Angeles International Airport was hijacked shortly after its 8:14 A.M. takeoff, between 8:42 and 8:46 A.M.. The airliner carried 65 people, including seven flight attendants and two pilots. The terrorists were Marwan al Shehhi, Fayez Banihammad, Mohand al Shehri, Ahemd al Ghamdi, and Hamza al Ghamdi. The hijackers used knives, pepper spray, and the threat of a bomb to take control of the flight and overcome the cockpit. The plane changed its path to head for New York City, and interestingly, barely missed crashing into two other airliners during this transition. The plane crashed into the 110-story tall World Trade Center South Tower at 9:03 A.M., killing all 66 people on board. The crash was seen across the world on television because many camera crews and news channels were covering the first attack. The building collapsed at 9:58 A.M..

American Airlines flight 77 from Washington, D.C.'s Dulles International Airport to Los Angeles International Airport was hijacked shortly after its 8:20 A.M. takeoff, between 8:51 and 8:54 A.M. The plane carried 64 people, including four flight attendants and two pilots. The terrorists were Khalid al Mindhar, Majed Moqed, Hani Hanjour, Nawaf al Hazmi, and Salem al Hazmi. The hijackers used box cutters and knives to take control of the flight and overcome the cockpit. The passengers were ordered to call their families and loved ones and tell them they were about to die. It is believed that the plane was headed for the White House but made a last-minute diversion and crashed into the Pentagon at 9:37 A.M. All 64 people on the airliner were killed, along with 125 people inside the Pentagon at the time of the attack.

United Airlines flight 93, from New Jersey's Newark International Airport to San Francisco's International Airport was hijacked shortly after its 8:42 A.M. takeoff. The plane carried 44 people, including five flight attendants and two pilots. The terrorists included Saeed al Ghamdi, Ahmed al Nami, Ahmad al Haznawi, and Ziad Jarrah. The hijackers used box cutters to take control of the flight and invaded the cockpit at 9:31 A.M. The terrorists ordered the passengers to call their families and loved ones and tell them they were about to die. During these conversations, the passengers learned about the World Trade Center attacks; it is believed that this is when some of the passengers decided to revolt against the terrorists and try to prevent the plane from hitting the White House, its intended target. After the plane began to head for Washington, the plane made several more turns and crashed into a field in Stony Creek Township, Pennsylvania, 80 miles southeast of Pittsburgh, at 10:06 A.M. All 45 people on the airliner were killed.

WTC NORTH TOWER

The mayhem and disorder that followed at the World Trade Center (WTC) and the Pentagon is almost unimaginable. When the first plane hit the WTC at 8:46 A.M., it cut through floors 93 to 99 of the North Tower. Hundreds of people were killed by the impact; the stairwells, the only way to safety, were blocked from the 92nd floor and above. A jet fuel ball exploded in many lower floors, including the 77th floor and the B4 level, which is four stories below ground, and a heavy cloud of black smoke engulfed the North Tower and made its way to the South Tower due to winds.

Immediately after the initial attack, numerous 911 calls were made from civilians inside the North Tower. The deputy safety director of the North Tower did not realize for approximately 10 minutes that a commercial jet had hit the building, although he did recognize that a major crisis had occurred. When he did make the emergency announcements, many floors did not hear it or the other announcements because of the amount of damage of the impact. The large volume of calls could not all be answered at 911 dispatch. When the calls were answered, the operators and the New York City Fire Department (FDNY) dispatchers did not know where the impact was and could not give any viable directions to the callers as to where to go. Because they did not know the fire's location, and if the callers were above or below the impact, many gave the general instructions for high-rise fires—stay low, remain where they were, and wait for emergency personnel. When the FDNY chiefs realized the magnitude of the incident, they enacted a full building evacuation; they also advised the Port Authority Police Department (PAPD) to evacuate the South Tower due to the damage caused by the first plane's impact. Many occupants tried to evacuate the building; others stayed where they were and waited for help or helped others in need. Many obstacles were in front of or on the way to exits. Some doors were assumed locked when, in fact, they were only jammed shut or stuck due to the structural damage caused by the plane's impact. Thick smoke and isolated fires were reported, especially on the upper floors. Some people, seeing the damage and the unlikelihood of making it out alive, jumped from upper-level windows.

WTC South Tower

Immediately after the attack, many people from the South Tower realized that a major incident or explosion had occurred on the upper levels of the North Tower and they evacuated. Morgan Stanley, which occupied 20 stories of the South Tower, evacuated all of its floors on recommendation from its company security officials. At about 8:49 A.M., a public announcement transmitted over the intercom system advised all occupants that the explosion had occurred in the North Tower and that occupants should remain on or return to their floors. At 9:02 A.M., immediately before the second plane hit the South Tower, another announcement was made over the intercom that advised an evacuation could be made if conditions warranted.

The plane hit the South Tower at 9:03 A.M. between the 77th and 82nd floors. The plane was angled on the floors, so one stairwell was open from at least the 91st floor and below. Hundreds of people, waiting to be evacuated at the 78th floor lobby, were trying to jam their way into elevators. Some began the descent in the stairway while others stayed and helped those who were injured and assisted people down the stairs. Some people from floors hit by the plane were able to be evacuated and those who descended from floors above the lower 70s floors had trouble navigating through the smoke; many attempted alternate routes.

At about 9:30 A.M. a "lock release" order, which allows all doors that are controlled by a computer inside the security system to unlock, was transmitted, but the damage caused by the plane's impact did not allow the system to work. As in the North Tower, people who called 911 were advised to stay where they were and wait for help, because the 911 operators were unaware of where the impact occurred. Although it is believed that the public address system did not work after the attack, evacuation tones are reported to have been heard above and below the impacted floors.

Response

The New York City Fire Department (FDNY)

Within five seconds of the plane hitting the North Tower, the FDNY began its response. Seven of the 11 most highly ranked chiefs in the department, with the Commissioner and many of his deputies, began their commute to the site from Brooklyn. During this trip, they had a good view of the World Trade Center and decided that it would be a rescue mission due to the magnitude and location of damage; they also called a fifth alarm, which would bring additional firefighters. In the initial response, firefighters approached the lobby of the North Tower and encountered badly burned civilians, blown out floor-to-ceiling windows, large marble tiles blown out of the walls, and an eleva-

The New York City Fire Department lost 343 firefighters in the attacks on the twin towers—the largest single loss of personnel in the history of the Department. *Photo by Andrea Booher/ FEMA News Photo.*

tor bank destroyed by the fireball. The firemen discovered that all 99 elevators were inoperable and that the sprinkler systems and standpipes might not have been working on the upper floors.

A crew began to ascend the stairwell, searching for the impact zone; other firefighters waited at the lobby for the search crew's response. At approximately 8:57 A.M., FDNY chiefs recommended that the South Tower evacuate due to the lack of safety from the damage to the North Tower. By 9:00 A.M., more than 200 firefighters were sent to the North Tower. Anecdotes from some FDNY chiefs acknowledge that they knew the dangers of the rescue mission and knew that they would probably lose some of their firefighters; however, they justified the decision based on estimates that they had 25,000 to 50,000 civilians to evacuate and rescue. No one imagined that the entire building would collapse. At approximately 9:30 A.M., a civilian falling from an upper floor landed on and killed the first firefighter of the day. By 10:00 a.m., one engine company had made it to the 54th floor, with other companies on the 44th floor and below of the North Tower.

After the second plane hit the South Tower, a second fifth alarm was activated to summon additional firefighters. Senior FDNY chiefs met and discussed their concerns, mainly communication and the lack of information about what was happening. Officials in the South Tower were frustrated by the lack of firefighters. It seems that the firefighters sent to the North Tower had not been reassigned to the South Tower after the second plane hit. The firefighters who had responded to the South Tower continued their evacuation and rescue mission. At about 9:50 A.M., firefighters found numerous seriously injured civilians on the 70th floor and even more were found trapped in an elevator on the 78th floor. A battalion chief made it to the 78th floor by the stairwell and reported that the 78th floor opened up into the 79th floor, well into the impact zone and that there were many fatalities in the area. By about 9:54 A.M., more than one-third of all FDNY companies had been dispatched to the WTC.

The New York City Police Department (NYPD)

Many NYPD officers witnessed the attack and called it into the communications center. At 8:50 A.M., the Aviation Unit of NYPD dispatched two helicopters to the roof of the North Tower to assess the damage and to see if a rooftop rescue was feasible. The NYPD pilots, in communication with the air traffic controllers at the three major local airports, learned that the controllers did not know that an airliner had crashed into the North Tower. At 8:58 A.M., the helicopters reported that a rooftop rescue could not be initiated due to heavy smoke and flames. Just before 9:00 A.M., a group of NYPD officers moved to the upper floors to set up a triage for the severely injured. A second group followed to assist in removing some of the victims. By 9:00 A.M., more than 900 police officers were dispatched to the North Tower. Officers were stationed around the complex to direct the evacuees. Subway stations around the area were shut down and evacuated. NYPD also closed down bridges and tunnels to expedite access by emergency personnel to the North Tower.

After the second attack, a second Level 4 mobilization was ordered, bringing the total number of police officers at the WTC to almost 2,000. The NYPD chief called for Operation Omega, a predetermined plan that called for the protection and evacuation of all sensitive locations around the city, including government and NYPD headquarters. NYPD officers ascended the stairs and made rescue and evacuation attempts in the South Tower. At 9:06 A.M., the NYPD Chief of Department ordered that no rooftop rescues would be made, although the two helicopters continued to fly over the Towers. At 9:51 A.M., one helicopter reported large pieces of debris hanging from the North Tower, although neither helicopter predicted that the tower would fall.

The Port Authority Police Department (PAPD)

The Port Authority's commanding officer was in the lobby of the North Tower when a fireball erupted from an elevator, causing him to dive for cover. He immediately contacted the WTC command center and set a meeting with other officers. One PAPD officer began ascending a stairwell while other officers began rescue and evacuation operation efforts on the ground floor and below the complex in the PATH (Port Authority Trans-Hudson). The PAPD did not have written instructions for personnel from outside commands responding to an incident at the WTC and some PAPD officers lacked compatible radio frequencies, which contributed to the lack of a coordinated PAPD response.

At 9:00 A.M., the PAPD commanding officer issued an evacuation order for the entire WTC complex over channel W, which could not be heard by the safety officer in the South Tower (and it can be assumed that many others didn't hear the order either). Officers who reported to the police desk were assigned to different evacuation areas including the stairwell, PATH station, plaza and the concourse. The PAPD did not have a predetermined plan on dealing with an incident of this magnitude, and had to create a plan on-site. By 9:58 A.M., one PAPD officer had reached the 44th floor of the North Tower, and another team had reached the mid-20s floors and below. Some

PAPD officers were climbing the South Tower; some were staying on ground floors of the complex to help with the evacuation.

Office of Emergency Operations (OEM)

Officials at OEM headquarters activated the Emergency Operations Center by 8:48 A.M., calling several agencies, including the FDNY, NYPD, Department of Health, and the Greater Hospital Association to send their representatives. They also called FEMA to send Urban Search and Rescue Teams. At about 8:50 A.M., a senior OEM representative arrived in the North Tower lobby and began to act as the OEM field responder to the incident. After the South Tower was hit, at 9:30 A.M., OEM decided to evacuate 7 WTC because a Secret Service agent told the senior OEM personnel that not all commercial planes had been accounted for.

COLLAPSE

At 9:37 A.M., a civilian on the 106th floor called 911 and reported that the "90-something floor" was collapsing. Due to miscommunication, this message was conveyed incorrectly and only to a few frequencies. At 9:58 A.M., the South Tower collapsed inside itself in 10 seconds. The collapse killed all civilians and first responders inside; many others on the concourse, at the Marriot next door, and on neighboring streets were also killed or injured. The collapse caused a massive cloud of debris and smoke. Some first responders in the North Tower did not realize that the South Tower had collapsed. FDNY chiefs immediately ordered a complete evacuation of the South Tower, although it is unknown if the order was heard by all units in that Tower. At 10:08 A.M., a helicopter pilot radioed that he did not think the North Tower would last much longer. The North Tower collapsed at 10:28 A.M., killing an unknown number of civilians and first responders inside the Tower and in the immediate vicinity of the Tower.

PENTAGON

The west part of the Pentagon was hit by American Airlines Flight 77 at 9:37 A.M.. The response was immediate and numerous organizations worked together. The Justice Department acted as the lead agency at the Pentagon, which houses all the components of the U.S. military. The response involved the Arlington County Fire Department among other local, state, and federal agencies. Other agencies that work at the Pentagon include the FBI, FEMA, ATF, the Virginia State Police, Metropolitan Washington Airports Authority, Ronald Reagan Washington National Airport Fire Department, Fort Meyer Fire Department, the Virginia Department of Emergency Management, National Medical Response Team, as well as other personnel from the Military District of Washington.

At 9:41 A.M., the initial Command was established; additional support was requested from fire departments in and around the Washington area. At 9:55 A.M., the incident commander ordered a full evacuation of the Pentagon because a collapse of the building

The plane striking the outer-ring of the Pentagon resulted in the loss of 125 lives within the building. *Photo Courtesy of Department of Defense.*

was imminent, and the Pentagon did partially collapse at 9:57 A.M.. No first responder was injured during this evacuation. The first of three evacuations of the command post was ordered at 10:15 A.M., due to reports of another hijacking coming into the area. All three of these reports, although false, were carried out in an efficient way and were well communicated.

The attack at the Pentagon was much different from the attack at the WTC, and this, along with the Pentagon being a powerhouse of military people, contributed to the efficiency and success of the response. The Pentagon attack occurred at relatively ground level, involved only one plane, and resulted in fewer deaths than the attacks on the WTC. Although it was a significant terrorist incident, it was not as complicated as the attacks on the WTC. Because the Pentagon is a federal government building, the plans of action in case of an attack or emergency were more detailed and agencies that helped in the aftermath worked together more efficiently than the agencies at the World Trade Center.

FEDERAL RESPONSE

On September 11, 2001, the airspace of the United States was managed and directed by two federal agencies: the Federal Aviation Administration (FAA) and the North American Aerospace Defense Command (NORAD). Every aircraft that travels above 10,000 feet is required to have a transponder transmit a unique signal to the FAA while in flight. On 9/11, terrorists on three of four flights turned off this transponder. The FAA has 22 Air Route Traffic Control Centers, which regularly receive information and make decisions independent of each other. The Control Centers in Boston, New York, Cleveland, and Indianapolis were the main points of contact between aircraft and the FAA on 9/11. Temporarily losing radio contact or even transponder signal with an aircraft or an aircraft deviating slightly from its course is not rare nor will it always cause alarm. It is when these things all happened simultaneously with multiple planes that the FAA and NORAD became alarmed.

Figure 2.1   Events of September 11, 2001

Time	
7:59	American Airlines flight 11 (AA11) takes off from Boston's Logan International Airport.
8:14	United Airlines flight 175 (UA175) takes off from Boston's Logan International Airport.
8:20	American Airlines flight 77 (AA77) takes off from Washington, D.C.'s Dulles International Airport.
8:41	Last communication from AA11 to air traffic control.
8:42	AA11 is hijacked.
8:42	United Airlines flight 93 (UA93) takes off from New Jersey's Newark International Airport.
8:42-8:46	UA175 is hijacked.
8:46	AA11 crashes into the World Trade Center's North Tower.
8:48	OEM Activates Emergency Operations Center, calling several agencies including the FDNY, NYPD, Department of Health, and the Greater Hospital Association to send representatives. Also called was FEMA to send Urban Search and Rescue Teams.
8:49	A public announcement transmitted over the loudspeakers in the South Tower advises all occupants to remain on or return to their floors.
8:50	NYPD aviation dispatches 2 helicopters to the North Tower to assess the damage and see if rooftop rescues are feasible.
8:50	A senior OEM representative arrives in the North Tower lobby and begins to act as OEM field responder to the incident.
8:51-8:54	AA77 believed hijacked.
8:57	FDNY Chiefs recommend evacuation of the South Tower due to lack of safety from the damage to the North Tower.
8:58	NYPD helicopters report that rooftop rescues from the North Tower would not be initiated due to heavy smoke and flames.
8:59	NYPD officers move to the upper floors of the North Tower to set up a triage for the severely wounded.
9:00	Over 200 FDNY firefighters sent to the North Tower.
9:00	Over 900 NYPD officers sent to North Tower.
9:00	Subway stations around the WTC complex are closed and stations are evacuated.
9:00	Port Authority Police Department commanding officer issues an evacuation order for the entire WTC complex, but because of the lack of coordinating radio frequencies, this order was not heard by the safety officer in the South Tower.
9:02	Announcement over the loudspeaker in the South Tower advises that a voluntary evacuation could begin if conditions warranted.
9:03	United Airlines 175 hits the South Tower, with the point of impact being between the 77th and 82nd floors. Becuase of the angle of the plane, at least one stairwell is still open, from the 91st floor down.
9:03	NYPD orders a second Level 4 mobilization, bringing the total number of police officers at the WTC to almost 2,000.
9:06	NYPD Chief of Department orders that no rooftop rescues would be made, although the 2 helicopters continued flying over the Towers.
9:27	UA 93 has last normal communication with air controller.
9:28	Possible screaming and a struggle is heard from the radio on UA 93 by other aircraft and air controllers; this is what is believed to be the beginning of the hijacking.

Figure 2.1, continued

9:30	A civilian falls from the tower, landing on and killing a firefighter; this is the first FDNY death of the day.
	OEM decides to evacuate 7 WTC because a Secret Service agent told senior OEM personell that not all commercial planes had been accounted for.
	A "lock-release" order, which allows doors that are locked or controlled by a computer inside the security system to unlock, is transmitted, but the damage caused by the plane's impact does not allow this order to work.
9:32	A transmission comes from UA 93 stating "We have a bomb onboard."
9:36	Cleveland Command Center tracking UA 93 and questions the FAA Command Center if the military has issued orders for military aircraft to intercept UA 93. Command Center tells Cleveland that higher ranked FAA officials are required to make the request for military assistance.
9:37	AA77 Crashes into the west wall of the Pentagon.
	A civilian on the 106th floor calls 911 and reports that the "90-something floor" was collapsing. Due to miscommunication, this message is conveyed wrongly and only to a few frequencies.
9:41	UA 93's transponder signal is lost and the Cleveland Command Center sees the plane change its route east, then south.
	Command Center for the Pentagon is arranged and numeorus agencies from the Virginia, and Washington DC areas, including military support.
9:50	Firefighters find numerous seriously injured civilians on the 70th floor of the South Tower, and even more civilians are found trapped on an elevator on the 78th floor. A battalion chief makes it up to the 78th floor by the stairwell and reports that the 78th floor opens up into the 79th floor, well into the impact zone and that there are many fatalities in the area.
9:51	An NYPD helicopter pilot reports large pieces of debris hanging from the North Tower.
9:53	FAA Headquarters discusses requesting military assistance to scramble fighter planes for UA 93.
9:54	More than 1/3 of all FDNY companies have been dispatched to the WTC.
9:55	Evacuation of the Pentagon is ordered, particularly the impact area.
9:57	Partial collapse of the Pentagon; no first responder injured or killed
9:58	Port Authority Police Department officer reaches the 44th floor of the North Tower.
	South Tower collapses into itself in ten seconds, killing civilians and first responders inside, on the concourse, at the Marriot next door, and on neighboring streets.
9:59	FDNY Chiefs immediately call a complete evacuation of the South Tower, although it is unknown if it is heard by all units in the South Tower.
10:00	One FDNY engine company makes it to the 54th floor of the North Tower, with other companies on the 44th floor and below.
10:01	A plane spotted UA Flight 93 "waving its wings," a term used to describe passengers attempting to take over the terrorists.
10:06	UA93 crashes into Stony Creek Township, Pennsylvania.
10:08	An NYPD helicopter pilot radioes that he does not think the North Tower will stay physically stable for much longer.
10:15	The Pentagon and Command Center at the Pentagon is evacuated due to reports from the FBI that a hijacked aircraft is approaching the area; this is the first of three such reports.
10:28	The North Tower collapses, killing an unknown number of civilians and first responders in and around the tower.

NORAD's main mission is to protect the United States' airspace from external threats. As of 9/11, there were seven sites, each with two fighter aircraft on alert; the United States is divided into three sectors of NORAD, and the actions on 9/11 all occurred in the Northeast Air Defense Sector (NEADS). The main threat anticipated by NORAD was cruise missiles, although scenarios that included using commercial aircraft as weapons had been developed. On 9/11, a command to shoot down a commercial aircraft would come from the President and Secretary of Defense.

American Airlines Flight 11

At 8:14, American Airlines Flight 11 did not increase its elevation to 35,000 feet as directed by the Boston Center air traffic controller. The controller repeatedly tried to contact the aircraft, especially after he tried to contact the pilot on the emergency frequency and received no response. At 8:21, when the flight turned off its transponder, there was increased concern, although the threat of a hijacking was not considered. The path of the flight began to change and the plane wandered into the paths of other flights. The controller had to change the paths of the flights in the interrupted path. At 8:24, a message came from Flight 11 that confirmed that the flight had been hijacked.

The controller followed FAA protocol for hijackings and between 8:24 and 8:32 notified the chain of command of the possible hijacking of AA Flight 11. At 8:28, the Herndon Command Center was informed of the possible hijacking and that it was believed that Flight 11 was headed toward New York airspace. The Herndon Command Center organized a conference call among the Boston, New York, and Cleveland Centers. At 8:32, the Command Center contacted the Operations Center at FAA headquarters. At 8:34, the Command Center contacted the military through FAA's Cape Cod facility. The final transmission from Flight 11 came to the controllers at 8:34, and a voice was heard instructing the plane's passengers "We are going back to the airport. Don't try to make any stupid moves."

At 8:37, the Command Center made contact with NEADS; this was the first notification to the military that Flight 11 had been hijacked. NEADS Battle Commander Colonel Robert Marr ordered the two F-15 aircraft at Otis Air Force Base in Falmouth, Massachusetts to battle stations. Marr then contacted Major General Larry Arnold, commanding general of the First Air Force and NORAD's Continental Region, to get authorization to scramble the fighter jets. The commanding general complied with the request and the

The F-15 fighter is the country's first line of air defense against an air or missile attack. There were jets in the air at about the same time that American Airlines Flight 11 struck WTC. It is questionable whether an order would have been given to shoot down the plane because America had never faced the actuality of such an event. In the aftermath of the attack it is clear that if a future threat emerges permission to down the threatening aircraft would come more quickly. *Photo Courtesy of Department of Defense.*

F-15 fighter jets were scrambled at 8:46 A.M. There was a lot of confusion because they did not know where Flight 11 was and, therefore, they did not know where to send the fighter jets. American Airlines Flight 11 hit the WTC at 8:46 A.M. NEADS personnel were informed at 8:50 A.M. that a plane hit the North Tower.

The F-15 fighter jets were airborne at 8:53 A.M., and, after they were informed that a plane hit the North Tower of the WTC, they were ordered to remain in the airspace until further notice.

United Airlines Flight 175

United Airlines Flight 175's last transmission to controllers occurred at 8:42 A.M., shortly after entering New York airspace. A voice is heard saying "We heard a suspicious transmission on our departure out of Boston, ah, with someone, ah, it sounded like someone keyed the mikes and said ah everyone ah stay in your seats." Within the next few minutes the plane abruptly turned southwest and its transponder code changed once, and then twice, at 8:47 A.M.. At 8:48 A.M., the air traffic control center was concentrating on finding American Flight 11, unaware that it had already crashed into the WTC. The controller looking for AA Flight 11 noticed at 8:51 that the transponder on UA Flight 175 had changed and immediately tried to contact the plane, with no response. The controller attempted several more times to make contact with the flight. He contacted another controller at 8:53 A.M., telling him that "we may have a hijack." The plane then began to head for New York City, and the controller contacted a New York manager at 8:55 to tell her that he believed UA Flight 175 had also been hijacked. The only knowledge by FAA Headquarters or the Herndon Command Center that there was a second hijacking was a phone conversation between 9:01 and 9:02 that said "We're, we're involved with something else, we have other aircraft that may have a similar situation going on here." Also at 9:01, the New York terminal approach located Flight 175 in rapid descent before it crashed into the South Tower at 9:03 A.M.

During this time, the Boston Command Center stopped all departures under New England Region's control. The Boston Command Center confirmed at 9:05 that the hijackers on AA Flight 11 said "we have planes," and the New York Center declared "ATC zero," an order to stop all departures, arrivals or travel through New York's airspace until further notice. After UA Flight 175 crashed into the South Tower, the Boston Command Center told its controllers to tell all active aircraft of the events at the WTC and implement heightened cockpit security.

The first notification to the military of a second hijacked flight occurred at 9:03 A.M., about the same time that UA Flight 175 hit the South Tower, when the New York Center contacted NEADS. At 9:08, when the mission crew commander of NEADS learned of the second impact, he decided that the fighter jets needed to be closer to Manhattan, and to coordinate that plan of action with the FAA. The fighter jets arrived in Manhattan airspace at 9:25 and made a combat air patrol (CAP) over the city. Due to refueling concerns, fighter jets from the Langley Air Force Base in Virginia were scrambled at 9:09.

American Airlines Flight 77

American Airlines Flight 77 slightly deviated from its flight path at 8:54 A.M., and then completely disappeared from radar two minutes later. The Indianapolis Center, which was tracking the flight, attempted contact with the flight via radio and, not knowing what was happening in New York, believed that the flight had experienced a serious mechanical or electrical malfunction. The Indianapolis Center contacted the Air Force Search and Rescue at Langley Air Force Base in Virginia at 9:08 A.M. to look for any downed aircraft. The Center also contacted West Virginia State Police and asked them to be on alert for any downed aircraft. At 9:09, the Indianapolis Center contacted the FAA regional center about the loss of contact with AA Flight 77, and the regional center then passed the information along at 9:24. The Indianapolis Center learned by 9:20 of the other hijacked aircraft and then began to doubt that AA Flight 77 had crashed. By 9:21, agencies including the Command Center, some FAA field offices, and American Airlines began to search for AA Flight 77, fearing that it had been hijacked. The Command Center notified FAA headquarters of the missing flight at 9:25. Although the Command Center knew that AA Flight 77 was missing, neither the Center nor FAA headquarters issued a warning or notified surrounding centers to look for the aircraft; the flight traveled, undetected, for 36 minutes on its way to Washington, DC.

At 9:25 A.M., the Command Center ordered a "nationwide ground stop." At 9:21, Dulles International Airport was notified of the missing flight and told to look for primary targets. A primary target was located at 9:32, going eastbound at a high rate of speed; Regan National Airport was notified, as well as the Secret Service. At 9:33, the Secret Service was notified that a suspicious aircraft was headed towards the White House, and right before an agent was to evacuate the Vice President, the plane turned south, away from the White House. After about a minute, the aircraft turned west and began to head for the White House again. The Vice President was evacuated from the White House at 9:36 and entered the underground shelter at 9:37. An unarmed National Guard C130H cargo aircraft was directed to find the primary target. The cargo aircraft identified the target as a Boeing 757, tried to follow it, and at 9:38 reported to the control tower "looks like that aircraft crashed into the Pentagon sir."

NORAD did not hear anything about the missing AA Flight 77, although the NEADS jets heard misinformation about AA Flight 11 at 9:21. It seems that the information that was transmitted was about AA Flight 77, although it was transmitted as AA Flight 11. At 9:23 the NEADS crew commander ordered F-15 jet fighters from Langley to scramble, and the fighter jets were airborne towards Baltimore at 9:30. At 9:34, NEADS contacted FAA headquarters about AA Flight 11 and learned, for the first time, that AA Flight 77 was missing. When the Langley fighters were called to head toward the White House, it was discovered that, due to miscommunication, they were over the Atlantic Ocean area and were 150 miles away when AA Flight 77 crashed into the Pentagon at 9:37 A.M.

Delta Airlines Flight 1989 was identified by the Boston Center as a possible hijacking. It, along with AA Flight 11 and UA Flight 175, was a transcontinental 767 jetliner that departed from Logan International Airport. The plane was tracked until it was determined that it had not been hijacked.

United Airlines Flight 93

At 9:27 A.M., United Airlines Flight 93 confirmed a message from the Cleveland Center controller and less than a minute later the controller and surrounding aircraft heard "a radio transmission of unintelligible sounds of possible screaming or a struggle from an unknown origin." When the Cleveland Center responded to this transmission, a second, similar transmission came into the Center. While the controllers at Cleveland Center were looking for the origins of the transmission, they noticed that UA Flight 93 had descended approximately 700 feet and there was no response when controllers tried multiple times to reach the flight. At 9:32, a transmission was heard with a voice saying "Keep remaining sitting. We have a bomb on board." By 9:34, FAA headquarters was informed that UA Flight 93 had been hijacked. Between 9:34 and 9:38, UA Flight 93 was observed ascending to 40,700 feet and controllers moved several planes out of the flight path. A fourth radio transmission was heard at 9:39 A.M., with the pilot confirming that a bomb was on board and to try to keep the passengers calm. From 9:34 until 10:08, FAA headquarters was kept aware of everything happening with UA Flight 93. The transponder signal was lost at 9:41 A.M. At 9:42, after the Command Center learned that an aircraft had struck the Pentagon, the FAA released an order for all aircraft to land immediately at the nearest airport, an unprecedented request (It is interesting to note that the air traffic control system effectively controlled about 4,500 flights that landed around the country).

At 9:49 A.M., the Cleveland Center inquired about getting the military involved; at 9:53 FAA headquarters was discussing scrambling planes. The Command Center then lost track of UA Flight 93 over Pittsburgh; at 10:01 a plane spotted UA Flight 93 "waving its wings," a term used to describe the passengers' attempt to take over the terrorists. UA Flight 93 crashed in a Pennsylvania field at 10:03 A.M. The first report of black smoke from the crash site was from the cargo plane that had been following AA Flight 77. The military had not been informed that UA Flight 93 had been hijacked until 10:07.

NEADS was attempting to locate the flight on radar, not realizing that the flight had crashed in Pennsylvania, and did not know it had crashed until 10:15 A.M.

Although the NEADS officers and commanders actively sought information, they had little, if any, awareness of the hijacked flights. NEADs knew about the hijacking of AA Flight 11 nine minutes before it crashed and had no notice before UA Flight 175, AA Flight 77, and UA Flight 93 crashed. It was only after all the aircraft had crashed that personnel at NEADS and FAA made an unprecedented move to implement a nationwide alert and land all active aircraft.

FEDERAL NOTIFICATION

No one in the White House, including the President, was aware of the hijacking before UA Flight 93 crashed into the North Tower at the WTC. In fact, most federal agencies were informed of the planes' crashes in New York from CNN. President Bush, in Sarasota, Florida at Emma E. Booker Elementary School, was told that a small twin engine plane had crashed into the WTC. The President believed that it must be from pilot error and, after speaking with National Security Advisor Condoleezza Rice at 8:55 A.M., continued his plans to read to a class at the school. At 9:05 A.M., the President was told that a second plane hit the South Tower. The President decided that he needed to stay calm and continued reading to the children for another five to seven minutes.

President Bush was briefed by his staff at about 9:15 A.M. and then spoke to Vice President Dick Cheney, National Security Advisor Condoleezza Rice, New York Governor George Pataki, and FBI Director Robert Mueller. The President made a brief statement at the school before leaving for the airport at 9:35; he reached the airport between 9:42 and 9:45. During this time, the President spoke with the Vice President and confirmed that he was informed of the attacks against the WTC and the Pentagon. Air Force One departed at 9:54, with no fixed destination.

Vice President Cheney, like many other Americans, watched the attack unfold on television. Viewing the damage from the first impact on the North Tower, he wondered how it could happen, and then a second plane hit the South Tower. After the second plane hit, many in the White House have said that they knew it was not an accident. Security precautions were taken by many, including the Secret Service who set up security precaution around the White House.

The FAA, White House, and Defense Department all set up multi-agency teleconferences, although none of them included the correct people before 10:00 A.M. At 9:20, the FAA set up a teleconference with several agencies, including the Defense Department that was fruitless. At approximately the same time, Special Assistant to the President Richard Clarke set up an interagency meeting with the CIA, FBI, Department of State, Department of Justice, Department of Defense, FAA and the White House shelter. At about 9:40, the safety of the President, the White House, and federal agencies was first discussed when it was reported that a plane crashed into the Pentagon. At 10:03, news of more hijacked aircraft reached the interagency meeting, as well as the combat air patrol set up over Washington. During this meeting, at 10:25 A.M., confirmation to shoot down the suspected hijacked aircraft came from the President, although that was being relayed to the Pentagon already.

The task of the National Military Command Center during an emergency is to establish the chain of command between the National Command Authority (made up of the President and Secretary of Defense) and those needed to carry out the orders. Secretary of Defense Donald Rumsfeld was in a briefing when he learned of the second strike in New York and helped with efforts after the Pentagon was hit. A "significant event" teleconference began at 9:29 A.M. with the events thus far being covered: two aircraft struck the World Trade Center, confirmed hijacking of American Flight 11, and jet fighters from Otis had been scrambled. The false information from the FAA concerning Flight 11 heading toward Washington, DC was covered in this meeting. The FAA had incorrectly not been added to the call, and therefore updated information from the agency had not been provided. The call ended at 9:34 A.M.

The "significant event" call resumed at 9:37, as an air threat conference call that included the President, Vice President, Secretary of Defense, Vice Chairman of the Joint Chiefs of Staff, and Deputy National Security Advisor Stephen Hadley, military personnel from the White House underground shelter and the President's military aide on Air Force One. The FAA was also included on the call at 10:17 after technical difficulties, although the representative had no relevant information about the situation or access to decisionmakers.

Between 10:10 and 10:15, the Vice President was informed that a suspicious aircraft (UAFlight 93) was 80 miles from Washington. He was asked for permission to engage the aircraft and he said "yes." Between 10:12 and 10:18, the military aide returned to confirm that the aircraft was 60 miles away and asked for authority to engage. The Vice President again confirmed engagement. After the second confirmation, White House Deputy Chief of Staff Joshua Bolten suggested that the Vice President call the President to confirm the engagement orders. Vice President Cheney called the President at 10:18 and received approval from the President. When the members in the shelter were informed that an aircraft had gone down in Pennsylvania, they wondered if it had been shot down by the U.S. military. At about 10:30 A.M., reports came in that another hijacked plane was only 5-10 miles outside the city. The Vice President again authorized to engage the aircraft. This aircraft was later identified as a medical evacuation (MEDEVAC) helicopter.

Figure 2.2   9/11 Action and Response by First Responders and the Federal Government

Time	
7:59	American Airlines flight 11 (AA11) takes off from Boston's Logan International Airport.
	United Airlines flight 175 (UA175) takes off from Boston's Logan International Airport.
8:14	American Airlines Flight 11 goes against procedure and does not increase elevation to 35,000 feet.
8:20	American Airlines flight 77 (AA77) takes off from Washington, D.C.'s Dulles International Airport.
8:21	AA Flight 11 turns off transponder.
8:24	Message is sent from AA Flight 11 to Boston Center air traffic control that confirms hijacking.
8:28	Boston Center air traffic control contacts Herndon Command Center, who organizes a conference call between Boston, New York, and Cleveland Centers.
8:32	Command Center contacts Operations Center at FAA headquarters.
8:34	Command Center contacts the military through the FAA's Cape Cod facility.
	Final transmission from AA Flight 11.
8:37	Command Center makes contact with NEADS. NEADS Battle Commander orders two F-15 aircraft at Otis Air Force Base to battle stations.
8:42	United Airlines flight 93 (UA93) takes off from New York's Newark International Airport.
	AA Flight 175's last transmission to controllers.
8:46	F-15 fighter jets are scrambled.
	American Airlines Flight 11 hits the North Tower of the World Trade Center.
8:47	AA Flight 175 abruptly turns southwest and transponder code changes twice.
8:48	Air traffic control is concentrating on finding Flight 11, unaware that it had already crashed into the World Trade Center.
8:50	NEADS personnel is informed that a plane hit the North Tower of the World Trade Center.
8:51	Controller looking for AA Flight 11 notices that AA Flight 175's code changed and tries to contact the aircraft.
8:53	F-15 fighter jets are airborne, then informed that a plane hit the World Trade Center. Ordered to remain in airspace until further notice.
	Controller contacts another controller, telling him "we may have a hijack," referring to UA 93.
	President Bush is informed by Senior Advisor to the President Karl Rove that a small twin-engine aircraft had struck the North Tower of the World Trade Center.
8:54	American Airlines flight 77 deviates slightly from its flight path.
8:55	Controller contacts New York manager to tell her that he believes Flight 175 has been hijacked.
	President Bush confers with National Security Advisor Condoleeza Rice, who informs him that it was actually a commercial flight that hit the building.
	President Bush believes the crash to be pilot error and continues with his plans to read to the children of Emma E. Booker Elementary in Sarasota, FL.
8:56	Flight 77 completely disappears from radar; Indianopolis Center attempts contact with flight via radio with no response.
9:00	Indianapolis Center begins contacting other agencies and informing them that Flight 77 was missing and possibly crashed.
9:01	Phone coversation to FAA headquarters and Herndon Command Center saying there was another plane in a similar situation as AA Flight 11.
	New York terminal locates Flight 175 in rapid descent before it crashes into the South Tower of the World Trade Center.

Figure 2.2, continued

9:03	Flight 175 crashes into South Tower of the World Trade Center.
9:05	President Bush is informed that a second plane has hit the South Tower of the World Trade Center.
9:08	Indianapolis Center contacts Langley Air Force Base to look for any downed aircraft.
	Indianapolis Center contacts West Virginia State Police and asks them to be on alert for downed aircraft.
	NEADS learns of second impact at World Trade Center and orders the jets from Otis Air Force Base to fly closer to Manhattan.
9:09	Fighter jets from Langley Air Force base are scrambled.
	Indianapolis Center contacts FAA regional center regarding loss of AA Flight 77.
9:15	President Bush meets with Vice President Dick Cheney, Condoleeza Rice, New York Governor George Pataki, and FBI Director Robert Mueller.
9:20	Indianapolis Center learns of the hijacking of AA Flights 175 and 11.
	FAA sets up a teleconference with several agencies, including the Defense Department.
	Special Assistant to the President Richard Clarke sets up an interagency meeting with the CIA, FBI, Department of State, Department of Justice, Department of Defense, the FAA, and the White House Shelter.
9:21	Dulles International Airport is notified of missing AA Flight 77 and told to look for primary targets.
	The Command Center and some FAA field offices begin to search for AA Flight 77, fearing it has been hijacked.
9:25	Otis Base fighter jets arrive in Manhattan airspace and makes a Combat Air Patrol over the city.
	The Command Center notifies the FAA headquarters of missing AA Flight 77.
	The Command Center orders a "nationwide ground stop."
9:27	United Flight 93 confirms a message from Cleveland Center controller.
9:28	Controller hears a radio transmission from UA Flight 93 of unintelligible sounds of possible screaming or a struggle.
9:30	Cleveland Center controllers notice UA Flight 93 had descended approximately 700 feet and is not responding to attempts to reach it.
9:32	A transmission is heard saying, " Keep remaining sitting. We have a bomb on board."
9:33	A primary target is located, going eastbound at a high rate of speed.
	Reagan National Airport and the Secret Service are notified of the primary target.
	Secret Service is notified that a suspicious aircraft is headed towards the White House.
9:34	FAA headquarters is informed that UA Flight 93 was hijacked.
9:35	President Bush leaves Emma E. Booker Elementary School.
9:36	Immediate evacuation of the Vice President is ordered.
9:37	AA 77 crashes into the Pentagon.
	Vice President enters the underground shelter.
9:38	National Guard C130H aircraft is advised to find the primary target reported to the control tower and to inform them that the target had crashed into the Pentagon.
9:39	Fourth transmission from UA Flight 93 heard, with the pilot trying to keep the passengers calm.
9:40	The safety of the President, White House, and federal agencies is discussed when it is reported that a plane had hit the Pentagon.
9:41	Transponder signal from UA Fflight 93 is lost.

Figure 2.2, continued

9:42	FAA releases an order for all aircraft to immediately land at the nearest airport.
9:49	Cleveland Center inquires about getting the military involved.
9:53	FAA headquarters discusses scrambling planes.
9:54	Air Force One departs from Florida, and is ordered to not return to Washington.
9:55	Command Center loses track of UA Flight 93 over Pittsburgh.
10:03	News of more hijacked airplanes reaches the FAA teleconference, as well as the combat air patrol set up over Washington.
10:06	UA 93 crashes into Stony Creek Township, Pennsylvania.
10:07	The military is informed of the hijacking of UA Flight 93.
10:15	NEADS is informed of the United 93 crash.
10:25	President gives confirmation to shoot down any hijacked aircraft.

ECONOMIC IMPACT

The 9/11 attacks focused the world's attention on the human and economic costs associated with violent acts of terrorism. Terrorism was certainly not a new phenomenon, but the gravity of the 9/11 attacks vividly illustrates the impact that terrorism has on the global economy. The costs are measured not only in financial terms and human suffering, but also in organizational policies and procedures of governments and the private sectors of countries throughout the world. Analysis of the costs associated with the WTC attacks provides an image of the impact of a massive catastrophe.

The causes and injustices that have led groups to choose violence as a means to rectify grievances (many of which are legitimate) can be debated. However, ultimately, those who suffer the most from terrorism are likely to be innocent citizens and public servants. The vast majority of the world's population want nothing more than to live in peace and pursue goals related to self-actualization and a better life for themselves and their families. The costs of terrorism throughout the world number in the billions of local and foreign currencies—ranging from the loss of income-producing family members and economic losses due to joblessness, to monumental costs in security requirements, government redeployment of funds and losses to private business enterprises.

The twentieth century was the most dynamic century in the history of mankind. More things changed with respect to daily living during the past one hundred years than occurred in any similar period of man's existence. The changes in communication alone have been phenomenal. In 1900 most people relied upon face-to-face conversation or the written word (assuming a person could

Osama bin Laden

Osama bin Laden was born on March 10, 1957 in Riyadh, Saudi Arabia. He studied business and project administration and in 1979, he earned a degree in civil engineering from King Abdul Aziz University in Jeddah, Saudi Arabia. In 1984, bin Laden established Maktab al Khadamat (MAK) to support the Afghans during the Afghan War against Russia. He did so by sending money, weapons, and Muslim fighters to assist in the opposition. In 1987 he left MAK to launch a crusade against Israel and the Western influence in Islamic countries. Based on these ideologies, al Qaeda was created in 1988. Bin Laden and al Qaeda's first known attack on the United States was on December 12, 1992 when they bombed the Gold Mihor Hotel in Aden, Yemen. The bombing killed approximately 100 American soldiers who were there in support of Operation Restore Hope. He is suspected of helping plan the 1993 attack on the World Trade Center. In 1994, Osama bin Laden's family publicly disowned him. Saudi Arabia revoked his citizenship after he admitted responsibility for the 1995 attacks on American and Saudi military bases in Riyadh and Dahran. In 1996, he was relocated to Afghanistan in an agreement between Saudi Arabia, Egypt, and the United States.

In 1998, Osama bin Laden and Ayman al Zawahiri signed a fatwa* that stated, "The ruling to kill the Americans and their allies—civilians and military—is an individual duty for every Muslim who can do it in any country in which it is possible to do it, in order to liberate the al-Aqsa Mosque (in Jerusalem) and the holy mosque (in Makka) from their grip, and in order for their armies to move out of all the lands of Islam, defeated and unable to threaten any Muslim. This is in accordance with the words of Almighty Allah, 'and fight the pagans all together as they fight you all together,' and 'fight them until there is no more tumult or oppression, and there prevail justice and faith in Allah.'"

Bin Laden is also wanted by the U.S. government also for his involvement in the bombings of two United States embassies in Dar es Salaam, Tanzania and Nairobi, Kenya. The bombings on August 7, 1998, killed 257 people and injured more than 5000. Osama bin Laden has been on the FBI's Ten Most Wanted Fugitives list since 1999. bin Laden and the al Qaeda terrorists are also wanted for their involvement in the October 2000 bombing of the USS Cole. After 9/11, the U.S. government immediately identified bin Laden as the number one suspect. He publicly released an interview wherein he stated, "I was not involved in the September 11 attacks in the United States nor did I have knowledge of the attacks." However, this statement was proven false when a videotape was found during a raid in Afghanistan. On the tape, Osama bin Laden is quoted as saying, "We calculated in advance the number of casualties from the enemy, who would be killed based on the position of the tower. We calculated that the floors that would be hit would be three or four floors. I was the most optimistic of them all. (. . . Inaudible . . .) Due to my experience in this field, I was thinking that the fire from the gas in the plane would melt the iron structure of the building and collapse the area where the plane hit and all the floors above it only. This is all we had hoped for."

Photo Courtesy of the Federal Bureau of Investigation, www.fbi.gov

---

* A Fatwa is a legal pronouncement or decree handed down by an Islamic scholar.

read) to communicate. A hundred years later even children regularly carry cell phones and use the Internet on a daily basis. Televisions can be carried in the hand, and powerful radios can fit into a pocket. In transportation the horse and train has (sic) been replaced by the car that can travel on almost any hard surface. People can fly to places in several hours that would have taken a week to travel a century ago. Weapons have become so sophisticated and commonplace that virtually anyone can obtain one capable of causing horrific damage. The attacks on the World Trade Center and the Pentagon are real examples of the way in which terrorists can use everyday tools as a means of conducting a terrorist attack (Dyson, 2001).

The impact of terrorism on other countries is significant. The total cost to the world is probably immeasurable, in the billions of dollars and loss of lives numbering in the hundreds of thousands. The cost to security forces and private companies is just beginning to be measured.

THE ECONOMIC DIMENSION

The world economy today touches almost every country. The main goods that are traded across borders include cars, trucks and car parts, petroleum products, textiles, footwear, and clothing. In addition, service related activities, such as tourism, communications and computer support, advertising, legal services, and entertainment make up a major part of the global economic environment.

A study released by the New York City Partnership shortly after 9/11 estimated that the damage to the New York economy would top $83 billion in losses. Even after payment of insurance claims, remaining losses would be more than $16 billion with a potential to go much higher depending on the performance of the total U.S. economy. In New York alone, in the fourth quarter of 2001, 125,000 jobs were lost. Lower Manhattan lost 30 percent of its office space thus putting at risk the remaining 270,000 jobs in the area. The study showed that the hardest hit sectors were tourism, retail, and financial services, and the ripple effect was tremendous.

Measuring the economic costs of terrorism goes far beyond financial considerations. The costs in terms of human suffering, loss of life, impact on family and friends, lost opportunities because of shifting priorities, the long-term psychological and sociological effects on whole societies, the impact on government decisions, and the burdens placed on public security forces can never be accurately measured. The list of financial costs resulting from a terrorist attack is lengthy. Some of the costs include:

Figure 2.3   9/11 Hijackers (see Appendix 2)

FLIGHT 11 HIJACKERS

| Mohamed Atta | Abdulaziz Alomari | Satam M. A. Al Suqami | Wail M. Alsheri | Waleed M. Alsheri |

FLIGHT 77 HIJACKERS

| Hani Hanjour | Khalid Almihdhar | Majed Moqed | Nawaf Alhazmi | Salem Alhazmi |

FLIGHT 93 HIJACKERS

  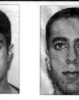 

| Ahmad Ibrahim Al Haznawi | Ahmed Alnami | Saeed Al-ghamdi | Ziad Samir Jarrah |

FLIGHT 175 HIJACKERS

| Ahmad Al-ghamdi | Mohand Alshehri | Hamza Al-ghamdi | Marwan Al-Shehhi | Fayez Rashid Ahmed Hassal Al Qadi Banihammad |

- Individual and family losses of "breadwinners"

- Insurance payouts and premium increases

- Travel related losses, especially air travel

- Losses in tourism

- Commercial business losses

- Increased security

- Higher costs for transportation of goods.

- Replacing facilities and damaged equipment

- Infrastructure repair

- Fuel costs

In the short term, some of the worst sufferers from a global down-turn will, as ever, be those who can least afford it. The countries that are accused of supporting terrorism are often among the worlds poorest. A large part of Afghanistan's problem is that it is not a participant in the global economy, and its [former] rulers have been eagerly taking it back into the dark ages, intellectually and economically. Other poor countries have enjoyed some economic growth through growing participation in the global economy, but a downturn will not only prejudice their economic prospects but imperil their political stability as well (Singleton-Green, 2001).

The 9/11 tragedy is perhaps most illustrative of global economic costs because it has received worldwide media coverage. Terrorist attacks in other countries have generally not received such international attention. The costs to airlines throughout the world were staggering. In Canada, 3,000 airline employees lost their jobs, and airlines in Canada, Switzerland, and Belgium were forced into bankruptcy (Robertson, 2001). An airport executive estimated that airports are expected to lose more than $2 billion in revenues and incur more than $1 billion in additional security costs in the 12 months following the September 11 attacks (Marchini, 2001).

In the United States, the unemployment rate reached its highest point in 20 years. An estimated nine million hotel and tourism workers lost their jobs according to another report (Hamid, 2001). The International Labour Union estimated that "24-million people worldwide could be fired this year" (*Business Day*, 2001).

World Bank President James Wolfensohn estimated that tens of thousands of children would die "and some ten million people are likely to be living below the poverty line of one (US) dollar per day because of the attacks." (*Ghanaian Chronicle*, 2001).

The costs of an attack on global communications networks are considerable. "The growing concern in the United States and elsewhere regarding the potential for information attacks against critical information structures needs to be addressed in light of both past experience and new conditions." (Rattray, 2001:66).

Key Concepts

- The 9/11 attacks were committed by al Qaeda and almost 3,000 were killed and thousands others injured at three sites: the World Trade Center in New York City, the Pentagon Building in Washington, DC, and a field in Stony Creek Township, Pennsylvania.

- Local agencies generally act as the first responders in disaster and emergency situations. This is evidenced by the initial response to the WTC site by the New York City Fire Department, New York City Police Department, Port Authority Police Department, and other agencies in the New York area.

- The coordinated effort at the Pentagon, which resulted in fewer deaths and injuries than the WTC site, is attributed to the less catastrophic impact of the plane, the more detailed plans of action for the building, and the efficiency different agencies working together.

- The federal response to the 9/11 attack has been accused of being inefficient, lacking adequate communication among agencies, and being unprepared for such an attack.

- The economic impact of the attacks is far reaching and, in New York City alone, is estimated to be upwards of $83 billion. Economic estimates do not solely include the financial losses, but also human suffering, loss of life, and the long term psychological and sociological ramifications.

Additional Readings

National Commission on Terrorist Attacks (2004). The 9/11 Commission Report: Final Report of the National Commission on Terrorist Attacks Upon the United States. New York, NY: W.W. Norton & Company.

CRS Report for Congress (2001). *Terrorism: Near Eastern Groups and State Sponsors, 2001.* Katzman, Kenneth.

Terrorist Attacks by Al Qaeda (2004). Congressional Research Service. Washington, DC

United States of America v. Zacarias Moussaoui.

Annual Country Reports on Terrorism, Title 22, Chapter 38. §2656f (2005).

Arlington County: After-Action Report on the Response to the September 11 Terrorist Attack on the Pentagon.

RELATED WEBSITES

Institute for the Study of Violent Groups http://www.isvg.org
(provides a comprehensive list of terrorist groups and other information and data related to terrorism throughout the world)

Port Authority PD (PAPD) http://www.panynj.gov/

The Office of Emergency Operation (OEM) http://www.nyc.gov/html/oem/home.html

Federal Aviation Association (FAA) FAA.gov

North American Aerospace Defense Command (NORAD) NORAD.mil

Northeast Air Defense Sector (NEADS) http://www.neads.ang.af.mil/

REFERENCES

Business Day (2001, November 9). "South Africa: Attacks Lead to Massive Jobs Losses." Africa News Service.

Cable News Network (2001, December 26).

Campbell, K.M. & M. Flournoy (2001*). To Prevail: An American Strategy for the Campaign Against Terrorism.* Washington, DC: The CSIS Press.

Dyson, W. (2001). Terrorism. Internet presentation for the Texas Commission on Law Enforcement Officer Standards and Education. Online.

Enders, W. & T. Sandler (1991). "Causality Between Transnational Terrorism and Tourism." *Terrorism: An International Journal*,14(1). New York: Crane, Russak and Co.

Ghanian Chronicle (2001, November 8). PanAfrica; Africa, America and the Terrorist Menace. Africa News Service. November 8, 2001.

Hamid, H. (2001, November 23). "Jobs Threat for 9M in World's Hotels, Tourism Industry." *New Straits Times Press*. (Malaysia) p. 2.

Jackson, B.A. (2001). "Technology Acquisition By Terrorist Groups." *Studies in Conflict & Terrorism*, 24(3):183-213.

Marchini, D. (2001, November 21). Airports Struggle Along with Airline Industry. *Cable News Network*. Transcript #112104cb.102.

NYC Partnership, *Economic Impact Analysis of the September 11th Attack on New York.* Executive Summary. November, 2001.

Rattray, G.J. (2001). *Strategic Warfare in Cyberspace*. Cambridge, MA: MIT Press.

Robertson, G. (2001, November 13). "Black Day for Airline Industry 'Imperiled' by New York Plane Crash." *Calgary Herald*. C1.

Singleton-Green, B. (2001, October 31). "Editorial—The Costs of Terror." *Financial Times* (London) Global News Wire. p.27.

NOTES

[1]   NY Times Article "A Nation Challenged: The Toll; In Cold Numbers, a Census of the Sept. 11 Victims" by Eric Lipton on April 19, 2002 in the Metropolitan Desk section.

[2]   As referred to by Jamal Ahmed Mohamed al-Fadl, a key government witness in the 1998 bombings of two U.S. embassies in Africa. According to al-Fadl, bin Laden made the following statement in 1993: "We have to stop the head of the snake . . . The snake is America and we have to stop them. We have to cut their head off and stop what they are doing in the Horn of Africa."

[3]   Several versions of the spelling of al Qaida have been published. The most common version used in the U.S. is "al Qaeda" and is the version used by this text.

[4]   Federal Bureau of Investigation (1998). *Terrorism in the United States 1998*. Washington, DC: U.S. Government Printing Office.

Chapter 3

The 9/11 Commission and the Department of Homeland Security

INTRODUCTION

The consequences of the 9/11 terrorist attacks will continue to resonate on political, social, economic, environmental, educational, and personal levels for generations. Traditional boundaries for cooperation and communication were transcended by a crisis, the magnitude of which conventional scenario planning and war gaming failed to accurately predict. The severity and visceral nature of the attacks, personalized by the tremendous loss of life introduced a sense of vulnerability and fear into American society which had no close parallel with the exception, perhaps, of disease epidemics in an earlier century.[1] Ever-present television coverage of the crime scenes and the seemingly endless search, first for survivors and subsequently for the recovery of victims, increased those feelings.

Policymakers across all strata of government—military, civilian, and law enforcement organizations—were compelled to react, at least initially, in a unilateral fashion, due to the urgency of the situation and to the lack of existing interagency relationships. The void was apparent organizationally by a lack of substantive knowledge about capabilities and resources within other agencies, and technologically by the inability to communicate across and, in many cases, among agencies on common or shared communication frequencies. Even if the attacks had not crippled the towers which supported communications, the lack of shared frequencies prevented real-time information related to operational needs being shared. Messengers were sent between command personnel both in New York and at the Pentagon site. The continuing absence of a redundant interoperable communications capability exposes a vulnerability to both criminal and terrorist organizations that must be resolved.

The absence of coordination and collaboration in the area of information and intelligence sharing contributed to the surprise nature of the attack. This is not a new issue: consider the last major surprise attack on U.S.

interests at Pearl Harbor: "Surprise, when it happens to a government, is likely to be a complicated, diffuse, bureaucratic thing. It includes neglect of responsibility but also responsibility so poorly defined or so ambiguously delegated that action gets lost. It includes gaps in intelligence, but also intelligence that, like a string of pearls too precious to wear, is too sensitive to give to those who need it." (Wohlstetter, 1962, Preface).[2]

The gaps in information sharing between and among agencies have been exhaustively chronicled in *The 9/11 Commission Report* and have been the foundation for sweeping legislative and organizational reform. In the weeks and months after the 9/11 attacks, and affirmed through recommendations in the *9/11 Commission Report*, was a series of national strategies to ensure the domestic security of the United States. These strategies, drafted by Bush Administration officials and staffers and released by the White House, provided the foundations for the creation of the Office of Homeland Security in October 2001, and eventually the Department of Homeland Security in March 2003. The first of these strategies was the National Strategy for the Homeland Security, which was released on July 16, 2002.

Homeland Security is defined within the National Strategy for Homeland Security as "a concerted national effort to prevent terrorist attacks within the United States, reduce America's vulnerability to terrorism, and minimize the damage and recover from attacks that do occur."[3] It is important to note that several definitions of terrorism are available and used interchangeably between agencies. The Homeland Security Act of 2002 defines terrorism in a slightly different way and encompasses both foreign and domestic entities: "terrorism" is defined as any activity that involves an act that is dangerous to human life or potentially destructive of critical infrastructure or key resources; and is a violation of criminal laws of the United States or any State, or subdivision; and appears to be intended to intimidate or coerce a civilian population; to influence the policy of a government by intimidation or coercion; or to affect the conduct of a government by mass destruction, assassination, or kidnapping.

The Homeland Security Act also specifies additional roles for the Department of Homeland Security, which include: carrying out all functions of entities transferred to the Department, including acting as the focal point regarding natural and manmade crisis and emergency planning; ensuring that the functions of the agencies and subdivisions within the Department that are directly related to securing the homeland are not diminished or neglected except by a specific act of Congress; and to monitor connections between illegal drug trafficking and terrorism, coordinate efforts to sever such connections, and otherwise contribute to efforts to interdict drug trafficking (Section 101, Executive Department; Mission).

The development and implementation of first, the Office, and then, the Department of Homeland Security, and an integrated National Strategy and supporting legislation encompass a wide range of tasks. It requires the reor-

ganization and realignment of the
missions of 22 separate agencies,
each with their own distinct organizational and jurisdictional
responsibilities, personnel policies, management systems,
recruitment and training standards, and individual agency
morale and loyalties. Institutionalized jurisdictional competitiveness has encumbered partnerships
and joint operations at a much
smaller scale and forecasts a magnitude of inevitable clashes. The

Former Director of Homeland Security Tom Ridge presents the
Homeland Security Advisory System March 12, 2002. *Courtesy of
the White House.*

lack of common insignia, common mission goals, and even similar equipment
and terminology contribute to the challenge of unity and focus on mission.

Building the Department of Homeland Security continues to be a work
in progress, with the development of new partnerships, normal attrition of
senior leadership, and demands for access and assistance from multitudes
of diverse customers. The organizational chart is complex. (See Figure 3.1)
As of November 2005, organizational changes were made to streamline
efficiency and effectiveness and to reduce overlap and duplication of effort.

One change is the appointment of a Chief Intelligence Officer who
reports directly to the Secretary of Homeland Security. The individual
appointed to the position was Charles E. Allen, a highly decorated veteran
of the Intelligence Community where he served for over four and a half
decades. Since 1988, he had been Assistant Director of Central Intelligence for Collection (AD/DCI/C) and Chair of the National Intelligence Collection Board. Mr. Allen was responsible for collection requirements and
collection integration across the entire intelligence community His appointment signaled a commitment to coordinate with the Intelligence Community
and to instill a collection-like discipline within the Department, including
a process for accessing and sharing information with state, local, and tribal
policing agencies.

The Homeland Security Act of 2002[4] recognized the fact that the federal
government uses intelligence collected pursuant to law enforcement activities as an important part of operations to prevent terrorist activity. Intelligence can be defined as the "collection and analysis of information to
produce an intelligence end product designed to inform law enforcement decisionmaking at both the tactical and strategic levels."[5] Law enforcement
agencies routinely collect information pursuant to public service activities.
They also collect information related to criminal activities and individuals
and organizations that violate the law.

Figure 3.1 Department of Homeland Security, November 2005

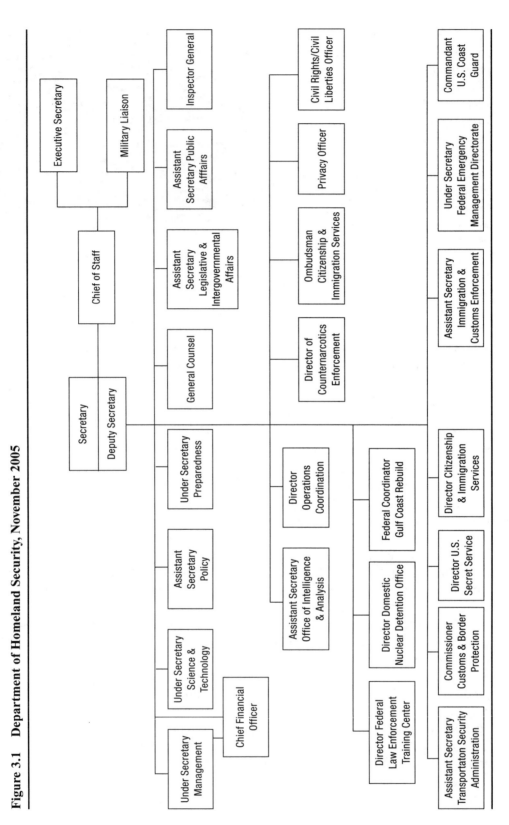

Historically, this information has not been shared across agencies, nor has there been a consistently reliable process for sharing it with the federal government or intelligence community. Similarly, there has not been a way for the federal government or intelligence community to share information with state and local agencies upon which decisionmaking could be better informed, situational awareness enhanced, and prevention actions undertaken.

Executive Order (EO) 13,356 passed September 1, 2004 directed all federal agencies possessing or acquiring terrorism related information to assist the Director of Central Intelligence (DCI) in developing common standards for information sharing. A key requirement of the E.O., related to the earlier Homeland Security Act, was to develop a standard for converting classified intelligence into an unclassified or "less classified" format for broader dissemination. This meant dissemination to state, local, and tribal policing organizations in a manner in which it could be used while still protecting from disclosure the means by which the information was obtained and collected.

Another change to the organization was the promotion of Matthew Broderick, a retired US Marine Corps (USMC) Brigadier General, former Director of the Homeland Security Operations Center (HSOC) to the Director of Operations, which also reported directly to the Secretary of DHS. This move signaled a consolidation of watch operations across the Department. A key responsibility will be the development and socialization of a common operating picture (COP) for the Secretary which enables the ability to visualize in real-time, in effect overlay assets, resources and capabilities across the 22 agencies. This improved situational awareness aims to enhance decisionmaking, reduce overlap and duplication, and improve response to disasters—either natural or of terrorist origin.

DHS became the latest partner in the Intelligence Community, joining 14 other agencies.[6] DHS's responsibilities in that arena include monitoring, assessing, and coordinating indications and warnings, maintaining real time intelligence connectivity to support situational awareness during the implementation of protective measures and incident management, and the gathering, analysis, and dissemination of threat information. These duties directly support the Secretary of DHS, who is responsible for implementation and oversight of the Homeland Security Advisory System. This system informs public safety officials and the citizenry whenever there is credible information to support a threat against the U.S. A visual symbol familiar to most is a color-coded chart which resembles an elongated traffic signal, changes to which are chronicled in national news reporting. In large measure the United States Government has consistently operated at an elevated level of threat (yellow), with few exceptions when the level was raised briefly to another level (orange). Additionally, DHS publishes threat advisories outlining actionable information related to threats against the nations' infrastructure which also contain suggested protective measures. DHS also publishes homeland security bulletins, comprehensive summaries of information which does not meet the threshold of warning, yet contains useful advisories on incident response and reporting

Homeland Security Advisory System

Specific guidance is provided to federal agencies for preparation and response to changing threat conditions In conjunction with the American Red Cross, DHS has also published guidance for the general public to consider when the threat level is elevated The American Society of Industrial Security (ASIS) published a Threat Advisory System Response (TASR) Guideline and a Business Continuity Guideline* to assist the private sector in the decision process in preparation for an elevation in threat conditions. The TASR developed a threat matrix geared to the private sector with suggested actions color-coded to match the national advisory system.

Guidance for Federal Departments and Agencies

The following Threat Conditions represent an increasing risk of terrorist attacks. Beneath each condition are some suggested protective measures, recognizing that the heads of federal departments and agencies are responsible for developing and implementing appropriate agency-specific measures:

1. **Low Condition (Green)**. This condition is declared when there is a low risk of terrorist attacks. Federal departments and agencies should consider the following general measures in addition to the agency-specific measures they develop and implement:

   - Refining and exercising, as appropriate, preplanned Protective Measures

   - Ensuring personnel receive proper training on the Homeland Security Advisory System and specific preplanned department or agency Protective Measures

   - Institutionalizing a process to assure that all facilities and regulated sectors are regularly assessed for vulnerabilities to terrorist attacks, and all reasonable measures are taken to mitigate these vulnerabilities

2. **Guarded Condition (Blue)**. This condition is declared when there is a general risk of terrorist attacks. In addition to the Protective Measures taken in the previous threat condition, federal departments and agencies should consider the following general measures in addition to the agency-specific measures they develop and implement:

   - Checking communications with designated emergency response or command locations

   - Reviewing and updating emergency response procedures

   - Providing the public with any information that would strengthen its ability to act appropriately

3. **Elevated Condition (Yellow)**. This condition is declared when there is a significant risk of terrorist attacks. In addition to the protective measures taken in the previous threat conditions, federal departments and agencies should consider the following general measures in addition to the agency-specific measures they develop and implement:

   - Increasing surveillance of critical locations

   - Coordinating emergency plans as appropriate with nearby jurisdictions

   - Assessing whether the precise characteristics of the threat require the further refinement of preplanned protective measures

   - Implementing, as appropriate, contingency and emergency response plans

*See ASIS GDL TASR,09 2004; Copyright 2004, ASAS international and ASIS GDL BC 01 2005; Copyright 2004 by ASIS International.

Homeland Security Advisory System, *continued*

4. **High Condition (Orange)**. This condition is declared when there is a high risk of terrorist attacks. In addition to the protective measures taken in the previous threat conditions, federal departments and agencies should consider the following general measures in addition to the agency-specific measures they develop and implement:

   • Coordinating necessary security efforts with federal, state, and local law enforcement agencies or any National Guard or other appropriate armed forces organizations

   • Taking additional precautions at public events and possibly considering alternative venues or even cancellation

   • Preparing to execute contingency procedures, such as moving to an alternate site or dispersing their workforce

   • Restricting threatened facility access to essential personnel only

5. **Severe Condition (Red)**. This condition reflects a severe risk of terrorist attacks. Under most circumstances, the protective measures for a severe condition are not intended to be sustained for substantial periods of time. In addition to the protective measures in the previous threat conditions, federal departments and agencies also should consider the following general measures in addition to the agency-specific measures they develop and implement:

   • Increasing or redirecting personnel to address critical emergency needs

   • Assigning emergency response personnel and pre-positioning and mobilizing specially trained teams or resources

   • Monitoring, redirecting, or constraining transportation systems

   • Closing public and government facilities

Citizen Guidance on the Homeland Security Advisory System Recommended Actions for Citizens••

Risk of Attack

GREEN Low Risk
Develop a family emergency plan. Share it with family and friends, and practice the plan. Create an "Emergency Supply Kit" for your household. Be informed. Know how to shelter-in-place and how to turn off utilities (power, gas, and water) to your home. Examine volunteer opportunities in your community, such as Citizen Corps, Volunteers in Police Service, Neighborhood Watch or others, and donate your time. Consider completing an American Red Cross first aid or CPR course , or Community Emergency Response Team (CERT) course .

BLUE Guarded Risk
Complete all steps listed in Level Green. Review stored disaster supplies and replace items that are outdated. Be alert to suspicious activity and report it to proper authorities.

YELLOW Elevated Risk
Complete all steps listed at levels green and blue. Ensure disaster supply kit is stocked and ready. Check telephone numbers in family emergency plan and update as necessary. Develop alternate routes to/from work or school and practice them. Continue to be alert for suspicious activity and report it to authorities.

**www.ready.gov. Visit the website for additional information.

Homeland Security Advisory System, *continued*

ORANGE High Risk
Complete steps listed at levels green, blue, and yellow. Exercise caution when traveling, pay attention to travel advisories. Review your family emergency plan and make sure all family members know what to do. Be Patient. Expect some delays, baggage searches and restrictions at public buildings. Check on neighbors or others that might need assistance in an emergency.

RED Severe Risk
Complete steps listed at levels green, blue, yellow, and orange. Listen to local emergency management officials. Stay tuned to TV or radio for current information/instructions. Be prepared to shelter-in-place or evacuate, as instructed. Expect traffic delays and restrictions. Provide volunteer services only as requested. Contact your school/business to determine status of work day.

Almost nothing about the bureaucratic character of government agencies makes them hospitable to interagency collaboration. The collaborative qualities value equality, adaptability, discretion, and results; the bureaucratic character venerates hierarchy, stability, obedience, and procedures. Making the transition from the existing way of doing agency business to a new and more collaborative way requires all personnel to withdraw from the bureaucratic personality. They must be willing to discard or break it up into components, some of which might warrant being salvaged or recycled (Bardach, 1998:232).

Accepting the seemingly difficult nature of bureaucracies, the challenges of joining together approximately 180,000 personnel from 22 separate agencies under one centralized organization would appear to be impossible. However, 11 days after the 9/11 attacks, President Bush announced the creation of an Office of Homeland Security (OHS) during his address to Congress. Executive Order (EO) 13228 followed on October 8, 2001, formalizing the duties and responsibilities of the Office and the creation of a Homeland Security Council (HSC).[7] The mission of the HSC—to advise and assist the President on all aspects of homeland security and to coordinate security policies among and between agencies and departments—signaled a first step towards development of a unified nationally led coalition for change.

With the passage of the Homeland Security Act of 2002, the mission of the HSC was further defined[8] and its membership was reduced to five primary members: The President, the Vice President, the Secretary of Homeland Security, the Attorney General, and the Secretary of Defense. The former Governor of Pennsylvania, Tom Ridge was appointed to the President's cabinet with the consent of the U.S. Senate. The Department of Homeland Security (DHS) became effective in March, 2003.

Homeland Security Operations Center (HSOC)

Homeland Security Operations Center (HSOC)

The Homeland Security Operations Center (HSOC) was created on July 8, 2004 and operates around the clock every single day of the year. It functions as the center of DHS for information sharing and domestic incident management, increasing the vertical coordination among federal, state, local, tribal policing and private sector partners with timely and credible reporting and dissemination of information. The HSOC is staffed by representatives from more than thirty-five agencies including federal, state, and municipal police agencies and others from the Intelligence Community. The HSOC issues threat advisories and bulletins,* which are coordinated with the Office of Information Analysis and contain guidance on protective measures to be considered, based on the identification and severity of the threat outlined by the advisory or bulletin.

The HSOC has two distinct components: Intelligence and Law Enforcement. These mirror one another, but with one primary and significant difference—access to classified information. The former concentrates on classified intelligence from a variety of sources to determine its potential contribution to credible threats to the homeland, while the latter focuses on the criminal activity and issues within the public safety realm which may have a connection to terrorist activity. In combination, the overall threat picture can be viewed in real-time to enhance warning and response.

One of the key areas of success is the capability of the HSOC, through its secure network, to disseminate information to consumers across the Country both in the public and private sector, each with a tiered access to information. This centralized dissemination eliminates inconsistent and incorrect information which in the past has caused unnecessary action, fear, and depletion of resources, as well as criticism leveled at the Government.

HSOC Information Sharing Tools**

The HSOC communicates in real-time to its partners by utilizing the Homeland Security Information Network's (HSIN) internet-based counterterrorism communications tool, supplying information to all 50 states, Washington, D.C., and more than 50 major urban areas. Threat information is exchanged with state and local partners at the Sensitive-but-Unclassified level (SBU) through this system. Future program expansion plans include linking additional cities and counties together, increasing communication capabilities at the classified SECRET level, and increasing the involvement and integration of the private sector. The system is encrypted using a secure network that includes a suite of applications including mapping and imaging capabilities. System participants include key homeland security partners, including governors, mayors, Homeland Security Advisors, state National Guard offices, Emergency Operations Centers, First Responders and Public Safety departments. Each receives training to participate in the information sharing network to combat terrorism and increase anti-terrorism situational awareness.

The HSIN-CI is specially designed to communicate real-time information to critical infrastructure owners and operators—80 percent of whom are part of the private sector. HSIN–CI has the capacity to send alerts and notifications to the private sector at a rate of:

- 10,000 simultaneous outbound voice calls per minute
- 30,000 inbound simultaneous calls (hot line scenario)

---

*See www.dhs.gov for additional information related to HSOC products. *Homeland Security Threat Advisories* are the result of information analysis and contain actionable information about an incident involving, or a threat targeting, critical national networks, infrastructures, or key assets. They often relay newly developed procedures that, when implemented, significantly improve security and protection. Advisories also often suggest a change in readiness posture, protective actions, or response.

**From www.dhs.gov. Please refer to website for additional information

Homeland Security Operations Center (HSOC), *continued*

- 3,000 outbound simultaneous faxes
- 5,000 outbound simultaneous Internet e-mail

The HSOC regularly disseminates domestic terrorism-related information generated by the Information Analysis and Infrastructure Protection Directorate, known as "products" to federal, state, and local governments, as well as private-sector organizations and international partners. Threat products come in two forms: Vulnerability Situational Awareness and Imagery Capability.

The Vulnerability Situational Awareness of the HSOC monitors vulnerabilities and compares them against threats, providing a centralized, real-time flow of information between homeland security partners. This data collected from across the country is then fused into a master template which allows the HSOC to provide a visual picture of the nation's current threat status. The HSOC has the capability to:

- Perform initial (first phase) assessment of the information to gauge the terrorist nexus
- Track operational actions taking place across the country in response to the intelligence information
- Disseminate notifications and alerts about the information and any decisions made

The Imagery Capability of the HSOC allows informational data shared across agencies to be cross-referenced against geospatial data that can then pinpoint an image down to an exact location. Satellite technology is able to transmit pictures of the site in question directly into the HSOC. This type of geographic data can then be stored to create a library of images that can be mapped against future threats and shared with our state and local partners. The "current operational picture" can be viewed using the geographical and mapping capabilities of 16 flat panel fifty-inch screens to monitor threat environment in real time Access to a significant portion of the District of Columbia's traffic cameras for real-time view of various transportation hubs

The HSOC is in constant communication with the White House, acting as the situational awareness conduit for the White House Situation Room by providing information needed to make decisions and define courses of action.

The Interagency Incident Management Group (IIMG) is a headquarters-level group comprised of senior representatives from DHS components, other federal departments and agencies, and non-governmental organizations. The IIMG provides strategic situational awareness, synthesizes key intelligence and operational information, frames operational courses of action and policy recommendations, anticipates evolving requirements, and provides decision support to the Secretary of Homeland Security and other national authorities during periods of elevated alert and national domestic incidents.

This list provides a sampling of the agencies which staff the HSOC and represent a cross-section of federal, state, and local policing, and includes representatives from the Intelligence Community. The contributing agencies have made a commitment to provide senior personnel which brings a great degree of experience to the center. Individuals work in close proximity to one another, reminiscent of a squad room configuration with access to common systems and to each other to enhance collaboration and to provide an all-source perspective on issues of concern as they arise.

Homeland Security Operations Center (HSOC), *continued*

Federal Bureau of Investigation	Alcohol, Tobacco, and Firearms
United States Coast Guard	Department of Defense
Postal Inspection Service	Department of State
Central Intelligence Agency	Department of Transportation
United States Secret Service	Department of Veterans Affairs
DC Metropolitan Police Department	National Capitol Region
Defense Intelligence Agency	Transportation Security Administration
Federal Protective Service	National Geospatial Intelligence Agency
New York Police Department	Department of Health and Human Services
National Security Agency	Federal Emergency Management Agency
Customs and Border Protection	National Oceanic Atmospheric Administration
Los Angeles Police Department	Public Affairs (DHS)
Immigration Customs Enforcement	State and Local Coordination Office
Department of Energy	Science and Technology Directorate
Environmental Protection Agency	Geo-spatial Mapping Office
Drug Enforcement Agency	Information Analysis Office
Department of Interior (US Park Police	Infrastructure Protection Office
Federal Air Marshal Service	

New partnerships and coalitions began to develop almost immediately. Organizational and jurisdictional lines appeared to blur and changes were based on anticipated mandates for collaboration in advance of policy or legal requirements. Agencies that had existed and functioned independently were forced into a paradigm for which they were wholly unprepared and with which they were, in most cases, uncomfortable. Change was being driven from the outside at the national level. The power structure within the organizations was being marginalized and the power base of regulators and those with congressional oversight were being eroded.

Budget

The 2006 Fiscal year budget of the Department of Homeland Security approved by Congress provided more than $30 billion to the Department. The budget allowed the most monies to Border and Transportation Security, followed by the Coast Guard, and to DHS Management. The 2006 budget, which is approximately $1.4 billion more in budget authority than the 2005 budget, allowed for increases in funding for Border and Transportation Security and a significant increase in budget for Science and Technology directorate (most earmarked for Development, Acquisition, and Operations). The nation is still at a vulnerable position for attacks and continuous efforts are being made to lessen these sensitive areas.

9/11 Commission Recommendations

The 9/11 Commission was created on November 27, 2002 through the National Commission on Terrorist Attacks upon the United States (Public Law 107-306). The Commission was formed to provide a complete account of the circumstances surrounding the September 11, 2001 terrorist attacks, including preparedness for and the immediate response to the attacks. The Commission was made up of 10 members and was chaired by Thomas H. Kean, a former governor of New Jersey and the President of Drew University. There were more than 70 staff members assigned to the Commission and, together, the 9/11 Commission worked for nearly 21 months to produce the report, of which the unclassified version was 567 pages long.

Unlike most government commission reports, the 9/11 Commission report reads like a novel and received considerable praise for its scope and detail. Even today, the 9/11 commission report is the most comprehensive account of the events of the 9/11 attacks and provides a careful post-mortem of the failings, both institutional and incidental, of the US national security apparatus. Beyond the narrative and descriptions of US government failings to identify and interdict the terrorist plots, the commission made 41 recommendations in Chapters 12 and 13 of the report that provided a roadmap for overhauling the national security apparatus to face the emerging threats of terrorism and weapons of mass destruction.

Photo Courtesy of the National Commission on Terrorist Attacks Upon the United States, www.911commission.gov

What follows is a presentation of the 41 recommendations and a brief discussion of the current status of the recommendations as of February 2006.

1. The U.S. government must identify and prioritize actual or potential terrorist sanctuaries. For each, it should have a realistic strategy to keep possible terrorists insecure and on the run, using all elements of national power. [The US] should reach out, listen to, and work with other countries that can help

2. If [Pakistan's President Pervez] Musharraf stands for enlightened moderation in a fight for his life and for the life of his country, the United States should be willing to make hard choices too, and make the difficult long-term commitment to the future of Pakistan. Sustaining the current scale of aid to Pakistan, the United States should support Pakistan's government in its struggle against extremists with a comprehensive effort that extends from military aid to support for better education, so long as Pakistan's leaders remain willing to make difficult choices of their own.

3. The President and the Congress deserve praise for their efforts in Afghanistan so far. Now the United States and the international community should make a long-term commitment to a secure and stable Afghanistan, in order to give the government a reasonable opportunity to improve the life of the Afghan people. Afghanistan must not again become a sanctuary for international crime and terrorism. The United States and the international community should help the Afghan government extend its authority over the country, with a strategy and nation-by-nation commitments to achieve their objectives.

4. The problems in the U.S.-Saudi relationship must be confronted, openly. The United States and Saudi Arabia must determine if they can build a relationship that political leaders on both sides are prepared to publicly defend—a relationship about more than oil. It should include a shared commitment to political and economic reform, as Saudis make common cause with the outside world. It should include a shared interest in greater tolerance and cultural respect, translating into a commitment to fight the violent extremists who foment hatred.

5. The U.S. government must define what the message is, what it stands for. The U.S. government should offer an example of moral leadership in the world, committed to treat people humanely, abide by the rule of law, and be generous and caring to our neighbors. America and Muslim friends can agree on respect for human dignity and opportunity. To Muslim parents, terrorists like Bin Laden have nothing to offer their children but visions of violence and death. America and its friends have a crucial advantage—it can offer these parents a vision that might give their children a better future. If the US heeds the views of thoughtful leaders in the Arab and Muslim world, a moderate consensus can be found.

6. Where Muslim governments, even those who are friends, do not respect these principles, the United States must stand for a better future. One of the lessons of the long Cold War was that short-term gains in cooperating with the most repressive and brutal governments were too often outweighed by long-term setbacks for America's stature and interests.

7. Just as in the Cold War, the U.S. must defend its ideals abroad vigorously. America does stand up for its values. The United States defended, and still defends, Muslims against tyrants and criminals in Somalia, Bosnia, Kosovo, Afghanistan, and Iraq. If the United States does not act aggressively to define itself in the Islamic world, the extremists will gladly do the job for us.

8. The U.S. government should offer to join with other nations in generously supporting a new International Youth Opportunity Fund. Funds will be spent directly for building and operating primary and secondary schools in those Muslim states that commit to sensibly investing their own money in public education.

9. A comprehensive U.S. strategy to counter terrorism should include economic policies that encourage development, more open societies, and opportunities for people to improve the lives of their families and to enhance prospects for their children's future.

10. The United States should engage other nations in developing a comprehensive coalition strategy against Islamist terrorism. There are several multilateral institutions in which such issues should be addressed. But the most important policies should be discussed and coordinated in a flexible contact group of leading coalition governments. This is a good place, for example, to develop joint strategies for targeting terrorist travel, or for hammering out a common strategy for the places where terrorists may be finding sanctuary.

11. The United States should engage its friends to develop a common coalition approach toward the detention and humane treatment of captured terrorists. New principles might draw upon Article 3 of the Geneva Conventions on the law of armed conflict. That article was specifically designed for those cases in which the usual laws of war did not apply. Its minimum standards are generally accepted throughout the world as customary international law.

12. Al Qaeda has tried to acquire or make weapons of mass destruction for at least 10 years. There is no doubt the United States would be a prime target. Preventing the proliferation of these weapons warrants a maximum effort—by strengthening counterproliferation efforts, expanding

the Proliferation Security Initiative, and supporting the Cooperative Threat Reduction program.

13. Vigorous efforts to track terrorist financing must remain front and center in U.S. counterterrorism efforts. The government has recognized that information about terrorist money helps us to understand their networks, search them out, and disrupt their operations. Intelligence and law enforcement have targeted the relatively small number of financial facilitators—individuals al Qaeda relied on for their ability to raise and deliver money—at the core of al Qaeda's revenue stream. These efforts have worked. The death or capture of several important facilitators has decreased the amount of money available to al Qaeda and has increased its costs and difficulty in raising and moving that money. Captures have additionally provided a windfall of intelligence that can be used to continue the cycle of disruption.

14. Targeting travel is at least as powerful a weapon against terrorists as targeting their money. The United States should combine terrorist travel intelligence, operations, and law enforcement in a strategy to intercept terrorists, find terrorist travel facilitators, and constrain terrorist mobility.

15. The U.S. border security system should be integrated into a larger network of screening points that includes our transportation system and access to vital facilities, such as nuclear reactors. The President should direct the Department of Homeland Security to lead the effort to design a comprehensive screening system, addressing common problems and setting common standards with system-wide goals in mind. Extending those standards among other governments could dramatically strengthen America and the world's collective ability to intercept individuals who pose catastrophic threats.

16. The Department of Homeland Security, properly supported by the Congress, should complete, as quickly as possible, a biometric entry-exit screening system, including a single system for speeding qualified travelers. It should be integrated with the system that provides benefits to foreigners seeking to stay in the United States. Linking biometric passports to good data systems and decision making is a fundamental goal. No one can hide his or her debt by acquiring a credit card with a slightly different name. Yet today, a terrorist can defeat the link to electronic records by tossing away an old passport and slightly altering the name in the new one.

17. The U.S. government cannot meet its own obligations to the American people to prevent the entry of terrorists without a major effort to collaborate with other governments. It should do more to exchange terrorist

information with trusted allies, and raise U.S. and global border security standards for travel and border crossing over the medium and long term through extensive international cooperation.

18. Secure identification should begin in the United States. The federal government should set standards for the issuance of birth certificates and sources of identification, such as driver's licenses. Fraud in identification documents is no longer just a problem of theft. At many entry points to vulnerable facilities, including gates for boarding aircraft, sources of identification are the last opportunity to ensure that people are who they say they are and to check whether they are terrorists

19. Hard choices must be made in allocating limited resources. The U.S. government should identify and evaluate the transportation assets that need to be protected, set risk-based priorities for defending them, select the most practical and cost-effective ways of doing so, and then develop a plan, budget, and funding to implement the effort. The plan should assign roles and missions to the relevant authorities (federal, state, regional, and local) and to private stakeholders. In measuring effectiveness, perfection is unattainable. But terrorists should perceive that potential targets are defended. They may be deterred by a significant chance of failure.

20. Improved use of "no-fly" and "automatic selectee" lists should not be delayed while the argument about a successor to CAPPS continues. This screening function should be performed by the TSA, and it should utilize the larger set of watchlists maintained by the federal government. Air carriers should be required to supply the information needed to test and implement this new system.

21. The TSA and the Congress must give priority attention to improving the ability of screening checkpoints to detect explosives on passengers. As a start, each individual selected for special screening should be screened for explosives. Further, the TSA should conduct a human factors study, a method often used in the private sector, to understand problems in screener performance and set attainable objectives for individual screeners and for the check-points where screening takes place.

22. As the President determines the guidelines for information sharing among government agencies and by those agencies with the private sector, he should safeguard the privacy of individuals about whom information is shared.

23. The burden of proof for retaining a particular governmental power should be on the executive, to explain (a) that the power actually mate-

rially enhances security and (b) that there is adequate supervision of the executive's use of the powers to ensure protection of civil liberties. If the power is granted, there must be adequate guidelines and oversight to properly confine its use.

24. At this time of increased and consolidated government authority, there should be a board within the executive branch to oversee adherence to the guidelines we recommend and the commitment the government makes to defend our civil liberties.

25. Homeland security assistance should be based strictly on an assessment of risks and vulnerabilities. Now, in 2004, Washington, D.C., and New York City are certainly at the top of any such list. We understand the contention that every state and city needs to have some minimum infrastructure for emergency response. But federal homeland security assistance should not remain a program for general revenue sharing. It should supplement state and local resources based on the risks or vulnerabilities that merit additional support. Congress should not use this money as a pork barrel.

26. Emergency response agencies nationwide should adopt the Incident Command System (ICS).When multiple agencies or multiple jurisdictions are involved, they should adopt a unified command. Both are proven frameworks for emergency response. The 9/11 Commission strongly supports the decision that federal homeland security funding will be contingent, as of October 1, 2004, upon the adoption and regular use of ICS and unified command procedures. In the future, the Department of Homeland Security should consider making funding contingent on aggressive and realistic training in accordance with ICS and unified command procedures.

27. Congress should support pending legislation which provides for the expedited and increased assignment of radio spectrum for public safety purposes. Furthermore, high-risk urban areas such as New York City and Washington, D.C., should establish signal corps units to ensure communications connectivity between and among civilian authorities, local first responders, and the National Guard. Federal funding of such units should be given high priority by Congress.

28. The 9/11 Commission endorsed the American National Standards Institute's recommended standard for private preparedness. The 9/11 Commissions believes that compliance with the standard should define the standard of care owed by a company to its employees and the public for legal purposes. Private-sector preparedness is not a luxury; it is a cost of doing business in the post-9/11 world. It is ignored at a tremendous potential cost in lives, money, and national security.

29. The 9/11 Commission recommended the establishment of a National Counterterrorism Center (NCTC), built on the foundation of the existing Terrorist Threat Integration Center (TTIC). Breaking the older mold of national government organization, this NCTC should be a center for joint operational planning *and* joint intelligence, staffed by personnel from the various agencies. The head of the NCTC should have authority to evaluate the performance of the people assigned to the Center.

30. The current position of Director of Central Intelligence should be replaced by a National Intelligence Director with two main areas of responsibility: (1) to oversee national intelligence centers on specific subjects of interest across the U.S. government and (2) to manage the national intelligence program and oversee the agencies that contribute to it.

31. The CIA Director should emphasize (a) rebuilding the CIA's analytic capabilities; (b) transforming the clandestine service by building its human intelligence capabilities; (c) developing a stronger language program, with high standards and sufficient financial incentives; (d) renewing emphasis on recruiting diversity among operations officers so they can blend more easily in foreign cities;(e) ensuring a seamless relationship between human source collection and signals collection at the operational level; and (f) stressing a better balance between unilateral and liaison operations.

32. Lead responsibility for directing and executing paramilitary operations, whether clandestine or covert, should shift to the Defense Department. There it should be consolidated with the capabilities for training, direction, and execution of such operations already being developed in the Special Operations Command.

33. Finally, to combat the secrecy and complexity we have described, the overall amounts of money being appropriated for national intelligence and to its component agencies should no longer be kept secret. Congress should pass a separate appropriations act for intelligence, defending the broad allocation of how these tens of billions of dollars have been assigned among the varieties of intelligence work.

34. Information procedures should provide incentives for sharing, to restore a better balance between security and shared knowledge.

35. The president should lead the government-wide effort to bring the major national security institutions into the information revolution. He should coordinate the resolution of the legal, policy, and technical issues across agencies to create a "trusted information network."

36. Congressional oversight for intelligence—and counterterrorism—is now dysfunctional. Congress should address this problem. The Commission considered various alternatives: A joint committee on the old model of the Joint Committee on Atomic Energy is one. A single committee in each house of Congress, combining authorizing and appropriating authorities, is another.

37. Congress should create a single, principal point of oversight and review for homeland security. Congressional leaders are best able to judge what committee should have jurisdiction over this department and its duties. But the Commission believed that Congress does have the obligation to choose one in the House and one in the Senate, and that this committee should be a permanent standing committee with a nonpartisan staff.

38. Since a catastrophic attack could occur with little or no notice, the disruption of national security policymaking should be minimized during the change of administrations by accelerating the process for national security appointments. The process could be improved significantly so transitions can work more effectively and allow new officials to assume their new responsibilities as quickly as possible.

39. A specialized and integrated national security workforce should be established at the FBI consisting of agents, analysts, linguists, and surveillance specialists who are recruited, trained, rewarded, and retained to ensure the development of an institutional culture imbued with a deep expertise in intelligence and national security.

40. The Department of Defense and its oversight committees should regularly assess the adequacy of Northern Command's strategies and planning to defend the United States against military threats to the homeland.

41. The Department of Homeland Security and its oversight committees should regularly assess the types of threats the country faces to determine (a) the adequacy of the government's plans—and the progress against those plans—to protect America's critical infrastructure and (b) the readiness of the government to respond to the threats that the United States might face.

These recommendations set the stage for the massive reorganization of the government and a broad range of domestic and international initiatives that impact local, state and federal responses to national emergencies. These initiatives also impact the private sector, the health care system, border security, infrastructure considerations, transportation and the role of individual citizens in emergency management. The inclusion of FEMA (Federal

Emergency Management Administration) in the new Department of Homeland Security also brought the federal response to natural disasters under the homeland security model.

Since the publication of the 9/11 Commission Report on July 22, 2004, there has been much debate about whether and how many of these recommendations should be implemented by the Bush administration. Not surprisingly, much of the criticism and analysis of the Bush Administration's implementation of the recommendations is wide ranging and partisan.

Intelligence Spending

For budgetary purposes, intelligence spending is divided between the National Intelligence Program (NIP) (formerly the National Foreign Intelligence Program (NFIP)), Tactical Intelligence and Related Activities (TIARA) (also known as intelligence-related activities), which covers programs supporting the operating units of the armed services, and the Joint Military Intelligence Program (JMIP), which covers programs, not necessarily tactical, that are of primary concern to the Defense Department.

Only a small part of the intelligence budget is made public; the bulk of the overall intelligence spending is contained within the DoD budget. Spending for most intelligence programs is described in classified annexes to intelligence and national defense authorization and appropriations legislation. Members of Congress all have access to these annexes, but must make special arrangements to read them.

Jurisdiction over intelligence programs is somewhat different in the House and the Senate. The Senate Intelligence Committee has jurisdiction only over the NIP but not JMIP and TIARA, whereas the House Intelligence Committee has jurisdiction over all three sets of programs. The preponderance of intelligence spending is accomplished by intelligence agencies within DoD and thus in both chambers the armed services committees are involved in the oversight process.

Other oversight committees are responsible for intelligence agencies that are part of departments other than DoD. Most appropriations for intelligence activities are included in national defense appropriations acts, including funds for the CIA, DIA, NSA, the NRO, and NGA. Other appropriations measures include funds for the intelligence offices of the State Department, the FBI, and the Department of Homeland Security. In the past, defense appropriations subcommittees have funded the intelligence activities of CIA and the DoD agencies (although funds for CIA have been included in defense appropriations acts, these monies are transferred directly).

Intelligence budgeting issues were at the center of the debate on intelligence reform legislation in 2004. On one hand, there was determination to make the new Director of National Intelligence (DNI) responsible for developing and determining the annual National Intelligence Program budget (which is separate from the JMIP and TIARA budgets that are prepared by the Secretary of Defense). The goal was to ensure a unity of effort that arguably has not previously existed and that may have complicated efforts to monitor terrorist activities. On the other hand, the intelligence efforts within the National Intelligence Program include those of major components of the Defense Department, including NSA, the NRO, and NGA, that are closely related to other military activities.

Some Members thus argued that even the National Intelligence Program should not be considered apart from the Defense budget. After considerable debate, the final version of the Intelligence Reform Act provides broad budgetary authorities to the DNI, but requires the President to issue guidelines to ensure that the DNI exercises the authorities provided by the statute "in a manner that respects and does not abrogate the statutory responsibilities of the heads of the Office of Management and Budget and Cabinet departments."

However, the 9/11 Commission members and staff have pushed to keep the report and its recommendations in the public spotlight long after their inquiry officially closed on August 21, 2004. The 9/11 Commission Chair and all the Commission members authored several reports and offered commentary on the current status of the report through the 9/11 Public Discourse Project, a 501(c)(3) organization created by the 10 commissioners.[10]

Figure 3.2   Final Report on 9/11 Commission Recommendations

Homeland Security and Emergency Response	
Radio spectrum for first responders	F/C*
Incident Command System	C
Risk-based homeland security funds	F/A*
Critical infrastructure assessment	D
Private sector preparedness	C
National Strategy for Transportation Security	C-
Airline passenger pre-screening	F
Airline passenger explosive screening	C
Checked bag and cargo screening	D
Terrorist travel strategy	I
Comprehensive screening system	C
Biometric entry-exit screening system	B
International collaboration on borders and document security	D
Standardize secure identifications	B-
Intelligence and Congressional Reform	
Director of National Intelligence	B
National Counterterrorism Center	B
New missions for CIA Director	I
Incentives for information sharing	D
Northern Command planning for homeland defense	B-
Full debate on USA PATRIOT Act	B
Privacy and Civil Liberties Oversight Board	D
Guidelines for government sharing of personal information	D
Intelligence oversight reform	D
Homeland Security Committees	B
Unclassified top-line intelligence budget	F
Security clearance reform	B
Foreign Policy and Nonproliferation	
Maximum effort to prevent terrorists from acquiring WMD	D
Afghanistan	B
Pakistan	C+
Saudi Arabia	D
Terrorist sanctuaries	B
Coalition strategy against Islamist terrorism	C
Coalition detention standards	F
Economic policies	B+
Terrorist financing	A-
Clear U.S. message abroad	C
International broadcasting	B
Scholarship, exchange, and library programs	D
Secular education in Muslim countries	D

*If pending legislation passes

On December 5, 2005, the 9/11 Public Discourse released their Report Card on Recommendations, which "graded" the U.S. government on its progress in implementing the 41 recommendations of their report. Of the 41 recommendations, only one, taking actions to interdict terrorist financing methods and freezing the assets of known terrorist organizations and their sympathizers, received a grade of A. 15 of the 41 recommendations received a grade of either F or D including recommendations related to airline passenger screening, critical infrastructure assessment, and efforts to prevent terrorists from acquiring weapons of mass destruction. All but two of the remaining recommendations were given a grade of either B or C.[9]

KEY CONCEPTS

- There are numerous definitions for the term "terrorism;" most definitions include components of violence and force; political motivations; fear and terror; threats; and psychological effects and reactions.

- The absence of coordination and collaboration (especially in the intelligence and information sharing sector) contributed to the surprise nature of the 9/11 attacks. Several agencies knew of the threat of Osama bin Laden and al Qaeda, but the organizations did not work together to try to understand or warn others of the high threat level posed by this group.

- The National Commission on Terrorist Attacks Upon the United States, commonly referred to as the 9/11 Commission, submitted 41 key recommendations. Many of these recommendations have been or are in the process of being implemented.

- The development of a complete Department of Homeland Security is ongoing and changes are continuously made in order to meet the missions of the organization: Prevent terrorist attacks within the United States, reduce America's vulnerability to terrorism, and minimize the damage from potential attacks and natural disasters.

- Some of the issues of reorganizing such a large amount of agencies include: differing jurisdictional responsibilities, personnel policies, and training standards; loyalties to original organization; and institutionalized competitiveness present in the singular agencies.

ADDITIONAL READINGS

Executive Order (EO) 13,228.

Centre for Economic Policy Research, Number 3791, *The Economic Effects of the 1918 Influenza Epidemic.*

Cilluffo, F., J.J. Collins, A. de Borchgrave, D., Goure, and M. Horowitz (2000). *Defending America in the 21st Century: New Challenges, New Organizations, and New Policies.* Center for Strategic and International Studies. Washington, DC.

The 2002 Olympic Winter Games Security Lessons Applied to Homeland Security (2002). Olympic Security Review Conference.

Homeland Security Act of 2002.

Kean, Thomas and Lee Hamilton (2006). *Without Precedent: The Inside Story of the 9/11 Commission.* New York, NY: Knopf.

RELATED WEBSITES

The Transportation Security Administration (TSA) www.tsa.gov

The Department of Homeland Security (DHS) www.dhs.gov

The National Counterterrorism Center www.nctc.gov

The Federal Emergency Management Agency (FEMA) www.fema.gov

Central Intelligence Agency (CIA) www.cia.gov

REFERENCES

The 9/11 Commission Report. National Commission on Terrorist Attacks Upon the United States. July, 2004.

Brian A. Jackson, D.J. Peterson, James T. Bartis, Tom LaTourette, Irene Brahmakulam, Ari Houser & Jerry Sollinger (2002). "Protecting Emergency Responders—Lessons Learned from Terrorist Attacks." Rand Science and Technology Policy Institute.

Bush, George W. The National Security Strategy of the United States of America, Washington, DC: The White House, September 2002.

Carter, David L. (2004). *Law Enforcement Intelligence: A Guide for State, Local, and Tribal Law Enforcement Agencies.* U.S. Department of Justice Office of Community Oriented Policing Services.

Department of Homeland Security Appropriations Bill. Conference Report (Fiscal Year 2006). Volume 5, No. 16

Donahue, L.K. & J.N. Kayyem (2002). Federalism and the battle over counterterrorist law: State sovereignty, criminal law enforcement, and national security. Studies in Conflict and Terrorism, Harvard University 25:1-18.

Gilmore Commission (2001). Third annual report to the president and the Congress of the advisory panel to assess domestic response capabilities for terrorism involving weapons of mass destruction. Washington, DC: U.S. Government.

Lois M. Davis, K. Jack Riley, Greg Ridgeway, Jennifer Pace, Sarah K. Cotton, Paul S. Steinberg, Kelly Damphousse & Brent L. Smith (2004). "When Terrorism Hits Home-How Prepared Are State and Local Law Enforcement?' Rand Infrastructure, Safety and Environment.

National Incident Management System (NIMS). Department of Homeland Security. March 2004.

National Response Plan (NRP). Department of Homeland Security. December 2004.

One Hundred and Seventh Congress of the United States of America, "H.R. 3162-The Uniting and Strengthening of America by Providing Appropriate Tools Required to Intercept and Obstruct Terrorism (USA PATRIOT) Act of 2001.

The White House, "Homeland Security Presidential Directive/HSPD-1: Organization and Operation of the Homeland Security Council," October 29, 2001.

The White House, "Homeland Security Presidential Directive/HSPD-5: Management of Domestic Incidents," December 17, 2003.

The White House, "Homeland Security Presidential Directive/HSPD-6: Integration and Use of Screening Information," September 16, 2003.

The White House, "Homeland Security Presidential Directive/HSPD-7: Critical Infrastructure Identification, Prioritization and Protection," December 17, 2003.

The White House. Homeland Security Presidential Decision Directive/HSPD-8, "National Preparedness." December 2003.

The White House, "Presidential Decision Directive/PDD-62: "Critical Infrastructure Protection," May 22, 1998.

The White House, "National Security Presidential Directive. NSPD-9: Combating Terrorism," October 25, 2001.

The White House (July 2002). *National Strategy for Homeland Security*. Washington, DC: Government Printing Office.

Wohlstetter, R. (1962). *Pearl Harbor: Warning and Decisions*. Stanford University Press.

NOTES

[1]   See Centre for Economic Policy Research, Number 3791, The Economic Effects of the 1918 Influenza Epidemic. The outbreak killed 40 million people worldwide including 675,000 in the United States, far exceeding the combined totals of World Wars, Korea, and Vietnam (abstract).

[2]   Wohlstetter, R. (1962). *Pearl Harbor: Warning and Decision*. Stanford University Press.

[3]   White House. (July 2002). *National Strategy for Homeland Security*. Washington, DC: Government Printing Office.

[4]   One of the requirements directed the President to develop procedures for the declassification and dissemination of intelligence information. An Executive Order (EO) followed, delegating the responsibility to the Department of Homeland Security-see E.O. No. 13,311, 68 Fed. Reg. 45149 (July 31, 2003).

[5]   Carter, David L. (2004). *Law Enforcement Intelligence: A Guide for State, Local and Tribal Law Enforcement Agencies*. US Department of Justice Office of Community Oriented Policing Services.

[6]   DHS's Directorate of Information Analysis and Infrastructure Protection (IA/IP) was designated as the 15th member of the Intelligence Community. The other members include: Air Force Intelligence; Army Intelligence; Central Intelligence Agency; Coast Guard Intelligence; Defense intelligence Agency; Department of Energy; Department of State; Department of Treasury; Federal Bureau of Investigation; Marine Corps Intelligence; National Geospatial Intelligence Agency; National Reconnaissance Office; National Security Agency and Navy Intelligence. The Drug Enforcement Administration is scheduled to become the 16th member of the IC in 2006.

[7]   Primary members included the President and Vice President of the United States; Secretary of the Treasury; the Secretary of Defense (SECDEF); the Attorney general (AG); the Secretary of Health and Human Services (HHS); the Secretary of Transportation (DOT); the director of the Federal Emergency Management Agency (FEMA); director of the Federal Bureau of Investigation (FBI); the director of Central Intelligence (CIA); and the Assistant to the President for Homeland Security. The Secretary of State, the Secretary of Agriculture, the Secretary of the Interior, the Secretary of Energy, the Secretary of Labor, the Secretary of Commerce, the Secretary of Veteran Affairs, the administrator of the Environmental Protection Agency (EPA), the assistant to the president for Economic Policy and the assistant to the President for Domestic Policy were invited to meetings pertaining to their responsibilities. Other cabinet and heads of executive departments were invited to attend when appropriate to the mission and responsibilities of their departments (Exec. Order No. 13,228, 5 (b). 66 Fed Reg. 196, 2002).

[8]   "For the purposes of more effectively coordinating the policies and functions of the United States government relating to homeland security, the Council shall (1) assess the objectives, commitments, and risks of the United States in the interest of homeland security and to make resulting recommendations to the President; (20 oversee and review homeland security policies of the federal government and to make resulting recommendations to the President; and (3) perform such other functions as the President may direct" (Homeland Security Act, 2002, 904).

[9]   Two recommendations were graded conditionally because their implementation was still be considered in current legislation at the time of the report.

[10]   Perhaps the best account of the 9/11 Commission and the U.S. government's implementation of the recommendations can be found in the new book *Without Precedent: The Inside Story of the 9/11 Commission*, by Thomas Kean & Lee Hamilton, the Chair and Vice Chair of the Commission.

Part II

The Homeland Security Transformation

The 9/11 Commission was specific in its recommendations about the flaws and vulnerabilities in the U.S. homeland security apparatus and urged major reforms in the intelligence community, the military, and the way that federal agencies interact with the private sector. Rather than leave these reforms to the bureaucrats within the intelligence community and military, Congress stepped in and passed legislation that guided the transformation of these agencies for homeland security.

The intelligence community was overhauled with the passage of the Intelligence Reform and Terrorism Prevention Act of 2004. For the first time in American history, direction of the U.S. Intelligence Community was taken from the Director of the Central Intelligence Agency and given to the Director of National Intelligence, a new post that reports directly to the President of the United States. The Federal Bureau of Investigation (FBI) was given more responsibility for the collection of intelligence domestically and was directed to make terrorism the primary investigative focus for the agency. This redirection of mission has resulted in a drop in the traditional types of crimes that the FBI had jurisdiction over, such as narcotics-related crime and financial fraud cases. Chapter 4 introduces the reader to the role of intelligence in national security and gives an overview of the current transformation in intelligence as a result of the Intelligence Reform and Terrorism Prevention Act of 2004.

The military underwent its greatest reorganization since the creation of the Joint Chiefs of Staff in 1986 with the creation of the Northern Command (NORTHCOM). NORTHCOM gave the military a unified command dedicated to securing the United States within its continental borders and increased coordination among three preexisting commands that had responsibilities related to homeland security. The deployment of the military on US soil presents some significant legal issues and it is forbidden, by the *Posse Comitatus* Act for the military to engage in any actions that are civilian in nature, such as law enforcement and order maintenance. The new homeland security legislation as it relates to the military and the creation of NORTH-COM will regularly be evaluated for legal compliance with these statutes.

Chapter 5 details the creation and responsibilities of the new Northern Command and places these new responsibilities within the existing legal framework of the *Posse Comitatus* Act and the exceptions to this legislation.

The final area of emphasis by the 9/11 Commission was the way that the agencies charged with homeland security interact with the private sector. The 9/11 Commission recognized that the private sector was a vastly underutilized resource for the U.S. law enforcement and intelligence communities and made specific recommendations to begin incorporating the private sector into homeland security strategies. Chapter 6 details the private-public partnerships that have been established since the 9/11 attacks and the initiatives created by the Department of Homeland Security to integrate the private sector into the homeland security architecture.

Chapter 4

The Intelligence Community

INTRODUCTION

The Intelligence Community (IC) was created under the National Security Act of 1947 and codified under Title 50, United States Code, National Security; membership is specified under Section 401 A. The IC was specifically tasked to conduct foreign intelligence in support of U.S. national security objectives. Both law and policy strictly regulate the role of the IC in domestic activities.

Since 2001, the IC has undergone intense scrutiny as a result of perceived failures leading up to the events of 9/11. Among other issues, investigations subsequent to 9/11 disclosed a failure to share information with other members of the IC, primarily the Federal Bureau of Investigation (FBI). Legislative action mandating intelligence sharing is a direct consequence of the exhaustive reviews of intelligence-related failures. Sweeping organizational reforms include restructuring the intelligence community, readjusting its traditional priorities, and requiring a broadening of its customer base to include federal, state, local, and tribal law enforcement, correctional officers, and the private sector. For the first time, there has been an acknowledgement of the need to use all intelligence resources in the domestic arena—human, technical, and open—to build and sustain a robust infrastructure capable of protecting the national security interests of the United States. [1]

This chapter will examine the role and responsibility of the IC, previously comprised of 14 members. The Department of Homeland Security became a new member under the Homeland Security Act (HSA) of 2002, signed into law by President Bush on November 25, 2002. The Drug Enforcement Administration (DEA) became part of the IC in April 2006, which was a logical addition given the global responsibilities of DEA and the clear nexus between criminal and terrorist activities and financing.[2]

Figure 4.1   Intelligence Community—Original Seals

Intelligence Community
Air Force Intelligence
Army Intelligence
Central Intelligence Agency
Coast Guard Intelligence
Defense Intelligence Agency
Department of Energy
Department of Homeland Security
Department of State
Department of the Treasury
Drug Enforcement Administration
Federal Bureau of Investigation
Marine Corps Intelligence
National Geo-Spatial Intelligence Agency
National Reconnaisance Office
National Security Agency
Navy Intelligence

Intelligence and Homeland Security

> Whatever the complexities of the puzzles we strive to solve, and
> whatever the sophisticated techniques we may use to collect the
> pieces and store them, there can never be a time when the thought-
> ful man can be supplanted as the intelligence device supreme.[3]

Sherman Kent, long acknowledged as the Father of Intelligence (and for
whom the Kent School of Intelligence was designed in tribute), recognized the unassailable value of the individual as a collector and evaluator
of intelligence. He also recognized the value of complex technical collection systems and apparatus as a piece in a larger, complex puzzle, for
which the trained individual was, in fact, the key. When the IC was created,
the primary threats to the United States and her national interests were well
outside her geographic boundaries. All of the IC's resources, both technical and human, were focused on identifying, disrupting, and defeating
foreign-based threats on foreign soil. The Department of Justice was primarily responsible for investigation into domestic-based terrorist threats[4]
and there was little collaboration between the agencies. Exchanges of per-

sonnel began to occur in the early 1990s with the establishment of the Counterterrorism Center (CTC) at CIA and today, the process is institutionalized with the exchange of senior and operational-level personnel from a broad array of federal agencies.

The coordinated attacks of September 11, 2001 were the first successful multiple terrorist events on domestic soil since the Civil War. This is not meant to diminish in any way the attack on the World Trade Center in February 1993: it should have been a signal for better intelligence sharing; more defined protocols for response and recovery; and an early warning of the scale of the intent by the financiers and implementers of the attack. The 1993 attack was designed to topple one tower into the other and to be the beginning of a coordinated set of attacks on the New York tunnels, the United Nations building, and the FBI office. Nine years later, the nation was still ill-prepared to respond to a domestic incident of the magnitude of 9/11. The gaps in preparedness and fore-knowledge have been well documented by the 9/11 Commission Report, countless reviews, and Congressional hearings.

The Intelligence Reform and Terrorism Prevention Act of 2004, Public Law 108-458, signed by the president on December 17, 2004, created the Office of the Director of National Intelligence (ODNI) and imbued it with

Intelligence and National Security Alliance (INSA)

The Intelligence and National Security Alliance (INSA) is a non-profit, non-partisan, professional association created to improve our nation's security through an alliance of intelligence and national security leaders in the private and public sectors. INSA understands the challenges of the increasing responsibilities of our nation's intelligence community, its role in the expanding demands of national security, at home and abroad, and that a strong advocacy voice for intelligence is the only way to ensure that critical capabilities are robust and able to meet these challenges. Through collaboration, INSA provides timely, practical solutions and insights to key policy, industry, and implementation issues affecting U.S. intelligence and national security. INSA is a resource for key decisionmakers at all levels of government, allowing for provision of alternative analyses of subjects or issues and capitalizing on an extensive network of members representing a broad base of experience. The central component is the INSA Forum, comprised of government, industry, and academic experts. The Forum provides thoughtful leadership, functional insight, and rigorous analysis that is then made available to decision leaders at all levels of government, industry, academia, and law enforcement and first responders. Along with the Forum, INSA sponsors Centers and Councils for directed work on some of the most vexing and critical issues facing the intelligence and national security communities. A key role for INSA is its advocacy for intelligence. Through papers, publications, testimonies, roundtables, symposia and conferences, INSA focuses the debate on important, critical issues, always rising above the political solution to highlight needs, capabilities, and support for those who, day-to-day, quietly protect our citizens, often with little tangible reward.

authority and responsibility which was unparalleled. The Director of National Intelligence (DNI) is a Presidential appointment requiring Senate confirmation. The DNI is the primary advisor on intelligence to the President, National Security Council, Homeland Security Council, Executive Branch department heads, Chairman of the Joint Chiefs of Staff, senior military commanders, and the Senate and House of Representatives and their committees. Additionally, he directs the National Intelligence Program,[5] has oversight of both the National Counterterrorism Centers (NCTC) and the National Intelligence Council (NIC),[6] and serves as the Chair of the Joint Intelligence Community Council.[7] The Joint Intelligence Community Council includes the Secretaries of State, Treasury, Defense, Energy, Homeland Security, and the Attorney General. The Council's primary responsibility is to assist the Director of National Intelligence in creating a federation of resources to protect national security. The Council supports the Director in such tasks as establishing requirements, developing budgets, managing finances, and supervising and evaluating the efficiency of the intelligence community. The Council also ensures that all programs, policies, and directives of the Director are implemented in a timely manner.

The National Counterterrorism Center (NCTC) is the principal organization responsible for analyzing and integrating all intelligence on terrorism and counterterrorism for the United States Government, excluding intelligence related to domestic terrorism and counterterrorism, authorities which are relegated to the FBI. Its head is appointed by the President and confirmed by the Senate and is the primary advisor to the DNI on counterterrorism. It is important to note that the NCTC has no authority to execute counterterrorism operations. There are five major functions of the NCTC:

1. Serve as the primary organization in the United States Government for analyzing and integrating all intelligence possessed or acquired by the United States Government pertaining to terrorism and counterterrorism, excepting purely domestic counterterrorism information. The Center may, consistent with applicable law, receive, retain, and disseminate information from any Federal, State, or local government, or other source necessary to fulfill its responsibilities concerning the policy set forth in section 1 of this order; and agencies authorized to conduct counterterrorism activities may query Center data for any information to assist in their respective responsibilities;

2. Conduct strategic operational planning for counterterrorism activities, integrating all instruments of national power, including diplomatic, financial, military, intelligence, homeland security, and law enforcement activities within and among agencies;

Figure 4.2   Office of Director of National Intelligence, 2005

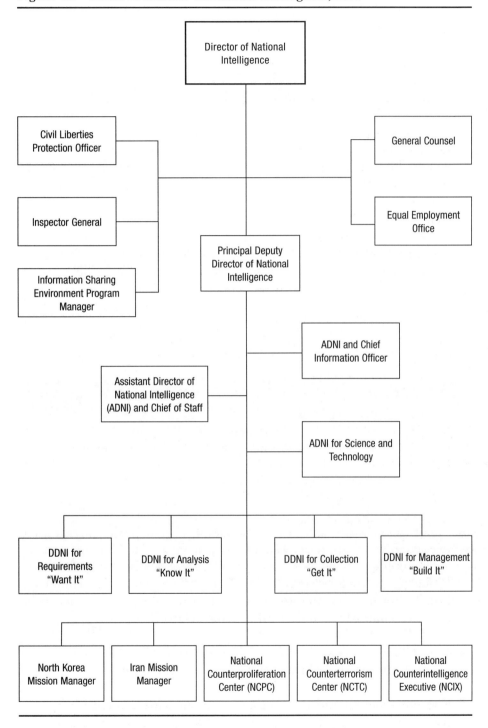

3. Assign operational responsibilities to lead agencies for counterterrorism activities that are consistent with applicable law and that support strategic plans to counter terrorism. The Center shall ensure that agencies have access to and receive intelligence needed to accomplish their assigned activities. The Center shall not direct the execution of operations. Agencies shall inform the National Security Council and the Homeland Security Council of any objections to designations and assignments made by the Center in the planning and coordination of counterterrorism activities;

4. Serve as the central and shared knowledge bank on known and suspected terrorists and international terror groups, as well as their goals, strategies, capabilities, and networks of contacts and support; and

5. Ensure that agencies, as appropriate, have access to and receive all-source intelligence support needed to execute their counterterrorism plans or perform independent, alternative analysis.[8]

The Intelligence Reform and Terrorism Act of 2004 amended the National Security Act of 1947 and redefined national intelligence.[9] Another significant change was the subordination of the Director of Central Intelli-

---

National Counterterrorism Center (NCTC)

The National Counterterrorism Center (NCTC) was established by Executive Order (EO) 13354. On December 6, 2004, all the authorities and responsibilities of the Terrorist Threat Integration Center (TTIC) were transferred to the NCTC. Effective June 17, 2005, the NCTC began operation under the joint authority of the Intelligence Reform and Terrorist Prevention Act and EO 13354. According to a Fact Sheet published by NCTC on January 6, 2006, the NCTC: serves as the principal advisor to the DNI on intelligence operations relating to counterterrorism; serves as the central and shared knowledge bank on terrorism information; provides an all-source intelligence support to government-wide counterterrorism activities; and establishes the information technology systems and architectures within the NCTC and between the NCTC and other agencies that enables access to, as well as integration, dissemination, and use of terrorism information. How they perform the mission is summarized below:

- Operates as a partnership of organizations to include: the Federal Bureau of Investigation; Central Intelligence Agency; and other entities that provide unique experience such as the Departments of Energy, Treasury, Agriculture, and Health and Human Services; Nuclear Regulatory Commission, and the U.S. Capitol Police.

- Produces an integrated and interagency-coordinated analytic assessment on terrorism issues and publishes terrorism warnings, alerts, and advisories.

- Maintains the National repository of known and suspected terrorism identities.

- Manages a 24/7 Operations Center that monitors and warns on worldwide terrorism-related issues and events.

gence (DCI) to the authority and oversight of the DNI. The title of the position was also modified to Director of the Central Intelligence Agency. Previously, the DCI served three primary roles as defined by Title 50 and Executive Order 12,333. The DCI served as the President's chief foreign intelligence advisor, Director of the Intelligence Community writ large, and Director of the CIA. The DCI was authorized to be the single voice for the IC and to take direction from the President on behalf of the IC. One of the key responsibilities of the position can be found in Executive Order 12,333, 1.5(h), 1981, which authorized the DCI to "ensure that programs are developed which protect intelligence sources, methods, and analytical procedures."

This presidential directed responsibility is one of the key justifications for limits imposed on the sharing and using of intelligence information in support of non-IC and DOD activities. The justifications were based on two important principles. The first, is that collections activities against foreign adversaries as extremely sensitive and fragile, and may take literally years to establish. The recruitment, development, and vetting of an intelligence source is time-consuming, dangerous, and costly process. The loss of a well placed source based on an intentional or inadvertent leak of information may impact on the ability of the source to provide additional information. Second, the sources of information are subject to denial and deception activities if their capabilities become known. Systems which cost billions of dollars to develop and to deploy could also be compromised if sources and methods are not assiduously protected. These same restrictions and potential impacts have complicated the issues surrounding the development of procedures to share an increased amount of intelligence related information with an expanded audience of consumers across the federal, state, local, tribal and international policing communities, as well as with a broader array of agencies within the Department of Homeland Security.

An additional complication is the authority basis for additional consumers of intelligence to actually receive it, both from a protocol perspective defined as a demonstrated "need to know" as well as from a legal standpoint which requires the acquisition of a national security clearance[10] and with it, the capability to receive, process, disseminate and store these materials, on the whole requirements which police departments are not funded nor resourced to establish and maintain. The sheer volume of law enforcement professionals with a potential need to know would, in fact, hobble the existing system requiring full background investigations and at some compartmentalized levels, polygraph examinations. Volume and cost are inhibitors as well as catalysts towards reducing the over-classification of materials and developing a standard which protects systems yet provides consistent and specific products to those who need them in a manner in which the products can be operationalized. A directive for this effort can be found in the specific language of the Executive Order No. 13,556.[11]

The classification system is derived from the potential damage that a compromise at different levels could inflict to the national security of the

United States. This includes both the source from which the information was collected and the method in which it was obtained. Lowenthal's work[12] provided the following quick review of classification levels:

> SECRET—information whose unauthorized disclosure "could be expected to cause damage to national security"

> TOP SECRET—information whose unauthorized disclosure "could be expected to cause serious damage to the national security"

In October 2005, the ODNI released The National Intelligence Strategy of the United States, subtitled: Transformation through Integration and Innovation. The titles are important, each signal the initial direction of a revamped intelligence community and a implied intention to essentially conduct business in a manner which looks outside the structural and cultural walls of the Intelligence Community for expertise, and moreover, affirmatively states a need to and willingness for engagement with domestic law enforcement and the private sector—both historically and intentionally kept at a distance and uninformed. The separation also meant a lack of a process for reciprocal information sharing from either of these vast communities, each with resources and capabilities of value. The acknowledgement of that value does not mean a complete change towards openness on the part of the IC to exchange information directly with either community. Mechanisms have been established with and through the Department of Homeland Security for that purpose. Exceptions related to the private sector may occur with the creation by the DNI of an open source intelligence component.

The words of Thomas Jefferson inscribed on the national memorial to him states "that the price of freedom is eternal vigilance." The National Intelligence Strategy indicates that vigilance alone is insufficient to combat current and emerging threats.[13] It acknowledges that existing organizational and institutional cultures developed for justifiable reasons at the time of their inception however in many cases the original catalysts for their formation and growth have either evolved or even perhaps, expired.[14] The recognition of the challenges posed by an enemy different then those engaged in the Cold War years, and one that has brought the fight to domestic soil has required an expansion of vision, the harnessing of proven technical and human capital, and the elimination of redundant resources or capabilities. A complete elimination of threats to the Nation is impossible, early knowledge and minimization is the goal. Emphasis is placed on analytical expertise and the exploration of alternative analysis—again harnessing resources to a greater degree then ever before which may exist outside of the intelligence community. A blending of cross-cutting new technology coupled with an enhanced collection both technical and human will drive the national will to prevent surprise such as those that occurred on 9/11.

Fifteen strategic objectives form the backbone of the newly released National Intelligence Strategy broken out as strategic and enterprise, developed to support five key mission objectives:

1. Collect, analyze, and disseminate accurate, timely, and objective intelligence, independent of political considerations, to the President and all who make and implement U.S. national security policy, fight our wars, protect our nation, and enforce our laws.

2. Conduct the U.S. government's national intelligence program and special activities as directed by the president.

3. Transform our capabilities in order to stay ahead of evolving threats to the United States, exploiting risk while recognizing the impossibility of eliminating it.

4. Deploy effective counterintelligence measures that protect our activities to ensure the integrity of the intelligence system, our technology, our armed forces, and our government's decision process.

5. Perform our duties under law in a manner that that respects the civil liberties and privacy of all Americans.

In order to meet the specific mission requirements, the following objectives supporting a timely and accurate intelligence process are identified:

1. Defeat terrorists at home and abroad by disarming their operational capabilities and seizing the initiative from them by promoting the growth of freedom and democracy.

2. Prevent and counter the spread of weapons of mass destruction.

3. Bolster the growth of democracy and sustain peaceful democratic states.

4. Develop innovative ways to penetrate and analyze the most difficult targets

5. Anticipate developments of strategic concern and identify opportunities as well as vulnerabilities for decision-makers.[15]

The 10 key enterprise objectives designed to outpace the capabilities of the adversary while protecting U.S. interests are identified as:

1. Build an integrated intelligence capability to address threats to the homeland, consistent with U.S. laws and the protection of privacy and civil liberties.

2. Strengthen analytical expertise, methods, and practices; tap expertise wherever it resides; and explore alternative analytical views.

3. Rebalance, integrate, and optimize collection capabilities to meet current and future customer and analytical priorities.

4. Attract, engage, and unify an innovative and results-focused Intelligence–Community workforce.

5. Ensure that Intelligence Community members and customers can access the intelligence they need when they need it.

6. Establish new and strengthen existing foreign intelligence relationships to help us meet global security challenges.

7. Create clear, uniform security practices and rules that allow us to work together, protect our nation's secrets, and enable aggressive counterintelligence activities.

8. Exploit path-breaking scientific and research advances that will enable us to maintain and extend intelligence advantages against emerging threats.

9. Learn from our successes and mistakes to anticipate and be ready for new challenges.

10. Eliminate redundancy and programs that add little or no value and re-direct savings to existing and emerging national security priorities.[16]

INTELLIGENCE REFORM AND TERRORISM PREVENTION ACT OF 2004

On December 7, 2004, the House of Representatives passed the Intelligence Reform and Terrorism Prevention Act of 2004 with a vote of 336-75. On December 8, 2004, the Senate also passed the Act with a vote of 89-2.

Prior to signing the Intelligence Reform and Terrorism Prevention Act, President Bush described the Act as "the most dramatic reform of our nation's intelligence capabilities since President Harry S. Truman signed the National Security Act of 1947." President Bush identified the main purpose of the Act as "to ensure that the people in government responsible for defending America have the best possible information to make the best possible decisions." Key tenets of the reform act are included to provide a macro view of the sweeping organizational changes which will reshape the entire intelligence community.

The most significant aspect of the Intelligence Reform and Terrorism Prevention Act of 2004 is the creation of a Director of National Intelligence (DNI). The Director oversees the intelligence community and is the primary national security advisor to the President, National Security Council (NSC), and the Homeland Security Council (HSC). The DNI is also responsible for the National Counterterrorism Center (NCTC) and the National Intelligence Council (NIC). This position serves as the information hub for the entire intelligence community and is in charge of the collection, analysis, and dissemination for all national intelligence.

With the creation of the DNI, the Office of the Director of National Intelligence was also developed and includes the Director of National Intelligence, the Principal Deputy Director of National Intelligence, the National Intelligence Council, the General Counsel, the Civil Liberties Protection Officer, the Director of Science and Technology, the National Counterintelligence Executive, and the Office of the National Counterintelligence Executive. The Office of the Deputy Director of Central Intelligence for Community Management has been moved to the Office of the Director of National Intelligence to assist the Director of National Intelligence in fulfilling his duties.

National intelligence, as defined by the Intelligence and Terrorism Prevention Act of 2004, refers to all intelligence that involves threats to the U.S., its people, property or interests; the development, proliferations, or use of weapons of mass destruction; or any other issue pertaining to national or homeland security. The sources of information and whether it is obtained within or outside the U.S. does not matter.

The National Intelligence Council includes senior analysts of the intelligence community and various specialists from the public and private sector, all of whom are appointed by and work under the Director of National Intelligence. The National Intelligence Council comprises estimates of national intelligence for the United States Government. The duties of the National Intelligence Council also include evaluating intelligence gathered by the intelligence community. The Council should be available to those within the intelligence community and those, deemed appropriate, who are not, such as policymaking officials.

The functions are also outlined in the Central Intelligence Agency (CIA) in the Intelligence and Terrorism Prevention Act of 2004 and includes all national intelligence gathered outside the U.S. is handled by the CIA and then the CIA informs the DNI. It also recommends several actions to transform the Agency, such as encouraging the hiring of diverse people and expanding the language program. It also seeks to develop a more efficient relationship between human and signals intelligence, and to create a more efficient balance between unilateral operations and liaison operations.

The Information Sharing Council (ISC) is responsible for directing the President and program manager on how to develop, improve, and maintain the information sharing environment (ISE). The program manager, who oversees the ISE, is responsible for disseminating information across the federal government. The ISC makes recommendations and implements new programs and initiatives to make information effective and is responsible for the information flow between federal agencies, as well as state and local agencies. Several guidelines have been developed to help the Council and the federal government improve efficiency:

- Define Common Standards for How Information is Acquired, Accessed, Shared, and Used within the ISE

- Develop a Common Framework for the Sharing of Information Between and Among Executive Departments and Agencies and State, Local, and Tribal Governments, Law Enforcement Agencies, and the Private Sector

- Standardize Procedures for Sensitive But Unclassified Information

- Facilitate Information Sharing Between Executive Departments and Agencies and Foreign Partners

- Protect the Information Privacy Rights and Other Legal Rights of Americans

- Promoting a Culture of Information Sharing.

National Counterterrorism Center

The National Counterterrorism Center (NCTC) is responsible for analyzing and integrating all terrorism and counterterrorism related intelligence in the U.S., except for intelligence that concerns domestic terrorism and counterterrorism. The NCTC has access to all levels of national power, including diplomatic, financial, military, intelligence, homeland security, and law enforcement tools. It also serves as the source of information for all international known and suspected terrorists and terror groups.

The Director of the NCTC reports directly to the Director of National Intelligence on all matters relating to counterterrorism, as well as pertinent terrorism information and current terror threat analysis.

The Terrorist Threat Integration Center (TTIC) is also included in the NCTC and is responsible for maintaining a current database with all intelligence on known or suspected terrorists. It also disseminates information regarding possible or real threats to national security to the private and public industry.

National Counterproliferation Center

The National Counterproliferation Center is responsible for evaluating and disseminating all intelligence relating to the proliferation of weapons of mass destruction, including the delivery of such weapons and technology used in the proliferation.

Joint Intelligence Community Council

The Joint Intelligence Community Council is responsible for creating and executing resources to protect national security and includes the DNI, Secretary of State, Secretary of Treasury, Secretary of Defense, Attorney General, Secretary of Energy, and the Secretary of Homeland Security. The Council establishes requirements, develops budgets, manages finances, supervises and evaluates the efficiency of the intelligence community, and ensures that all programs are carried out in a timely manner.

Criminal Justice Information Services (CJIS)

The Federal Bureau of Investigation (FBI) established a Criminal Justice Information Services (CJIS) Division to serve local, state and federal law enforcement. The CJIS Division manages some of the largest information systems available to law enforcement in the United States, such as:

IAFIS—Integrated Automatic Fingerprint Identification System
NCIC—National Crime Information Center
UCR—Uniform Crime Reporting Program
NICS—National Instant Criminal Background Check System

While only a federal agency such as the FBI has the resources to create and maintain these large systems, the majority of the information contained in them comes from the local and state law enforcement agencies throughout the nation. The FBI created the CJIS Advisory Process to obtain advice from local, state, and federal user agencies that supply the information to these systems. The underlying philosophy of the CJIS Advisory Process is that of shared management, where the stakeholders assist in the management of these critical information systems.

In 1992 when the FBI established the CJIS division, there were two separate advisory groups that gave advice to the Bureau. The National Crime Information Center Advisory Policy Board, established in the 1960s, provided guidance on the NCIC system, fingerprint systems and identification systems. The second advisory board was the UCR Data Providers Advisory Policy Board, created in 1988 to provide the FBI Director with advice and guidance. By 1994, in consultation with some of the largest police organizations in the country, the two boards were combined to form the current CJIS advisory process.

The CJIS advisory board consists of representatives from all 50 states. There are also representatives from the U.S. Territories, federal law enforcement agencies, the Royal Canadian Mounted Police and various large criminal justice organizations including the International Association of Chiefs of Police (IACP), Major City Chiefs (MCC), the National Sheriffs Association, Corrections and Parole, the federal court systems, the National District Attorney Association and many others; in total there are approximately 180 members.

The advisory process has three separate levels. The first consists of five regional working groups (RWG's). The Nation is divided into four geographic regions, representing all 50 states: the northeast, southern, north central and the western region. Each of these four regions has two representatives from each state, one representing local law enforcement agencies and one, a state law enforcement agency. The fifth region is composed of various federal agencies that have a law enforcement mission such as ATF, ICE etc.

Issues are debated at the regional level so that law enforcement agencies can have input; the views expressed at the five regions are then sent to the second level of the process, APB (Advi-

Criminal Justice Information Services (CJIS), *continued*

sory Police Board) Sub-Committees. Sub-committees handle various areas of concern such as fingerprint-based identification, the NCIC system and UCR. Any misuse of the systems is reported to a sanctions sub-committee. Recommendations from the sub-committees go to the third step of the process, the Advisory Policy Board. The APB is composed of elected members of the geographic regions plus representatives of the major police groups such as IACP, Major City Chiefs MCC, The National Sheriffs Associations, etc.

The APB elects a Chairperson that under the By-Laws may speak on behalf of the process. Once a recommendation is made through this process it has been vetted by approximately 180 members representing thousands of law enforcement agencies. The recommendations then go to the Director of the FBI for action. The 2006 Chair of the APB, Chief Frank Sleeter of the Sun Prairie Wisconsin Police Department, said: "Whenever a police officer requests one of the millions of NCIC warrant checks that occur daily or an agency electronically sends a fingerprint to the FBI and gets a response back in minutes these transactions do not occur by magic but instead are the results of a lot of hard work from dedicated law enforcement officials involved in the FBI CJIS Advisory Process."

The Intelligence Reform and Terrorism Prevention Act of 2004 also provides harsher punishments for those convicted of Obstruction of Justice and False Statements in Terrorism Cases (Section 6703, U.S. Code) has been increased to five years, and up to eight years if the offense involves international or domestic terrorism.

The Weapons of Mass Destruction Prohibition Improvement Act of 2004 allows imprisonment up to 20 years in the offense of providing material support or resources to a nuclear weapons program or other weapons of mass destruction program of a foreign terrorist power, or the attempt or conspiracy to do so. Those convicted of this charge may also be charged up two million dollars.

The Human Smuggling and Trafficking Center (HSTC) is operated by the Secretary of State, the Secretary of Homeland Security, and the Attorney General. The Center was created to help deter and prevent terrorists traveling and the smuggling of persons.

KEY CONCEPTS

- There are 16 members of the Intelligence Community:
    - Air Force Intelligence
    - Army Intelligence
    - Central Intelligence Agency (CIA)
    - Coast Guard (now part of DHS)
    - Defense Intelligence Agency (DIA)
    - Drug Enforcement Administration (DEA)

- • Energy Department
- • Federal Bureau of Investigation
- • Department of Homeland Security
- • Marines Intelligence
- • National Geospatial-Intelligence Agency (NGA)
- • National Reconnaissance Office (NRO)
- • National Security Agency (NSA)
- • Navy Intelligence
- • State Department's Bureau of Intelligence and Research (INR)
- • Department of the Treasury

- The Office of the Director of National Intelligence, created in 2004, oversees all matters and organizations related to national intelligence. The Office was created by the Intelligence Reform and Terrorism Prevention Act of 2004.

- Effective intelligence requires not only the collection of vital information, but also the analysis and dissemination to proper agencies of such information.

- The *Intelligence Reform and Terrorism Prevention Act of 2004* made several contributions to the Intelligence Community, including an updated definition of national intelligence and the creation of the Director of National Intelligence.

- The disclosure of intelligence failures after 9/11 led to a major reorganization of how intelligence agencies function, including modified priorities and a broadening of its consumer base.

ADDITIONAL READINGS

EO 12333, "United States Intelligence Activities," 04 December 1981.

EO 12958, "Classified National Security Information," 12 April 1995.

EO 13292, "Classified National Security Information," 25 March 2003.

EO 13311, "Homeland Security Information Sharing," 29 July 2003.

Abbas Amanat, "Empowered Through Violence: The Reinventing of Islamic Extremism," in Strobe Talbott and Nayan Chanda, Editors, *The Age of Terrorism: America and the World After September 11*, pp. 23-52.

Homeland Security Act (HSA) of 2002.

Intelligence Reform and Terrorism Prevention Act of 2004.

Laqueur, Walter (1985). *A World of Secrets: The Uses and Limits of Intelligence*. New York: Basic Books.

Lowenthal, Mark M. (2003). *Intelligence From Secrets to Policy*.Washington, DC: CQ Press.

Lowenthal, Mark M. (1992). *U.S. Intelligence: Evolution and Anatomy*, Second Edition. Westport, CT: Praeger.

National Security Act of 1947.

Patterns of Global Terrorism 2004 (April 2005). Washington, DC: United States Department of State.

Pillar, Paul R. (2003). "Terrorism, The United States, and World Order," Chapter 3 in *Pillar, Terrorism and United States Foreign Policy*, pp. 41-72. Washington, DC: Brookings Institution Press.

Stern, Jessica (2003). "Territory," in *Terror in the Name of God: Why Religious Militants Kill.* Harper Collins.

U.S. Department of Justice, Office of the Inspector General, The Federal Bureau of Investigation's Efforts to Improve the Sharing of Intelligence and Other Information, Audit Report No. 04-10, December 2003.

U.S. Department of Justice, Office of Justice Programs, The National Criminal Intelligence Sharing Plan, Version 1.0, October 2003.

Weapons of Mass Destruction Prohibition Improvement Act of 2004.

Wohlstetter, Roberta (1962). *Pearl Harbor: Warning and Decision.* Stanford, CA: Stanford University Press.

RELATED WEBSITES

Federal Bureau of Investigation (FBI) www.fbi.gov

Intelligence Community (IC) www.intelligence.gov

Office of the Director of National Intelligence (ODNI) www.dni.gov

National Intelligence Council (NIC) www.cia.gov/nic

Central Intelligence Agency (CIA) www.cia.gov

National Counterterrorism Center (NCTC) www.nctc.gov

REFERENCES

http://www.dni.gov/DNI.html

http://www.dni.gov/release_letter_103105.html

http://www.whitehouse.gov/news/releases/2004/12/print/20041217-1.html

http://www.gpoaccess.gov/serialset/creports/intel_reform.html

(TTIC) http://www.house.gov/gibbons/072203b.asp

CRS Report for Congress (2001). *Terrorism: Near Eastern Groups and State Sponsors, 2001.* Katzman, Kenneth.

Intelligence and the New National Security Environment (2004). AFCEA International Committee.

Office of the Director of National Intelligence (2005). *The National Intelligence Strategy of the United States of America: Transformation through Integration and Innovation.*

Teitelbaum, L. (2005). *The Impact of the Information Revolution on Policymakers' Use of Intelligence Analysis.* Arlington, VA: Pardee Rand Graduate School.

NOTES

1   See Final Report of the Homeland Security Advisory Council (HSAC) on Intelligence and Information Sharing Initiative, dated December 2004. There are specific recommendations to leverage the existing law enforcement knowledge and experience base by developing a comprehensive, consistent, multi-disciplinary approach to domestic intelligence collection effort consistent with 28CFR, part 23. The report specifically recommends that the collection effort must not compromise the ability to carry out routine policing responsibilities.

2   House Report 109/118—Science, State, Justice, Commerce, and Related Agencies Appropriations Bill, Fiscal Year 2006.

3   Kent, *Strategic Intelligence for American World Policy*, preface to the 1965 edition, p. xviii.

4   Memorandums of Understanding (MOUs) were developed to identify and resolve jurisdictional and organizational rivalries between agencies in investigations which involved the criminal misuse of explosives. The MOU outlines the primacy of agencies when there is a clear delineation of motivation, intent, and/or responsibility. Examples included within the MOU are related to bombings directed at health care facilities providing abortion services, bombings committed by environmentalists, and bombings directed against government facilities. Signatories to a 1973 MOU included the Federal Bureau of Investigation; the Bureau of Alcohol, Tobacco, and Firearms; and the United States Postal Investigations Service. Oftentimes, there is a joint investigative process to the point of prosecution.

5   According to the National Security Act of 1947, the National Intelligence Program (formerly the National Foreign Intelligence Program) "refers to all programs, projects, and activities of the intelligence community, as well as any other programs of the intelligence community designated jointly by the Director of Central Intelligence and the head of a United States department or agency or by the President. Such term does not include programs, projects, or activities of the military departments to acquire intelligence solely for the planning and conduct of tactical military operations by United States Armed Forces."

6   The National Intelligence Council is comprised of senior analysts of the Intelligence Community and experts from the public and private sector. It is responsible for developing National Intelligence Estimates (NIEs); advising the Directorate of National Intelligence; assessing the capabilities and needs of intelligence community analysts; and communicating with senior intelligence consumers on a regular basis, supporting their current and long-term needs and addressing their concerns.

7   See Subtitle C, Intelligence Reform and Terrorism Act of 2004.

8   See Executive Order 13354: National Counterterrorism Center, Section 2. August 27, 2004.

9   Paragraph (5) of section 3 of the National Security Act of 1947 (50 U.S.C. 4101) was amended to read: The terms 'national intelligence' and 'intelligence related to national security' refer to all intelligence, regardless of source from which derived and including information gathered within or outside the United States, that (A) pertains, as determined consistent with any guidance issued by the President, to more than one United States Government Agency; and (B) that involves (i) threats to the United States, its people, property, or interests; (ii) the development, proliferation, or use of weapons of mass destruction; or (iii) any other matter bearing on United States national or homeland security.

[10] See Executive Order 12958 dated April 17, 1995 for description of classification levels and definitions.

[11] Executive Order No. 13,556, 69 Fed. Reg. 53599 (September 1, 2004).

[12] Mark M. Lowenthal, Intelligence from Secrets to Policy, Second Edition, CQ Press, 2003, p. 58.

[13] See page 2 of Foreword in National Intelligence Strategy which also acknowledges that risk is a natural amnd permanent field of action for the Intelligence Community which requires a proactive, dynamic, and sustainable approach to effectively identify and defeat current and emergent threats.

[14] National Intelligence Strategy, ODNI, October, 2005.

[15] See National Strategy for Homeland Security, July 2002.

[16] See National Strategy for Homeland Security, July 2002.

Chapter 5

The Role of the U.S. Military in Homeland Security

INTRODUCTION

> "Our most important contribution to the security of the U.S. homeland is our capacity to disrupt and defeat threats early and at a safe distance, as far from the U.S. and its partners as possible. Our ability to identify and defeat threats abroad—before they can strike—while making critical contributions to the direct defense of our territory and population is the sine qua non of our nation's security."[1]

Including a brief overview on the role of the United States Military in a textbook on homeland security may at first glance appear to be incongruous; however, the inclusion is deliberate and significant. The U.S. Military has, throughout history, performed a critical role in ensuring the nations' safety from foreign aggression and by means of legislated authority has a significant support role in the domestic arena. Structurally, since the end of WWII, the military has been defined as an instrument of national power used for the projection of power and secondarily as a defensive mechanism. The Goldwater-Nichols Act of 1986 (which amended Title 50, USC), placed a great deal of emphasis on the construct of jointness, with no service having primacy and the majority of commands having a geographic focus. Operational authority was centralized through the Chairman of the Joint Chiefs as opposed to the service chiefs. The chairman was designated as the principal military advisor to the president, National Security Council and secretary of defense. The act established the position of vice-chairman and streamlined the operational chain of command from the president to the secretary of defense to the unified commanders.

Commands were defined as warfighting commands, which uses forces, and force-providers. Each combatant commander has subunified command forces, usually Army, Navy, Air Force, and Marine at his disposal. The military has had to make major changes in the mindset of its personnel to support current DoD missions in which the military is not the primary instrument of power but serves in a support role as it does in the domestic arena.

There is a clear distinction legally and organizationally between homeland security and homeland defense missions, authorities, and responsibilities. Homeland security is defined within the National Homeland Security Strategy[2] as "a concerted national effort to prevent terrorist attacks within the United States, reduce America's vulnerability to terrorism, and minimize the damage and recover from attacks that do occur." That mission is inextricably linked with other national prerogatives related to national security and homeland defense, each and all concerned with the protection of freedom and sovereignty.

The DoD Strategy for Homeland Defense and Civil Support outlines the distinction with the following definition: homeland defense is "the protection of U.S. sovereignty, territory, domestic population, and critical defense infrastructure against external threats and aggression."[3] However clear the distinction is, there are equally clear and legally codified authorities that allow the military to support civilian authorities when directed to do so by either the President of the United States or the Secretary of Defense in specific areas to include disasters, chemical, biological, radiological incidents, epidemics, and civil disturbances. Within those authorities are additional responsibilities to include the support of counter-drug operations and protection of elements of the defense industrial base. This chapter defines the role of the Department of Defense (DOD) in Homeland Defense; the creation of a new combatant command authority; and the relationships with, and distinctions from homeland security. A legislative history will also be provided to illustrate the intended clear separation of military authority and jurisdiction codified into law.

THE CREATION OF NORTHERN COMMAND

Even before the creation of the Department of Homeland Security, the military was reorganized to better combat terrorism abroad and to protect U.S. citizens at home. Through the signing of the Defense Department Unified Command Plan, which was signed into law on April 25, 2002, the U.S. Northern Command (NORTHCOM) was created and given the responsibility for defense of the United States, including land, aerospace, and sea defenses, as well as to provide military assistance to civil authorities, including immediate crisis and subsequent consequence management operations. The creation of NORTHCOM represented the largest unified command reorganization since WWII.

Officially, NORTHCOM began operations on October 1, 2002 at its headquarters on Peterson Air Force Base in Colorado Springs, Colorado. As of November 2005, NORTHCOM was staffed by approximately 1,200 active duty, reserve military, and civilian personnel. According to a 2005 report by the Congressional Research Service, the estimated annual budget for NORTHCOM is roughly $70 million.[4]

It is important to note that NORTHCOM was not the first foray into homeland defense for the military, rather it took control of the three pre-existing homeland defense organizations; all of which had distinct missions under homeland defense prior to creation of NORTHCOM. The first of these homeland defense organizations was the Joint Forces Headquarters—Homeland Security (JFHQ-HS), based at Norfolk, VA. This

command was the homeland security component of the U.S. Joint Forces Command (JFCOM) that coordinates the land and maritime defense of the continental United States and military assistance (for operations such as disaster relief) to civil authorities. JFHQ-HS was quickly stood up in the weeks following the 9/11 attacks and has played key roles in major national-level events such as coordinating military support for security missions during Super Bowl XXVI in New Orleans, LA and the XIX Winter Olympics in Salt Lake City, Utah. JFHQ-HS has since been disbanded and replaced with the Standing Joint Force Headquarters North (SJFHQ-N) and the Joint Force Headquarters National Capital Region (JFHQ-NCR).

NORTHCOM also took control of the Joint Task Force for Civil Support (JTF-CS) at Ft. Monroe, VA. JTF-CS provides military support to civil authorities responding to weapons of mass destruction. The task force provides more than 150 military and civilian personnel for command and control of DoD assets deployed to support the leading federal agency (which would more than likely be the Federal Emergency Management Administration [FEMA]) managing the consequences of a weapons of mass destruction attack or mass casualty event. The JTF-CS is the only military organization dedicated solely to planning and integrating Department of Defense (DoD) forces for consequence management support to civil authorities in such a situation. Although, thankfully, JTF-CS has never been deployed to a CBRNE (chemical, biological, radiological, nuclear, explosive) situation, the task force was mobilized in the weeks following Hurricane Katrina in late August 2005.

Joint Task Force North (JTF-N) at Ft. Bliss, TX was the third command that fell under NORTHCOM control once it was established in October 2002.[5] JTF-N is comprised of approximately 160 soldiers, sailors, airmen, marines, and civil servants. This task force was originally established on November 13, 1989 by President George H. W. Bush to support the nation's federal law enforcement agencies in the war on drugs. JTF-N was established to serve as the planning and coordinating operational headquarters to support local, state, and federal law enforcement agencies within the Southwest border region to counter the flow of illegal drugs into the United States.

The task force's original area of operations consisted of the four border states of California, Arizona, New Mexico and Texas—a land area of more than 580,000 square miles. In February 1995, by directive of the commanding general U.S. Army Forces Command, JTF-N's area of responsibility was expanded to include the entire continental United States, Puerto Rico, and the U.S. Virgin Islands. In June 1997, responsibility for Puerto Rico and the U.S. Virgin Islands was transferred to the U.S. Southern Command. Since its inception and until its redesignation in 2004, JTF-N completed over 5,800 missions in support of more than 430 federal, state, and local law enforcement agencies and counterdrug task forces. JTF-N has also had its mandate widened to include some homeland defense responsibilities beyond counterdrug operations. The task force aids federal law enforcement agencies protecting U.S. borders from transnational threats, which include international terrorism, the proliferation of weapons of mass destruction, delivery systems for those weapons and organized crime. Task force operations include: fixed and rotary wing aircraft reconnaissance missions to locate drug operations; border detection missions to interdict drug smuggling; and engineering missions to build fences, lights, and roads.

Beyond assuming control for the preexisting homeland defense commands in the United States, NORTHCOM has international responsibilities for coordinating defense efforts with Canada and Mexico. NORTHCOM is working with its Canadian counterparts to review the more than 600 agreements between the countries and is looking to expand the cooperative defense agreement from beyond air and space to include the maritime domain. Mexican and U.S. forces regularly cooperate on anti-drug trafficking operations. NORTHCOM has begun what it describes as the process of building further ties with Mexico. NORTHCOM has held senior officer visits with Mexican counterparts, invited Mexican participation in exercises, and continues to work on security assistance issues.

Figure 5.1   International Terrorist Attacks 1982-2003

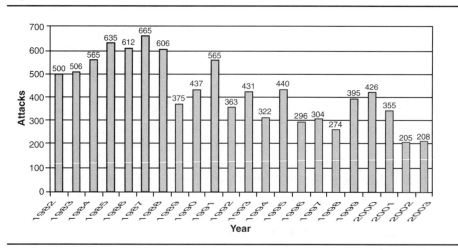

In its liaison and support role to the civilian U.S. homeland security apparatus, NORTHCOM has to pay close attention to its relationships with other law enforcement and homeland security agencies. One way NORTHCOM has done this is to permanently assign military personnel to support DHS components such counterdrug and counterterrorism security operations. Unfortunately, the interagency relationships are not always as strong as they could be. For example, since the 9/11 attacks, procedures have been put in place to allow Federal Aviation Administration (FAA) air traffic controllers to speak directly to NORTHCOM if something seems out of the ordinary. As a result, U.S. Air Force fighters have checked out more than 1,500 suspicious flights since 9/11. During the June 2004 ceremonies marking President Reagan's death, the NORTHCOM Commander had to consider whether to order the shoot-down of an unidentified plane violating Washington, D.C. airspace. It turned out that the FAA had given the plane overflight permission without telling the military.

The Role of NORTHCOM in Counterterrorism

Counterterrorism operations, when conducted on U.S. soil, are primarily law enforcement actions, so the involvement of U.S. military units are limited to support roles subsequent to being requested by civil authorities and approved by the Secretary of Defense. The Federal Bureau of Investigation is the lead federal agency in all terrorism-related investigations. The specific circumstances which require military assistance to domestic law enforcement are outlined below:

1. Providing technical support and assistance to law enforcement and other crisis response personnel (crisis response)

2. Interdicting an event and apprehending those responsible (crisis response)

3. Restoring law and order following an incident (consequence management), and

4. Abating the consequences of a terrorist attack (consequence management)

Military technical assistance to law enforcement authorities can include: loaning equipment, facilities or personnel. The Secretary of Defense has the final approval authority for any requests for potentially lethal support, all support for counterterrorism operations, and certain support in situations involving WMD.[6] The use of military personnel, equipment, and technical assistance in non-hostile situations is allowed, but must be determined jointly by the Attorney General and Secretary of Defense.

In an emergency situation, 18 U.S.C. Section 831 authorizes the Attorney General to request DoD law enforcement assistance when nuclear materials are involved. 10 U.S.C. Section 382 authorizes assistance when chemical or biological weapons are involved. When providing assistance under these statutes, the military units and personnel will remain under the military chain of command at all times. The senior on-scene federal law enforcement official (the FBI is usually designated as the on-scene commander [OSC] in most cases), may request support directly from the senior military commander at the crisis site. The planning and execution of all military support will remain the responsibility of the military commander. Any disagreements between the OSC and the military commander regarding the request for support will be referred to the Secretary of Defense and the Attorney General for resolution.

The commander of the military unit determines the appropriate technical assistance procedures based on the following priorities:

1. Protection of human life or prevention of injuries, including injury to the military personnel involved

2. Preventing the use of a chemical, biological, or nuclear weapon

3. Mitigating the consequences in the event of a the use of a chemical, biological, or nuclear weapon

4. Protecting property

Normally, military units providing technical assistance to federal law enforcement authorities will not be armed unless specifically requested through the military chain of command and authorized in advance by the Secretary of Defense and agreed to by the OSC.

Members of military units, whether armed or not, will not be placed in hostile fire situations and are only authorized to use force in self-defense as defined in the Chairman of the Joint Chiefs of Staff Peacetime Rules of Engagement. The rules specify self-defense as the reasonable, necessary, and proportional force to defend himself or herself and to defend the unit against hostile intent and/or acts. The use of deadly force is authorized against any person demonstrating hostile intent or committing hostile acts if there is a reasonable belief that the person poses an imminent danger of death or serious physical injury to the member or to another person. When providing technical assistance to the FBI or other law enforcement agencies, DoD expects the controlling agency to have made the incident area safe for assistance operations prior to admitting the military.

Searches and Evidence

Military personnel may search non-DoD property during an emergency involving WMD when there is reason to suspect that the area contains booby traps and trained FBI personnel are not available. The FBI may ask the military to clear the area of hazardous devices prior to a law enforcement search of the area. Possible criminal evidence encountered during the search may be brought to the attention of the FBI. The FBI and the senior military commander will determine the procedures to use when performing the technical assistance requested based on safety to the public, the unit, and surrounding property. The military may consider preservation of forensic evidence when choosing the assistance technique. Military personnel will not compromise safety standards in order to enhance the survival or collection of evidence for law enforcement purposes. This distinction is a particularly important in terms of subsequent prosecution of culpability in legal proceedings.

Disposition and Transportation of a WMD

When a suspected or actual WMD is rendered inert or otherwise made safe for transportation, federal law enforcement officials are responsible for obtaining approval to dispose of the device, including approval of the ultimate disposal site. If the FBI specifically requests DoD assistance through the Attorney General in the transportation and disposal of the WMD, it must be approved by the Secretary of Defense. The transportation of the WMD from the incident site is not viewed as technical assistance under 10 U.S.C. Section 382 or 18 U.S.C. Section 831. As such, it must be authorized and funded under a different authority. The specific nature of the device (chemical, biological, radiological, or nuclear) is a critical factor when considering disposition and transport. Also, the evidentiary imperatives of the law enforcement process are considered before deciding on the disposal location and method of transportation.

Training

DoD requires that all personnel likely to participate in providing assistance to federal law enforcement agencies be adequately trained and meet the minimum operational standards set within each military unit. Specialized units may train in methods for defeating WMD devices to prepare for possible employment in domestic law enforcement situations. The Department of Justice, in coordination with the FBI, provides the military with an orientation package addressing how military members may participate in the

Air Force F-15 Eagle fires an air-to-air missile during an exercise. *Courtesy of Department of Defense, photo by Master Sgt. Michael Ammons, U.S. Air Force.*

search and seizure of evidence or take the necessary precautions to avoid degrading or destroying the evidence. All military personnel likely to support law enforcement agencies are also trained in the rules of engagement they are to follow when assisting civil law enforcement members in the performance of their duties. This is particularly important when the Secretary of Defense has authorized that the military personnel be armed when performing their duties because of the danger involved in the mission.

Requests for Tactical Assistance

Employing a military tactical force in response to a domestic law enforcement emergency concerning terrorism and WMD could take place in two situations:

1. Armed conflict-like situations that threaten the continuity of government and

2. A threat endangering public safety that is beyond the tactical response capability of law enforcement.

The deployment of a tactical response to supplement law enforcement is designed to be short in duration until civilian control is firmly established.

LEGAL FRAMEWORK FOR MILITARY INTERVENTION IN HOMELAND DEFENSE

The deployment of U.S. Military forces on American soil for the purposes of performing tasks of civilian government, i.e., law enforcement, order maintenance, or compel state officials to perform federally imposed duties, is forbidden through the *Posse Comitatus* Act (PCA). The reason for this proscription is that Congress, in 1878 following the Reconstruction period, wanted to prohibit Federal troops from supervising elections in former Confederate states. There are however, several exceptions to the PCA that allow for the use of the U.S. Military for enforce law and conduct duties of civilian authorities. There are specific exceptions to the PCA enacted by the U.S. Congress that are related to counter drug assistance to law enforcement (Title 10 USC, Section 381); Insurrection (Title 10 USC, Sections 331-335); emergency assistance in the theft of nuclear materials (Title 18, USC, Section 831); and emergency situations involving chemical or biological weapons of mass destruction (Title 10, USC, Section 382). In the case of the last two situations both the Attorney General of the United States and the Secretary of Defense must agree that the conditions exceed the capabilities and resources of civilian law enforcement personnel and require assistance from DoD.

The Insurrection Statutes

Title 10 U.S.C. Sections 331-334, known as the Insurrection Statutes, authorize the President to seek military assistance to support civilian law enforcement authorities when confronted with a rebellion, unlawful obstruction, or combination of assemblage which makes enforcement of the law by duly constituted civilian authorities impracticable.

If the President found it necessary to employ the military in a domestic situation involving terrorism and WMD, invoking the Insurrection Statutes could allow the military to operate outside the traditional military support to law enforcement (technical assistance) and the prohibitions of the *Posse Comitatus* Act. The President may, when requested by a state legislature or governor when the legislature cannot be convened, send active military forces to suppress an insurrection against state authority. Normally the state authorities will specify to the President that the violence cannot be brought under control by state and local law enforcement agencies and the state National Guard. The President may also take unilateral action by invoking Sections 332 and 331 of the Insurrection Statutes when he finds that widespread unlawful activities "make it impracticable to enforce the laws of the United States" or when the violence "hinders the execution of the laws of that State, and of the United States within that State" or obstructs the execution of federal law.

If the President either receives a request for assistance from a state or decides to take unilateral action under the Insurrection Statutes, he would execute the process in two steps following 10 U.S.C. Section 334, *Proclamation to Disperse*. First, the President would issue a proclamation commanding all persons engaged in acts of domestic violence and disorder in the affected area to cease and desist and to leave the area peaceably. The President would then immediately issue an executive order authorizing the Secretary of Defense to use active duty members of the armed forces to suppress the violence described in the proclamation. The Secretary would be authorized to determine when the active military forces should be withdrawn from the area. The order would also require the Secretary to coordinate law enforcement policies with the Attorney General.

Military Tactical Assistance Operational Response

If military force is authorized by the President, DoD has a variety of options. The most likely option in the case of terrorism (especially a WMD situation) would involve tactical assistance in the form of a Joint Special Operations Task Force (JSOTF). The task force is an agile, highly trained special mission force available to the FBI if a threat or an actual incident of domestic terrorism is considered beyond the tactical response capability of

law enforcement. In such a case, the FBI On-Scene Commander would request that the FBI Director recommend that the Attorney General seek DoD support for the situation.

The FBI would normally ask for military support only if its assets are overwhelmed by multiple threats or incidents, or if the specific target, including a suspected or known WMD, is beyond the capability of FBI tactical and technical assets. The JSOTF may include or have immediate access to specially trained personnel capable of dealing with various

U.S. Air Force Senior Airman Chris Johnson demonstrates how this robot holds C4 explosives. The robots can disassemble improvised explosive devices and perform reconnaissance by searching the area for more hazards. *Courtesy of Department of Defense, photo by Senior Airman Colleen Wronek.*

types of WMD. The Attorney General will begin the process by conferring with the Secretary of Defense to determine if military support is appropriate using the same criteria employed in a technical assistance situation. The OSC will also request that the FBI Director ask the Attorney General to deploy the emergency support team if it has not already been launched to the incident site. The DoD component of the DEST will include liaison officers familiar with the capabilities of the military units most likely to be tasked to support the FBI in a potentially hostile domestic terrorism situation. The launching of the DEST aircraft and all DoD personnel assigned to the team must be authorized by the Secretary of Defense. The military liaison officers assigned to the DEST are allowed to report directly to DoD and contingency planning for possible military intervention may begin. The commander of the JSOTF is integrated directly into the command group of the FBI JOC in order to gain first-hand knowledge of the tactical situation.

Technical assistance operations may run in concert with military tactical assistance planning. DoD may undertake precautionary steps, such as the pre-positioning of a limited number of military forces near the incident site with the approval of DOJ and the OSC. When the OSC anticipates that federal military assistance is necessary to resolve the incident, he will immediately notify the FBI Director who will advise the Attorney General of the situation. After consultation with the Secretary of Defense, the Attorney General will advise the President that conditions warrant the employment of federal military forces. If the President decides to approve the use of military force, he invokes the Insurrection Statutes as previously discussed. The Attorney General, through the FBI, remains responsible for coordinating all activities for federal, State, and local agencies assisting in the resolution of the incident and the administration of justice in the affected area. When presidential approval to use military force is granted, the Attorney General will advise the FBI who will notify the OSC. The Secretary of Defense will advise the commander of the military task force who in turn will begin coordination with the OSC for transfer of operational control of the incident site to the military.

Responsibility for the tactical phase of the operation is transferred to military authority when the OSC relinquishes command and it is accepted by the military commander. The OSC may revoke the military authority at any time prior to the assault phase of the operation if he determines that military intervention is no longer required provided that the military commander agrees a withdrawal of forces can be accomplished without endangering the safety of his personnel. Once the incident is resolved, the military commander will return on-scene authority and responsibility to the OSC. The military forces will normally evacuate the area to a mutually agreed upon relocation site to prepare for redeployment to their home station. However, key military personnel may be requested to remain at the incident site if the OSC determines their presence is necessary in the investigative process. The FBI will provide the military members the appropriate constitutional and procedural safeguards, including the presence of military counsel if required by the circumstances. The FBI will also, to the extent

---

Military Guide to Terrorism in the 21st Century

Counterterrorism Measures and Methods

- Deny terrorists superior target intelligence to select targets, circumvent security, and plan operations.

- Information includes any record of surveillance incidents directed against U.S. diplomatic or commercial activities; correlation of confirmed surveillance against these potential targets permits a deployed unit to identify personnel, vehicles, and techniques in use in that area prior to arrival.

- Deter attacks by simple variations in a unit's operational patterns.

- Exploitation of media coverage.

- Terrorism definition "The calculated use of unlawful violence or threat of unlawful violence to inculcate fear; intended to coerce or to intimidate governments or societies in the pursuit of goals that are generally political, religious, or ideological," from Joint Pub 1-02 (DoD).

permitted by law, protect the identity of the military members participating in the event and any sensitive tactics, techniques, and procedures used by the military during the operation. The decision to employ active military forces against a target in the United States, especially if it involves American citizens, remains a sensitive and complicated issue with numerous potential political and legal ramifications. Questions remain concerning the appropriateness of the use of federal troops and how military force should be employed in the United States.

KEY CONCEPTS

- Department of Defense (DoD)

- Department of Defense Directive (DoDD)

- Homeland Defense (HD)

- Secretary of Defense (SECDEF)

- Command, Control, Communications, and Intelligence (C31)

- Command, Control, communications, Computers, Intelligence, and Reconnaissance (C4ISR)

- Chemical, Biological, Radiological, Nuclear, Explosive (CBRNE)

- Critical Infrastructure Assurance Office (CIAO)

- Commander in Chief (CINC)

- Consequence Management (CoM)

- Continental United States (CONUS)

- Defense Coordinating Officer (DCO). The single point of contact at an incident management location for coordinating and validating the use of DoD resources. The DCO works directly with the FCO or designated Federal representative, and coordinates requests for assistance with the joint force commander, where a JTF is tasked to an incident response.

- Defense Threat Reduction Agency (DTRA)

- Field Training Exercise (FTX)

- Federal Coordinating Officer (FCO). A federal representative who manages Federal resource support activities related to the Stafford Act disasters and emergencies; supports and is subordinate to the Principal Federal Official (PFO) when one is designated by DHS.

- Joint Chiefs of Staff (JCS)

- Joint Forces Command (JFCOM)

- Joint Information Center (JIC)

- Joint Task Force Civil Support (JTF/CS)

- Joint Worldwide Intelligence communications System (JWICS)

- Military Support to Civil Authorities (MSCA)

- Military Assistance for Civil Disturbances (MACDIS)

- Principal Federal Official (PFO). Senior representative of Secretary of Homeland Security and lead federal officer on-scene to coordinate Federal domestic incidents management and resource allocations on-scene.

- U.S. Northern Command (USNORTHCOM)

ADDITIONAL READINGS

Department of Defense, Quadrennial Defense Review Report (Government Printing Office, 30 September 2001).

Bowman, Steve (2003). "Homeland Security: The Department of Defense's Role." Congressional Research Service Report for Congress, Order Code RL 31615, 7, 14 May 2003.

Donald H. Rumsfeld (2002). "Transforming the Military," Foreign Affairs, Vol. 81, No. 3 (May/June 2002):20-32.

Thomas P. M. Barnett (2004). *The Pentagon's New Map: War and Peace in the Twenty-First Century*. New York: G.P. Putnam's Sons.

U.S. Department of Defense, Report to Congress on the Role of the Department of Defense in Supporting Homeland Security. Washington, D.C., September 2003.

The Posse Comitatus Act, 18 U.S.C. 1385

The Robert T. Stafford Disaster Relief and Emergency Assistance Act, 42

U.S.C. 5121-5206

RELATED WEBSITES

http://www.northcom.mil

http://www.usarmy.mil

http://www.adtdl.army.mil

REFERENCES

A Military Guide to Terrorism in the 21st Century, August 15, 2005 (http://www.fas.org/irp/threat/terrorism/guide.pdf).

CRS Report for Congress; Homeland Security: Establishment and Implementation of Northern Command, updated May 14, 2003 (http://www.fas.org/man/crs/RS21322.pdf).

CRS Report for Congress; Terrorism and the Military's Role in Domestic Crisis Management: Background and Issues for Congress, April 19, 2001 (http://www.fas.org/irp/crs/RL30938.pdf).

CRS Report for Congress; Terrorism: Some Legal Restrictions on Military Assistance to Domestic Authorities Following a Terrorist Attack, May 27, 2005 (http://www.fas.org/sgp/crs/natsec/RS21012.pdf).

http://www.NORTHCOM.mil/.

Notes

1   Ibid. National Defense Strategy, as quoted in Strategy for Homeland Defense and Civil Support, Department of Defense, Washington, DC, June 2005, p. 5.

2   National Strategy for Homeland Security, Office og Homeland Security, Washington, D.C. July 2002, p. 14.

3   Strategy for Homeland Defense and Civil Support, Department of Defense, Washington, D.C. 2005, p. 5.

4   See CRS Report #RS21322 *Homeland Security—Establishment and Implementation of Northern Command* by Christopher Bolkcom, Lloyd DeSerisy, and Lawrence Kapp.

5   JTF-North was formerly known as Joint Task Force-Six, but was officially renamed JTF North on September 28, 2004.

6   See 10 U.S.C. Section 382, *Emergency Situations Involving Chemical or Biological Weapons of Mass Destruction* and 18 U.S.C. Section 831, *Prohibited Transactions Involving Nuclear Materials.*

Chapter 6

Public–Private Partnerships

INTRODUCTION

The answer to an attack on our freedom is more freedom, not less. Freedom is not vulnerability, but strength. In the 1940s, American businesses built an "arsenal of democracy" to win the war. Today they're building an "arsenal of security"—exciting, nimble, cutting-edge products that can cut response time and save lives. Homeland security requires innovation and imagination. And businesses need the opportunity—the opportunity to do well by doing good. It can give us not just a safer, more secure America, but a more competitive and prosperous America.[1]

This chapter examines the development and maturation of public/private partnerships in the post-9/11 world, and addresses the critical role of the citizenry in an integrated homeland security strategy. Involving the citizenry is not a new or novel idea but has been foundational in a democratic society, codified by the U.S. Constitution and addressed in the Bill of Rights. Involvement, however, requires knowledge and education to build trust, commitment, and inspire action. It requires honest brokers on both sides to diminish the inherent fears of overregulation, the protection of proprietary information and hence competition for profit, as well as vulnerabilities associated with the compromise of security systems and inadvertent misuse of information. In an earlier era when the country was faced with a different form of crisis in the homeland, President Abraham Lincoln commented: "I am a firm believer in the people. If given the truth, they can be depended upon to meet any national crisis. The great point is to bring them the real facts."

THE FEDERAL GOVERNMENT AND THE PRIVATE SECTOR

Building a business case for increasingly active involvement of the private sector from the perspective of both the architects of the National Homeland Security and Intelligence Community Strategies, and those in the private sector makes sense. It is an acknowledgment that all of the requirements for building a security-based infrastructure are not naturally resident within the confines of government agencies but rather extend to corporations, research laboratories, and academia, each of which has unique capabilities to identify risks and vulnerabilities within their respective domains, and have the knowledge and technological capabilities to protect those interests. In the technology area, these capabilities often surpass those utilized within the public sector which is harnessed with complex acquisition and procurement procedures. As well, resident in the private sector, particularly in universities and laboratories is a historical research and reference repository for adding knowledge value to a host of issues ranging from anthrax to the root causes of terrorism. Eighty-five percent of critical infrastructure is owned by the private sector, which includes the interdependent fiber optic, twisted wire, and wireless systems that support utilities, communications, energy, and transportation systems. Elements of the national security agencies and the Department of Defense (DoD) are supported by these same technological platforms, and any interference on their functionality has a potential collateral impact on the operability of national level offensive and defensive capabilities and thus on national and homeland security concerns. A necessary first step in establishing a balance between the needs of the private sector and the requirements for an integrated homeland security strategy framework involves identifying and diminishing the potentially contradictory motivations resident in each. Each sector has been exclusionary, albeit for dissimilar reasons: the private sector, due to competitiveness and the fiscal bottom line; and the public sector, as a result of a host of reasons related to information protection and jurisdictional responsibilities, mandates, and inherent organizational impediments.

Homeland Security Secretary Michael Chertoff acknowledged the inherent friction and took a business case approach to the new challenges presented:

> And I know that there was an understandable tendency on the part of some people right after 9/11 to take the attitude that protection overrides everything. But I think we understand now that this has got to be a long-term strategy, you've got to be structured for a long-term war against terror, and that means we cannot destroy our way of life in order to save it. So whenever we make a risk analysis, we have to also make a cost-benefit analysis. And we have to say how much risk are we prepared to tolerate or should we tolerate in order to make sure we have a free flow of commerce.[2]

Chertoff further explained the logic supporting the business case for a public-private partnership in part as an inextricably intertwined network involving individuals, organizations, and systems in this way:

> We want a homeland security strategy that is sustainable over the long run, which balances the need for security with a need to preserve our freedom, our privacy, and our prosperity. We want to look ultimately to creating a security envelope, within which we have a high degree of confidence that people and goods are vetted, are not threats to our society nor to our people, and therefore can move efficiently and effectively without paying high transaction costs.[3]

Secretary of Department of Homeland Defense Michael Chertoff. *Courtesy of Department of Homeland Security.*

BORDER SECURITY

Building relationships among and between public and private sector entities is not limited to the domestic arena, as commerce is dependent upon trade relationships with foreign partners. Logic defies the construction of a sustainable homeland security apparatus without serious consideration of the partners with which the United States shares geographical borders and trade relationships vital to the economies of each. Increased cooperation in the areas of trade, coupled with the streamlining of industrial production and emphasis on "just in time" deliveries of products, has accelerated trade and has also likely contributed to an increased access through borders for criminal and terrorist elements. In turn, this has necessitated the broadening of relationships with law enforcement agencies and establishing a higher level of reciprocity between them to include the areas of technology, intelligence, and tactical cooperation agreements. Flynn (2002), in his seminal work on border issues, provided a glimpse of the magnitude of the problem set confronting the guardians of homeland security—inside and outside of the government with the following statistics: in the calendar year 2000 alone, 489 million people, 127 million passenger vehicles, 11.6 million maritime containers, 11.5 million trucks, 2.2 million railroad cars, 829,000 planes, and 211,000 vessels passed through U.S. border inspection systems. In the year 2004, those numbers were part of a regulatory system completely incapable of anything but a rudimentary inspection of the contents of most of the conveyances.

A specific case cited by Flynn is the bridge between Canada and Detroit where approximately 5,000 trucks pass from Canada to the U.S. on a daily basis and inspection procedures average two minutes per truck. A thorough examination for contraband of either a 40-foot container or 18-wheel truck would require five inspectors working full-time for three hours according to Flynn. The appetite for the time delay and inconvenience is nonexistent in a world where lost time equates to lost money in the private sector. Unfortunately, this attitude exposes vulnerability for exploitation by a criminal/terrorist organization willing to risk the odds of any but pro-forma scrutiny. The delays caused by the increased inspection at the borders immediately following the events of September 11, 2001, compelled the Ford Motor Company to idle five assembly plants at the cost of $1 million per hour per plant. As Flynn commented: "Nineteen men wielding box-cutters ended up accomplishing what no adversary of the world's sole superpower could have ever aspired to: a successful blockade of the U.S. economy."[4]

Jihadist websites publicized comments by bin Laden lauding the collateral impact on the economy which continues to resonate across its sectors four years after the attack. Bin Laden wrote that the economic consequences of the attacks of September 11, 2001 equaled an amount upwards of $1 trillion. He also spoke of the need to boycott any Western products and praised the militants fighting the Bush administration and the United States.

> Those who were killed in the World Trade Center towers were an economic power, not a school for children or a house. Those who were in the center backed the biggest economic power in that world that sows corruption on earth.[5]

In response to the enormity and the complexity of securing international borders from the importation of weapons, weapon systems, and/or chemical, biological, radiological, nuclear, or explosive materials, partnerships have been developed between the government and the private sector. Trade relationships with foreign governments have been broadened, with the addition of enhanced security awareness and procedures which focus on the maritime elements of international trade. The imposition of security requirements was designed and launched by the U.S. Customs Service to balance the imperatives for safety with the business need for efficiency. The successful interdiction at the earliest possible

An estimated 16 million cargo containers cross border control points each year.

level, usually at the point of origin was a catalyst for a now mature program which identifies high-risk countries, ports, shippers, vessels, and financiers— every spoke in the wheel of commerce. This targeting and deployment of resources allows for the focused application of resources and technology on the highest risk areas which are exploitable by terrorist organizations.

Approximately 90 percent of the world's cargo moves by container, and each year more than 16 million containers arrive in the United States via ship, truck, or rail.[6] The Container Security Initiative (CSI) is a model program that has built partnerships with the largest seaports in the world that ship cargo via the container system into the U.S. The CSI is organized around the following four core elements with the principal goal of detecting and interdicting contraband at the earliest opportunity:

1. The use of automated information to identify and target high-risk containers,

2. Prescreening those containers identified as high-risk before they arrive at U.S. ports,

3. Using detection technology to quickly prescreen high-risk containers, and

4. Using smarter, tamper proof containers.

Establishing sustainable partnerships between the public and private sectors in consonance with the requirements for a homeland security structure necessitates identifying and defining a common ground. Developing a mechanism that not only identifies best practices but also interprets or translates the assortment of available technologies, organizational processes, and interoperability of systems is paramount. A number of key partnerships have been developed and programs have been implemented by the Department of Homeland Security to establish the common ground that benefits the private sector in relation to the expedient movement of goods and services while simultaneously reducing the potential threat of compromise to critical infrastructure, either by the conveyance itself or at the point of delivery.

TERROR ATTACKS ON AMERICAN INTERESTS ABROAD

The American focus on consumerism and freedom portrayed by the advertisement industry and media are inconsistent with the belief systems of Muslim-fundamentalist terrorist organizations. A review of the annual report,[7] entitled *Patterns of Global Terrorism*, yielded an increase in the targeting of business enterprises by international terrorist groups in 2001 and an increase in the number of American casualties during the same period.[8] Subsequent years show an escalation and a direct targeting of non-combatants and an increase in casualties and property damage directed against U.S. interests and against perceived support to U.S. interests by Israel. According to the U.S. State Department, "the term noncombatant is interpreted to include, in addition to civilians, military personnel who at the time of the incident are unarmed and/or not on duty."[9]

Figure 6.1   Total Significant Terrorist Attacks Involving a U.S. Citizen and/or U.S. Facility, by Region, 2004

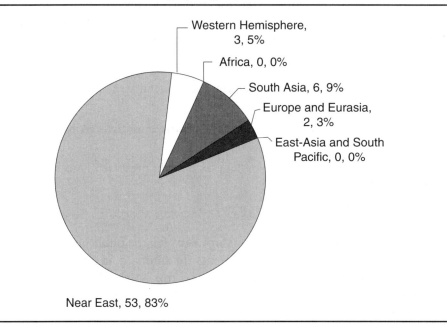

Western Hemisphere, 3, 5%

Africa, 0, 0%

South Asia, 6, 9%

Europe and Eurasia, 2, 3%

East-Asia and South Pacific, 0, 0%

Near East, 53, 83%

Targeting by terrorist groups tends to be symbolic and is directed against the symbols that represent what they abhor about the power and influence of the American culture and way of life. In many cases, the targeting is based on perceived injustice, retaliation, and often, revenge. The mastermind of the 1993 attack on the World Trade Center, Ramzi Yousef desired to topple the twin towers which were viewed as an a affront to Allah, and to kill 250,000 people, a number he based on the number killed by the Americans in Hiroshima and Nagasaki, believing it would take an act that large to make Americans realize they were involved in a war.[10] Miscalculations and a fundamental misunderstanding about the construction of the trade center towers foiled Yousef's plans at the time.[11] However, the cycle of targeting American interests continued unabated with attacks planned, such as the series of attacks in 1995 on airliners in the Bojinka plot[12] or executed, including in 1998 those directed against the U.S. Embassies in Africa[13] on the eighth anniversary of the arrival of American troops in Saudi Arabia, and two years later on an American naval ship, resulting in the death of 17 military personnel. In the year 1999, a Customs agent alerted by heighten intelligence foiled the millennium plot directed against Los Angeles International Airport.

Deparment of Homeland Security Outreach Programs

> We want a homeland security strategy that is sustainable over the long run, that balances the need for security with a need to preserve our freedom, our privacy, and our prosperity. We want to look ultimately to creating a security envelope, a worldwide security envelope, within which we have a high degree of confidence that people and goods are vetted, are not threats to our society or to our people, and therefore can move efficiently an effectively without paying high transaction costs . . . But much of the most critical infrastructure is in private hands, and there, a lot of what we have to offer is not direct grants or money, but it is preparedness, it is setting standards, to help you do the job. It is working through the sector councils to coordinate. And it is also in creating a set of priorities that state and local governments can use to work with private partners in determining how we allocate our resources to protect infrastructure.[14]

Information Sharing and Analysis Center (ISAC)

The major communication components of the Department of Homeland Security are the Information Sharing and Analysis Centers (ISACs) that act as the information hub for many public and private industries. There are numerous ISACs, each separate by area of industry or concentration. There are currently 14 ISACs in operation from the Department of Homeland Security, and several other ISACs are in development. These centers concentrate on sharing critical information and intelligence with each other and combine efforts in case of a terror attack or other disaster. ISACs communicate within each other, with other ISACs, with government agencies, and the private sector about threats.

The private and public sector work together to notify critical infrastructure organizations, government agencies, and public groups in situations that jeopardize national security, and other emergency situations that may have social, physical or economic consequences. ISACs are available 24 hours a day to ensure real time warnings and threat assessments.

ISACs were developed by Presidential Decision Directive 63 (PDD-63) in 1998 that requested the public and private sector to produce a partnership that was concerned with communicating any information regarding physical and cyber threats, vulnerabilities, or acts to protect the infrastructure of the U.S. PDD-63 was updated in 2003 with President Bush's Homeland Security Presidential Directive (HSPD-7). There is a fully functioning ISAC for all the critical infrastructure sectors except defense industrial base and postal and shipping. These 12 functioning ISACS are briefly described below:

- Chemical Sector ISAC
    - Developed in 2002 by the Chemical Transportation Emergency Center (CHEMTREC) and the National Infrastructure Protection Center (NIPC), the Chemical ISAC is concerned with chemical, physical, and cyber threats.

- Food Industry ISAC
    - The Food Industry ISAC was created in 2002 to provide protection and threat assessment for the food and agriculture infrastructure by making it a difficult and undesirable target for terror attacks.

- Water ISAC
    - The Water ISAC was formed in 2002 to prevent contamination of the water supply and to recommend security measures for water system vulnerabilities.

- Emergency Fire Services ISAC
    - The Emergency Fire Services was developed in 2002 to assess threats made against critical infrastructure, respond to emergency situations, and sustain effective communication among fire departments.

- State Government
    - The Multi-State ISAC was developed in 2003 to encourage and facilitate communication between the 50 states and territories in the U.S. This ISAC was formed in response to the need for states to communicate with each other as well as the federal government without duplicating information and to participate in training and simulation exercises to test communication abilities among the states.

- Information Technology ISAC
    - Created in 2000, the Information Technology ISAC seeks to protect, prevent and report any threats made to the cyber infrastructure. This ISAC also uses a scale to determine the level of threat posed to the cyber world, much like the scale used in the Homeland Advisory System. The Information Technology ISAC is concerned with physical threats, and is not limited to cyber threats.

- Telecommunications ISAC
  - The Telecommunications ISAC, referred to and developed from the NCC-ISAC (National Coordinating Center for Telecommunications) is concerned with vulnerabilities, assessment, prevention and response to potential or real threats or attacks on the telecommunications infrastructure.

- Research and Education Network ISAC
  - In 2003, the Research and Education Network ISAC was developed to communicate within and between several areas, including the cyber infrastructure, education facilities, and research facilities.

- Electric Power ISAC
  - The Electric Power ISAC (NERC) was formed to address threats and attacks related to the electric power infrastructure, including cyber, physical, and operational security.

- Energy ISAC
  - The Energy (oil and gas) ISAC was developed in 2001 to asses, prevent, and respond to any threats or attacks made against the Energy infrastructure.

- Surface Transportation ISAC
  - The Surface Transportation ISAC, which includes rail and non-rail transportation, was formed to assess, prevent, and respond to any threats or attacks made against the transportation infrastructure.

- Financial Services ISAC
  - The Financial Services ISAC was developed in 1999 in response to and in preparation for Y2K. It is concerned with both physical and cyber threats and attacks.

- Real Estate ISAC
  - The Real Estate ISAC, formed in 2003, seeks to protect buildings and the individuals who occupy them by assessing and responding to any threats made against the real estate sector.

- Emergency Law Enforcement ISAC

Office of the Private Sector

The Office of the Private Sector is made up of five categories: Border and Transportation Security; Emergency Preparedness and Response; Science and Technology; Information Analysis and Infrastructure Protection;

and Regulation Review and Analysis. These groups allow private businesses and corporations to work directly with the Department of Homeland Security to foster the development of effective policies and programs. These relationships also work to promote public-private partnerships and allow the private sector to work with federal labs, research centers and the academic world to produce efficient and positive outcomes and programs. The open relationship that exists between the private sector and the federal government via the Department of Homeland Security will also encourage an open dialogue and communication from the private sector to the Secretary of DHS on the potential effects and results of policies and programs. The major tenet of this program is that the federal government and private sector should work together to develop programs and policies that will be effective for the government, private sector, and the public.

Protected Critical Infrastructure Information (PCII) Program

One of the programs under the Information Analysis and Infrastructure Protection component of the Office of the Private Sector is the Protected Critical Infrastructure Information (PCII) Program. This program was established in February 2002 from the Critical Infrastructure Information Act of 2002 (CII Act) and encourages the private sector to voluntarily share vital information with the federal government, particularly information regarding infrastructure and security concerns. The PCII program was developed in response to the critical needs of the infrastructure of the United States, particularly with regard to terrorist attacks. According to estimates of the PCII, more than 85 percent of the critical infrastructure in the nation is owned by the private sector. A concern for many members of the private sector is the sensitive information of infrastructure and many were hesitant to provide certain information to the federal government out of disclosure concerns. The PCII program will not publicly disclose any information voluntarily provided by the private sector if it meets the requirements outlined by the CII Act.

The PCII program uses the information provided by the private sector to analyze and secure critical infrastructure as well as to determine any threats against or vulnerabilities of the infrastructure. This information is only provided to members of the federal government who are committed to keeping the information provided confidential from the public. According to the program, regulations and limitations under the Freedom of Information Act, state and local sunshine laws, and civil litigation cannot be applied to information submitted under the PCII program. Sensitive information regarding infrastructure and the private sector must be kept confidential from the public because of economic and stability concerns.

Office of Interoperability and Compatibility

The Office of Interoperability and Compatibility, part of the Science and Technology component of DHS, was launched on October 1, 2004 to oversee the interoperability management of issues regarding public safety and emergency personnel. The Office seeks to improve the communications ability between different agencies and departments, particularly in an emergency or critical situation. It concentrates on the communication as well as equipment, training, and other necessary tools to improve the interoperability of multiple agencies. The Office focuses on first responders and the communication infrastructure capabilities in emergency situations, and strives to provide coordinated responses to future terrorist attacks and other emergency situations.

SAFECOM Program Office

Established in the spring of 2002, SAFECOM is a program developed under the Office of Interoperability and Compatibility to improve the wireless communication abilities among public safety personnel and first responders. The goals, according to the program, include providing "research, development, testing and evaluation, guidance and assistance for local, tribal, state, and federal public safety agencies working to improve public safety response through more effective and efficient interoperable wireless communications." SAFECOM recognizes the vulnerabilities and weaknesses in the current communications system and seeks to rectify these issues by updating and developing more efficient technology in the wireless communication sphere.

InfraGard

InfraGard was started in 1996 as a collaborative effort between private sector cyber professionals and the FBI field office in Cleveland Ohio. The dramatic success of this initial effort inspired the FBI to expand the program to every field office in the country.

In 1998, InfraGard become part of the National Infrastructure Protection Center (NIPC). While under the direction of NIPC, the focus of InfraGard was cyber infrastructure protection. After September 11, 2001 NIPC expanded its efforts to include physical as well as cyber threats to critical infrastructures. InfraGard's mission expanded accordingly.

Ultimately, NIPC was reconstituted under DHS and in response to the changing federal landscape InfraGard adapted. In 2003 the private sector members of InfraGard formed the InfraGard National Members Alliance (INMA). The INMA is a non-profit Delaware LLC with 501c3 status. The

INMA LLC is comprised of 84 separate InfraGard Member Alliances (IMAs) that represent more than 13,000 Subject Matter Experts (SMEs) nation wide. All InfraGard Member SMEs are vetted by an FBI records check and by a local peer group.

It is important to note that the INMA Board of Directors continues to work very closely with FBI Headquarters and that all 84 IMAs in the country have a local FBI coordinator. However, the formalization of InfraGard's private sector corporate structure allows the INMA and its member IMAs to engage federal, state, and local stakeholders in new and productive programs that are outside the purview of law enforcement. This makes the program flexible and agile enough to meet the needs of a wide range of stakeholders in the public and private arena.

> The hurdles that impede effective "public-private" collaboration revolve around non-trivial issues of trust. Unfortunately, many of the countries "information sharing" efforts seek to employ technology to overcome an inherently human problem. InfraGard seeks to remedy this error by concentrating on the development of individual relationships between private sector subject matter experts and government personnel. These relationships grow and prosper at InfraGard Member Alliance meetings across the country. Ultimately, the infrastructure is going to be protected locally by people who trust each other. InfraGard is developing thousands of trusted relationships across all of the infrastructure sectors and at the local level . . . where it will do some good if a disaster strikes.
>
> Robert Schmidt, President; InfraGard National Members Alliance.

Information Technology Acquisition Center

The Information Technology Acquisition Center (ITAC), under the Office of Procurement Operations (OPO) in the Department of Homeland Security, is responsible for two programs, EAGLE and FirstSource, which will establish contracts based on the Information Technology (IT) field and concentration. The programs, although not completed, began development in August 2005.

EAGLE

The Enterprise Acquisition Gateway for Leading Edge (EAGLE) program is focused on Information Technology (IT) contracts with competitive bid solicitations and breaks down needs into five functional service categories (FCs): Engineering Design, Development, Implementation and Integration

(FC1); Operations and Maintenance (FC2); Independent Test, Evaluation, Validation and Verification (FC3); Software Development (FC4); and Management Support Services (FC5). EAGLE welcomes large and small businesses, and offers partial small business set-asides. This program is based on the service needs of the government.

First Source

The First Source program concentrates on IT supplies and commercial products. The program will include items such as IT equipment and software, networking equipment, wireless technology, imaging products, voice recognition technology, and online data reporting services. It is conducted by the Information Technology Acquisition Center, which is under the Department of Homeland Security. First Source encourages small business participation and is concentrating on companies with fewer than 150 employees.

Citizen-Ready Initiatives of DHS

Citizen Corps

Citizen Corps, an element of USA Freedom Corps which was developed in January 2002, provides an outlet for citizens to volunteer time, supplies, and money to victims of terror attacks, natural disasters, and other disasters. Its main goal is to promote open communication and dialogue among members of the community to prevent, prepare for and act in response to disasters. It promotes interoperability between the government, first responders, volunteers, and communities. Citizen Corps uses publications and training programs to promote volunteerism and preparing for disasters.

Community Emergency Response Team (CERT)

The Community Emergency Response Team (CERT) trains and educates citizens about disaster response skills, such as fire safety, search and rescue, and emergency medical procedures. The CERT program is taught by first responders and the citizens that complete this program can support first responders in the case of an emergency. Those that complete the program can also participate in projects that improve the safety and preparedness of their communities and CERT is a program of Citizen Corps.

Fire Corps

Fire Corps is a program to help fire departments constrained by budget and manpower limitations by having citizen volunteers participate in community outreach programs. These programs can concentrate on fire prevention, fire safety, youth outreach, and administrative support.

Coast Guard Auxiliary

The Coast Guard Auxiliary was created on February 23, 1939 when a legislative mandate was passed that gave the Coast Guard authority to use civilian volunteers to promote safety on the nation's waterways. The Auxiliary has a long and detailed history in the United States and actively participated in World War II, among other duties. The Coast Guard Authorization Act of 1996 outlined that the Auxiliary will assist the Coast Guard "in performance of any Coast Guard function, duty, role, mission, or operation authorized by law."

Homeland Security Advisory System

The Homeland Security Advisory System was developed in March 2002 to communicate threat levels to local and state agencies, the private sector, and the community. The system uses a color coded guide to describe the seriousness of the threat. Green is the lowest level of threat and is "low risk," blue is "guarded risk," yellow is "elevated risk," orange is "high risk," and red is "severe risk." Each level of risk has corresponding suggested actions to take. The Homeland Security Advisory System can be seen on many media outlets, including television, newspapers, and Internet websites. Many Americans are familiar with this program and the system is prominent in many of the resources that individuals use to get their news.

Homeland Security Information Network (HSIN)

The Homeland Security Information Network (HSIN) is a threat level communication program between the Department of Homeland Security and the state and local public sector as well as the private sector. The program provides real-time information sharing to members on the network. The HSIN combines technology and preparedness to develop this threat awareness program. In case of a disaster, first responders, law enforcement, government agencies, and citizens will be notified through this network immediately.

Ready Campaign

Developed in February 2003, the Ready Campaign serves as a public safety reminder to the community of what action to take in case of a terror attack, natural disaster, or other emergency. The program includes guides and how-to's for actions to take in case of an emergency and also provides detailed information on what to expect and descriptions of chemical and biological agents. The Listo Campaign was launched in December 2003, which serves as the Spanish-language version of the Ready Campaign. Programs focusing on businesses and children are also in development. The Ready Campaign uses publications and advertising to promote education and preparation of disasters.

Transit and Rail Inspection Pilot (TRIP) Program

The Transit and Rail Inspection Pilot (TRIP) program is in development and will seek to screen all passengers and baggage attempting to board rail systems. The program uses technology to provide an efficient yet thorough check for prohibited items, specifically explosives and weapons. The TRIP program works in conjunction with the Transportation Security Administration.

LAW ENFORCEMENT AND SECURITY OFFICERS WORKING TOGETHER

Another often overlooked opportunity for bridging private and public sector relationships is the partnering of sworn law enforcement officers with private security officers. Both professions are integral to protecting not only people but property and information systems. With approximately 800,000 sworn law enforcement personnel and an estimated 2 million security officers, there is a business case for establishing a strong partnership to assist in meeting the myriad homeland security challenges while still carrying out traditional responsibilities of each profession. Private security firms, like law enforcement firms, are uniquely positioned to serve as early warning of problems—whatever the origin simply because trained personnel are always on duty, and moreover, because these individuals have the detailed knowledge of their areas—which responders particularly in a major disaster may not.

Private security firms, in fact, are responsible for the safeguarding of critical elements of the nation's infrastructure and defense industrial base, including many government facilities, each of which are vulnerable targets. With additional training, these individuals could serve to assist uniformed personnel with orderly evacuation, transportation, sheltering, and in providing information to reduce fear and panic which always accompany a disaster. Developing a partnership between the professions would have the impact of a force multiplier and could considerably shorten the reporting and response cycle when a problem occurs. The idea is not without obstacles, which include actual and perceived differences in training and professionalism; use of force; legal authorities and powers of arrest; and a lack of interoperable communications and standardized training. This issue was the subject of a Department of Justice funded initiative[15] led by the COPS (Community Oriented Policing) Office and the International Association of Chiefs of Police. Sponsors included the following three leading private sector consortiums: American Society of Industrial Security (ASIS); International Security Management Association (ISMA); and the National Association of Security Companies (NASCO).

A national policy summit, concentrated on the issue of public-private partnerships, was held and at its conclusion, five recommendations were highlighted:

- Leaders of the major law enforcement and private security organizations should make a formal commitment to cooperation.

- The Department of Homeland Security and/or Department of Justice should fund research and training on relevant legislation, private security, and law enforcement-private security cooperation.

- The Department of Homeland Security and/or Department of Justice should create an advisory council to oversee the day-to-day implementation issues of law enforcement-private security partnerships.

- The Department of Homeland Security and/or Department of Justice, along with relevant membership organizations, should convene key practitioners to move this agenda forward in the future.

- Local partnerships should set priorities and address key problems as identified by the summit. Examples of local and regional activities that can and should be undertaken immediately include the following:
  - Improve joint response to critical incidents
  - Coordinate infrastructure protection
  - Improve communications and data interoperability
  - Bolster information and intelligence sharing
  - Prevent and investigate high-tech crime
  - Devise responses to workplace violence

Building and sustaining this type of partnership over time will yield a greater security envelope with increased levels of redundancy and heightened threat awareness and reporting.

KEY CONCEPTS

- The security of the nation's infrastructure relies on the cooperation and collaboration with the federal government and private sector. The private sector controls approximately 85 percent of the critical infrastructure and provides information such as technological advances and research.

- To expedite and improve border security and cargo checks, the Container Security Initiative (CSI) was implemented and uses technology provided by the private sector to ensure cargo safety.

- Information Sharing and Analysis Centers (ISACs) provide up to date information to the critical infrastructure organizations, government agencies, and public groups regarding national security or emergency vulnerabilities or situations.

- Department of Homeland Security has programs focused on the government working closely working with the private sector to expand the knowledge and support for the Department's missions; there are also several programs aimed at the general public to get involved with the Department and assist in emergency or disaster situations.

- The relationship between public law enforcement and private security should be encouraged to meet the needs of homeland security. Both groups have similar training and goals, and this partnership is vital to provide assistance in case of homeland security emergency.

ADDITIONAL READINGS

Bardach, E. (2001). "Development Dynamics: Interagency Collaboration as an Emergent Phenomenon." *Journal of Public Administration Research and Theory*, 11(2):149-164.

Coast Guard Authorization Act of 1996.

Critical Infrastructure Information Act of 2002 (CII Act).

DOJ COPS Office, National Policy Summit. Building Private Security/Public Policing Partnerships to Prevent and Respond to Terrorism and Public Disorder, Cooperative Agreement Number 2003-CKWX-0242. Vital Issues and Policy Recommendations 2004.

Federal Emergency Management Agency, "Reference Manual to Mitigate Potential Attacks Against Buildings," December 2003.

Homeland Security Presidential Directive (HSPD-7).

Presidential Decision Directive 63 (PDD-63).

United States Department of Justice, Office of Community Oriented Policing Services. "What Is Community Policing," http://www.cops.usdoj.gov/default.asp?Item=36 (accessed 20 August 2005).

U.S. Department of Justice, Office of Community Oriented Policing Services, COPS INNOVATIONS, "A Closer Look, Law Enforcement Responds to Terrorism: Lessons in Prevention and Preparedness," Washington, DC, 2002.

U.S. Department of Homeland Security, "The National Strategy for the Physical Protection of Critical Infrastructures and Key Assets," February 2003.

RELATED WEBSITES

American Society for Industrial Sciences www.asisonline.org

InfraGard www.infragard.net

Citizen Corps www.citizencorps.gov

Community Emergency Response Team (CERT) www.citizencorps.gov/cert/

Fire Corps www.firecorps.org

Ready Campaign www.ready.gov

Transportation Security Administration (TSA) www.tsa.gov

U.S. Customs www.customs.gov

SAFECOM Program Office www.safecomprogram.gov

Coast Guard Auxillary nws.cgaux.org

REFERENCES

Benjamin, Daniel & Steven Simon (2002). *The Age of Sacred Terror*, p. 7 New York: Random House.

Cilluffo, F., J.J. Collins, A. de Borchgrave, D. Goure & M. Horowitz (2000). *Defending America in the 21st Century: New Challenges, New Organizations, and New Policies.* Washington, DC: Center for Strategic and International Studies.

DOJ COPS Office, National Policy Summit (2004). Building Private Security/ Public Policing Partnerships to Prevent and Respond to Terrorism and Public Disorder, Cooperative Agreement Number 2003-CKWX-0242. Vital Issues and Policy Recommendations.

U.S. Customs Service (USCS) (2002, August 21). Retrieved November 21, 2002 from http://www.customs.ustreas.gov/hot-news/pressrel2002/0821-00.html

U.S. Department of Homeland Security, Office for Domestic Preparedness (2003). *Office for Domestic Preparedness Guidelines for Homeland Security: Prevention and Deterrence.*

U.S. Department of Homeland Security (2004). *Securing our Homeland: U.S. Department of Homeland Security Strategic Plan.*

The Role of "Home" in Homeland Security. The Federalism Challenge: The Challenge for State and Local Government (2003). The Nelson A. Rockefeller Institute of Government. Albany, NY.

NOTES

[1] Remarks from former Director of Homeland Security Tom Ridge at the The Associated Press Annual Luncheon, The Hilton New Orleans Riverside Hotel, New Orleans, LA, April 29, 2002.

[2] (April 13, 2005, Testimony by Secretary Michael Chertoff Before the House Homeland Security Committee).

[3] April 29, 2005, Secretary of Homeland Security Michael Chertoff at the U.S. Chamber of Commerce.

[4] Flynn, p. 61.

[5] Bin Laden, January 21, 2003 (SITE Institute).

[6] U.S. Customs Service (USCS). (2002, August 21). Customs set to begin phase 3 of customs-trade partnership against terrorism. Author. Retrieved November 21, 2002 from http://www.customs.ustreas.gov/hot-news/pressrel2002/0821-00.html

[7] This report is submitted in compliance with Title 22 USC, Section 2656 f (a), which requires the Department of State to provide to Congress a full and complete annual report on terrorism, which includes detailed assessments of foreign countries where significant terrorist acts occurred and countries which have been identified as repeatedly providing state support for international terrorism. In 1996, Congress amended the reporting requirements to include information on the extent to which other countries cooperate with the U.S. in apprehending, convicting, and punishing terrorists responsible for attacking U.S. citizens or interests (U.S. Government, 2002).

[8] In 2001, there were a total of 397 businesses attacked, up from 383 in 2000; there was also an increase in the amount of American casualties from 23 in the year 2000, to approximately 3,240 in the year 2001. Initially a figure of 3,000 was used as the total of casualties including the terrorist attacks of 9/11/2001, however, subsequent reporting on fraudulent claims filed for alleged victims of the attacks reduced that figure to 2, 792, see Murray, 2003.

[9] From the 2003 *Patterns in Global Terrorism* Report.

[10] Daniel Benjamin and Steven Simon: The Age of Sacred Terror. Random House, New York, 2002, p. 7.

[11] Ibid, p.14 when he avowed : "Unfortunately, our calculations were not very accurate this time; however, we promise you that next time, it will be very precise and WTC will continue to be one of our targets unless our demands are met."

[12] Ibid, pp20-26. The plot was geared to the destruction of up to 12 U.S. owned jumbo jets while in flight over the Pacific Ocean. Yousef tested one device by smuggling it aboard an airliner, concealing it beneath a passenger seat and then exiting at a stopover. The device functioned and resulted in the death of an innocent traveler, and served as a case-study for Yousef and his colleagues on the manufacture and concealment of improvised explosive mixtures.

13   See Benjamin and Simon, pp. 26-27: The bombing directed against the embassy in Nairobi was known as Operation Kaaba, after the cubic structure at the center of the Grand Mosque in Mecca, the holiest of holy sites in the Muslim world; and the attack against the embassy in Dar es Salaam, was known as Operation al-Aqsa, so named after the mosque in Jerusalem, the third holiest spot.

14   Secretary of Homeland Security Michael Chertoff, at the U.S. Chamber of Commerce, April 29, 2005.

15   See DOJ COPS Office, National Policy Summit. Building Private Security/ Public Policing Partnerships to Prevent and Respond to Terrorism and Public Disorder, Cooperative Agreement Number 2003-CKWX-0242. Vital Issues and Policy Recommendations, 2004.

Part III

Homeland Security Strategies and Initiatives

The Bush Administration and the newly established Department of Homeland Security began their task of improving the security of the continental U.S. with an assessment of the vulnerabilities in critical infrastructure and in the policies that direct homeland security efforts. As the U.S. learned from the 9/11 attacks, a massive terrorist event that results in significant loss of life is devastating in human terms but can be more destructive to the economy and psyche of a country. A direct terrorist attack, or even a natural disaster, against a critical infrastructure component can result in the crippling of one or more industries with economic implications that would ripple throughout the world.

The Bush Administration made assessing and securing the critical infrastructure of the United States one of its first priorities following the 9/11 attacks. The National Strategy for the Physical Protection of Critical Infrastructures and Key Assets was one of the first strategic documents released by the Bush Administration for creating the nation's homeland security apparatus. In this document, the various sectors of critical infrastructure were defined and the threats to these sectors were identified. The National Strategy discussed which government agencies are responsible for securing and protecting each infrastructure sector and listed present and future security initiatives underway. Chapters 6, 7, and 8 provide detailed overviews of each critical infrastructure sector. Two sectors in particular, Transportation and Border Security and Communications and Information Technology, are discussed in greater detail because they are widely considered to be the sectors with the most direct impact on U.S. national security.

In addition to the National Strategy for the Physical Protection of Critical Infrastructures and Key Assets, the Bush Administration and homeland security policymakers released strategies for counterterrorism and weapons of mass destruction. The counterterrorism strategy presented a roadmap for defeating al-Qaeda and the global jihadist-movements that are inspired by al-Qaeda's ideology. The strategy made specific mention about confronting the sponsorship and support of terrorist groups and laid out plans to ensure the protection of Americans and American interests at home and abroad. Chapters 10 and 11 introduce the national strategies for counterterrorism and weapons of mass destruction and review the implementation of these plans. The al-Qaeda threat is discussed in detail and tactical interdictions in terrorist financing and the structures of the groups are reviewed.

Chapter 7

Critical Infrastructure Protection

INTRODUCTION

The cornerstone of any homeland security strategy must be the ability to protect the most valuable and vulnerable institutions, networks, and systems that allow a society to function successfully. In the United States, these institutions and networks, known as infrastructure components, are incredibly complex and oftentimes interrelated, which poses significant challenges to policymakers and leaders responsible for homeland security. The realities of limited budgets and a newly organized Department of Homeland Security require policymakers to examine each infrastructure component to determine those that are most important to the safety and security of the country. This select group of valuable and often vulnerable infrastructure components has come to be designated as *critical infrastructure* for the United States. At present, there are 13 sectors designated as critical infrastructure, although this has not always been the case. Each of these sectors has its own vulnerabilities and associated risks, and the Department of Homeland Security has developed strategies for protecting these sectors from threats to homeland security by terrorism, espionage, sabotage, and attacks by foreign governments. This chapter examines the U.S. critical infrastructure sectors, the threats posed to each of these sectors, and the strategies developed by the Department of Homeland Security to ensure the protection of American society.

WHAT IS CRITICAL INFRASTRUCTURE?

According to the *American Heritage Dictionary of the English Language*, the term *infrastructure* has been used in the United States since 1927 to refer collectively to the roads, bridges, rail lines, and similar public works that are required for an industrial economy, or a portion of it, to function. This definition probably contributed to the commonly held conception that "infrastructure" was synonymous with maintaining the adequacy of the nation's public works and economy.

In a 1983 report, *Public Works Infrastructure: Policy Considerations for the 1980s*, the Congressional Budget Office (CBO) broadly defined "infrastructure" as facilities with "the common characteristics of capital intensiveness and high public investment at all levels of government. They are, moreover, directly critical to activity in the nation's economy." This definition stressed that infrastructure was related to the activity of the nation's economy and specified that highways, public transit systems, wastewater treatment works, water resources, air traffic control, airports, and municipal water supply were in this category. The CBO also noted that the concept of infrastructure applied broadly to social facilities as schools, hospitals, prisons, and industrial capacities.

In 1984, Congress enacted a bill that established the National Council on Public Works Improvement and mandated a report on the state of public works infrastructure systems (P.L. 98-501). This report stressed the need to designate as infrastructure any "physical asset that is capable of being used to produce services or other benefits for a number of years." The category of infrastructure was expanded to include roadways, bridges, airports and airway facilities, mass transportation systems, solid waste, hazardous waste services, wastewater treatment or related facilities, water resources projects, hospitals, resource recovery facilities, public buildings, space or communication facilities, railroads, and federally assisted housing. Taken as a whole, infrastructure was defined as facilities, services and installations that form the underpinnings of the nation's defense, a strong economy, and our health and safety.

This view of infrastructure began to change in the mid-1990s with the growing threat of international terrorism. Attacks against U.S. interests overseas and the 1995 bombing of the Murrah Federal Building in Oklahoma City led policy makers to reconsider the definition of "infrastructure" in the context of homeland security. Decisions were made about the security of various sectors that make up the United States infrastructure, and the designations of "critical" infrastructures were discussed.

On July 15, 1996, President Clinton signed Executive Order 13010 establishing the President's Commission on Critical Infrastructure Protection (PCCIP). This Executive Order (E.O.) defined "infrastructure" as:

> The framework of interdependent networks and systems comprising identifiable industries, institutions (including people and procedures), and distribution capabilities that provide a reliable flow of products and services essential to the defense and economic security of the United States, the smooth functioning of government at all levels, and society as a whole.

This definition of "infrastructure" is consistent with the broad definitions from the 1980s.

Critical Infrastructure Sectors

- Agriculture
- Food
- Water
- Public Health
- Emergency Services
- Government
- Defense Industrial Base
- Information and Telecommunications
- Energy
- Transportation
- Banking and Finance
- Chemical Industry and Hazardous Materials
- Postal and Shipping

Critical Infrastructure

In response to the terror attacks of September 11, 2001, Congress passed the USA PATRIOT Act of 2001(P.L. 107-56). The PATRIOT Act was intended to "deter and punish terrorist acts in the United States and around the world, to enhance law enforcement investigatory tools, and for other purposes." In its findings, P.L. 107-56 states that:

> Private business, government, and the national security apparatus increasingly depend on an interdependent network of critical physical and information infrastructures, including telecommunications, energy, financial services, water, and transportation sectors (Sec. 1016(b)(2)).

The act goes on to define "critical" infrastructure as systems and assets, whether physical or virtual, so vital to the United States that the incapacity or destruction of such systems and assets would have a debilitating impact on security, national economic security, national public health or safety, or any combination of those matters (Sec. 1016(e)).

This definition was adopted, by reference, in the Homeland Security Act of 2002 (P.L. 107-296, Sec. 2(4)) establishing the Department of Homeland Security (DHS). The Homeland Security Act also formally introduced the concept of "key resources," defined as "publicly or privately controlled resources essential to the minimal operations of the economy and government" (Sec. 2(9)).

Key Assets

After identifying what may be considered a critical infrastructure, a protection strategy must identify which elements of the infrastructure are critical to its function or pose the most significant danger to life and property. Not all assets may be critical, and some may be more so than others. However, the size and complexity of these infrastructures can make identifying which assets of an infrastructure are critical a daunting task.

For example, a recent report by the National Research Council (NRC) characterizes the extent of the U.S. domestic transportation system as follows:

> The U.S. highway system consists of 4 million interconnected miles of paved roadways, including 45,000 miles of interstate freeway and 600,000 bridges. The Freight rail networks extend for more than 300,000 miles and commuter and urban rail system's cover some 10,000 miles. Even the more contained civil aviation system has some 500 commercial-service airports and another 14,000 smaller general aviation airports scattered across the country. These networks also contain many other fixed facilities such as terminals, navigation aids, switch yards, locks, maintenance bases and operation control centers.

Left out of this description of the transportation system is a large maritime infrastructure of inland waterways, ports, and vessels.

Similarly, the electric power infrastructure includes 92,000 electric generating units (including fossil fueled, nuclear, and hydroelectric units), 300,000 miles of transmission lines, and 150 control centers, regulating the flow of electricity. The nation's water infrastructure includes 75,000 dams and reservoirs, thousands of miles of pipes and aqueducts, 168,000 public drinking water facilities, and 16,000 publicly owned waste water treatment facilities. The chemical industry includes thousands of chemical facilities that handle hazardous or toxic substances.

Fortunately, a considerable amount of information that can be used to categorize infrastructure is already available at the federal level. For example, the Federal Highway Administration classifies highways by type and produces copious statistics about them. Some of this information could be quite useful in a discussion about which parts of the transportation infrastructure are most critical. The National Highway System, which is a category of roads that includes the interstate highway system, constitutes only 4 percent of the nation's public road mileage, but carries over 44 percent of all travel. A similar situation exists in the aviation system. Of the 546 commercial airports that had airline service in April 2001, fully 70 percent of all airline passenger boardings occurred at just 31 airports.

Key assets represent individual targets whose destruction could cause large-scale injury, death, or destruction of property, and/or profoundly damage our national prestige, and confidence. Such assets and activities alone may not be vital to the continuity of critical services on a national scale, but an attack on any one of them could produce, in the worst case, significant loss of life and/or public health and safety consequences. This category includes such facilities as nuclear power plants, dams, and hazardous materials storage facilities. Other key assets are symbolically equated with traditional American values and institutions or U.S. political and economic power. National symbols, icons, monuments, and historical attractions preserve history, honor achievements, and represent the natural grandeur of our country. They also celebrate American ideals and way of life—a key target of terrorist attacks. Successful terrorist strikes against such assets could profoundly impact national public confidence.

Monuments and icons, furthermore, tend to be gathering places for large numbers of people, particularly during high-profile celebratory events—a factor that adds to their attractiveness as targets.

CRITICAL INFRASTRUCTURE SECTORS

The Department of Homeland Security has classified the national assets in thirteen sectors and established a strategy for protecting US critical infrastructure based on these assessments. There are thirteen official critical infrastructure sectors listed in The National Strategy for Homeland Security.

This chapter briefly addresses 11 of the 13 critical infrastructure sectors as described in the National Strategy for Homeland Security. The Transportation and Information and Telecommunications sectors will be discussed in greater detail in the next two chapters.

Agriculture and Food

The agriculture and food sectors are a source of essential commodities in the U.S., and they account for close to one-fifth of the Gross Domestic Product. A significant percentage of that figure also contributes to the national export economy, as the U.S. exports approximately one quarter of its farm and ranch products to foreign countries. The Agriculture and Food Sectors include:

- The supply chains for feed, animals, and animal products;
- Crop production and the supply chains of seed, fertilizer, and other necessary related materials; and
- The post-harvesting components of the food supply chain, from processing, production, and packaging through storage and distribution to retail sales, institutional food services, and restaurant or home consumption.

The greatest threats to the food and agricultural systems are disease and contamination, in which case, sector decentralization represents a challenge to assuring their protection. Government and industry have worked together in the past to deal with isolated instances of deliberate food tampering. The effectiveness of the food safety system with regard to preventing, detecting, and mitigating the effects of unintentional or isolated contaminations offers a foundation to build upon for countering deliberate acts to corrupt the food supply. Because of the food system's many points of entry, detection is a critical tool for securing the agriculture and food sectors.

The Department of Agriculture (USDA) is the lead agency responsible for the safety and security of the agriculture and food critical infrastructure sectors. To date, the USDA has worked with the Department of Homeland Security (DHS) and the Department of Health and Human Services (HHS) to evaluate the vulnerabilities to terrorism and disease outbreak and conducted risk assessments to identify these vulnerabilities. Recognizing the vulnerability of the supply chain, USDA has worked with the Department of Transportation standardize the methods that the USDA reports truck hijackings and cargo thefts.

Water

The U.S. water sector is critical from both a public health and an economic standpoint. The water sector consists of two basic, yet vital, components: fresh water supply and wastewater collection and treatment. Sector infrastructures are diverse, complex, and distributed, ranging from systems that serve a few customers to those that serve millions. On the supply side, the primary focus of critical infrastructure protection efforts is the Nation's 170,000 public water systems.

These utilities depend on reservoirs, dams, wells, and aquifers, as well as treatment facilities, pumping stations, aqueducts, and transmission pipelines. The wastewater industry's emphasis is on the 19,500 municipal sanitary sewer systems, including an estimated 800,000 miles of sewer lines. Wastewater utilities collect and treat sewage and process water from domestic, commercial, and industrial sources. The wastewater sector also includes storm water systems that collect and sometimes treat storm water runoff. The water sector has taken great strides to protect its critical facilities and systems. For instance, government and industry have developed vulnerability assessment methodologies for both drinking water and wastewater facilities and trained thousands of utility operators to conduct them. In response to the Public Health Security and Bioterrorism Preparedness and Response Act of 2002, the Environmental Protection Agency (EPA) has developed baseline threat information to use in conjunction with vulnerability assessments. Furthermore, to defray some of the cost of those studies, the EPA has provided assistance to drinking water systems to enable them to undertake vulnerability assessments and develop emergency response plans.

The basic human need for water and the concern for maintaining a safe water supply are driving factors for water infrastructure protection. Public perception regarding the safety of the Nation's water supply is also significant, as is the safety of people who reside or work near water facilities. In order to set priorities among the wide range of protective measures that should be taken, the water sector is focusing on the types of infrastructure attacks that could result in significant human casualties and property damage or widespread economic consequences. In general, there are four areas of primary concentration:

- Physical damage or destruction of critical assets, including intentional release of toxic chemicals;

- Actual or threatened contamination of the water supply;

- Cyber attack on information management systems or other electronic systems; and

- Interruption of services from another infrastructure.

To address these potential threats, the sector requires additional focused threat information in order to direct investments toward enhancement of corresponding protective measures. The water sector also requires increased monitoring and analytic capabilities to enhance detection of biological, chemical, or radiological contaminants that could be intentionally introduced into the water supply. Some enterprises are already in the process of developing advanced monitoring and sampling technologies, but additional resources from the water sector will likely be needed. Environmental monitoring techniques and technologies and appropriate laboratory capabilities require enhancement to provide adequate and timely analysis of water samples to ensure early warning capabilities and assess the effectiveness of cleanup activities should an incident occur. Specific innovations needed include new broad spectrum analytical methods, monitoring strategies, sampling protocols, and training.

Photo Courtesy of National Weather Service.

The operations of the water sector depend extensively on other sectors. The heaviest dependence is on the energy sector. For example, running pumps to move water and wastewater and operating drinking water and wastewater treatment plants require large amounts of electricity. To a lesser extent, the water sector also depends on the transportation system for supplies of water treatment chemicals, on natural gas pipelines for the energy used in some operational activities, and on the telecommunications sector. Water and wastewater systems are increasingly automated and controlled from remote locations for efficiency.

The Environmental Protection Agency (EPA) is the lead agency responsible for the safety and security of the water critical infrastructure sector. The EPA is actively working with DHS to improve site security at key points of storage and distribution such as dams, pumping stations, chemical storage facilities, and treatment plants. The water sector is often interdependent on other sectors, so threats and the protection from threats often require cross-sector coordination.

Public Health

The public health sector is vast and diverse. It consists of state and local health departments, hospitals, health clinics, mental health facilities, nursing homes, blood-supply facilities, laboratories, mortuaries, and pharmaceutical stockpiles. Hospitals, clinics, and public health systems play a critical role in mitigating and recovering from the effects of natural disasters or deliberate attacks on the homeland. Physical damage to these facilities or disruption of their operations could prevent a full, effective response and exacerbate the outcome of an emergency situation. Even if a hospital or public health facility were not the direct target of a terrorist strike, it could be significantly impacted by secondary contamination involving chemical, radiological, or biological agents.

In addition to established medical networks, the U.S. depends on several highly specialized laboratory facilities and assets, especially those related to disease control and vaccine development and storage, such as the HHS Centers for Disease Control and Prevention, the National Institutes of Health, and the National Strategic Stockpile.

Public health workers are accustomed to placing themselves in harm's way during an emergency. They may be unlikely, however, to view themselves as potential targets of terrorist acts. Most hospitals and clinics are freely accessible facilities that provide the public with an array of vital services. This free access, however, also makes it difficult to identify potential threats or prevent malicious entry into these facilities. This fact, combined with a lack of means and standards to recognize and detect potentially contaminated individuals, can have an important impact on facility security and emergency operations. Another significant challenge is the variation in structural and systems design within our hospitals and clinics. On one hand, so-called "immune buildings" have built-in structural design elements that help prevent contamination and the spread of infectious agents to the greatest extent possible.

Such features include controlled airflow systems, isolation rooms, and special surfaces that eliminate infectious agents on contact. At the other extreme are buildings with relatively little built-in environmental protection. Protection of this category of facility presents the greatest challenge.

During an epidemic, infectious individuals who continue to operate in the community at large may pose a significant public health risk. The sector needs to develop comprehensive protocols governing the isolation of infectious individuals during a crisis.

Additional public health sector challenges relate to the maintenance, protection, and distribution of stockpiles of critical emergency resources. Currently, other than the National Strategic Stockpile, there are limited resources for rotating and replenishing supplies of critical materials and medicines. Supply chain management for medical materials also requires greater attention to ensure secure and efficient functioning during an emergency. Potential solutions to these problems are impacted by complex legal and tax issues. Currently, the federal government has only limited regulatory authority to request information from companies concerning their available inventory of medical supplies and their capacity to produce them. Since pharmaceutical companies are taxed on their product inventories, they try to avoid stockpiling finished goods and meet demand through "just-in-time" manufacturing.

Sector-specific legal and regulatory issues also tend to impede the effective protection of assets and services. The *Emergency Medical Treatment and Active Labor Act* requires hospitals to treat patients requiring emergency care regardless of their insurance status. Disaster situations involving mass casualties tax the resources of critical facilities in terms of manpower, medical supplies, and space. As patients are stabilized, it is often necessary to transfer them to other hospitals to free up critical resources for newly arriving casualties. With respect to disaster victims without insurance, however, once treatment is no longer an emergency, hospitals are not bound to treat them. As a result, many second-tier, non-critical hospitals will not or cannot accept uninsured patients, thereby requiring the critical hospital by default to continue non-emergency treatment. Additionally, privacy rules mandated in the *Health Insurance Portability and Accountability Act* should be reviewed to determine whether they could prevent the sharing of critical data in the event of an epidemic.

Existing security challenges have focused the public health sector on assessing its ability to deliver critical services during a crisis. Many hospitals, however, are faced with operating at limited profit margins and, therefore, have difficulty making appropriate security investments.

Finally, specialized medical and pharmaceutical laboratories merit special attention—particularly those handling highly toxic or infectious agents. These facilities are mission-critical with respect to identifying hazardous agents should an attack or outbreak occur. These facilities also enable the containment, neutralization, and disposal of such hazardous materials.

Overcoming the protection challenges associated with securing these specialized assets is a top priority.

The HHS is the lead agency with responsibility for the safety and security of the public health critical infrastructure sector. In the case of a biological, chemical, or radiological attack by a terrorist organization, HHS would likely become the most critical infrastructure and, for a short time, would be the sole first responder capable of handling the situation. The HHS and DHS have been working together to ensure the protection of the national emergency stockpiles of medical supplies and international pharmaceutical manufacturing facilities. HHS has been working with state and local health officials to develop isolation and quarantine standards to improve the protection of the unaffected population during a public health crisis.

Emergency Services

The emergency services infrastructure consists of fire, rescue, emergency medical service (EMS), and law enforcement organizations that are employed to save lives and property in the event of an accident, natural disaster, or terrorist incident.

Lessons learned from the September 11 attacks indicate that the most pressing problems to be addressed in this sector include: inadequate information sharing between different organizations—particularly between law enforcement and other first responders; telecommunications problems, such as a lack of redundant systems; and the challenge of enhancing force protection through such measures as stronger crime scene control and enhanced security to mitigate secondary attacks. Terrorists pose a major challenge to our national emergency response network. Although the existing infrastructure is sufficient for dealing with routine accidents and regional disasters, the September 11 attacks revealed shortfalls in its specific capabilities to respond to large-scale terrorist incidents and other catastrophic disasters requiring extensive cooperation among local, state, and federal emergency response organizations. Most pressing among these shortfalls has been the inability of multiple first-responder units, such as police and fire departments, to coordinate their efforts—even when they originate from the same jurisdiction.

Major emergencies require cooperation by multiple public agencies and local communities. Systems supporting emergency response personnel, however, have been specifically developed and implemented with respect to the unique needs of each agency. Such specification complicates interoperability, thereby hindering the ability of various first responder organizations to communicate and coordinate resources during crisis situations.

Robust communications systems are essential for personnel safety and the effective employment of human resources during a crisis or an emergency. Failure of communications systems during a crisis impedes the speed of response and puts the lives of responders at risk. Another important issue is the extent to which emergency response communications depend on key physical nodes, such as a central dispatcher, firehouse, or 9-1-1 call center.

Unlike most critical infrastructures, which are closely tied to physical facilities, the emergency services sector consists of highly mobile teams of specialized personnel and equipment. Another challenge for the emergency services sector, therefore, is assuring the protection of first responders and critical resources during emergency response operations. Future terrorist incidents could present unseen hazards at incident sites, including the risk of exposure to CBR agents. Moreover, past experience indicates that emergency services response infrastructure and personnel can also be the targets of deliberate direct or secondary attacks, a bad scenario that could be made worse by communication difficulties and responding units that are ill-prepared for such a likelihood.

The Department of Justice (DOJ) is the lead agency with responsibility for the safety and security of the emergency services critical infrastructure sector. Almost immediately after the September 11, 2001 attacks, DOJ and the (then) Office of Homeland Security began to work on developing interoperable communications systems and redundant communications networks. DHS was tasked, by the President, to inventory and analyze the vulnerability of the national emergency response infrastructure and to work with state and local officials to ensure the safety of first responder personnel.

Defense Industrial Base

The defense and military strength of the United States rely primarily on the Department of Defense (DoD) and the private sector defense industry that supports it. Without the important contributions of the private sector, DoD cannot effectively execute its core defense missions, including mobilization and deployment of our nation's military forces abroad. Conversely, private industry and the public at large rely on the federal government to provide for the common defense of our Nation and protect our interests both domestically and abroad. Success in the war on terrorism depends on the ability of the United States military to mount swift, calculated offensive and defensive operations. Ensuring that our military is well trained and properly equipped is critical to maintaining that capability. Private industry manufactures and provides the majority of the equipment, materials, services, and weaponry used by our armed forces. For several decades, DoD has worked to identify its own critical assets and systems. It has also begun to address its dependency on the defense industrial base, and is now taking the concerns of private industry into consideration in its critical infrastructure protection assessment efforts.

Market competition, consolidations, globalization, and attrition have reduced or eliminated redundant sources of products and services and therefore increased risk for DoD. Outsourcing and complex domestic and foreign corporate mergers and acquisitions have made it even more difficult for DoD to be assured that its prime contractors' second-, third-, and fourth-tier subcontractors understand its security requirements and are prepared to support them in a national emergency.

Over the past 20 years, DoD's dependency on the private sector has greatly increased. Outsourcing has caused the department to rely increasingly on contractors to perform many of the tasks that were once under the exclusive purview and control of the military. Even the utilities that service many of the nation's important military installations are being privatized. Because of market competition and attrition, DoD now relies more and more on a single or very limited number of private-sector suppliers to fulfill some of its most essential needs. DoD, unlike other federal government agencies, requires strict adherence to military product specification and unique requirements for services. Select private-industry vendors may be the only suppliers in the world capable of satisfying these unique requirements. Many of these sources have single manufacturing and distribution points that warrant additional security review and assessment.

A related problem involves the current process through which DoD contracts with the private sector to provide critical services and supplies. Most often the procurement process is based on cost and efficiency. Such an approach may not always take into account the vendor's critical infrastructure protection practices (e.g., workforce hiring, supplier base) and its ability to supply products and services and provide surge response during an emergency or exigent circumstances.

Finally, there are also growing concerns within the private sector regarding the potential for additional costs and risks resulting from federal mandates that require private industry to implement enhanced infrastructure protection measures.

The Department of Defense is the lead agency responsible for the safety and security of the Defense Industrial Base critical infrastructure. As much of the threat and vulnerabilities are related to the private sector contactors and supporting corporations, the key to its homeland security strategy is working with DHS, law enforcement agencies with DOJ, and the intelligence community to be able to monitor, collect, and analyze security-related information within the defense industry.

Energy

The energy sector is commonly divided into two segments in the context of critical infrastructure protection: electricity and oil and natural gas. The electric industry services almost 130 million households and institutions. The

United States consumed nearly 3.6 trillion kilowatt hours in 2001. Oil and natural gas facilities and assets are widely distributed, consisting of more than 300,000 producing sites, 4,000 off-shore platforms, more than 600 natural gas processing plants, 153 refineries, and more than 1,400 product terminals, and 7,500 bulk stations.

Electricity

Almost every form of productive activity—whether in businesses, manufacturing plants, schools, hospitals, or homes—requires electricity. Electricity is also necessary to produce other forms of energy, such as refined oil. Were a widespread or long-term disruption of the power grid to occur, many of the activities critical to the national economy and national defense—including those associated with response and recovery—would be impossible.

The North American electric system is an interconnected, multi-nodal distribution system that accounts for virtually all the electricity supplied to the United States, Canada, and a portion of Baja California Norte, Mexico. The physical system consists of three major parts: generation, transmission and distribution, and control and communications.

Generation assets include fossil fuel plants, hydroelectric dams, and nuclear power plants. Transmission and distribution systems link areas of the national grid. Distribution systems manage and control the distribution of electricity into homes and businesses. Control and communications systems operate and monitor critical infrastructure components.

In addition to these components, the electric infrastructure also comprises ancillary facilities and systems that guarantee fuel supplies necessary to support electricity generation, some of which involve the handling of hazardous materials. The electricity sector also depends heavily on other critical infrastructures for power generation, such as telecommunications and transportation.

The North American electric system is the world's most reliable, a fact that can be attributed to industry led efforts to identify single points of failure and system interdependencies, and institute appropriate back-up processes, systems, and facilities.

The electricity sector is highly regulated even as the industry is being restructured to increase competition. The Federal Energy Regulatory Commission (FERC) and state utility regulatory commissions regulate some of the activities and operations of certain electricity industry participants. The Nuclear Regulatory Commission (NRC) regulates nuclear power reactors and other civilian nuclear facilities, materials, and activities.

Oil & Gas

The oil and natural gas industries are closely integrated. The oil infrastructure consists of five general components: oil production, crude oil transport, refining, product transport and distribution, and control and other external support systems. Oil and natural gas production include: exploration, field development, on- and offshore production, field collection systems, and their supporting infrastructures. Crude oil transport includes pipelines (160,000 miles), storage terminals, ports, and ships. The refinement infrastructure consists of about 150 refineries that range in size and production capabilities from 5,000 to more than 500,000 barrels per day. Transport and distribution of oil includes pipelines, trains, ships, ports, terminals and storage, trucks, and retail stations.

The natural gas industry consists of three major components: exploration and production, transmission, and local distribution. The U.S. produces roughly 20 percent of the world's natural gas supply. There are 278,000 miles of natural gas pipelines and 1,119,000 miles of natural gas distribution lines in the U.S.

Distribution includes storage facilities, gas processing, liquid natural gas facilities, pipelines, city gates, and liquefied petroleum gas storage facilities. City gates are distribution pipeline nodes through which gas passes from interstate pipelines to a local distribution system. Natural gas storage refers to underground aquifers, depleted oil and gas fields, and salt caverns.

The pipeline and distribution segments of the oil and natural gas industries are highly regulated. Oversight includes financial, safety, and sitting regulations. The exploration and production side of the industry is less regulated, but is affected by safety regulations and restrictions concerning property access.

Protection of critical assets requires both heightened security awareness and investment in protective equipment and systems. One serious issue is the lack of metrics to determine and justify corporate security expenditures. In the case of natural disasters or accidents, there are well-established methods for determining risks and cost-effective levels of investments in protective equipment, systems, and methods for managing risk (e.g., insurance). It is not clear what levels of security and protection are appropriate and cost effective to meet the risks of terrorist attack.

The first responders to a terrorist attack on most oil and natural gas sector facilities will be local police and fire departments. In general, these responders need to improve their capabilities and preparedness to confront well-planned, sophisticated attacks, particularly those involving CBR weapons. Fortunately, because of public-safety requirements related to their operations and facilities, the oil and natural gas industries have substantial protection programs already in place.

Quick action to repair damaged infrastructure in an emergency can be impeded by a number of hurdles, including the long lead time needed to obtain local, state, and federal construction permits or waivers; requirements for environmental reviews and impact statements; and lengthy processes for obtaining construction rights-of-way for the placement of pipelines on adjoining properties if a new path becomes necessary. The availability of necessary materials and equipment, and the uniqueness of such equipment are also impediments to rapid reconstitution of damaged infrastructure.

The Department of Energy (DOE) is the lead agency responsible for the safety and security of the energy critical infrastructure sector. DOE and DHS are currently working with industry partners to identify equipment stockpile requirements and develop regional and national programs for identifying spare parts, requirements, notifying parties of their availability, and distributing them in an emergency. Given the DOE responsibility for maintaining the U.S. nuclear arsenal, the DOE works closely with the DoD and the intelligence community identify vulnerabilities and threats from foreign agents.

Banking and Finance

The banking and financial services sector infrastructure consists of a variety of physical structures, such as buildings and financial utilities, as well as human capital. Most of the industry's activities and operations take place in large commercial office buildings. Today's financial utilities, such as payment and clearing and settlement systems, are primarily electronic, although some physical transfer of assets does still occur. The financial utilities infrastructure includes such electronic devices as computers, storage devices, and telecommunication networks. In addition to the sector's key physical components, many financial services employees have highly specialized skills and are, therefore, considered essential elements of the industry's critical infrastructure

The financial industry also depends on continued public confidence and involvement to maintain normal operations. Financial institutions maintain only a small fraction of depositors' assets in cash on hand. If depositors and customers were to seek to withdraw their assets simultaneously, severe liquidity pressures would be placed on the financial system. With this in mind, federal safeguards are in place to prevent liquidity shortfalls. In times of crisis or disaster, maintaining public confidence demands that financial institutions, financial markets, and payment systems remain operational or that their operations can be quickly restored.

With regard to retail financial services, physical assets are well distributed geographically throughout the industry. The sector's retail niche is characterized by a high degree of substitutability, which means that one type of payment mechanism or asset can be easily replaced with another during a short-term crisis. For example, in retail markets, consumers can make payments through cash, checks, or credit cards.

The banking and financial services industry is highly regulated and highly competitive. Industry professionals and government regulators regularly engage in identifying sector vulnerabilities and take appropriate protective measures, including sanctions for institutions that do not consistently meet standards.

Like the other critical sectors, the banking and financial services sector relies on several critical infrastructure industries for continuity of operations, including electric power, transportation, and public safety services. The sector also specifically relies on computer networks and telecommunications systems to assure the availability of its services. The potential for disruption of these systems is an important concern. For example, the equity securities markets remained closed for four business days following September 11, not because any markets or market systems were inoperable, but because the telecommunications lines in lower Manhattan that connect key market participants were heavily damaged and could not be restored immediately. As a mitigation measure, financial institutions have made great strides to build redundancy and backup into their systems and operations.

Overlapping federal intelligence authorities involved in publicizing threat information cause confusion and duplication of effort for both industry and government. The Department of the Treasury organized the Financial and Banking Information Infrastructure Committee (FBIIC) as a standing committee of the PCIPB. The FBIIC comprises representatives from 13 federal and state financial regulatory agencies. The FBIIC is currently working with the National Infrastructure Protection Center, the Financial Services ISAC (FS-ISAC), and the OHS to improve the information dissemination and sharing processes.

The Department of the Treasury (TREAS) is the lead agency responsible for the safety and security of the Financing and Banking critical infrastructure sector. The primary vulnerability to this sector is the security of the information systems and networks from domestic and international threats for the purposes of hacking, identity theft, and industrial espionage. TREAS is working closely with law enforcement agencies within the Department of Justice and the private sector to enhance the exchange of security-related information relevant to this sector.

Chemical and Hazardous Materials

The chemical sector provides products that are essential to the U.S. economy and standard of living. The industry manufactures products that are fundamental elements of other economic sectors. For example, it produces fertilizer for agriculture, chlorine for water purification, and polymers that create plastics from petroleum for innumerable household and industrial products. Additionally, more than $97 billion of the sector's products go to health care alone.

Currently, the chemical sector is the Nation's top exporter, accounting for 10 cents out of every dollar sold abroad. The industry is also one of the most innovative in the United States. It earns one out of every seven patents issued in the U.S., a fact that enables our country to remain competitive in the international chemical market.

The sector itself is highly diverse in terms of company sizes and geographic dispersion. Its product and service-delivery system depends on raw materials, manufacturing plants and processes, and distribution systems, as well as research facilities and supporting infrastructure services, such as transportation and electricity products.

Public confidence is important to the continued economic robustness and operation of the chemical industry. Uncertainty regarding the safety of a product impacts producers as well as the commercial users of the product. With respect to process safety, numerous federal laws and regulations exist to reduce the likelihood of accidents that could result in harm to human health or the environment. However, there is currently no clear, unambiguous legal or regulatory authority at the federal level to help ensure comprehensive, uniform security standards for chemical facilities.

In addition to the economic consequences of a successful attack on this sector, there is also the potential of a threat to public health and safety. Therefore, the need to reduce the sector's vulnerability to acts of terrorism is important to safeguard our economy and protect our citizens and the environment.

The EPA is the lead agency responsible for the safety and security of the Chemical and Hazardous Materials critical infrastructure sector. The most important initiative in this sector is the promotion of site security to prevent spillage, leaking, misuse, or theft of the large quantities of hazardous materials often stored near large population centers.

Postal and Shipping

Americans depend heavily on the postal and shipping sector. Each day, more than two-thirds of a billion pieces of mail flow through the U.S. postal system; and each day more than 300,000 city and rural postal carriers deliver that mail to more than 137 million delivery addresses nationwide. In all, the vast network operated by the United States Postal Service (USPS) consists of a headquarters in Washington, D.C., tens of thousands of postal facilities nationwide, and hundreds of thousands of official drop-box locations. USPS employs more than 749,000 full-time personnel in rural and urban locations across the country and generates more than $60 billion in revenues each year. Together, USPS and private-industry mailing and shipping revenues exceed $200 billion annually.

The postal system is highly dependent on and interconnected with other key infrastructure systems, especially the transportation system. USPS depends on a transportation fleet composed of both service-owned and contractor-operated vehicles and equipment. Mail also travels daily by commercial aircraft, truck, railroad, and ship. Because of these dependencies, many key postal facilities are co-located with other transportation modalities at various points across the United States.

The expansiveness of the national postal facilities network presents a significant, direct protection challenge. Additionally, the size and pervasiveness of the system as a whole have important implications in terms of the potential secondary effects of a malicious attack. The Fall 2001 anthrax attacks underscore this concern. In addition to localized mail stoppages across the U.S., the tainted mail caused widespread anxiety that translated into significant economic impact.

Historically, the American public has placed great trust, confidence, and reliance on the integrity of the postal sector. This trust and confidence are at risk when the public considers the mail service to be a potential threat to its health and safety. Consequently, USPS continues to focus on the specific protection issues facing its sector and is working diligently to find appropriate solutions to increase postal security without hampering its ability to provide fast, reliable mail service.

USPS has identified five areas of concern for the postal system:

- Points of entry and locations of key facilities;
- The mail's chain of custody;
- Unique constitutional and legal issues;
- Interagency coordination; and
- The ability to respond in emergency situations.

The fact that there are numerous points of entry into the postal system complicates its protection.

Compounding this problem is the fact that these access points are geographically dispersed, including the multitude of postal drop boxes nationwide. Effective, affordable technology to scan mail and provide early warning of potential hazards is under current evaluation.

The location of many key postal service facilities can also aggravate risk-management challenges. Several major USPS facilities are co-located with or adjacent to other government agencies or major transportation hubs. Relocating these facilities to mitigate risk is often constrained by limited resources, a lack of available, alternative sites, and other pressing local imperatives.

Another factor affecting postal security is the fact that USPS does not always maintain control of the mail during its entire chain of custody. Oftentimes, independent contractors transport mail for USPS. Because

USPS utilizes hundreds of long-haul mail carriers, mail moves into and out of USPS control along its route. To address this issue, USPS transportation purchasing requirements call for all transportation vendors, their employees, and subcontractors to submit to criminal and drug background checks. These checks include fingerprinting and follow-up if necessary by the Postal Inspection Service.

The Department of Homeland Security is the lead agency responsible for the safety and security of the postal and shipping critical infrastructure sector. The greatest challenge to the USPS is the lack of control it has over the mail once it enters the USPS system. DHS is working with the Postal Inspection Service and other law enforcement agencies within the DOJ to clarify and formalize responsibilities for assuring the security of mail transiting US borders. The security of key facilities within the USPS system are frequently inspected and evaluated to identify vulnerabilities.

KEY CONCEPTS

*   Infrastructures are the facilities, services, and installations that form national defense, economy, and the health and safety of citizens. These include roads, rail lines, bridges, public transit systems, water resources, airports, communication facilities, hazardous waste services, and public buildings.

*   Critical infrastructures are infrastructures whose systems and assets are so vital to the nation that their incapacity or destruction would be disastrous and have a negative impact on national security, economic security, and/or national public health or safety. There are currently eleven critical infrastructures, including:

    > Agriculture and Food
    > Water
    > Public Health
    > Emergency Services
    > Defense Industrial Base
    > Telecommunications
    > Energy
    > Transportation
    > Banking and Finance
    > Chemical Industry and Hazardous Materials
    > Postal and Shipping

*   Threats to these critical infrastructures include anything that will harm or disrupt their continued and effective missions. Such threats include terrorism, espionage, sabotage, and attacks by foreign governments.

*   The key assets to critical infrastructures are individual targets whose destruction could cause large scale injury, death, destruction of property and damage the national prestige and confidence. Key assets may be facilities with critical missions such as nuclear power plants and dams, or areas of national tradition or values, such as monuments and historical attractions.

- Each critical infrastructure has its own method and goals of preventing compromise or destruction of assets and to reduce the vulnerabilities of the structure. This can include target hardening, detection, monitoring of infrastructures, information sharing, and protective equipment and systems.

ADDITIONAL READINGS

Public Works Infrastructure: Policy Considerations for the 1980s

USA PATRIOT Act of 2001

The National Strategy for Homeland Security

Public Health Security and Bioterrorism Preparedness and Response Act of 2002

The Emergency Medical Treatment and Active Labor Act

The Health Insurance Portability and Accountability Act

RELATED WEBSITES

U.S. Department of Agriculture (USDA) www.USDA.gov

Department of Health and Human Services www.hhs.gov

Environmental Protection Agency (EPA) www.epa.gov

Department of Justice (DOJ) www.usdoj.gov

Department of Defense (DOD) www.dod.gov; www.defenselink.mil

Department of Energy (DOE) www.energy.gov

Federal Energy Regulatory Commission (FERC) www.ferc.gov

Nuclear Regulatory Commission (NRC) www.nrc.gov

The Department of the Treasury (TREAS) www.ustreas.gov

The Financial and Banking Information Infrastructure Committee (FBIIC) www.fbiic.gov

REFERENCES

The National Strategy for the Physical Protection of Critical Infrastructures and Key Assets (2003). The White House. Washington, DC.

Public Works Infrastructure: Policy Considerations for the 1980s. 1983 Report by the Congressional Budget Office (CBO).

U.S. Department of Homeland Security (2004). *Securing Our Homeland: U.S. Department of Homeland Security Strategic Plan.* USA PATRIOT Act of 2001 (P.L. 107-56).

Chapter 8

Transportation Infrastructure in the U.S.

INTRODUCTION

The years after World War II led the United States into an era of massive public works projects in which many of the country's critical infrastructures, such as the communications networks and national medical system, were upgraded. Chief among these, the transportation infrastructure was dramatically expanded to increase interstate and international trade and for national defense purposes.

The most important developments in transportation infrastructure during this time were the expansion of the highways and the emergence of commercial aviation. The modern-day highway system was created with President Dwight D. Eisenhower's signing of a bill that created the National System of Interstate and Defense Highways on June 29, 1956. This bill authorized the creation of nearly 41,000 miles of roads within the United States to better facilitate troop and personnel movement across the country. Commercial aviation emerged in the 1950s as a way of using the surplus of military aircraft and aviation production capacity from World War II. Heavy and superheavy bomber airframes like the B-29 were easily converted into commercial aircraft for transporting people and materials. By the end of the 1950s, the computer had been introduced into aviation, which revolutionized the way that U.S. airspace was controlled.

Today, the transportation infrastructure is a massive multi-modal network that includes the national airspace systems, airlines, and aircraft, and airports; roads and highways, trucking and personal vehicles; ports and waterways and the vessels operating thereon; mass transit, both rail and bus; pipelines, including natural gas, petroleum, and other hazardous materials; freight and long haul passenger rail; and delivery services.

This first part of this chapter will introduce the six main modes of transportation infrastructure, as identified by the National Strategy for the Physical Protection of Critical Infrastructure and Key Assets, and address the roles of the government agencies charged with protecting and regulating the transportation critical infrastructures. This includes the current and future threats to transportation infrastructures and the initiatives that the U.S. has undertaken to improve transportation safety.

The second part of the chapter focuses on the land and sea borders and the various ports of entry into the U.S. as well as the unique threats that the U.S. borders pose to homeland security. The chapter concludes with an explanation of the various border security initiatives that the U.S. has implemented since 9/11.

TRANSPORTATION INFRASTRUCTURE

The U.S. transportation infrastructure is the most complex and technologically advanced in the world and is one of the most important components in maintaining the country's dominant economic and geopolitical position in the world. Any attack or disruption in the transportation infrastructure would have immediate and lasting economic effects on the economies of the U.S. and the rest of the world, which makes attacking or disrupting the transportation infrastructure an alluring prospect for a terrorist or sub-state actor.

Transportation infrastructure essentially consists of six general areas: Air, Roads/Highways, Ports and Waterways, Mass Transit, Pipelines, and Freight and Long-Haul Passenger Rail. Each of these areas has unique vulnerabilities and therefore pose unique challenges to homeland security agencies and officials.

Air Infrastructure

The air transportation infrastructures were, until the 9/11 attacks, some of the most vulnerable targets in the entire transportation system. Much of the security at airports was privatized and there was very little technology employed to meaningfully screen the passengers and luggage of individuals boarding airplanes. On the aircraft themselves, there was very little physical security separating the airplane's cockpit from the service and passenger cabins. In fact, it was not unusual for the captain or the co-pilot to leave the cockpit door open for portions of the flight or for him/her to walk around the cabin to mingle with the passengers. Hijackings were considered to be a rare occurrence and it was generally accepted that hijackings were committed for some political purpose, such as seeking asylum or demanding freedom for political prisoners. There was very little serious thought that terrorists might turn an airplane into a tactical missile to bring down a tall tower or building. Given these circumstances, it is not difficult to imagine why Osama bin Laden and al-Qaeda's operational planners chose to strike the U.S. via the transportation infrastructure.

Securing the air infrastructure of the United States is a daunting task, as homeland security and other public officials quickly found out in the weeks and months after the 9/11 attacks. First, the U.S. air infrastructure consists primarily of commercial aviation, which includes the airlines that provide passenger transportation (i.e., Delta, Continental, American, and United Airlines), and general aviation, which includes everything from personal aviation to crop dusting aircraft. According to the 2004 Bureau of Transportation Statistics, there are nearly 70 airline carriers (nearly 219,426 aircraft) in the United States which, together, make up more than 99 percent of the total domestic scheduled-service passenger revenues and employ more than 618,000 individuals. General aviation, on the other hand, consists of more than 209,000 aircraft, nearly 70 percent of which are single engine piston planes (FAA, 2005).

Photo Courtesy of NASA.

There are more than 19,000 airports in the United States, of which nearly 14,000 are privately owned (Statistical Abstract of the U.S., 2003). Altogether, these airports, airlines, and aircraft service more than 612 million paying individuals in the United States through more than 9 million aircraft departures annually. The sheer size and scope of the air infrastructure in the U.S. makes it impossible, and certainly impractical, to try to inspect every passenger and every piece of luggage on every flight operating in U.S. airspace.

Road/Highway Infrastructures

The roads and highways in the United States make U.S. citizens some of the most mobile individuals on the planet and are the key to the single largest international trading relationships in the whole world: the cross-border trade between the U.S. and Canada and the U.S. and Mexico. As of 2004, the U.S. interstate system contained more than 42,700 miles (68,500 km) of roads, all at least four lanes wide, and has cost nearly $114 million to build and maintain.

Ports and Waterways

The maritime shipping infrastructure includes ports and their associated assets, ships and passenger transportation systems, coastal and inland waterways, locks, dams and canals, and the network of railroads and pipelines that connect these waterborne systems to other transportation networks. There are 361 seaports in the United States, and their operations range widely in size and characteristics. Most ports have diverse waterside facilities that are owned, operated, and accessed by diverse entities. State and local governments control some port authority facilities, while others are owned and operated by private corporations. Most ships are privately owned and operated. Cargo is stored in terminals at ports and loaded onto ships or other vehicles that pass through them on their way to domestic and international destinations.

The Department of Defense has also designated certain commercial seaports as strategic seaports, which provide facilities and services needed for military deployment. The size, diversity, and complexity of this infrastructure make the inspection of all vessels and cargo that passes through our ports an extremely difficult undertaking. Current inspection methods—both physical and technological—are limited and costly. As with other modes of transportation that cross international borders, we must manage the tension between efficient processing of cargo and passengers and adequate security.

Major portions of the maritime industry's operations are international in nature and are governed by international agreements and multinational authorities, such as the International Maritime Organization. Negotiation of maritime rules and practices with foreign governments lies within the purview of the Department of State. Often these international efforts involve extended negotiation timelines. The Department of Transportation currently recommends guidelines for passenger vessel and terminal security, including passenger and baggage screening and training of crews. The industry requires research and development for cost-effective technologies for the rapid detection of explosives and other hazardous substances, as well as for new vessel designs to minimize the likelihood of a ship sinking if it were attacked.

The U.S. Coast Guard has primary responsibility for protecting the coastline and waterways. *Photo Courtesy of the White House, www.whitehouse.gov*

Much of the port system represents a significant protection challenge, particularly in the case of high consequence cargo. Physical and operational security guidelines have undergone a comprehensive review, from which the Department of Transportation and DHS will issue guidance and recommendations for appropriate protective actions. Efforts to increase the security of the maritime industry must also consider infrastructures subject to multi-agency jurisdictions and the international framework in which the industry operates.

Mass Transit

Each year passengers take approximately 9.5 billion trips on public transit. In fact, mass transit carries more passengers in a single day than air or rail transportation. If the effect on air transportation resulting from the September 11 attacks is an indicator, then a terrorist attack on a major mass transit system could have a significant regional and national economic impact. Mass transit systems are designed to be publicly accessible. Most are owned and operated by state and local agencies. A city relies on its mass transit system to serve a significant portion of its workforce in addition to being a means of evacuation in case of emergency.

Mass transit is regulated by various agencies. These agencies must communicate and work together effectively to allow the transit structure to work as a system rather than in separate modes. Mass transit is funded and managed at the local level, and operated as a not-for-profit entity. The Federal Transit Authority has limited legislative authority to oversee the security planning and operations of transit systems. Mass transit systems were designed for openness and ease of public access, which makes monitoring points of entry and exit difficult. Protecting them is also expensive. Transit authorities must have the financial resources to respond to emergencies and maintain adequate security levels to deter attacks over broad geographic areas. The cost of implementing new security requirements could result in significant financial consequences for the industry. Each city and region has a unique transit system, varying in size and design. No one security program or information sharing mechanism will fit all systems. Despite these differences, as a general rule, basic planning factors are relatively consistent from system to system.

Photo Courtesy of Federal Highway Administration, Department of Transportation, Photo by Fluor Daniel.

Pipelines

The United States has a vast pipeline industry, consisting of many hundreds of thousands of miles of pipelines, many of which are buried underground. These lines move a variety of substances such as crude oil, refined petroleum products, and natural gas. Pipeline facilities already incorporate a variety of stringent safety precautions that account for the potential effects a disaster could have on surrounding areas. Moreover, most elements of pipeline infrastructures can be quickly repaired or bypassed to mitigate localized disruptions. Destruction of one or even several of its key components would not disrupt the entire system. As a whole, the response and recovery capabilities of the pipeline industry are well proven, and most large control-center operators have established extensive contingency plans and backup protocols.

Pipelines are not independent entities, but rather integral parts of industrial and public service networks. Loss of a pipeline could impact a wide array

of facilities and industrial factories that depend on reliable fuel delivery to operate. Several hundred thousand miles of pipeline span the country, and it is not realistic to expect total security for all facilities. As such, protection efforts focus on infrastructure components whose impairment would have significant effects on the energy markets and the economy as a whole. For the pipeline industry, determining *what* to protect and *when*

Photo Courtesy of U.S. Department of Transportation, www.dot.gov to protect it is a factor in cost-effective infrastructure protection. During periods of high demand—such as the winter months—pipeline systems typically operate at peak capacity and are more important to the facilities and functions they serve.

Freight and Long-Haul Passenger Rail

During every hour of every day, trains traverse the United States, linking producers of raw materials to manufacturers and retailers. They carry mining, manufacturing, and agriculture products; liquid chemicals and fuels; and consumer goods. Trains carry 40 percent of intercity freight—a much larger portion than is moved by any other single mode of transportation. About 20 percent of that freight is coal, a critical resource for the generation of electricity. More than 20 million intercity travelers use the rail system annually, and 45 million passengers ride trains and subways operated by local transit authorities. Securing rail sector assets is critical to protecting U.S. commerce and the safety of travelers.

The U.S. railway system is vast and complex, with multiple points of entry. Differences in design, structure, and purpose of railway stations complicate the sector's overall protection framework. The size and breadth of the sector make it difficult to react to threats effectively or efficiently in all scenarios. This fact complicates protection efforts, but it also offers certain mitigating potential in the event of a terrorist attack. For example, trains are confined to specific routes and are highly controllable. If hijacked, a train can be shunted off the mainline and rendered less of a threat. Similarly, the loss of a bridge or tunnel can impact traffic along major corridors; however, the potential for national-level disruptions is limited.

The greater risk is associated with rail transport of hazardous materials. Freight railways often carry hazardous materials that are essential to other sectors and public services. The decision-making process regarding their transport is complex and requires close coordination between industry and government. A sector-wide information sharing process could help prevent over-reactive security measures, such as restricting the shipment of critical hazardous materials nationwide as a blanket safety measure in response to a localized incident.

Photo Courtesy of Wisconsin Department of Transportation, www.dot.wisconsin.gov

Security solutions to the container shipping challenge should recognize that, in many cases, commerce, including essential national security materials, must continue to flow. Stifling commerce to meet security needs simply swaps one consequence of a security threat for another. In the event that a credible threat were to necessitate a shutdown, well-developed continuity of operations procedures can mitigate further unintentional negative consequences. For example, contingency planning can help determine how quickly commerce can be resumed; whether rerouting provides a measure of protection; or what specific shipments should be exempt from a shutdown, such as national defense critical materials.

REGULATORY AGENCIES FOR TRANSPORTATION INFRASTRUCTURE

DHS is the primary agency responsible for the security of the borders and transportation infrastructure. The Homeland Security Act of 2002 transferred the relevant funding and most of the personnel of 22 agencies and offices to the newly created Department of Homeland Security. DHS was organized into four main directorates: Border and Transportation Security (BTS); Emergency Preparedness and Response (EPR); Science and Technology (S&T); and Information Analysis and Infrastructure Protection (IAIP).

Border security functional responsibilities are at their most vivid at the point at which goods or people are expected to cross borders. The border and transportation security responsibilities of DHS are primarily located within the BTS Directorate. The Coast Guard is a stand alone agency within DHS, but has significant border security responsibilities.

Within the BTS Directorate, Customs and Border Protection (CBP) has responsibility for security at and between ports-of-entry along the border. These responsibilities include inspecting people and goods to determine if they are authorized to enter, and maintaining border crossing stations to process persons seeking entry to the U.S. The inspection and border-related functions of the Customs Service; the inspection functions of the former Immigration and Naturalization Service; the Border Patrol; and the inspection functions of the Animal and Plant Health Inspection Service (APHIS) program are consolidated under the CBP. Within CBP, the United States Border Patrol (USBP) is the agency responsible for the enforcement of federal immigration laws between ports of entry. As currently comprised, the USBP's primary mission is to detect and prevent the entry of terrorists, weapons of mass destruction, and unauthorized aliens into the country, and to interdict drug smugglers and other criminals.

Also within BTS, the bureau of Immigration and Customs Enforcement (ICE) focuses on enforcement of immigration and customs laws within the United States, as well as investigations into such activities as fraud, forced labor, trade agreement noncompliance, smuggling and illegal transshipment of people and goods, and vehicle and cargo theft. In addition, this bureau oversees the building security activities of the Federal Protective Service, formerly of the General Services Administration; the operations of the Air and Marine Operations unit; and the Federal Air Marshals Service (FAMS), that was transferred to ICE from Transportation Security Administration (TSA) in August of 2003. The bureau combined the investigations and intelligence functions of the U.S. Customs Service and the former INS, the air and marine interdiction functions of those agencies, and the immigration detention and removal programs, as well as the operations of the Federal Protective Service. ICE conducts investigations to develop intelligence to reduce illegal entry into the United States, and is responsible for locating and removing illegal aliens by inspecting places of employment for undocumented workers. ICE is responsible for identifying and finding persons who have overstayed their visas, and the Bureau also develops intelligence to combat terrorist financing and money laundering, and to enforce export laws against smuggling and fraud.

The TSA, created by the Aviation and Transportation Security Act, was established to increase the protection of people and commerce as they traveled into and throughout the United States. TSA's primary focus in the aftermath of the 9/11 attacks has been aviation security, which includes protecting the air transportation system against terrorist threats, sabotage and other acts of violence through the deployment of passenger and baggage screeners; detection systems for explosives, weapons, and other contraband; and other security technologies. TSA also has responsibilities for marine and land modes of transportation including assessing the risk of terrorist attacks to all non-aviation transportation modes, issuing regulations to improve the security of the modes, and enforcing these regulations to ensure the protection of the transportation system. TSA is further charged with serving as the primary liaison for transportation security to the law enforcement and intelligence communities, and with conducting research and development activities to improve security technologies.

The Coast Guard is the lead federal agency for the maritime component of homeland security. As such, it is responsible for border and transportation security as it applies to U.S. ports, coastal and inland waterways, and territorial waters. The Coast Guard also performs other missions, including some (such as fisheries enforcement and marine rescue operations) that are not related to homeland security. The law that established DHS directed that the Coast Guard be maintained as a distinct entity within DHS and that the Commandant of the Coast Guard report directly to the Secretary of DHS. Accordingly, the Coast Guard exists as its own agency within DHS and is not part of DHS's border and transportation security directorate. The Coast Guard does, however, work closely with the BTS directorate.

The Department of State (DOS) and the Department of Justice (DOJ) also have a role to play in border security. Foreign nationals not already legally residing in the United States who wish to come to the United States generally must obtain a visa to be admitted. Under current law, three departments— DOS, DHS, DOJ—play key roles in administering the law and policies on the admission of aliens. DOS's Bureau of Consular Affairs is responsible for issuing visas. DHS's Citizenship and Immigration Services Bureau (USCIS) is charged with approving immigrant petitions. In addition, DOJ's Executive Office for immigration Review (EOIR) plays a significant policy role through its adjudicatory decisions on specific immigration cases.

BORDER SECURITY

Securing the national borders of the United States is one of the most difficult homeland security tasks faced by U.S. authorities, and is due, in large part, to the size of the United States and its geography within North America. The U.S. shares a 2,000 mile border with Mexico to the South and a 5,500-mile border with Canada to the North, as well as a maritime border with more than 95,000 miles of shoreline and navigable waters. Beyond these physical borders, there are inland borders, known as points of entry, usually at the major international airports within the United States, such as O'Hare International Airport in Chicago, IL and Bush Intercontinental Airport in Houston, TX. Through these borders, more than 500 million people enter the United States every year, of which, nearly 330 million are not U.S. citizens. America's borders are also integral to maintaining the economic engine that sustains the U.S. position in the world. It is estimated that more than $1.35 trillion in trade is imported into the U.S. each year, while nearly $1 trillion in exports leave the country for consumption overseas.

BORDER SECURITY INITIATIVES SINCE 9/11

One of the first actions taken by the Bush administration in the months after the September 11, 2001 attacks was an initiative to dramatically increase border security and to deploy technology to develop a "smart" border system for managing and securing the transnational flow of goods and

individuals. The implementation of these border security initiatives began with an influx of funding in the 2003 fiscal year budget of more than $11 billion. The funding for border security increased in 2004 and 2005 as the Department of Homeland Security's bureaucracy became more settled and is training, operations, and technology programs began to mature. Within the Department of Homeland Security, the Border and Transportation Security Directorate was formed to consolidate the disparate agencies with responsibilities related to homeland security. Enhanced-tech-

President George W. Bush signs the Maritime Transportation Security Act of 2002 in the Oval Office, Nov. 25, 2002. *Courtesy of the White House, photo by Paul Morse.*

nology initiatives like US-VISIT, the Container Security Initiative, SENTRI, and NEXUS were given priority and have been developed and partially implemented.

Expansion of ICE and CBP

Two key agencies, U.S. Immigration and Customs Enforcement (ICE) and the U.S. Customs and Border Protection (CBP), were given primary responsibility for securing and managing the borders of the United States. The creation of these two agencies is considered to be one of the most important realignments under the new Department of Homeland Security. These two agencies represent the combination of the United States Customs Service (formerly within the Department of Treasury), the Immigration and Naturalization Service and Border Patrol (formerly Department of Justice), the Animal and Plant Health Inspection Service (formerly Department of Agriculture), and the Transportation Security Administration (formerly Department of Transportation). The Federal Protective Service (formerly General Services Administration) was also added to the Border and Transportation Directorate of the Department of Homeland Security to perform the additional function of protecting government buildings.

ICE is the largest investigative arm of the United States Department of Homeland Security (DHS), and is responsible for identifying and shutting down vulnerabilities in the nation's border, economic, transportation and infrastructure security. ICE, which employs more than 15,000 people, is tasked with the enforcement of immigration and customs laws within the

United States and the protection of specified federal buildings. ICE is headed by an assistant secretary who reports to the undersecretary of homeland security for border and transportation security.

CBP is charged with preventing terrorists and terrorist weapons from entering the United States. CBP is also responsible for apprehending individuals attempting to enter the United States illegally, stemming the flow of illegal drugs and other contraband; protecting the United States agricultural and economic interests from harmful pests and diseases; protecting American businesses from theft of their intellectual property; and regulating and facilitating international trade, collecting import duties, and enforcing U.S. trade laws.

To accomplish its missions, CBP has a workforce of more than 40,000 employees, including inspectors, canine enforcement officers, Border Patrol agents, aircraft pilots, trade specialists, and mission support staff. Presently there are 317 officially designated ports of entry and an additional 14 pre-clearance locations in Canada and the Caribbean. CBP is also in charge of the Container Security Initiative, which identifies and inspects foreign cargo in its mother country before it is to be imported into the United States.

CBP became an official agency of the United States Department of Homeland Security on March 1, 2003, combining employees from the United States Department of Agriculture, the United States Immigration and Naturalization Service, United States Border Patrol and the United States Customs Service.

Both ICE and CPB have become managers of several technology-enhanced security initiatives designed to improve security at the national borders. Initiatives such as US-VISIT, SENTRI, and NEXUS were all designed to bolster existing border protection procedures and use technology to enhance the accuracy and speed with which the large amounts of transnational trade and migration are screened. Together, these initiatives represent more than $1 billion in federal funding since the creation of the Department of Homeland Security.

US-VISIT

The U.S. Visitor and Immigrant Status Indicator Technology, commonly known as US-VISIT, is a massive federal program launched in 2003 to overhaul the nation's border management and immigration systems. It is a three tier continuum of biometrically enhanced security measures that begins outside U.S. borders and continues through a visitor's arrival in and departure from the United States.

The first tier is a pre-entry screening process that begins when a non-U.S. citizen applies for a visa to enter the United States. A visa is a document issued by the United States giving a certain individual permission to formally request entrance to the U.S. during a given period of time and for certain purposes. When the US-VISIT program was announced, the U.S. Department of State set new standards for international passports that required digital photographs of the individual possessing the passport and machine readable pages for ease of processing.

Upon entry into the United States, visitors must show their passport with a valid visa issued by the U.S. Department of State. At the point of entry, the visitor will be photographed and biometric identifiers will be taken. In July 2005, DHS Secretary Chertoff announced that the US-VISIT program would be expanded to require 10 finger scans for all first time visitors to the United States. All subsequent entries and exits at air, sea, and land border ports will require that two fingers be scanned for verification. It is hoped that these increased identification procedures will make it virtually impossible for someone to use a false identity or to claim the identity of another visitor.

The final phase of the US-VISIT program occurs at points of exit from the United States. It is very important that the departure from the United States be confirmed and documented so that DHS and the U.S. Department of State can keep track of who is in the country. Currently, these exit procedures are performed by comparing arrival and department manifest data provided by airlines and cruise lines to determine when someone exited the country. It is hoped that technology integration will dramatically improve the ability of the US-VISIT program to track the entry and exit of individuals from the country. One possible solution is the implementation of radio-frequency identification technology (RFID) to automatically detect a visitor (at a distance of up to 100 feet) and to automatically review entry and exit information previously collected by the US-VISIT system. This proposed system is being pilot tested in several locations throughout the United States.

US-VISIT biometric entry procedures are currently in place at 115 airports, 15 seaports and in the secondary inspection areas of 154 land ports of entry. US-VISIT exit procedures are operating at 12 airports and two seaports. Since its inception in 2003, the US-VISIT program has received more than $1 billion in federal funding.

SENTRI

SENTRI, the Secure Electronic Network for Travelers Rapid Inspection, is a program implemented by the U.S. Customs and Border Protection (CBP) service to increase the speed and accuracy of inspecting individuals and vehicles that traverse the southern borders of the United States. SENTRI is a border management process designed to allow vigorous enforcement of the law while swiftly accelerating the inspections of certain low risk, pre-enrolled crossers at ports of entry. The system identifies travelers who pose little risk to border security, verifies their low-risk status through extensive record checks, and screens approved participants, and their vehicles, each and every time they enter the United States. The SENTRI system acts as an automated dedicated commuter lane for low-risk travelers into the United States, using advanced Automatic Vehicle Identification (AVI) technology modified to meet the stringent law enforcement needs at the border, while at the same time providing a more efficient means of traffic management, thereby reducing congestion.

International travelers who wish to participate in the SENTRI program must apply for the program at one of the offices in either El Paso, Texas or in Otay Mesa, California. The application process requires international visitors to submit proof of citizenship or naturalization, a valid passport and/or visa, evidence of lawful residence in the U.S., a valid U.S. driver's license, proof of current vehicle registration and insurance, and evidence of financial support/employment. After making an application, SENTRI takes the applicants photograph and fingerprints, and conducts a complete inspection of the applicant's vehicle. Once the applicant is approved and enrolled in the SENTRI system, he/she will be able to cross U.S. borders without enduring the long lines and inspection procedures reserved for non-approved visitors.

The Customs and Border Protection service describes the technical process behind the SENTRI system:

> When an approved international traveler approaches the border in the SENTRI lane, the system automatically identifies the vehicle and validates the identity of the occupants of the vehicle. This is accomplished three ways: 1) through data maintained in a SENTRI enrollment system computer (which includes digitized photographs of the vehicles occupants); 2) from data accessed by a magnetic stripe reader and the border crosser's Identification Number; and 3) by an inspector's visual comparison of the vehicle and its passengers with the data on a computer screen. Simultaneously, automatic digital license plate readers and computers perform queries of the vehicles and their occupants against law enforcement databases that are continuously updated. A combination of electric gates, tire shredders, traffic control lights, fixed iron bollards, and pop-up pneumatic bollards ensure physical control of the border crosser and their vehicles.

NEXUS

Similar to SENTRI, the NEXUS system is an alternative inspection program that allows pre-screened, low-risk travelers to be processed with little or no delay by United States and Canadian border officials. Travelers make an application to either the U.S. Customs and Border Protection service or the Canada Border Services Agency. In the application, they must certify their citizenship in either the U.S. or Canada and provide evidence of residence and financial support/employment. The vehicle will be subject to a thorough inspection and officials from CPB or the Canada Border Services Agency will then certify the applicant and provide a NEXUS ID card. A certified NEXUS ID card allows travelers to use the NEXUS commuter lane and avoid the full inspection and questioning procedures that are required of non-NEXUS certified travelers. NEXUS travelers are still required to make customs declarations when crossing the border and are subject to identification and questioning.

KEY CONCEPTS

*   Transportation can be broken down into six categories: air, roads/highways, ports and waterways, mass transit, pipelines, and freight and long haul passenger rail. Each sector has its separate functions and security concerns.

*   The Department of Homeland Security has the primary responsibility for border security and transportation infrastructure. This aspect of homeland security is organized in the Border and Transportation Security (BTS) Directorate; the Coast Guard, which is a stand-alone agency, also has significant border security responsibilities.

*   Immigration and Customs Enforcement (ICE) and Customs and Border Protection (CBP) are the main agencies tasked with securing and managing the borders of the U.S. ICE is responsible for identifying and shutting down vulnerabilities in the nation's border, economic, transportation, and infrastructure sectors. CBP is responsible for preventing and apprehending terrorists and their weapons, illegal immigrants, illegal drugs, and contraband from illegally entering the U.S., and collecting import duties and enforcing trade laws.

*   The Transportation and Security Administration was created to better protect people and commerce as they traveled into and throughout the U.S. The main focus of TSA has been aviation security, although it also has responsibility for marine and land modes of transportation.

*   Several technology-based initiatives for border security were introduced shortly after 9/11, including US-VISIT, Container Security Initiative, SENTRI, and NEXUS.

ADDITIONAL READINGS

The Homeland Security Act of 2002.

The Aviation and Transportation Security Act.

U.S. Department of Homeland Security (2004). *Securing our Homeland: U.S. Department of Homeland Security Strategic Plan.*

RELATED WEBSITES

The Federal Aviation Administration (FAA) www.faa.gov

Bureau of Transportation Statistics www.bts.gov

The Department of Transportation (DOT) www.dot.gov

The Department of Defense (DOD) www.dod.gov

The UN's International Maritime Organization www.imo.org

The Department of Homeland Security (DHS) www.dhs.gov

The Federal Transit Administration www.fta.dot.gov

The Animal and Plant Health Inspection Service (APHIS) www.aphis.usda.gov

U.S. Immigration and Customs Enforcement (ICE) www.ice.gov

The Transportation Security Administration (TSA) www.tsa.gov

U.S. Customs and Border Protection (CBP) www.cbp.gov

Department of State (DOS) www.state.gov

Department of Justice (DOJ) www.usdoj.gov

DHS's Citizenship and Immigration Services Bureau (USCIS) www.uscis.gov

DOJ's Executive Office for Immigration Review (EOIR) www.usdoj.gov/eoir

DHS's Bureau of Consular Affairs www.travel.state.gov

REFERENCES

The *National Strategy for the Physical Protection of Critical Infrastructure and Key Assets*.

The Homeland Security Act of 2002.

Federal Aviation Administration. FAA Aerospace Forecasts—Fiscal Years 2005-2016. March 2005.

Statistical Abstract of the United States: 2004.

Chapter 9

Communications and Information Technology

THREAT AND VULNERABILITY ASSESSMENT

Our Nation's critical infrastructures consist of the physical and cyber assets of public and private institutions in several sectors: agriculture, food, water, public health, emergency services, government, defense industrial base, information and telecommunications, energy, transportation, banking and finance, chemicals and hazardous materials, and postal and shipping. Cyberspace is the nervous system of these infrastructures—the control system of our country. Cyberspace comprises hundreds of thousands of interconnected computers, servers, routers, switches, and fiber optic cables that make our critical infrastructures work. Thus, the healthy functioning of cyberspace is essential to our economy and our national security. Unfortunately, recent events have highlighted the existence of cyberspace vulnerabilities and the fact that malicious actors seek to exploit them.

Most critical infrastructures, and the cyberspace on which they rely, are privately owned and operated. The technologies that create and support cyberspace evolve rapidly from private sector and academic innovation. Government alone cannot sufficiently secure cyberspace.

For the United States, the information technology revolution quietly changed the way business and government operate. Without a great deal of thought about security, the Nation shifted the control of essential processes in manufacturing, utilities, banking, and communications to networked computers. As a result, the cost of doing business dropped and productivity skyrocketed. The trend toward greater use of networked systems continues. By 2003, our economy and national security became fully dependent upon information technology and the information infrastructure.

A network of networks directly supports the operation of all sectors of our economy—energy (electric power, oil and gas), transportation (rail, air, merchant marine), finance and banking, information and telecommunications, public health, emergency services, water, chemical, defense

175

industrial base, food, agriculture, and postal and shipping. The reach of these computer networks exceeds the bounds of cyberspace. They also control physical objects such as electrical transformers, trains, pipeline pumps, chemical vats, and radars.

Terrorist groups today frequently use the Internet to communicate, raise funds, and gather intelligence on future targets. Although there is no published evidence that computers and the Internet have been used directly, or targeted in a terrorist attack, malicious attack programs currently available through the Internet can allow anyone to locate and attack networked computers that have security vulnerabilities, and possibly disrupt other computers without the same vulnerabilities. Terrorists could also use these same malicious programs, together with techniques used by computer hackers, to possibly launch a widespread cyber attack against computers and information systems that support the U.S. critical infrastructure.

The federal government has taken steps to improve its own computer security and to encourage the private sector to also adopt stronger computer security policies and practices to reduce infrastructure vulnerabilities. In 2002, the Federal Information Security Management Act (FISMA) was enacted giving the Office of Management and Budget (OMB) responsibility for coordinating information security standards and guidelines developed by civilian federal agencies. In 2003, the National Strategy to Secure Cyberspace was published by the Administration to encourage the private sector to improve computer security for the U.S. critical infrastructure by having federal agencies set an example for best security practices.

However, despite growing concerns for national security, computer vulnerabilities persist, the number of computer attacks reported by industry and government has increased every year, and federal agencies have, for the past two years, come under criticism for the ineffectiveness of their computer security programs. In addition, a study by one computer security organization found that, during the latter half of 2002, the highest rates for global computer attack activity were directed against critical infrastructure industry companies, such as power, energy, and financial services. In January 2003, an Internet worm reportedly entered the computer network at a closed nuclear power plant located in Ohio, and disrupted its computer systems for more than 5 hours. Also, during the August 14, 2003 power blackout, the Blaster computer worm may have degraded the performance of several communications lines linking key data centers used by utility companies to manage the power grid.

It is first important to note that no single definition of the term "terrorism" has yet gained universal acceptance. Additionally, no single definition for the term "cyber terrorism" has been universally accepted. Also, labeling a computer attack as "cyber terrorism" is problematic, because it is often difficult to determine the intent, identity, or the political motivations of a computer attacker with any certainty until long after the event has occurred.

There are some emerging concepts, however, that may be combined to help build a working definition for cyber terrorism. Under 22 U.S.C., section 2656, terrorism is defined as premeditated, politically motivated violence perpetrated against noncombatant targets by sub national groups or clandestine agents, usually intended to influence an audience. The term "international terrorism" means terrorism involving citizens or the territory of more than one country. The term "terrorist group" means any group practicing, or that has significant subgroups that practice, international terrorism.

The National Infrastructure Protection Center (NIPC), now within DHS, defines cyber terrorism as "a criminal act perpetrated through computers resulting in violence, death and/or destruction, and creating terror for the purpose of coercing a government to change its policies."

By combining the above concepts, "cyber terrorism" may also be defined as the politically motivated use of computers as weapons or as targets, by subnational groups or clandestine agents intent on violence, to influence an audience or cause a government to change its policies. The definition may be extended by noting that DOD operations for information warfare also include physical attacks on computer facilities and transmission lines.

Finally, other security experts reportedly believe that a computer attack may be defined as cyber terrorism if the effects are sufficiently destructive or disruptive enough to generate fear potentially comparable to that of a physical act of terrorism.

WHY COMPUTER ATTACKS ARE SUCCESSFUL

Networked computers with exposed vulnerabilities may be disrupted or taken over by an attacker. Computer hackers opportunistically scan the Internet looking for computer systems that do not have necessary or current software security patches installed, or that have improper computer configurations leaving them vulnerable to potential security exploits. Even computers with up-to-date software security patches installed may still be vulnerable to a type of attack known as a "zero-day exploit."

This may occur if a computer hacker discovers a new vulnerability and launches a malicious attack program onto the Internet before a security patch can be created by the software vendor and made available to provide protection to software users. Should a terrorist group attempt to launch a coordinated attack against computers that manage the U.S. critical infrastructure, they may copy some of the tactics now commonly used by computer hacker groups to find computers with vulnerabilities and then systematically exploit those vulnerabilities.

WHY COMPUTER VULNERABILITIES PERSIST

Vulnerabilities provide the entry points for a computer attack. Vulnerabilities persist largely as a result of poor security practices and procedures, inadequate training in computer security, and poor quality in software products. For example, within some organizations, an important software security patch might not get scheduled for installation on computers until several weeks or months after the security patch is made available by the software product vendor. Sometimes this delay may occur if an organization does not actively enforce its own security policy, or if the security function is under-staffed, or sometimes the security patch itself may disrupt the computer when installed, forcing the systems administrator to take additional time to adjust the computer configuration to accept the new patch. To avoid potential disruption of computer systems, sometimes a security patch is tested for compatibility on an isolated network before it is distributed for installation on other computers. As a result of delays such as these, the computer security patches that are actually installed and protecting computer systems in many organizations, at any point in time, may lag considerably behind the current cyber threat situation.

Whenever delays for installing important security patches are allowed to persist in private organizations, in government agencies, or among home PC users, some computer vulnerabilities may remain open to possible attack for long periods of time. Many security experts also emphasize that if systems administrators received proper training to adhere to strict rules for maintenance, such as installing published security patches in a timely manner or keeping their computer configurations secure, then computer security would greatly improve for the U.S. critical infrastructure.

Commercial software vendors are often criticized for consistently releasing products with errors that create vulnerabilities. Government observers have reportedly stated that approximately 80 percent of successful intrusions into federal computer systems can be attributed to software errors, or poor software quality.

Richard Clarke, former Whitehouse cyberspace advisor under the Clinton and Bush Administrations (until 2003), has reportedly said that many commercial software products have poorly written, or poorly configured security features. There is currently no regulatory mechanism or legal liability if a software manufacturer sells a product that has design defects. Often the licensing agreement that accompanies the software product includes a disclaimer protecting the software vendor from all liability.

Many major software companies now contract for development of large portions of their software products in countries outside the United States. Offshore outsourcing may give a programmer in a foreign country the chance to secretly insert a Trojan Horse or other malicious trapdoor into a new commercial software product. In 2003, GAO reportedly began a review of DOD reliance on foreign software development to determine the adequacy of measures intended to reduce these related security risks in commercial software products purchased for military systems.

POSSIBLE EFFECTS OF CYBER ATTACKS

A cyber attack has the potential to create economic damage that is far out of proportion to the cost of initiating the attack. Security experts disagree about the damage that might result from a cyber attack, and some have reportedly stated that U.S. infrastructure systems are resilient and could possibly recover easily from a cyber terrorism attack, thus avoiding any severe or catastrophic effects.

Physical Security: Lower Risk, but Less Drama

Tighter physical security measures now widely in place may actually encourage terrorists in the future to explore cyber terror as a form of attack that offers lower risk of detection to the attackers, with effects that could possibly cascade to disrupt other information systems throughout the critical infrastructure. A successful cyber attack that targets vulnerable computers, causing them to malfunction, can result in corrupted flows of information that may disable other downstream businesses that have secure computer systems previously protected against the same cyber threat. For example, cyber attacks that secretly corrupt secure credit card transaction data at retail Internet sites, could possibly cause that corrupted data to spread into banking systems and could erode public confidence in the financial sector, or in other computer systems used for global commerce. Also, some security experts reportedly have stated that because technology continuously evolves, it is incorrect to think that future cyber attacks will always resemble the past annoyances we have experienced from Internet hackers.

However, other security observers disagree, stating that terrorist organizations might be reluctant to use the Internet itself to launch an attack. Some observers believe that terrorists will avoid launching a cyber attack because it would involve less immediate drama, and have a lower psychological impact than a traditional physical bombing attack. These observers believe that unless a computer attack can be made to result in actual physical damage or bloodshed, it will never be considered as serious as a nuclear, biological, or chemical terrorist attack. Unless a cyber terror event can be designed to attract as much media attention as a physical terror event, the Internet may be better utilized by terrorist organizations as a tool for surveillance and espionage, rather than for cyber terrorism.

SCADA Systems

Supervisory Control And Data Acquisition (SCADA) systems are computer systems relied upon by most critical infrastructure organizations to automatically monitor and adjust switching, manufacturing, and other process control activities, based on feedback data gathered by sensors. Some experts believe that these systems may be vulnerable to cyber attack, and that their importance for controlling the critical infrastructure may make them an attractive target for cyber terrorists. SCADA systems once used only proprietary computer software, and their operation was confined largely to isolated networks. However, an increasing number of industrial control systems now operate using Commercial- Off-The-Shelf (COTS) software, and more are being linked via the Internet directly into their corporate headquarters office systems. Some observers believe that SCADA systems are inadequately protected against a cyber attack, and remain vulnerable because many of the organizations that operate them have not paid proper attention to computer security needs.

However, other observers disagree, suggesting that the critical infrastructure and SCADA systems are more robust and resilient than early theorists of cyber terror have stated, and that the infrastructure would likely recover rapidly from a cyber terrorism attack. They note, for example, that in the larger context of economic activity, water system failures, power outages, air traffic disruptions, and other cyberterror scenarios are routine events that do not always affect national security. System failure is a routine occurrence at the regional level, where service may often be denied to customers for hours or days. Highly skilled engineers and technical experts who understand the systems would, as always, work tirelessly to restore functions as quickly as possible. Cyber terrorists would need to attack multiple targets simultaneously for long periods of time, perhaps in coordination with more traditional physical terrorist attacks, to gradually create terror, achieve strategic goals, or to have any noticeable effects on national security.

Several simulations have been conducted to determine the effects that an attempted cyber attack might have on U.S. defense systems and the critical infrastructure. In 1997, DOD conducted a mock cyber attack to test the ability of DOD systems to respond to protect the national information infrastructure. That exercise, called operation "Eligible Receiver 1997" revealed dangerous vulnerabilities in U.S. military information systems. In October 2002, a subsequent mock cyber attack against DOD systems, titled "Eligible Receiver 2003," indicated a need for greater coordination between military and non-military organizations to deploy a rapid computer counter-attack, or pre-emptive attack.

In July 2002, the U.S. Naval War College hosted a three-day seminar-style war game called "Digital Pearl Harbor." The objective was to develop a scenario for a coordinated, cross-industry, cyber terrorism event involving mock attacks by computer security experts against critical infrastructure systems in a simulation of state-sponsored cyber warfare attacks. The exercise concluded that a "Digital Pearl Harbor" in the United States was only a small possibility. However, a survey of war game participants after the exercise indicated that 79 percent believed that a strategic cyber attack would be likely within the next 2 years. Fortunately, this did not occur.

The U.S. Naval War College simulation showed that cyber attacks directed against SCADA systems controlling the electric power grid were only able to cause disruption equivalent to a temporary power outage that consumers normally experience. Simulated attempts to cripple the telecommunications systems were determined to be unsuccessful because system redundancy would prevent damage from becoming too widespread. The computer systems that appeared to be most vulnerable to simulated cyber attacks were the Internet itself, and systems that are part of the financial infrastructure

Some news sources have reported that al Qaeda operatives are not currently involved with high technology. Many captured computers contain files that are not encrypted, or that use encryption that is easily broken, and many of al Qaeda's "codes" consist of simple word substitutions, or flowery Arabic phrases. However, Osama Bin Laden reportedly has taken steps to improve organizational secrecy through more clever use of technology.

Several experts have also observed that al Qaeda and other terrorist organizations may begin to change their use of computer technology:

- seized computers belonging to al Qaeda indicate its members are now becoming familiar with hacker tools that are freely available over the Internet;

- as computer-literate youth increasingly join the ranks of terrorist groups, what may be considered radical today will become increasingly more mainstream in the future;

- a computer-literate leader may bring increased awareness of the advantages of an attack on information systems that are critical to an adversary, and will be more receptive to suggestions from other, newer computer-literate members; once a new tactic has won widespread media attention, it likely will motivate other rival groups to follow along the new pathway; and,

- potentially serious computer attacks may be first developed and tested by terrorist groups using small, isolated laboratory networks, thus avoiding detection of any preparation before launching a widespread attack.

Possible Links Between Hackers and Terrorists

Hacker groups are numerous, and have differing levels of technical skill. Membership in highly skilled hacker groups may be exclusive, and limited only to individuals who develop and share their own closely guarded set of sophisticated hacker tools. These exclusive hacker groups are more likely not to seek attention because secrecy allows them to be more effective.

Some hacker groups may be globally dispersed, with political interests that are supra-national, or based on religion or other socio-political ideologies. Other groups may be motivated by profit, or linked to organized crime, and may be willing to sell their computer skills to a sponsor, such as a nation state or a terrorist group, regardless of the political interests involved. For instance, it has been reported that the Indian separatist group, Harkat-ul-Ansar, attempted to purchase military software from hackers in late 1998.

In March 2000, it was reported that the Aum Shinrikyo cult organization had contracted to write software for up to 80 Japanese companies, and 10 government agencies, including Japan's Metropolitan police department; however, there were no reported computer attacks related to these contracts. Linkages between hackers, terrorists, and terrorist-sponsoring nations may be difficult to confirm, but cyber terror activity may possibly be detected through careful monitoring of network chat areas where hackers sometimes meet anonymously to exchange information. The Defense Advanced Research Projects Agency (DARPA) has conducted research and development for systems, such as the former Terrorism Information Awareness Program.

Managing threat and reducing vulnerability in cyberspace is a particularly complex challenge because of the number and range of different types of users. Cyberspace security requires action on multiple levels and by a diverse group of actors because literally hundreds of millions of devices are interconnected by a network of networks. The problem of cyberspace security can best be addressed on five levels.

Level 1, the Home User/Small Business

Though not a part of a critical infrastructure the computers of home users can become part of networks of remotely controlled machines that are then used to attack critical infrastructures. Undefended home and small business computers, particularly those using digital subscriber line (DSL) or cable connections, are vulnerable to attackers who can employ the use of those machines without the owner's knowledge. Groups of such "zombie" machines can then be used by third-party actors to launch denial-of-service (DoS) attacks on key Internet nodes and other important enterprises or critical infrastructures.

Level 2, Large Enterprises

Large-scale enterprises (corporations, government agencies, and universities) are common targets for cyber attacks. Many such enterprises are part of critical infrastructures. Enterprises require clearly articulated, active information security policies and programs to audit compliance with cybersecurity best practices. According to the U.S. intelligence community, American networks will be increasingly targeted by malicious actors both for the data and the power they possess.

Level 3, Critical Sectors/Infrastructures

When organizations in sectors of the economy, government, or academia unite to address common cybersecurity problems, they can often reduce the burden on individual enterprises. Such collaboration often produces shared institutions and mechanisms, which, in turn, could have cyber vulnerabilities whose exploitation could directly affect the operations of member enterprises and the sector as a whole. Enterprises can also reduce cyber risks by participating in groups that develop best practices, evaluate technological offerings, certify products and services, and share information. Several sectors have formed Information Sharing and Analysis Centers (ISACs) to monitor for cyber attacks directed against their respective infrastructures. ISACs are also a vehicle for sharing information about attack trends, vulnerabilities, and best practices.

Level 4, National Issues and Vulnerabilities

Some cybersecurity problems have national implications and cannot be solved by individual enterprises or infrastructure sectors alone. All sectors share the Internet. Accordingly, they are all at risk if its mechanisms (e.g., protocols and routers) are not secure. Weaknesses in widely used software and hardware products can also create problems at the national level, requiring coordinated activities for the research and development of improved technologies. Additionally, the lack of trained and certified cybersecurity professionals also merits national level concern.

Level 5, Global

The Worldwide Web is a planetary information grid of systems. Internationally shared standards enable interoperability among the world's computer systems. This interconnectedness, however, also means that problems on one continent have the potential to affect computers on another. We therefore rely on international cooperation to share information related to cyber issues and, further, to prosecute cyber criminals. Without such cooperation, our collective ability to detect, deter, and minimize the effects of cyber-based attacks would be greatly diminished.

The *National Strategy to Secure Cyberspace* articulates five national priorities including:

I.   A National Cyberspace Security Response System;

II.   A National Cyberspace Security Threat and Vulnerability Reduction Program;

III.   A National Cyberspace Security Awareness and Training Program;

IV.   Securing Governments' Cyberspace; and

V.   National Security and International Cyberspace Security Cooperation.

The first priority focuses on improving our response to cyber incidents and reducing the potential damage from such events. The second, third, and fourth priorities aim to reduce threats from, and our vulnerabilities to, cyber attacks. The fifth priority is to prevent cyber attacks that could impact national security assets and to improve the international management of and response to such attacks.

Key Concepts

- Cyberspace is made up of hundreds of thousands of interconnected computers, servers, routers, switches, and fiber optic cables, and its functions are essential to the nation's economy and security. Critical infrastructure systems rely on cyberspace for numerous functions, and the compromise of cyberspace systems can be detrimental.

- Although there is no universally accepted definition of terrorism or cyber terrorism, cyber terrorism may be loosely defined as the politically motivated use of computers as weapons or as targets, by sub-national groups or clandestine agents intent on violence, to influence an audience or cause a government to change its policies. It is very difficult to categorize certain acts or events as cyber terrorism, but several acts and concepts are seeking to make it easier to accurately define certain behavior in this category.

- Supervisory Control and Data Acquisitions (SCADA) systems are the computer systems relied upon by many critical infrastructure organizations to monitor and track process control activities. SCADA systems have been accused of being vulnerable to and under-prepared for cyber attacks.

- Terrorist organizations recognize the vulnerabilities of cyberspace and are beginning to concentrate on cyber attacks to illicit fear among the masses and disrupt critical infrastructures and other functions.

- Hacker groups are numerous and can be motivated by social-political ideologies or profit. These groups can target all levels of cyberspace security, including the home user/small business, large enterprises, critical sectors/infrastructures, national levels, and global system.

ADDITIONAL READINGS

Federal Information Security Management Act.

U.S. Department of Homeland Security (2004). *Securing our Homeland: U.S. Department of Homeland Security Strategic Plan.*

Federal Efforts to Collect and Analyze Information on Foreign Science and Technology (1993).

Protecting America's Freedom in the Information Age (2002). The Markle Foundation: Task Force on National Security in the Information Age.

RELATED WEBSITES

The Office of Management and Budget (OMB) www.whitehouse.gov/omb/

The Department of Homeland Security (DHS) www.dhs.gov

The Department of Defense (DOD) www.dod.gov

U.S. Naval War College www.nwc.navy.mil

The Defense Advanced Research Projects Agency (DARPA) www.darpa.mil

REFERENCES

The National Strategy to Secure Cyberspace (2003). The White House. Washington, DC.

Chapter 10

Counterterrorism and
Homeland Security

INTRODUCTION

The term counterterrorism connotes a great many activities, ranging from intelligence to target-hardening. In its narrowest sense it refers to the investigation of terrorist threats prior to their commission, and investigation following an incident. In essence, homeland security encompasses the broader aspects of terrorism, much of which is covered in other chapters in this book. The following chapter addresses the organization, intelligence function, and operational aspects of investigations concerning specific threats, potentially violent groups, and investigative techniques.

At the outset it should be noted that counterterrorism efforts involve, to some degree, local, state, federal and private initiatives, particularly from an information and intelligence standpoint. Unlike most criminal investigations, that involve handling a case after an event has occurred, the most successful terrorism investigations involve prevention of the occurrence of an act. Virtually all of the literature in the field stresses the importance of intelligence, which may be defined as:

> A body of evidence and the conclusions drawn therefrom that is acquired and furnished in response to the known or perceived requirements of consumers. It is often derived from information that is concealed or not intended to be available for use by the acquirer. Raw intelligence is information that is collected from a single source and quickly evaluated. Reports may be produced from this intelligence and delivered to consumers if the information is time sensitive. Finished intelligence is more fully analyzed and evaluated information. It is usually based upon raw intelligence collected from many (or all) sources and analyzed in this context.[1]

The 9/11 Commission, on the subject of intelligence, notes:

> Since the Pearl Harbor attack of 1941, the intelligence community has devoted generations of effort to understanding the problem of forestalling a surprise attack. Rigorous analytic methods were developed, focused in particular on the Soviet Union, and several leading practitioners within the intelligence community discussed them with us. These methods have been articulated in many ways, but almost all seem to have at least four elements in common: (1) think about how surprise attacks might be launched; (2) identify telltale indicators connected to the most dangerous possibilities; (3) where feasible, collect intelligence on these indicators; and (4) adopt defenses to deflect the most dangerous possibilities or at least trigger an earlier warning.[2]

Counterterrorist investigations may be viewed as beginning at the point where information or intelligence analysis identifies a potential threat that puts in motion a more sustained effort to more clearly analyze and assess the probability of the threat being real. Instances of potential threats by individuals and groups, which were not submitted for further investigation, proved to be a major criticism of the 9/11 Commission.[3] For example, four of the 9/11 hijackers were linked to al Qaeda more than a year before the attack by a military intelligence agency, but the information was not passed to the FBI. (Jehl, P.1)[4] Passage of the USA PATRIOT Act (see Chapter 13) has broadened the investigative and intelligence gathering abilities of the government.

Reorganization of the intelligence community has centralized much of the information and intelligence capabilities of the government, and reported threats are now investigated by one of the appropriate investigative units. For example:

- The recently established Office of the Director of National Intelligence serves as the head of all national intelligence agencies and is the communication portal for all intelligence information.

- The Directorate of Intelligence at the Federal Bureau of Investigation (FBI) has responsibility for meeting current and emerging national security and criminal threats through investigative work, implementing policies, and providing information and analyses to national security, homeland security and law enforcement communities. (FBI.gov)

- Immigration and Customs Enforcement (ICE) is an investigative agency with the responsibility of investigating immigration issues, transnational crimes, and identifying and correcting vulnerabilities of America's borders.

- The Customs and Border Patrol (CBP) is an enforcement agency and provides security to America's borders and ports and enforces immigration laws.

- The Postal Inspection service investigates matters involving fraud and other illegal activity that uses the mail, as well as certain Internet-related cases.

- The Drug Enforcement Administration (DEA) investigates cases that involve drugs and their relationship to terrorist activity, financial crimes, and production.

- Financial Crimes Enforcement Network (FinCEN) is a network that works to investigate and fight money laundering.

- The Defense Department has several military investigative units, each with its own unique priorities and concentration.

  ○ The Office of Special Investigations (OSI) of the U.S. Air Force focuses on criminal investigation and counterintelligence services, particularly in matters relating to the Air Force.

  ○ The U.S. Army's Criminal Investigative Command (CID) investigates crimes that are or may be related to the Army, including intelligence, forensics, and serious crimes.

  ○ The Naval Criminal Investigative Service (NCIS) is a branch of the U.S. Navy that is concerned with law enforcement and counterintelligence measures for matters involving or possibly involving the Navy or Marine Corps.

Counterterrorist investigations rely on a variety of techniques, including surveillance (physical and electronic), informants, background and records checks, and financial activity and support investigations. Where a potentially real threat is identified it will come under the jurisdiction of the appropriate agency and a team of investigators, usually one of the FBI's terrorist task forces, which will handle the criminal investigation.

William Dyson, a retired FBI special agent in charge of a joint terrorism task force (JTF), in his book *Terrorism: An Investigator's Handbook,* notes that terrorism investigations are markedly different than those of a traditional criminal nature.

> Unlike common criminals with whom law enforcement deals on a regular basis, terrorists represent a true threat to the very nature and structure of the country. They do not intend to use the democratic process to achieve their ends. They want a change, and they will use extreme violence to get what they want. They may claim that they do not wish to harm innocent people; however, to many terrorists, the ends justify the means. Consequently, if inno-

cent parties are harmed, that is acceptable. Terrorists are selfish and self-righteous. They know what they want, they are certain that they are correct, and they intend to get what they want regardless of who is harmed (page v).

TYPES OF COUNTERTERRORISM INVESTIGATIONS

The primary goal of a counterterrorism investigation is to make a criminal case against individuals who violate one or more criminal laws, and to accomplish this prior to the commission of a violent act. In such cases the following crimes outlined in the U.S. Code of Federal Regulations are frequently pursued:

- Murder
- Assault
- Assault with Attempt to Murder
- Kidnapping
- Conspiracy
    - Conspiracy to Commit Identification Document Fraud
    - Conspiracy to Kill United States Nationals
    - Conspiracy to Murder and Kidnap and Maim at places outside the United States
    - Conspiracy to Use Weapons of Mass Destruction to Destroy Buildings and Property of the United States
    - Conspiracy to Commit Armed Bank Robbery
    - Conspiracy to destroy property affecting interstate commerce
    - Conspiracy to use a Destructive Device
    - Conspiracy to Commit Offense or Defraud the United States
- Attempted Arson
- Solicitation to Commit a Crime of Violence
- Unlawful Procurement of Naturalization, Materially False Statements, False Oath in Matter Relating to Naturalization
- Possession or use of illegal materials, such as bombs, firearms, or other weapons
- Possession of a Destructive Device

- Possession of an Unregistered Firearm

- Money laundering

- Illegal immigration

- Arson (particularly for environmental terrorists)

- Attempted acts listed above

Following a terrorist attack or action individuals may be charged with one or more of the crimes listed above. Most terrorism investigations involve more than one individual, and in the case of more complex terrorist organizations a planned action may involve cells which may or may not be linked to a central group. For example, al Qaeda operations involve a planning cell, a logistics cell, and an action cell (that carries out the attack). Additionally, there may be other individuals who provide support, often without knowledge of the terrorist's mission. This may involve housing, transportation, monetary contributions, providing information, and assistance in gaining entry into the country.

Al Qaeda, and affiliated or support-related terrorist groups, represent the most serious and immediate threat to the homeland security of the United States.

Figure 10.1 Methods Used in the 651 Significant International Terrorist Attacks Involving Worldwide Victims, 2004

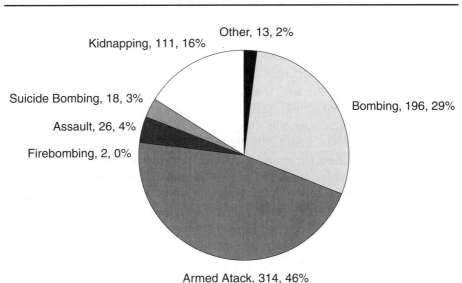

Information from the U.S. State Department, Country Reports on Terrorism 2004. April 2005.

Figure 10.2 Total Significant Terrorist Attacks Involving a U.S. Citizen and/or U.S. Facility, by Region, 2004

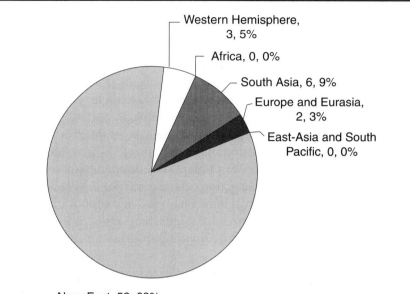

Western Hemisphere, 3, 5%

Africa, 0, 0%

South Asia, 6, 9%

Europe and Eurasia, 2, 3%

East-Asia and South Pacific, 0, 0%

Near East, 53, 83%

Information from the U.S. State Department, Country Reports on Terrorism 2004. April 2005.

AL QAEDA

Background

The al Qaeda (Arabic for "the base") movement began in 1988 following the Afghan victory over Russia, it was initially supported by the United States (due to its participation in overcoming Russian communism). Within Afghanistan a feud between the Taliban, led by Mullah Mohammad Omar, and the Northern Alliance movement, led by Afghanistan President Buranuddin Rabbani, had divided the country. Bin Laden and his al Qaeda movement sided with the Taliban. The main tenet of al Qaeda is to remove all Western, especially American, influence from Muslim countries. This includes the culture, politics, individuals and economy of the Western world. The group's ideology is best illustrated by its leader, Osama bin Laden's 1998 fatwa: "We call on every Muslim who believes in God and wishes to be rewarded to comply with God's order to kill the Americans and plunder their money wherever and whenever they find it." By September 2001, bin Laden and the movement were known to American intelligence authorities and the intelligence agencies of other countries, particularly in western nations.

Al Qaeda Attacks

Al Qaeda has been linked directly or indirectly to a series of attacks throughout the world including:

- The December 1992 bombings targeting U.S. troops in Aden, Yemen. No casualties reported.
- The 1993 bombing of the World Trade Center that killed 6 and injured about 1,000 people.
- The October 1993 firefight in Mogadishu, Somalia that shot down 2 Black Hawk helicopters and killed 18 U.S. Special Forces troops with 79 injured.
- The November 1995 car bomb outside a Saudi-U.S. joint training facility in Riyadh, Saudi Arabia that killed 5 Americans and 2 Indian officials.
- The June 1996 truck bomb in the Khobar Towers that housed U.S. Air Force personnel in Dhahran, Saudi Arabia that killed 19 U.S. citizens and wounded 515 people, including 372 Americans.
- The attacks on the American embassies in Kenya and Tanzania on August 7, 1998 that killed 301 and injured more than 5,000.
- The October 12, 2000 attacks on the USS Cole in Aden, Yemen, which killed 17 and injured 39 U.S. Navy personnel.
- 11 April 2002: Al Qaeda reportedly firebombed a synagogue in Tunisia, killing 19 and injuring 22.
- 6 October 2002: Al Qaeda reportedly directed a suicide attack on a French oil tanker off the coast of Yemen, killing 1 and injuring 4.
- 8 October 2002: Al Qaeda reportedly attacked U.S. military personnel in Kuwait, killing 1 and injuring 1.
- 12 October 2002: Al Qaeda reportedly supported an attack (primarily carried out by Jemaah Islamiya) on a nightclub in Bali, Indonesia, killing approximately 180 people.
- 28 November 2002: Al Qaeda reportedly bombed an Israeli-owned/patronized hotel in Mombasa, Kenya, killing 15 and injuring 40. Simultaneously, al Qaeda operatives unsuccessfully attempted to shoot down an Israeli chartered plane using a surface-to-air missile as it departed the airport in Mombasa, Kenya.
- 12 May 2003: Al Qaeda reportedly supported suicide attacks on three Western housing compounds in Riyadh, Saudi Arabia, that killed 34 people, including 8 Americans.
- 16 May 2003: Fourteen suicide bombers, members of a local group (Al-Salafiyyah al-Jihadiyah, or "Salafia Jihadia") allegedly connected to al Qaeda, carried out nearly simultaneous attacks on five Western and Jewish targets in Casablanca, killing 45 people and injuring more than 100.
- 15 November 2003: A group called the Abu Hafs al-Masri Brigades, which reportedly has connections to al Qaeda, carried out twin suicide truck bomb attacks on synagogues in Istanbul. Twenty-five people were killed and more than 300 were injured.
- 20 November 2003: An organization called the Great Eastern Islamic Raiders' Front (or IBDA-C), which reportedly may have received logistical training and support from al Qaeda, carried out suicide attacks against the British Consulate and the HSBC bank in Istanbul, Turkey.
- 11 March 2004: Simultaneous bombings of four packed commuter trains in Madrid killed 190 people and injured more than 1,400. Evidence is still being gathered; however, Spanish police have in custody a number of Moroccan and other Islamist radicals who are reportedly members of organizations such as Al-Salafiyyah al-Jihadiyah, the group that carried out the Casablanca attacks and which reportedly has links with al Qaeda.

Attempted and not completed terror attacks by al Qaeda include the following.[5]

- Assassination of Pope John Paul II during his visit to the Philippines in 1994
- Assassination of President Bill Clinton during his visit to the Philippines in 1995
- Bombing of numerous U.S. trans-Pacific flights in 1995
- The attempted bombing of Los Angeles International Airport in 1999 by Ahmed Ressam (see Chapter 1)
- The attempted bombing of a transatlantic flight from Paris to Milan by Richard Colvin Reid in December 2001

It is difficult to estimate or determine the attacks committed by al Qaeda and its associates since September 11, 2001. Attacks have been committed almost solely in the Middle East, particularly Iraq, where U.S. and coalition forces are deployed. However, al Qaeda has been linked, directly or indirectly, to a number of international attacks in Indonesia, Spain, India, Turkey, Morocco, Jordan, Saudi Arabia, Kenya, Kuwait, Tunisia, Yemen, and England.

Group Characteristics

Since the 9/11 attacks, al Qaeda has been a terrorist group in transition. At the time of the attacks on the World Trade Center and the Pentagon, al Qaeda was a typical decentralized cellular terrorist organization. Osama bin Laden and his top lieutenants were responsible for operational planning for the group, resource procurement, fundraising, propaganda distribution, and terrorist training. It was a very complex organization that took advantage of the latest technology to exploit weaknesses in the global community and in the national security structures of Western countries. However, the U.S. offensive in Afghanistan from 2003-2005 that crushed the Taliban and disrupted al Qaeda's base of operation severely crippled the terrorist group. Official U.S. reports indicate that more than 75 percent of al Qaeda's leadership has been killed or captured since the 9/11 attacks, including Khalid Sheikh Mohammed and Ramzi bin al-Shib (the operational planners of the 9/11 attacks), Mohamed Atta (al Qaeda's Military Chief), and Abu Zubaydah (one of bin Laden's chief operational planners). Although Osama bin Laden and his Afghanistan network of al Qaeda fighters have been disrupted, the al Qaeda ideology has grown and inspired numerous terrorist groups throughout the world to conduct attacks in the name of al Qaeda.

Al Qaeda is now a nebulous decentralized movement with cells located throughout the world; estimates vary, but there are reportedly several hundred to several thousand members affiliated with the al Qaeda movement. It is unknown how much direction and support these cells receive from Osama bin Laden, but it is clear that they benefit from his international network and sympathizers. Attacks on subway stations in Madrid, Spain and London, England, on hotels and resorts in Bali, Indonesia, and Sharm el-Sheikh, Egypt are indicative of how al Qaeda's ideology, training, and resources are being used by the global-jihadist movement. Whether al Qaeda as a singular terrorist group exists or whether it has been reduced to a movement, the hallmarks of an al Qaeda terrorist operation remain.

One of the primary characteristics of al Qaeda is a detailed planning capability and intense training of those who carry out the attacks. In addition to comprehensive training manuals, the group has established sophisticated training facilities in the mountains of Afghanistan and now in the remote areas of Iraq and Iran. Captured documents and films indicate the sophisticated nature of al training, which involves a loosely connected group of organizations and people in countries worldwide. Many of these organizations, such as the Muslim Brotherhood and Muslim American Society, had been in existence many years before al Qaeda was established, but, unlike al Qaeda, their activities were generally limited to their own country or, in the case of Hamas, to their geographic region.

Group Financing

Al Qaeda is not financed by bin Laden's personal fortune, as it was once believed. Instead, most of the money needed to sustain the organization comes from donations and the operation of private corporations.[6] Donations are made to al Qaeda by individuals, groups, and Muslim charitable organizations. The group maintains legitimate businesses such as a construction company and a bank. Other sources of income include the trading of illegally mined gems and diamonds; operation of ostrich farms and shrimp boats in Kenya; forestry in Turkey; and farming in Tajikistan. Al Qaeda receives money from donors and charities, mostly in the Gulf states (especially Saudi Arabia), to maintain their (estimated) $30 million a year operation. The only government entity to support al Qaeda financially at the time of the 9/11 attacks was the Taliban. The group moved its money by way of hawala, a financial trading system that allows large amounts of money to be moved around the world with trust as the basis for transaction. Al Qaeda funds were used for many things, including terrorist operations, training camps, jihadists' family members, equipment, arms, vehicles; money also went to the Taliban in return for providing a safe haven.

The growing effectiveness of American security and intelligence has made communication between groups more difficult, and individuals or cells may be more likely to act in greater isolation, without the support that occurred in the 9/11 attacks. Generally, individual cells will not be aware of the activities or plans of other cells in the organization. The so-called "single cell" operation involves one or more individuals carrying out less targeted attacks. An example is the London bombing cases in 2005, in which two groups of four individuals attacked the transport system. These cells were supplied and directed from a single source, but the selection of targets, subways and buses, were random, at least insofar as a specific train or bus was targeted. The threats of individual cells, particularly "lone wolf" operations (for instance the case of Richard Reid, the so-called shoebomber), make counterterrorist investigations difficult because communication is limited. Such investigations underscore the importance of developing information from the community and other private sources that may view the actions of an individual as being suspicious.

Investigators must also be aware of other sources that might provide leads, such as purchases of weapons or bomb making or hazardous materials, unusual travel activities, attendance at specific types of functions or meetings, taking photos of sensitive locations, money transfers, suspicious internet communications, evidence of inflammatory statements, and unusual communications. Of particular concern to the investigator must be the recognition that in a free society many such activities may be nothing more than coincidence or the exercise of free association and free speech. Although this may be difficult at times, the investigator should realize that an overzealous approach may actually work to hamper an investigation.

On a broader scale, investigations of illegal money transactions or the solicitation of funds to support a terrorist enterprise provide a better understanding of the way violent groups operate. Funding for terrorism in the U.S. has a long history, from donations to the Irish Republican Army, to support for Middle Eastern terrorist groups such as Hamas, as well as al Qaeda. In many cases individuals providing funds are not aware of the final destination of their contribution, believing they are providing humanitarian aid.

On the front line in the fight against domestic and international terrorism are the FBI's Joint Terrorism Task Forces, or JTTFs.

Joint Terrorism Task Forces (JTTFs)

The Joint Terrorism Task Force (JTTF) concept was developed in 1979 in response to a high number of bank robberies in the New York area. The cooperation and relationship between the New York City Police Department (NYPD) and the Federal Bureau of Investigation (FBI) made the concept of the JTTF a success, and a second group followed in Chicago. The program has grown tremendously, especially since the terror attack of September 11. The original JTTF was comprised of 22 members, with 11 officers from NYPD and eleven agents from the FBI. The number of JTTFs has almost doubled since September 11, 2001, with currently more than 100 programs nationwide. There are currently more than 3,700 members nationwide, including more than 2,000 Special Agents, 800 local law enforcement officers, and approximately 700 members from other government agencies. Numerous federal and local agencies are involved with the JTTFs, including the U.S. Marshals Service; CIA; Department of Homeland Security; Transportation Security Administration; Bureau of Alcohol, Tobacco, Firearms, and Explosives; Immigration and Customs Enforcement; Customs and Border Protection; and the U.S. Secret Service.

In 2002, the FBI created a National JTTF at their command center in Washington, D.C. The National JTTF includes almost 30 agencies at federal, state, and local levels of law enforcement. The National JTTF acts as the communication portal for all pertinent and intelligence-related information that concerns the JTTFs. The National Center can then inform local JTTFs of any relevant situations or investigations. This approach increases communication and efficiency of the program and is used as a safeguard to ensure that information is transmitted in an effective manner. The mission of the JTTF is to investigate and prevent acts of terrorism. Following the attacks on the World Trade Center in 1993, the JTTF became an integral part in the intelligence and investigation after the attack, and was responsible for the arrests of four terrorist suspects just one month after the attack. These four individuals were each sentenced to 240 years in prison and a $250,000 fine for their participation in the terror attacks. Also, during the investigation of the 1993 World Trade Center bombings, the JTTF discovered that a radical

Islamic terrorist group was planning several other attacks in New York City and the surrounding area. Specifically, the terrorists were planning to bomb the Lincoln and Holland tunnels, the United Nations headquarters building, and the federal building where the FBI New York Field Office is located. Upon learning of their plan, JTTF members raided the terrorists' safe house and discovered terrorists making bombs to use in the attacks. Fifteen arrests were made by the JTTF, preventing the Islamic extremists from conducting the attacks.

JTTFs serve a crucial role in combating terrorism and the investigations of terror attacks. They combine numerous federal, state, and local agencies to work together in the fight against terrorism and provide an effective communication strategy to increase the efficiency of terror investigations.

Terrorist organizations have increasingly used other forms of criminal activity to fund their activities. Drug trafficking, illegal smuggling of cigarettes and other types of contraband, and the smuggling of people have been linked to suspect groups. Terrorist groups also use legitimate businesses, religious donations and charities, oil revenues and other means to raise funds. Loretta Napoleoni, an economist and terrorism researcher notes that, "Together with the illegal economy, the New Economy of terror amounts to nearly $1.5 trillion, well over 5 percent of the world economy" (2005:106).

FINANCING TERRORISM

As world business leaders moved to cope with a global economic recession, fueled in large part by the 9/11 attacks, government leaders and global organizations moved to cut off the financing of terrorist groups. "At least three groups have the potential to act on terrorist financing: the United Nations, the Financial Action Task Force, and the IMF [International Monetary Fund]" (Fidler, 2001).

The financing of terrorism takes many forms, and represents an economic structure that has many of the same characteristics as international organized crime. Despite the passage of new laws regarding money laundering in several countries, the ability to investigate such transactions is difficult at best. Terrorist and organized crime activities, although in the millions, represent a minute portion of the trillions of dollars in the global banking systems.

The cost of maintaining a terrorist network and, in particular, the cost of carrying out a terrorist attack is relatively small. Admittedly, a well organized and financed group may spend millions of dollars, but even this is insignificant by comparison with the cost of combating it. A primary concern, however, is the threat of weapons of mass destruction—which do generally involve higher developmental and training costs. In this regard, the involvement of state sponsored or supported terrorism is an important consideration.

Major sources of income for terrorist groups are organized crime and the trafficking of weapons and drugs. The United Nations estimates that the drug trade involves about $400 billion a year, and the trade in light weapons has increased significantly following the end of the 'cold war' (Dyson, 2005). Terrorist groups in Colombia and Peru, for example, are funded in part by drug trafficking, and the drug trade supports groups in the Middle and Far East.

Funding al Qaeda takes many forms. Although many early reports attributed the funding of al Qaeda almost solely to the personal fortune of bin Laden, more recent research suggest that such funding takes many forms. It has been reported, particularly by the 9/11 Commission Report, that al Qaeda gets much of its financial support from donations from individuals and Muslim charitable organizations, as well as from illegal operations of drug trafficking and illegally mined gems and diamonds, and from legitimate business ventures, including a construction company and bank.

Where a terrorist group reaches the stage at which its finances go beyond support for a small group of individuals—usually volunteers who may hold regular jobs—and has had some success in carrying out attacks, the need for funding increases (Campbell & Flournoy, 2001:130).

> Organizations must raise funds to purchase the materials or weapons necessary for their innovative activities and gain access to the knowledge to put those materials to work. As a result, terrorist groups that are financially secure . . . have a distinct advantage (Jackson, 2001:201).

For most groups funding will come from one or more sources usually related to:

- State sponsorship.
- Global fund raising.
- "Legitimate" business enterprises.
- Sophisticated organized crime enterprises.
- Drug trafficking.
- Local fund raising.
- Common criminal activity (robbery, shakedowns).

With the exception of local fund-raising and common criminal activity the use of banks to launder and transfer funds is not unusual. A classic case is that of the Irish Republican Army (IRA), which drew much of its funding from donations in the United States into the 1970s, usually through front groups. When government and public pressure was successful in curtailing this funding, the organization moved into small-time criminal activity such as smuggling, protection, extortion, and fraud. By threatening cab and bus companies they were successful in operating cab and bus companies, raising millions of dollars (Dishman, 2001:48).

Over the past decade terrorist groups have increasingly moved into the drug trade to finance operations. Such has been the case in Peru with the Shining Path; Colombia with the M-19 and FARC (Revolutionary Armed Forces of Colombia) organizations; Myanmar with the Karen Rebel Movement and the LTTE (Liberation Tigers of Eelam) in Sri Lanka. Allegations of groups involved in drug trafficking also include groups in Bosnia and Afghanistan—which is one of the largest opium producing countries in the world. Dishman (2001) contends that most of these groups do not affiliate with organized crime entities, but develop their own criminal networks.

Figure 10.3 illustrates the more traditional models for the evolution of funding for terrorist groups. The al Queda network, which has also evolved over time has taken a different approach, and although it is believed that early funding came from a network of "charitable" organizations—many set up by Saudi Arabian interests.

Figure 10.3 The Evolution of International Terrorist Funding

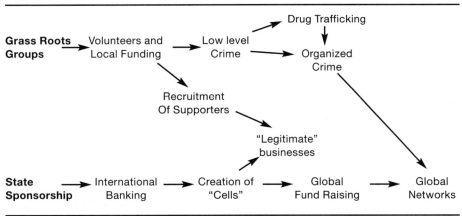

State sponsorship of terrorist organizations generally takes one of two forms, the first being the establishment of an organization by the rogue country, and the second, the agreement to support an existing movement. In either case the sponsoring state is capable of providing funding, as well as technical resources, training, and upscale weapons. Since the end of the "cold war" state sponsorship of terrorist activities has shifted from Europe to several countries in the Middle East and Africa. And as state sponsorship of terrorism has declined there are a growing number of individuals and loosely tied groups who oppose globalization.

The pressure put on by the U.S. and other governments in attacking banking interests and suspect charitable organizations involved in the funding of groups, such as al Qaeda, Hamas, and Hizbollah through these mechanisms has shifted in the case of al Qaeda which has moved toward a more loosely knit structure in which individual cells or groups raise their own funding for operations. The declaration of a war against terrorism by President George W. Bush following the 9/11 attacks has marked a major change in the monetary policies of numerous governments, shifting the primary focus to more local operations.

What role al Qaeda plays today is open to speculation. But, there is evidence that attacks in Spain, Indonesia and England were funded by local groups, perhaps with direct or indirect links to al Qaeda. An exception to this is in Iraq, where insurgent groups are believed to have closer ties to al Qaeda and may be funded by Iran and, to a lesser degree, Syria.

TOWARD NEW MODELS OF TERRORIST FUNDING AND OPERATIONS

Although the initial focus was on al Qaeda as a major source of planning and funding operations, cooperative efforts with other countries has changed the global picture. The economic costs of terrorism now run into trillions of dollars throughout the world when one takes into account the security and loss factors associated with international terrorism. Pressure put on the main organizational structure of al Qaeda and more effective intelligence and field successes has crippled the group's ability to communicate with support groups and cells in other countries. A number of experts maintain that al Qaeda as an operational entity is severely limited, and more recent attacks have not been planned or funded by bin Laden and his operatives. Indeed, some speculate that the so-called command or headquarters structure of al Qaeda is virtually defunct, bin Laden may have been severely wounded in an American attack on Tora Bora in December 2001. Other experts surmise that al Qaeda's *modus operandi* has historically been on large scale well planned attacks aimed at America's economic structure. They warn of the danger of another attack, such as 9/11, perhaps using weapons of mass destruction. In 2006 bin Laden, in a message on *Al Jazeera* television warned of another attack against America.

At the same time the world has seen a number of bombing attacks in other countries that are either supportive of the U.S., or where tourism attracts Americans. These locally sponsored attacks may or may not be directed by al Qaeda, but ultimately they are supportive of bin Laden's philosophy of attacking western interests in the Middle East and countries where there are large Muslim populations.

Although terrorism is not new, the advent of new weapons, new tactics and different targets have increased the threat. No country can really go it alone in mounting a counter terrorism effort, for we live today in an interdependent world community. Ultimately, the only hope for success in reducing terrorism lies in cooperation among all countries involved in combating terrorism.

Another component of terrorist investigations involves legal and illegal immigration. As America has tightened legal immigration greater emphasis has been placed on illegal immigration. The relatively porous borders of the country make it possible for individuals intent on committing violence to enter the country with relative ease. However, this threat depends also largely on suspects to have contacts for support once in the country. In many cases such individuals are not very familiar with American culture and, despite training, will frequently stand out. Here again, successful investigations depend in large measure on information from the public, or from local police who may come into contact with them.

Where a suspect has been identified the investigation will depend largely on surveillance, frequently with the cooperation of local authorities. The types of surveillance available and the methods of investigation are beyond the scope of this book. Nevertheless, it is important to recognize that continued improvements in training, the use of technology, and better intelligence and analysis, as well as new investigative methods will increase effectiveness. In this regard, it is important that one recognizes the flexible capability and innovative strategies of terrorists, and be willing to think "outside the box" in developing a counterterrorism model.

In large measure the front-line personnel of law enforcement and the private sector represent a key component of the homeland security effort. The information that they provide, as well as receive from the intelligence structure lays the ground work for an effective counterterrorism approach. This will depend in large measure on the ability to better utilize available technology, for the complexity of the problem is enormous. Both from a vulnerability standpoint, as well as the varied tactical and weapons capabilities of terrorist groups.

It is also important to recognize that terrorism, while a global phenomenon currently centered largely in the Middle East, the country is also vulnerable to threats from within. In addition to a relatively large infrastructure of radical Muslim support groups, many of whom were born in the United States or hold citizenship, there are also domestic groups as well as a well organized recruiting effort in the prisons. In some case their ideologies may be different, but the goals are the same—to attack and change or bring down the government. Overall, the numbers of people is small, representing less than one percent of the population, but their ability to create chaos is great.

Understanding the goals of terrorist organizations is important, for it will frequently serve to identify tactics. For example, the goal of al Qaeda, as stated by Osama bin Laden, is to weaken and destroy the economic structure to bring down capitalism; whereas the goal of domestic groups is largely focused on single issues, such as abortion, ecology, or animal rights. A growing movement against the economic powers of the West has also fostered a violent protest movement that is growing in the U.S., as well as England, France, Germany and other countries.

Many would argue that once a plot has been initiated it is difficult, if not impossible, to prevent a violent attack.[7] It has been estimated that 50,000 Muslims went through training camps, and America's infrastructure and transportation facilities are vulnerable. Undoubtedly, the task is a difficult one, but the potential threat—given the capability for a massive attack—emphasizes the need to continuously strive to develop better counterterrorist efforts at all levels of government and society.

KEY CONCEPTS

- Counterterrorism involves intelligence and information about terrorist groups and acts before and after an incident. It is a multi-functional field and involves local, state, federal, and private initiatives. Its main function is to prevent future terrorist attacks through the use of intelligence and attention to threats.

- Many counterterrorism investigations involve more than one person and the purpose of these investigations is to make a criminal case against involved individuals. Some of the charges against individuals in counterterrorist investigations include murder, assault, conspiracy, kidnapping, money laundering, illegal immigration, and possession of illegal materials or destructive device.

- Al Qaeda is a decentralized organization with cells located around the world; the group has been linked to numerous attacks around the world, dating back to 1992 and including the 9/11 attacks. The group is financed by donations from private individuals and groups, as well as from the operation of illegal enterprises.

- Joint Terrorism Task Forces (JTTFs) combine numerous federal, state, and local agencies to work together to combat terrorism and investigate terror attacks. The New York City JTTF was a vital part in the investigation of the 1993 WTC attacks.

- Terrorist organizations and attacks are relatively inexpensive, especially when compared to the amount of money spent on combating terrorism. Terrorism financing can take many forms, including global and local fundraising, drug and human trafficking, legitimate business enterprises, state sponsorship, organized crime enterprises, and common criminal activities.

ADDITIONAL READINGS

The 9/11 Commission Report. National Commission on Terrorist Attacks Upon the United States. July, 2004.

Posner, Richard (2005). *Preventing Surprise Attacks: Intelligence Reform in the Wake of 9/11.*

U.S. Department of Homeland Security, Office for Domestic Preparedness (2003). *Office for Domestic Preparedness Guidelines for Homeland Security: Prevention and Deterrence.*

Treverton, G.F. (2005). *Making Sense of Transnational Threats. Workshop Reports.* Arlington, VA: RAND National Security Research Division.

Target Capabilities List: Version 1.1 (2005). U.S. Department of Homeland Security, Office of State and Local Government Coordination and Preparedness. Washington, DC.

Risk Management Series: Reference Manual to Mitigate Potential Terrorist Attacks Against Buildings (2003). U.S. Department of Homeland Security, FEMA.

V. Forging America's New Normalcy: Securing Our Homeland, Preserving Our Liberty (2003). Arlington, VA: RAND Corporation.

Davis, L.M., Riley, K.J., Ridgeway, G., Pace, J., Cotton, S.K., Steinberg, P.S., Damphousse, K., Smith, B.L. *When Terrorism Hits Home: How Prepared Are State and Local Law Enforcement?* (2004). Arlington, VA: RAND Corporation.

RELATED WEBSITES

Office of the Director of National Intelligence www.dni.gov

Federal Bureau of Investigation (FBI) www.fbi.gov

U.S. Immigration and Customs Enforcement (ICE) www.ice.gov

U.S. Customs and Border Protection (CBP) www.cbp.gov

Drug Enforcement Administration (DEA) www.dea.gov

Financial Crimes Enforcement Network (FinCEN) www.fincen.gov

Air Force's Office of Special Investigations (OSI) public.afosi.amc.af.mil

Army's Criminal Investigative Command (CID) www.cid.army.mil

Naval Criminal Investigative Service (NCIS) www.ncis.navy.mil

New York Police Department (NYPD) www.nyc.gov/html/nypd/home.html

REFERENCES

Cronin, A.K., H. Aden, A. Frost, and B. Jones. *Foreign Terrorist Organizations.* CRS Report for Congress. Congressional Research Service, The Library of Congress.

CRS Report for Congress (2001). *Terrorism: Near Eastern Groups and State Sponsors, 2001.*

Dyson, William E. (2005). *Terrorism: An Investigator's Handbook,* Second Edition. New York, NY: LexisNexis/Anderson Publishing.

Katzman, K. (2005). *Al Qaeda: Profile and Threat Assesment.* CRS Report for Congress. Congressional Research Service, The Library of Congress.

Kushner, Harvey with Bart Davis (2004). *Holy War on the Home Front: The Secret Islamic Terror Network in the United States Sentinel.* New York: Penguin Group.

Jehl, Douglas, "4 in 9/11 Plot Are Called Tied to al Qaeda in '00." *New York Times.* August 9, 2005, P.1.

Napoleoni, Loretta (2005). *Terror Incorporated: Tracing the Dollars Behind the Terror Networks.* New York: Seven Stories Press.

9/11 Commission Report.

Posner, Richard (2005). *Preventing Surprise Attacks: Intelligence Reform in the Wake of 9/11.* Maryland, New York: Bowman and Littlefield Publishers.

Terrorist Attacks by al Qaeda (2004). Congressional Research Service. Washington, DC.

NOTES

[1]   From intelligence.gov.

[2]   From the 9/11 Commission Report, Page 346.

[3]   The 9/11 Commission Report cites examples of instances in which threats are not reported or followed up on, including threats that al Qaeda planned to hijack a plane in order to free U.S. held prisoners; using an aircraft filled with explosives, and then blowing up the aircraft over a U.S. city; and hijacking planes and flying them into U.S. assets, such as the World Trade Center and CIA headquarters. There are also numerous examples of federal agencies failing to work together to investigate claims and threats including the CIA not watchlisting known or suspected terrorists; the CIA not notifying the FBI when these known or suspected terrorists have valid U.S. visas; and the FBI not acknowledging the threat or investigating Zacarias Moussaoui.

[4]   The information was not shared because the four individuals were in the U.S. on valid passports, and at the time American law prohibited singling out U.S. citizens and "green card" holders in intelligence investigations. See Jehl, P.1.

[5]   Estimates and attack details are reported from the March 31, 2004 Congressional Research Service (CRS) Report.

[6]   From the February 6, 2004 Congressional Research Service (CRS) Report for Congress *Foreign Terrorist Organizations.*

[7]   See, for example, Posner, Richard, *Preventing Surprise Attacks: Intelligence Reform in the Wake of 9/11.* MD, NY: Bowman and Littlefield Publishers. See also Kushner, Harvey with Bart Davis (2004). *Holy War on the Home Front: The Secret Islamic Terror Network in the U.S. Sentinel.* New York, NY: Penguin Group.

Chapter 11

Weapons of Mass Destruction

> There is a consensus among nations that proliferation cannot be tolerated. Yet this consensus means little unless it is translated into action. Every civilized nation has a stake in preventing the spread of weapons of mass destruction.
>
> —President George W. Bush

> There is no greater threat the nation faces than the combination of terrorists and nuclear weapons.
>
> —Amitai Etzioni

INTRODUCTION

The risk of a weapon of mass destruction attack against the United States is the most serious threat in the post-9/11 world and is one of the strongest strategic issues guiding American domestic and foreign policy. In 2003, the U.S. invaded Iraq ostensibly to prevent the spread of weapons of mass destruction to terrorists and rogue states. The second major commission since the 9/11 attacks was directly focused on the issue of the nation's preparedness to combat weapons of mass destruction, and nearly every national strategy has addressed this issue in one form or another.

However, for most individuals, weapons of mass destruction (WMD) are vastly misunderstood in their description and in the specific threat that each weapon type poses to the United States. While uncommon, there have been several attacks using WMD in the past 10 years including a chemical attack on the Japanese subway system and a biological attack against politicians and public figures in the United States in the weeks after the 9/11 attacks. These attacks did not kill many people, but they did instill fear in a large population and affected the way that a large section of society lived their lives for a period of time.

This chapter provides an overview of chemical, biological, radiological, and nuclear weapons of mass destruction and the strategies that the United States is taking to identify, combat, and respond to these threats. The main

WMD threats are discussed in a context to help the reader better judge the significance of the threat by understanding the challenges posed by deploying each specific type of WMD.

WORST CASE SCENARIOS

The high potential for violence and catastrophe in a weapon of mass destruction attack often frames any discussion of these events in terms of the worst case scenario. This is understandable given the level of shock and disbelief at the carnage caused by the 9/11 attacks. Three worst case scenarios have caught the attention of U.S. policymakers and the public at large and are worth discussing here for a better understanding of the popular conception of the WMD threat. Each scenario involves a nuclear/radiological WMD device being delivered at a different location, each with devastating results.

The first scenario, described by Dr. Stephen Flynn in his book *America the Vulnerable*, involves a dirty-bomb attack that brings the nation's transportation system to a standstill. In this scenario, al Qaeda operatives acquire radioactive material from the Ukraine, which is incorporated into an explosive device, creating a "dirty bomb." The target for this dirty bomb is the Los Angeles Airport, chosen largely because al Qaeda has shown a determination to hit targets that have been unsuccessful in the past. Flynn's scenario is well thought out and comprehensive in design walking the reader through the existing overseas and domestic homeland security apparatus to highlight the inadequacies and vulnerabilities of the U.S. current efforts to protect the homeland.

The second scenario, portrayed in a 45-minute film titled *Last Best Chance*, was produced by the Nuclear Threat Initiative (NTI), a 501 (c) 3 public charity initially funded by donations from Mr. Ted Turner and others. In this film, al Qaeda becomes a nuclear power after acquiring a Hiroshima-sized nuclear weapon from the theft of fissile material in an unsecured location in Belarus that is eventually assembled and concealed as carry-on luggage. Ultimately the nuclear bomb is delivered by an innocuous-looking Canadian couple driving a large SUV across the border into America. This worst case scenario highlights the very real threat of loose nuclear material throughout the world and supposed ease of acquiring it if a subnational group or individual has the right amount of money and/or connections.

The third scenario, a 90-minute film produced by the British Broadcasting Corporation (BBC) titled *Dirty War*, tells the hypothetical story of the planning and execution of a "dirty bomb" attack on central London by radical Islamist terrorists. In this film, a terrorist cell reaches the operational stage in a terrorist attack they have been planning for several years. The counterterrorism authorities have virtually no intelligence on the plot and are completely unprepared for the attack. The attack is successfully conducted outside a major transportation station when suicide bombers detonate a large bomb mixed with radioactive material, killing scores of commuters and sending a radioactive plume high into the morning sky. This worst-case scenario highlights the challenges of identifying and interdicting a terrorist attack using WMD as well as the complicated issues involved in responding to it.

In each of these scenarios, the WMD of choice for the terrorists/sub-state actors is a radiological/nuclear device, which is consistent with the threat assessments of WMD attacks by many of the intelligence, law enforcement, and homeland security officials in the U.S. However, nuclear and radiological devices are just one type of WMD that the U.S. must prepare for in homeland security.

Altogether there are four main families of weapons of mass destruction: Chemical, Biological, Radiological, and Nuclear; each with their own operational advantages and disadvantages and challenges for homeland security. What follows is a discussion of each of these four categories of WMD and specific examples within each type. Understanding the operational realities of each type of WMD will help to place the WMD threat into perspective for homeland security.

CHEMICAL WEAPONS OF MASS DESTRUCTION

Chemical weapons of mass destruction are weapons that use the toxic properties of chemical substances to kill, injure, or incapacitate another person or group of people. They differ from conventional weapons in that the destructive effects are not caused primarily by explosive material. Under the Chemical Weapons Convention, which is a convention of international law signed in 1993, chemical weapons include any toxic chemical, regardless of its origin, that is used for anything other than research, medical, pharmaceutical or protective purposes; this includes the use of *nonliving* toxic products produced by living organisms (the use of *living* toxic products produced by organisms are considered to be biological weapons of mass destruction [see the next section]).

There are hundreds of chemical agents that have been used in warfare, whether it was the traditional battles of World War I and II or the asymmetric forms of modern warfare such as terrorism and insurgency. Some of the common chemical agents that are considered serious WMD threats to homeland security include Sarin, Ricin, VX gas, and Tabun. Most chemical agents fall into one or more of the following classes depending on how the chemicals affect a human body: blister agents, blood agents, choking agents, nerve agents, lacrimators, vomiting agents, irritants, and psychotropic compounds (Langford, 2004). However, vomiting agents, irritants, and psychotropic compounds have little utility for terrorists and other subnational groups that pose a threat to U.S. homeland security.

Figure 11.1 WMD Agents—Ease of Acquisition

Chemical Agents, Biological Agents, Toxins Potential Terror Use					
	Ease of Acquisition	Public Health Impact	Vaccine Availability	Resistance to Medical Treatment	Ease of Distribution	Weaponized
CHEMICAL AGENT						
Nitrogen Mustard	+	+	-	+	+	-
Sulfur Mustard	+	+	-	+	+	-
Sarin	O	+	-	O	O	-
VX	—	+	-	+	+	-
Ammonia	+	0	-	+	—	-
Chlorine	+	0	-	+	—	-
Cyanogen Chloride	+	0	-	—	—	-
Hydrogen Cyanide	+	0	-	—	—	-
BIOLOGICAL AGENT (DISEASE)						
Pneumonic Plague (*Yersinia pestis*)	+	+	O	O	+	Weapon
Dengue hemorrhagic fever	O	+	O	+	O	Research
Eastern equine encephalitis	O	+	O	+	O	Research
Russian spring-summer encephalitis	O	O	O	+	+	Research
Anthrax (*Bacillus anthracis*)	+	+	—	O	+	Weapon
Q fever (*Coxiella burnetti*)	+	+	O	—	+	Weapon
Ebola hemorrhagic fever	—	+	+	+	+	Research
Marburg hemorrhagic fever	—	+	+	+	+	Weapon
Glanders (*Burkholderia mallei*)	+	+	+	O	+	Weapon
Venezuelan equine encephalitis	O	—	O	+	O	Weapon
Typhoid fever	+	O	—	—	—	Unknown
Cholera (*Vibrio cholerae*)	+	—	—	—	+	Unknown
Monkeypox	—	+	—	O	+	Unknown
Smallpox (*Variola major*)	—	+	—	O	+	Weapon
Tularemia (*Francisella tularenis*)	O	+	O	—	+	Weapon
Enscherichia coli O157:H7	+	—	+	+	—	Unknown
Shigella dysenteriae	O	+	+	—	—	Unknown
TOXIN						
Ricin	+	+	O	+	O	Weapon
Aflatoxins	O	—	+	+	O	Weapon
Shigatoxin	+	+	+	+	O	Unknown
Abrin	+	+	+	+	O	Unknown

KEY:

EASE OF ACQUISITION:
  + = easily obtained, manufactured, grown, or bought; few side products in production; not widely dangerous
  O = obtained, manufactured, grown, or bought with some difficulty; can produce poisonous or harmful side effects or products during manufacture; grown in remote areas
  — = very difficult or harmful to obtain, manufacture, grow, or buy; can create lethal side products during manufacture; found in few places

PUBLIC HEALTH IMPACT:
  + = significant harmful health impact
  O = moderate harmful health impact
  — = relatively insignificant health impact

VACCINE AVAILABILITY:
  + = no vaccine available
  O = potential vaccine that does not have approval by Food and Drug Administration
  — = vaccine available
  - = no information available

RESISTANCE TO MEDICAL TREATMENT:
  + = no cure available, only supportive treatment
  0 = can be treated with specific (sometimes unproven) medical treatment within immediate timeframe
  — = can be effectively cured or treated (without limitations of a timeframe)

EASE OF DISTRIBUTION:
  + = agents can be distributed through close contact or in contact with skin
  0 = agents can be passed on as an aerosol and inhaled or ingested; can also use when contaminate food or drink
  — = large amounts of vapor or aerosol must be inhaled; ingested through food or drink; or may need to use an animal vector (insect)

WEAPONIZATION:
  - = information not available1

Information from Shea, Dana A. and Gottron, Frank. (June 23, 2004). Small Scale Terrorist Attacks Using Chemical and Biological Agents: An Assessment Framework and Preliminary Comparisons.

Blister agents are either inhaled or spread through physical contact, but they do not often result in death. Instead, these agents are often used to harass or adversely affect the intended target, resulting in skins burns and blisters or causing damage to the eyes, airway, or lungs and other organs. The most common form of blister agents are those derived from *mustard gas*, which can be manufactured with relative ease, but also require large quantities of precursor chemicals. The production and transfer of CW precursor chemicals is internationally monitored under the Chemical Weapons Act providing some degree of control over their distribution (GAO, 1999).

Blood agents are chemical weapons that are usually inhaled and produce their effects by preventing the body from utilizing oxygen. These agents work very quickly and can cause cessation of respiration within one minute and death by cardiac failure within a few minutes. The most common blood agent is the *cyanide* group of chemicals, which are colorless and can sometimes have a faint, bitter, almond-like odor. Terrorist groups like al Qaeda have acquired and experimented with cyanide chemicals. Several videotapes seized in Afghanistan showed al Qaeda's testing of chemical weapons on caged dogs; some experts believed that cyanide was one of the gases used in these tests. Ahmed Ressam, the al Qaeda operative convicted of trying to blow up the air traffic control tower at Los Angeles Airport (LAX) in 2000, testified that al Qaeda had conducted tests using cyanide to kill dogs (Robertson, 2002).

Choking agents (also known as pulmonary agents) are designed to impede an intended target's ability to breathe, resulting in suffocation. Most choking agents produce severe vomiting and death can follow instantly or within three hours depending on the agent used and the amount of exposure. *Chlorine gas* is the best known choking agent due to its wide use by the Germans in World War I. In fact, the use of chlorine gas on April 22, 1915 by the Germans marked the very first time that chemical weapons were used against humans (Cook, 1999). Al Qaeda has also shown an interest in using chlorine gas, but its effectiveness as a terrorist weapon is doubtful for the following reasons (CCC, 2005):

- Chlorine gas is heavier than air and therefore remains low and hugs the ground.

- When chlorine is released from a pressurized container the remaining chlorine gets colder and ices as the pressure inside the container gets lower—this effect slows the release rate over time. Chlorine gas supports combustion—if released via explosion, the chlorine gas will be consumed by the heat of the resulting fire.

- Chlorine gas would not be a wise terrorist's choice because it can be quickly and easily identified by a strong odor at extremely low concentrations allowing for an immediate response and action to leave the area. At higher concentrations it is also visible as a yellow/green color. Terrorists, intent on inflicting human and economic pain, are likely to choose an insidious and undetectable chemical weapon.

Nerve Agents are considered to be the most dangerous form of chemical weapons because they can cause loss of consciousness and convulsions within seconds and death within minutes of exposure. Nerve agents are similar to blister agents in that they are effective when inhaled or passed through physical contact with the agent; the more potent nerve agents can penetrate clothing, skin, and mucous membranes (Langford, 2004). When compared to other types of chemical weapons, nerve agents are more difficult to produce, and require synthesizing multiple precursor chemicals. This requires high-temperature processes and creates dangerous by-products, which makes the production of many nerve agents unlikely outside an advanced laboratory.

In broad terms, there are two main categories of nerve agents, G-series and V-series agents. *G-series agents* were developed first, either during or shortly after the second world war, and include Sarin, Tabun, and Soman. The three are still considered to be some of the deadliest types of WMD in existence. *Sarin* is a clear, colorless, and tasteless liquid that has no odor in its pure form, although Sarin can be evaporated into a vapor (gas) and spread into the environment. It is one of the most volatile nerve agents and dissipates once released, quickly diminishing its potency and the threat of exposure. To date, Sarin is the only chemical weapon that has been used in a terrorist attack. The doomsday cult, Aum Shinrikyo, used Sarin in two terrorist attacks in Japan in 1994 and 1995. The 1995 attack on the Tokyo subway system resulted in more than 5500 people seeking medical attention (Sidell, 2005).

V-series agents are known as persistent agents, meaning that they do not degrade or wash away easily, and can therefore remain on clothes and other surfaces for long periods. The most common v-series agent is *VX*, which is an odorless and tasteless oily liquid that is amber in color and very slow to evaporate. Under very high temperatures VX can be evaporated to a vapor which can then be released. VX is one of the deadliest nerve agents created to date with as little as 10 mg being enough to kill an average person. According to the Council on Foreign Relations (2005), it is doubtful that al Qaeda or other terrorist groups would be able to create and deploy VX because it is very complicated and extremely dangerous to synthesize. It requires the use of toxic and corrosive chemicals and high temperatures in a sophisticated chemical laboratory.

Lacrimatory agents are chemical weapons more commonly known as *tear gasses*. These agents are inhaled and usually have some type of odor, although they rarely cause death to their intended targets. Instead, lacrimatory agents usually cause profuse crying, severe cough, involuntary defecation, and vomiting; however, these effects usually last less than 30 minutes. Given the lack of injury and decreased lethality of tear gasses, this chemical agent holds very little attraction for terrorists. Terrorist groups that conduct paramilitary-type training might be interested in using lacrimatory agents for disabling or subduing individuals during the course of a terrorist operation. For instance, it has been reported that some form of noxious chemical spray, believed to be tear gas or *pepper spray,* was used on the American 11 and United 175 flights to keep passengers out of the first-class cabin during the 9/11 attacks. The 9/11 Commission Report (2004) revealed that pepper spray was found in the luggage of Mohamed Atta's checked luggage that was found at Logan Airport.

Although understanding the different types of chemical weapons is critical, it is equally important to understand how chemical weapons are delivered because that will ultimately determine the effectiveness of a chemical weapons attack. As was seen with the Sarin gas attack on the Tokyo subway, even the most lethal types of chemical weapons can be rendered useless without a proper *delivery method.*

The traditional method of delivering chemical weapons was through *munitions*; such as artillery shells, bombs, and missiles; that allow dissemination at a distance and *spray tanks* which disseminate from low-flying aircraft. Although these techniques were developed and used in World War I with limited effectiveness, they are still attractive delivery methods for terrorists and sub-state actors. For instance, it was widely reported that Zacarias Moussaoui was inquiring about the availability of crop duster aircraft, presumably for the delivery of chemical weapons.

The principal method of disseminating chemical agents has been the use of explosives. These usually have taken the form of central bursters expelling the agent laterally, although the efficiency of this practice is doubtful given that a good deal of the agent is lost by incineration in the initial blast and by being forced onto the ground.

It is generally accepted that the best way to deliver a chemical weapon is in an aerosolized form, although the best method of aerosolizing weapons is still subject to much debate. To aerosolize a weapon is to break it down into tiny particles so that the chemical or biological weapon can become airborne and inhaled by the intended target. There are several methods for aerosolizing weapons, i.e., thermal, flashing, aerodynamic dispersion, but it is sufficient to state that aerosolized weapons are more effective the finer their particles become.

Aerosolizing a chemical weapon is only one step in the delivery process. Once the chemical weapon is aerosolized, a wide range of factors affecting the delivery must be taken into account. For instance, if an aerosolized form of VX was to be delivered via a fired mortar canister, factors such as wind speed, wind direction, level of humidity, and the compactness of the space would all affect the effectiveness of the delivery.

BIOLOGICAL WEAPONS OF MASS DESTRUCION

Biological weapons of mass destruction are weapons that use any infectious microorganisms (bacteria, virus or other disease-causing organism) or toxin found in nature, that reproduce within the host to cause an incapacitating or fatal illness. Weight-for-weight, biological weapons agents are hundreds to thousands of times more potent than the most lethal chemical warfare agents, making them true weapons of mass destruction with a potential for lethal mayhem that can exceed that of nuclear weapons (Office of Technology Assessment, 1993).

Biological agents which may be used as weapons, of which there are hundreds of agents and strains, generally fall into one of six categories: bacteria, viruses, rickettsiae, chlamydia, fungi, and toxins (NATO, 1996). The U.S. strategy for defending the homeland from biological weapons specifically addresses the following biological agents that can readily be weaponized: Anthrax, Botulism, Brucellosis, Cholera, Plague, Q Fever, Ricin Intoxication, Staphylococcal Enterotoxin B Disease, Tricothecene, Mycotoxicosis, Tularemia, Variola (Smallpox), and Venezuelan Equine Encephalitis. Four main categories of biological agents will briefly be discussed, with special attention paid to the agents designated as serious threats to U.S. homeland security.

Bacterial Agents

Bacteria are small free-living organisms consisting of nuclear material, cytoplasm, and cell membrane. The diseases they produce often respond to specific therapy with antibiotics and it is often possible to manufacture vaccines for preventing bacteria-based outbreaks. Some of the most common biological weapons are bacterium, including anthrax, tularemia, brucellosis, cholera, and plague.

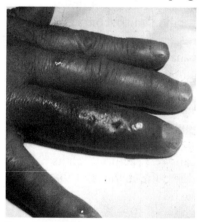

Example of effects of cutaneous anthrax. *Photo Courtesy of UCSF Medical Canter Infection Control, http://infectioncontrol.ucsf medicalcenter.org*

Anthrax is perhaps the best known of the bacteria biological agents because of its use in the first biological attack in the 21st century when five people were killed over several weeks beginning September 18, 2001. The anthrax in these attacks was a weaponized strain, known as the Ames strain, and was delivered through the U.S. Postal Service to several news media offices and the offices of two U.S. Senators.

Anthrax is a zoonotic disease, meaning an animal disease that can be transferred to humans, caused by the bacterium *Bacillus anthracis* and is contracted by humans cutaneously (through physical contact) and through inhalation. Nearly 95 percent of all cases of anthrax in humans are the result of *cutaneous anthrax*, which has an incubation period of 1-6 days and results in a small elevated lesion on the skin (Kushner, 2004). *Inhalation anthrax* is far more deadly than cutaneous anthrax because the bacterial organism enters the lungs, making it more difficult to identify and diagnose. In cases of inhalation anthrax, death often occurs within 24-36 hours of the infection setting in (FAS, 2005). It is important to note that anthrax itself is not contagious, rather it is the spreading of the bacterium spores that transfers the disease from person to person and animal to animal.

Tularemia (also known as rabbit fever) is a lesser known zoonotic disease, caused by the bacterium *Francisella tularensis,* that can be weaponized as a biological agent. It is one of the most infectious diseases known to man and is considered to be endemic in North America and parts of Europe. The main carriers of tularemia are ticks and deer flies, with common animals such as deer, rabbits, and rodents being the most common host animals. Similar to anthrax, tularemia can be contracted through cutaneous contact or inhalation, but it can also be ingested. Similar to anthrax, tularemia has an incubation period, although it is a good deal longer ranging from 1-14 days after exposure. If used in a biological attack, tularemia could be expected to have a fatality rate higher than the 5-10 percent experienced in natural exposure to the bacterium.

There have not been any known terrorist attacks using tularemia; however, there have been several outbreaks of the disease since 2000. In the summer of 2000, a 43-year-old house painter was killed and nine other individuals fell ill after being exposed to tularemia while working and performing various tasks outdoors (Burrell & Barry, 2000). An investigation by the Centers for Disease Control and Prevention (CDC) determined that Martha's Vineyard was one of the only places in the world where inhalation tularemia could be contracted as a result of lawn mowing.

On September 24, 2005, several chemical and biological WMD sensors went off the morning after a book fair and anti-war demonstration on the National Mall in Washington, D.C. The sensors all indicated that small levels of tularemia had been detected throughout the mall area although no cases of tularemia infection were reported (Levine & Horwitz, 2005).

Brucellosis (also known as Undulant fever or Malta fever) is an infectious zoonotic disease, caused by the *Brucella* bacteria, where the organisms are acquired by humans via the oral route through the ingestion of unpasteurized milk and cheese, via inhalation of aerosols generated on farms and in slaughterhouses, or via inoculation of skin lesions in persons with close animal contact (USAIID, 2005).

Brucellosis has an incubation period ranging from 1 to 6 weeks and the onset of the disease is characterized by malaise, fever, chills, sweating, headache, and fatigue, with a rising and falling fever being the dominant symptom (Byrnes, Tierno & King, 2003). Death is most common when the infection reaches the lining of the heart of the membranes of the brain, but the death rate is less than one percent.

Cholera (also known as Asiatic cholera) is an infectious disease, caused by bacteria that are typically ingested by drinking water that is contaminated by improper sanitation, or by eating improperly cooked fish and shellfish; it is rarely spread person to person. In a weaponized form, cholera would most likely be used to contaminate a water supply, although it would require a considerable amount of planning to control conditions if the supply was large.

Symptoms include diarrhea, abdominal cramps, nausea, vomiting, and dehydration, but cholera can have a high death rate (as high as 50%) due to dehydration if there is no treatment administered. The incubation period can be as short as 4 hours or as long as 5 days. Cholera has not been seen in the United States since the beginning of the twentieth century, but pandemic outbreaks have been recorded in South America as recently as 1994 when Peru had more than 1 million identified cases (Lama, 1999) and thousands of deaths.

Plague (also known as Bubonic plague, Pneumonic plague, and Septicemic plague, depending where in the body the infection occurs) is an infectious disease caused by the bacterium *Yersinia pestis*. Compared to the other bacterium biological weapons that do not form spores, plague is considered to be quite resilient. The Soviet Union was able to weaponize plague for their biological warfare arsenals; a feat that U.S. scientists were reportedly unable to master for mass production (Croddy, 2001).

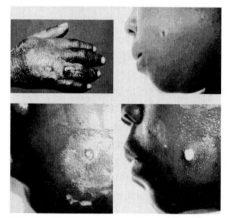

Effects of bubonic plague. *Photo Courtesy of UCSF Medical Center Infection Control, http://infectioncontrol.ucsfmedicalcenter.org*

If left untreated, plague can have a mortality rate of more than 50 percent for bubonic forms and near 100 percent for pneumonic forms. The incubation period for plague can range from 2-10 days depending on the type of plague contracted and is highly infectious for interpersonal transmission (Cashman, 2000). If plague were to be used in a biological attack it would most probably have to be disseminated through aerosol in a closed or semi-closed space because of the volatility of the bacterium to environmental stresses such as exposure to sunlight.

Viral Agents

Viruses are organisms which require living cells in which to replicate and are therefore intimately dependent upon the cells of the host which they infect. Diseases produced by viruses generally do not respond to antibiotics but may be responsive to antiviral compounds, which tend to be of little availability and limited use. The viral biological weapons that are considered to be top threats to homeland security include Smallpox and Venezuelan Equine Encephalitis.

Smallpox is a highly contagious virus that is transmitted only through human-human contact and causes high fever with flu-like symptoms which are immediately followed by a quick-spreading rash of red bumps and pustules (CDC, 2005). Although smallpox transmission is limited to humans, it can be contracted through inhalation, ingestion, physical contact, or through indirect contact with smallpox affected objects such as bedding or clothing.

After transmission, smallpox has an incubation period of between 10 and 17 days during which the intended target will be primarily asymptomatic. The fatality rate for smallpox is usually between 30 and 40 percent for individuals who are not vaccinated, which would constitute a large segment of the current U.S. population because routine smallpox vaccinations ceased in the U.S. in 1972. Further, anyone vaccinated before 1972 would no longer be protected from smallpox because boosters were not provided following the World Health Organization announcement in 1980 that smallpox had been eradicated from the planet (Croddy, 2001). This means that virtually all of the world's civilians are now susceptible to the disease.

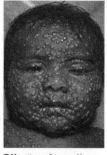

Effects of smallpox. *Photo Courtesy of Albert Einstein College of Medicine of Yeshiva University, www.aecom.yu.edu*

Smallpox is known to exist in two places in the world: the U.S. Centers for Disease Control and Prevention (CDC) in Atlanta, Georgia, and at Vector, a biological research laboratory in Novosibirsk, Russia (Tucker, 2001). Although both the U.S. and Russia have agreed to destroy their stockpiles, the threat of smallpox programs in North Korea and Iraq have given pause to the destruction timetables of the smallpox stockpiles (Croddy, 2001).

The Council on Foreign Relations (2005a) addressed the issue of weaponized smallpox for use by terrorist organizations. They argued that while smallpox is small enough to be effectively aerosolized for inhalation, it is less readily available than many other biological agents, such as anthrax and plague. Acquiring, storing, and transporting large quantities of the smallpox virus would require special skills that most transnational terrorist organizations do not have; although, the sophistication shown by al Qaeda in its ability to conduct information warfare, collect intelligence on potential targets, and plan complex multi-phase attacks suggest that this is not beyond the capability of the upper echelon terrorist organizations. The dangerousness of smallpox may make it an irresistible method of asymmetric warfare for groups and individuals within the al Qaeda network.

Venezuelan Equine Encephalitis (VEE) is an arthropod-borne (transmitted by organisms like spiders, ticks, crustaceans, centipedes, and other insects) alphavirus that is endemic in northern South America, Trinidad, Central America, Mexico, and Florida. The primary natural transmitter of this agent is mosquitos, although the agent can be transmitted person-to-person or through aerosol. The U.S. successfully weaponized VEE during the 1950s and 1960s as a part of its biological warfare programs, and it is assumed that other countries have been or are suspected of having weaponized this agent as well (State of North Dakota, 2005).

There is an incubation period of between 1 and 5 days, but unlike many of the previous biological agents, VEE has a relatively low fatality rate of usually less than 1 percent. If VEE progresses into full-blown encephalitis, then the fatality rate increases to around 20 percent. Following the incubation period, the intended target will experience flu-like symptoms that persist and eventually worsen; as encephalitis sets in, the intended target often slips into a coma.

Rickettsiae

Rickettsiae are microorganisms which have characteristics common to both bacteria and viruses. They are similar to bacteria in that they possess metabolic enzymes and cell membranes, utilize oxygen, and are susceptible to broadspectrum antibiotics. Rickettsiae are similar to viruses in that they grow only within living cells. These type of diseases are most often transmitted by the bite of infected ticks, fleas, or lice. The most well-known rickettsiae biological agent is Q-Fever.

Q-Fever (also known as query fever)is a zoonotic disease caused by the microorganism *Coxiella Burnetti*, which is most commonly found in sheep, cattle, and goats, although infection has been noted in a wide variety of animals. Humans are very susceptible to the disease and can be infected by inhaling particles contaminated with the organisms. Q-Fever makes an attractive biological agent because it is highly resistant to heat, drying, and many common disinfectants. Once infected, an individual has only a slight chance of death; however, they are at a much greater risk of contracting chronic Q-Fever, which is a much more serious disease. As many as 65 percent of persons with chronic Q-Fever may die from the disease. It has been estimated that 50 kilograms of dried, powdered *Cokiella Burnetti* would produce casualties at a rate equal to that of similar amounts of anthrax or tularemia organisms (Weintraub, 2002). There have not been any known terrorist attacks using Q-Fever, although it was widely reported that Aum Shinrikyo had been experimenting with several dispersal methods for the delivery of weaponized Q-Fever (Olson, 1999).

Toxins

Toxins are poisonous substances produced and derived from living plants, animals, or microorganisms like bacteria or fungi; some toxins may also be produced or altered by chemical means. Toxins are some of the most dangerous substances known to man, with effects ranging from disabling to acutely toxic. They are considered to be more potent than chemical weapons because they require less material to produce an equivalent number of casualties; however, they are not self reproducing, so they require more weaponized material than for an attack using a more traditional biological agent. Three toxins, Ricin, Botulinum, and Staphylococcal Enterotoxic B (SEB), are considered to have the highest potential for use by terrorists and sub-state actors.

Ricin is a potent plant toxin found in the seeds of the castor plant whose lethality and ease of production has long made it a favorite biological weapon of terrorists and governments. Ricin is often referred to as the "poor man's poison" because it requires little sophistication and can be produced by a relative novice after reading a few passages from books like *The Poisoner's Handbook, Silent Death,* and *Catalogue of Silent Tools of Justice.* Now, instructions for producing ricin from the castor bean are widely available on the Internet and have been posted on many jihadist websites (SITE, 2005).

The Bulgarian secret police used Ricin to assassinate a Soviet dissident, Georgi Markov, in London by injecting him with a pellet containing a few hundred millionths of a gram delivered from a weapon disguised as an umbrella. Terrorists and extremists have also shown a great interest in using Ricin as an offensive weapon. In the United States, extremists with links to right wing and Neo-Nazi groups have been arrested with ricin or have had ricin producing materials in their homes. Al Qaeda has also shown a strong interest in producing ricin for use in terrorist attacks, as indicated by the arrest of an Algerian cell suspected to be linked to al Qaeda in Britain in 2003 and in reports that Ansar al-Islam was testing ricin on animals like donkeys and chickens.

Ricin exposure in humans can be accomplished through ingestion, injection, and even inhalation if the ricin is weaponized. Once exposed, ricin can kill an individual in less than 36 hours and involves severe respiratory distress, organ failure, and severe internal and external bleeding. That said, many experts believe that ricin would make for a poor weapon of mass destruction because it is difficult to expose large numbers of people to the toxin. One report estimated that it would take more than 8 metric tons to cover a 100 km^2 with enough toxin to kill 50 percent of the people in that area (Kortepeter & Parker, 1999).

Botulinum is a toxin produced by the bacterium *Clostridium botulinum* and is considered to be the second most toxic substance known behind plutonium. Botulinum toxin causes the disease *Botulism* in humans, which is a potentially fatal but noncontagious disease marked by muscle paralysis. It is extremely potent, which has led it to be one of the most researched biological agents for use in warfare. The Journal of the American Medical Association (JAMA) formed a working group on Civilian Biodefense and specifically addressed the threat of botulinum toxin as a weapon of mass destruction. JAMA reported that a single gram of crystalline botulinum toxin, if evenly dispersed and inhaled, would kill more than one million people (Arnon et al., 2001). To put the potency of boulinum toxin in perspective with some of the previously discussed agents, it is 275 times more toxic than cyanide, and 100,000 times more toxic than sarin nerve gas, which was used by Aum Shinrikyo to attack the Tokyo subway system (Weintraub, 2002).

Contemporary History of Ricin Use

In 1978, ricin was used to assassinate Bulgarian dissident Georgi Markov in London. A novel, umbrella-based weapon was used to inject a pellet containing ricin into Markov (Shea & Gottron, 2004).

In 1983, Montgomery Todd Meeks, 19, was tried for attempting to murder his father with ricin. He claimed that the act was motivated by his father's abuse. He conducted research on poisons, decided on ricin, and then purchased the material from Aardvark Enterprises in Louisville, Kentucky, for $200. A classmate went to Kentucky to pick up the purchase, but emptied the vial of ricin into a toilet when he returned to Orlando International Airport. It was alleged that Meeks continued with the murder plan and ceased only when a friend went to the police (CNS, 2004).

In 1983, two brothers were arrested by the FBI for producing an ounce of pure ricin, which they stored in a 35-mm canister. Officials were directed to the brothers after receiving a tip from an informant. The FBI took the material to the U.S. Army laboratories at Ft. Detrick where it was destroyed (CNS, 2004).

In 1982 Texas attorney William A. Chanslor, 50, was sentenced to jail for three years and fined $5,000 for plotting to kill his 39-year-old wife with ricin. He claims that he wanted the ricin to assist his wife in committing suicide. She was paralyzed after having a stroke in 1979. She begged the jury not to convict Chanslor. He put ads in two paramilitary magazines, *Soldier of Fortune* and *Gung Ho*. His ads said, "Wanted: experts in poisons and chemical agents with access to same." He also read at least one book that included information on the toxin. When Chanslor contacted the author of a book on toxins, regarding the acquisition of ricin, the author contacted Canadian law enforcement officials. Police then recorded a meeting between the two where Chanslor purchased a tablet supposedly containing ricin for $2,500. On 4 August 1982, facing a penalty of 20 years in prison, Chanslor was sentenced to three years in prison and fined $5,000 (CNS, 2004).

In 1993, a retired electrician who had worked the trans-Alaska pipeline and was arrested in 1993 after Canadian customs officials found his car loaded with guns, 20,000 rounds of ammunition, neo-Nazi literature, instruction manuals for chemical and biological weapons, and a bag full of ricin. He told authorities he was preparing to control the coyote problem on his farm. (Weintraub, 2002).

In 1994 and 1995, members of a tax-resistance group, the Minnesota Patriots Council, were found in possession of 0.7 grams of ricin. They were arrested and convicted for the possession of a lethal poison for use as a weapon, a violation of the Biological Weapons Anti-Terrorism Act of 1989 (P.L. 101-298) (Shea & Gottron, 2004).

In August 1995, Dr. Ray W. Mettetal, Jr., a 44-year-old neurologist at Rockingham Memorial Hospital in Harrisonburg, Virginia, was apprehended at Vanderbilt University Medical Center in Nashville, Tennessee, carrying a six-inch veterinarian's syringe with a four-inch needle filled with boric acid and salt water (contact lens solution), which could prove lethal if injected into the heart. He allegedly planned to use the syringe to murder Dr. George S. Allen, his former supervisor when he was a neurology resident at Vanderbilt in the 1980s. After the arrest, police searched a storage unit rented by Mettetal in Harrisonburg, Virginia, in which they found toxic chemicals and several books on assassination and producing chemical and biological agents. Also among the items was a small glass jar containing the toxin ricin, notes documenting Allen's whereabouts, maps of the campus where Allen worked, and photographs of his house. These notebooks alleged that Mettetal planned to soak pages of a book with a ricin-solvent mixture that could promote the movement of the toxin through the skin once introduced. After the ricin was discovered in his possession, a federal case was brought against Mettetal. He was also charged with the federal offense of providing false information (e.g., the false identity of Steven Ray Maupin) to the U.S. Postal Service (CNS, 2004).

In December 1995, Thomas Lewis Lavy was arrested while crossing into Canada from Alaska. Canadian customs officials seized a

Contemporary History of Ricin Use, *continued*

white powder later determined to be 130 grams of ricin. Mr. Lavy was later arrested for possession of a lethal poison for use as a weapon. His intentions for the ricin are unknown, as he committed suicide while in detention (Shea & Gottron, 2004).

In August 1995, Michael Farrar, a 40-year-old cardiologist, was hospitalized with a mysterious illness. On two additional occasions, Farrar was hospitalized for exhibiting similar unexplained symptoms. At first, doctors believed his problems were connected to his recent trip to South America, and it was not until 25 September 1995 that ricin was considered the cause. On that day, Farrar called police during a domestic dispute with his estranged wife, Debora Green, a 44-year-old non-practicing oncologist. The police report stated that due to her bizarre behavior, Green was taken to a psychiatric clinic that night. Finding castor beans in his wife's purse, Farrar turned the beans and sales receipt over to police. Green had purchased the castor beans through special order from a garden center in Kansas City, Missouri, and placed them in Farrar's food. It is unclear if she extracted the ricin or merely added the beans to the food. Later, Farrar had to undergo multiple heart and brain surgeries related to the poisoning (CNS, 2004).

In January 1997, Thomas Leahy was arrested for shooting his stepson in the face. In the basement of Leahy's home was a makeshift laboratory where, tests indicated, he had produced ricin. Mr. Leahy pleaded guilty to violating the Biological Weapons Anti-Terrorism Statute (Shea & Gottron, 2004).

In 1997, Internal Revenue Service (IRS) investigators searched the home of James Dalton Bell, a 39-year-old electronics engineer, and discovered a cache of chemicals, which included sodium cyanide (500 grams), diisopropyl flourophosphate, and a range of corrosive acids. Subsequent analysis of computer files confiscated from the residence revealed that Bell engaged in e-mail communications with a friend, Robert East, a 46-year-old merchant marine radio operator, that expressed a desire to obtain castor beans to see if they could extract ricin. Bell had already acquired the home addresses of nearly 100 federal employees from the Federal Bureau of Investigation (FBI), IRS, and Bureau of Alcohol, Tobacco and Firearms; and computer files from voter registration. Bell was in the process of producing and acquiring chemical and biological agents (CNS, 2004).

In 1998, three members of a splinter group of the North American Militia in Michigan were arrested on weapons and conspiracy charges. The April 1998 indictment was the result of an investigation involving an Alcohol, Tobacco, and Firearms (ATF) agent who infiltrated the group in March 1997. When federal law enforcement raided the homes of these men, they discovered an arsenal of weapons and a videotape. Produced in a cooking-show format, the tape gave instructions on how to manufacture bombs and other assorted militia-type weaponry, including a feature segment on how to extract ricin from castor beans. During the court proceedings, prosecutors drew attention to the ricin segment, stating that the men were "collecting information on the manufacture and use of ricin." However, other than the videotape, no materials associated with ricin production were found in any of the raids (CNS, 2004).

In 1998, Dwayne Lee Kuehl, 38, was arrested in Escanaba, Michigan, for producing ricin with intent to use it against an Escanaba city official. Keuhl was under investigation in connection with a 1 February 1988 fire that destroyed a business that he owned. While carrying out a search warrant at Kuehl's home and his rental property, police interviewed him. During the interview, Kuehl indicated that he had obtained the recipe and ingredients for the manufacture of ricin and made the poison in 1993. He also admitted that he made the ricin in order to kill James O'Toole, an Escanaba housing inspector. Police later found the ingredients for ricin manufacture, along with other toxic substances, at two separate residences owned by Keuhl (CNS, 2004).

In 2000, a South African expatriate, Dr. Larry Ford, killed himself in Orange County, California, apparently because he was sus-

Contemporary History of Ricin Use, *continued*

pected in the attempted murder of his business partner two days earlier. A biotechnology entrepreneur, Ford also happened to be a white supremacist with a passion for neo-Nazi William Pierce's novel "*The Turner Diaries*." He also had ties to several anti-government extremist groups. Investigations after his death revealed that Ford possessed an unusual and deadly arsenal that ranged from machine guns and explosives to biological agents and quantities of ricin (Anti-Defamation League, 2005).

In 1999, press reports indicated that FBI agents had apprehended a man in Tampa, Florida, for threatening to kill court officials and "wage biological warfare" in Jefferson County, Colorado. James Kenneth Gluck, 53, a former Colorado resident, sent a 10-page letter to Jefferson County judges threatening to kill them with a biological agent. He specifically identified one judge by name. FBI agents arrested Gluck on 5 November 1999 as he left a public library near his home in Tampa. Police, fire, and hazardous materials (HazMat) crews responded to the scene along with the FBI and blocked off Gluck's street. Upon searching his residence the next day, agents discovered that Gluck had the necessary ingredients to make ricin, though no refined ricin was actually found. They also found test tubes and beakers, as well as the "anarchist's cookbook" and books on biological toxicology, in a makeshift laboratory in his home (CNS, 2004).

In August 2001, the FSB (Russian Federal Security Service) told the Itar-Tass news service it had intercepted a recorded conversation between two Chechen field commanders in which they discussed using homemade poisons against Russian troops. According to Itar-Tass, Chechen Brigadier General Rizvan Chitigov asked Chechen field commander Hizir Alhazurov, who is now living in the United Arab Emirates, for instructions on the "homemade production of poison" for use against Russian soldiers. Russian authorities reportedly raided Chitigov's home and seized materials, including instructions on how to use toxic agents to contaminate consumer

goods, a small chemical laboratory, three homemade explosives, two land mines, and 30 grenades. The confiscated papers reportedly also contained instructions on how to produce ricin from castor beans (CNS, 2004).

In 2002, Kenneth Olson was arrested for producing small amounts of ricin. He was found guilty of possession of a biological agent or toxin for use as a weapon, and sentenced to 13 years imprisonment (Shea & Gottron, 2004).

In January 2003, six Algerians were arrested at their apartment in London, United Kingdom on charges of "being in the possession of objects which give rise to reasonable suspicions of the intention of carrying out preparing, or instigating an act of terrorism" and for trying to "develop or produce a chemical weapon." Following the arrests, authorities discovered traces of ricin in the apartment located in Wood Green, located in northern London. They also discovered castor oil beans and equipment for crushing the beans. Those arrested are believed to be part of a terrorist cell known as the "Chechen network" which may have ties to the Algerian group behind the millennium bomb plots in the United States. Members of the cell are Algerians who received training in Chechnya and the former Soviet republic of Georgia. Five of the six arrested were identified as Mustapha Taleb, Mouloud Feddag, Sidali Feddag, Samir Feddag, and Nasreddine Fekhadji. Authorities arrested the suspects following a tip by French intelligence agencies, which had been following two of the men. Authorities stated that they believe the ricin discovered was only part of a larger batch that they believe was removed from the apartment before the arrests. Police stated that they were continuing to search for the missing ricin (CNS, 2004).

In October 2003, ricin was detected on an envelope processed in a Greenville, South Carolina mail facility. While no postal workers showed symptoms of ricin exposure, the facility was closed until environmental testing concluded that no facility contamination existed. The individual who mailed the ricin has not been identified. The Federal Bureau of

Contemporary History of Ricin Use, *continued*

Investigation has offered a $100,000 reward for information leading to the individual's arrest (Shea & Gottron, 2004).

In November 2003, the Secret Service reportedly intercepted an envelope addressed to the White House that contained ricin. The letter accompanying the ricin shared similar demands as those found in the South Carolina letter (Shea & Gottron, 2004).

In March 2003, FBI agents arrested Bertier Ray Riddle in Omaha, Arkansas on suspicion that he sent an envelope to the FBI field office in Little Rock that claimed to contain ricin. The front of the envelope sent on 19 February, reportedly stated that the letter was from a "Lee Alexander Hughes." The return address on the letter was Riddle's, but was signed "Sincerely not Bertie Ray Riddle." The front of the envelope also contained the phrase "If you make me have to claim to be my kidnapper's son, while depriving me of my correct identity you are going to hell!" The back of the envelope reportedly stated "Caution: contents contain ricin." A plastic bag containing a powder and dark flakes was discovered inside of the envelope. Test on the substance revealed that it was not ricin. On 12 March 2003, Riddle was indicted on two charges, one of mailing a threatening communication and the other of insulting a federal law enforcement officer and threatening to use a weapon of mass destruction (CNS, 2004).

In February 2004, ricin was detected in the Dirksen Senate Office Building in Washington, DC. It was believed that the toxin was mailed to the offices of the Republican Majority Leader Senator Bill Frist. The source of the ricin and motivation behind the letters still remains unknown (Shea & Gottron, 2004).

Additionally, reports have placed trace amounts of ricin in various locales in Afghanistan, and have claimed that Al Qaeda allied groups in Kurdish controlled areas of northern Iraq have experimented with ricin production.

Botulinum toxin exposure in humans can come as result of ingestion or inhalation. Inhalation represents the most threatening form of exposure, although it is considered to be quite difficult to disperse botulinum toxin through aersolized dispersal. JAMA reported that Aum Shinrikyo recognized the value of botulinum toxin early on and attempted aersol dispersal of the toxin at multiple sites between 1990 and 1995, including attempts on a U.S. military installations (Arnon et al., 2001). Iran, North Korea, and Syria are all believed to be in the process of developing and weaponizing botulinum toxin. According to the CIA, botulinum toxin would, at best, be effective in small-scale poisoning or through an aerosol attack in an enclosed space like a movie theatre (CIA, 2003).

Staphylococcal Enterotoxic B (SEB) is the toxin produced by the bacterium *Staphylococcus aureus* and causes the disease SEB intoxification, which is non-lethal but can cause incapacitating effects on the respiratory and gastro-intestinal systems. SEB occurs naturally and is one of the leading causes of food poisoning in the U.S. each year; however, SEB has been extensively studied for use as a bioweapon. In a weaponized form, SEB can be potentially life threatening producing a severe toxic shock. Any terrorist application of SEB would likely be to contaminate a food or low volume water supply, given the ease of production and its resistance to high temperatures and decontaminants (Cordas, 2003).

RADIOLOGICAL AND NUCLEAR WEAPONS OF MASS DESTRUCTION

As indicated by their popularity in worst case scenarios, radiological and nuclear weapons have recently joined chemical and biological weapons as the chief WMD threat to the United States. Radiological weapons use conventional high explosives to disperse radioactive material over an area. Although they can cause high casualty rates, radiological weapons are useful primarily as an area denial weapon, forcing evacuation and extensive decontamination. Nuclear weapons, which are completely different from radiological weapons, refer specifically to true nuclear warheads as opposed to nuclear material and are considered to be highly unlikely weapons for a terrorist organization because of their complexity, scarcity, and difficulty to locate and transport clandestinely.

While a nuclear weapon is the most destructive of all WMD, obtaining one poses the greatest difficulty for terrorist groups. The key obstacle to building such a weapon is the availability of a sufficient quantity of fissile material—either plutonium or highly enriched uranium. There are very few terrorist groups or sub-state actors that could create a crude nuclear weapon if given access to the necessary quantities of fissile material. A much less difficult nuclear option is a radiological weapon using conventional high explosives to disperse any type of radioactive material. This obviates the need for fissile material and the complexity of a nuclear bomb. A radiological device is unlikely to cause mass casualties, but it could still have very significant radiation contamination effects if well-targeted.

The chief radiological or nuclear threat to homeland security is the detonation of a "dirty bomb." Also known as a radiological dispersal device (RDD), a dirty bomb combines a conventional explosive, such as dynamite, with radioactive material. This is very different from a nuclear weapon, which requires a much greater level of expertise to develop and detonate. In most instances, the conventional explosive itself would have more immediate lethality than the radioactive material. The radiation level created by most radiological sources would not produce enough radiation to kill people or cause severe illness. However, certain radioactive materials, dispersed in the air, could contaminate up to several city blocks, creating fear and possibly panic and requiring potentially costly cleanup. Prompt, accurate, non-emotional public information might prevent the panic sought by terrorists.

U.S. STRATEGIES TO COMBAT WEAPONS OF MASS DESTRUCION

The U.S. strategy for interdicting weapons of mass destruction is based largely on two documents, the National Strategy to Combat Weapons of Mass Destruction, released by the White House in 2002, and the report of the Commission on the Intelligence Capabilities of the United States Regarding Weapons of Mass Destruction, which was released in an unclassified form in March 2005. Both of these reports outlined failures of the U.S. law enforcement and intelligence communities in combating WMD and made recommendations for how the U.S. can improve its overall effectiveness.

The White House presented an approach to combating WMD that was based on three pillars:

1. Counterproliferation

2. Nonproliferation

3. WMD Consequence Management

Counterproliferation is the offensive strategy of the United States to actively counter the threat and use of WMD by states and terrorists against the U.S. and its interests. Included in counterproliferation is an active effort to interdict the spread of WMD between and among states, terrorist organizations, and criminal groups. This effort will be largely based on the work of U.S. intelligence agencies and personnel to support military operations that will eliminate individuals, sub-state groups, and even hostile nations that actively proliferate WMD material. Counterproliferation will require an open policy of deterrence so that hostile forces seeking to use WMD against the U.S. will recognize that they will face overwhelming force, including the potential use of nuclear weapons by the U.S. In instances where deterrence is not an achievable strategy (i.e., when dealing with groups like al Qaeda whose operatives are not usually concerned with death), counterproliferation includes taking a defensive posture that can help mitigate the effects of a WMD attack. Programs like advanced air defense and the development of new technologies to defeat WMD capabilities of hostile forces will be developed.

Nonproliferation is the diplomatic strategy of the United States that supports and advocates its counterproliferation policies. In short, this means working diplomatically to dissuade supplier states (such the nuclear supply network from Dr. A. Q. Kahn in Pakistan) from cooperating with proliferant states (such as North Korea, Iran, and Syria) and induce proliferant states to end their WMD and missile programs. There are several existing diplomatic regimes through which the United States will focus its nonproliferation diplomacy. To combat nuclear nonproliferation, the International Atomic Energy Agency and the Nuclear Nonproliferation Treaty will be strengthened

Figure 11.2 CBRNE Threat Spectrum

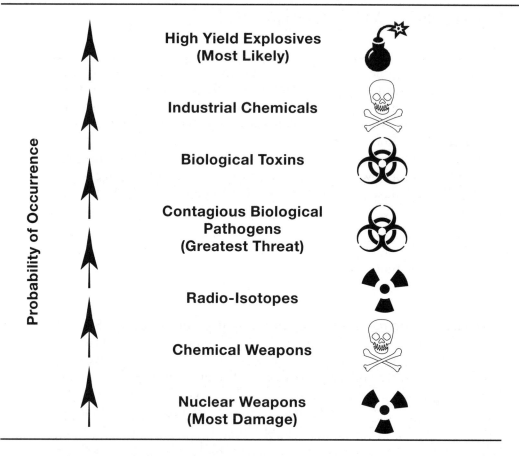

through the passage of additional diplomatic protocols and appropriate increases in funding. To combat chemical and biological proliferation, the United States will try to strengthen the Biological Weapons Convention and the international organizations that work to end the use of chemical and biological weapons. Missile proliferation will be combated by strengthening the Missile Technology Control Regime and urging universal adherence to the International Code of Conduct Against Ballistic Missile Proliferation.

WMD Consequence Management is the homeland security component of the U.S. Strategy to Combat WMD and is concerned with domestic preparedness for responding to a WMD attack on U.S. soil or against U.S. interests abroad. Beginning with the creation of the National Incident Management System (NIMS), the Department of Homeland Security has taken the lead in responding to a possible WMD event. Steps taken to date include:

- Working with the providers to prepare them for responding to a catastrophic terrorist event

- Working to enable stable and interoperable communication systems for first responders

- Augmenting national vaccine and pharmaceutical stockpiles that would be necessary for responding to a biological or chemical attack

- Train first responders in handling mass decontamination for exposure to chemical, biological, or radiological agents

- Increasing the role of the U.S. military in civil support operations for responding to a WMD attack

Beyond the creation of national strategies to combat, respond, and manage WMD events, the most important work to date on the issue of WMD has been the workings of the Commission on the Intelligence Capabilities of the United States Regarding Weapons of Mass Destruction. This commission, following in the steps of the 9/11 Commission, examined the capabilities and challenges of the U.S. Intelligence Community to collect, process, analyze, produce, and disseminate information concerning the capabilities, intentions, and activities of such foreign powers relating to the design, development, manufacture, acquisition, possession, proliferation, transfer, testing, potential or threatened use, or use of Weapons of Mass Destruction, related means of delivery, and other related threats of the 21st century. The WMD Commission report made 74 recommendations to the President, the majority of which advised on how to best reconfigure and manage the U.S. Intelligence Community. Those that deal specifically with the WMD threat will be reviewed here.

The WMD Commission recommended to the President that a National Counterproliferation Center (NCPC) be created to replace the Counterproliferation Center that existed at the CIA. Unlike the National Counterterrorism Center, which has operational, as well as managerial, roles the NCPC should primarily play a management and coordination function by overseeing analysis and collection on nuclear, biological, and chemical weapons across the Intelligence Community. The NCPC was officially created in June 2005 and will reportedly have fewer than 100 people assigned.

Biological and Nuclear weapons were specifically singled out in the WMD Commission report as areas of emphasis for the U.S. Intelligence Community. The Commission recommended that the U.S. work to expand its resources within the biological sciences community to meet the threat that biologi-

U.S. Marines from the Combined Joint Task Force along with Australian service members join together in training while wearing Nuclear, Biological, Chemical (NBC) suits at Camp Doha, Kuwait during Operation Enduring Freedom. *Courtesy of Department of Defense, photo by CWO2 William D. Crow, USMC.*

cal agents pose to homeland security. The Departments of Homeland Security and Health and Human Services have been directed to work with the Director of National Intelligence to create a Community-wide National Biodefense Initiative. The WMD Commission also recommended monitoring insecure nuclear weapons and materials, or "loose nukes"—mainly in the former Soviet Union but also potentially in other nations. Private proliferation networks such as those run by Pakistani nuclear scientist A.Q. Khan are also priorities for U.S. counterproliferation efforts.

KEY CONCEPTS

- The use of Weapons of Mass Destruction (WMDs) is the most serious threat since 9/11, although such use is quite rare. Several worst case scenarios have been presented regarding WMDs, and each scenario used a radiological/nuclear device.

- Chemical WMDs use toxic properties of chemical substances to kill, injure, or incapacitate others. There are eight classes of chemical WMDs including blister agents (mustard gas), blood agents (cyanide), choking agents (chlorine gas), nerve agents (sarin and VX), lacrimators (pepper spray), vomiting agents, irritants, and psychotropic compounds. There are several ways to disseminate chemical weapons, including explosives or munitions in an aerosolized form.

- Biological WMDs use infectious microorganisms (bacteria, virus, or other disease-causing organism) or toxin found in nature that reproduces within the host to cause an incapacitating or fatal illness. There are six classes of biological WMDs, including bacterial agents (anthrax, plague), viruses (smallpox), rickettsiae (Q-fever), toxins (ricin), Chlamydia, and fungi.

- Radiological WMDs use conventional high explosives to disperse radioactive material over an area. Nuclear WMDs refer to true nuclear warheads as opposed to nuclear material. The main threat is form the detonation of a "dirty bomb," also known as a radiological dispersion device (RDD) which combines a conventional explosive with radioactive material.

- The approach taken by the White House to combat weapons of mass destruction includes counterproliferation, nonproliferation, and WMD consequence management.

ADDITIONAL READINGS

America the Vulnerable by Stephen Flynn.

Chemical Weapons Convention (signed in 1993).

9/11 Commission Report.

The National Strategy to Combat Weapons of Mass Destruction.

Nuclear Nonproliferation Treaty.

RELATED WEBSITES

Federation of American Scientists (FAS) www.fas.org

Center for Disease Control and Prevention (CDC) www.cdc.gov

North Atlantic Treaty Organization (NATO) www.nato.int

Journal of the American Medical Association (JAMA) www.jama.ama-assn.org

Central Intelligence Agency (CIA) www.cia.gov

International Atomic Energy Agency (IAEA) www.iaea.org

FEMA's National Incident Management System (NIMS) www.fema.gov/nims

REFERENCES

Arnon, S.S, R. Schecte, T.V. Inglesby, D.A. Henderson, J.G. Bartlett, M.S. Ascher, E. Eitzen, A.D. Fine, J. Hauer, M. Layton, S. Lillibridge, M.T. Osterholm, T. O'Toole, G. Parker, T.M. Perl, P.K. Russell, D.L. Swerdlow, and K. Tonat (2001). "Botulinum Toxin as a Biological Weapon." *Journal of the American Medical Association*, 285:8.

Anti-Defamation League (2005). "Extremists and the Ricin Threat." Retrieved December 1, 2005 from: http://www.adl.org/learn/news/ricin_threat.asp?print=true.

Byrnes, M.E., P.M. Tierno, and D.A. King (2003). *Nuclear, Chemical, and Biological Terrorism*. CRC Press: Boca Raton, FL.

Cashman, J.R. (2000). *Emergency Response to Chemical and Biological Agents*. CRC Press: Boca Raton, FL.

Center for Nonproliferation Studies (2004). Chronology of Incidents Involving Ricin. Retrieved December 1, 2005 from: http://cns.miis.edu/pubs/reports/ricin_chron.htm.

Central Intelligence Agency (2003). Terrorist CBRN: Materials and Effects. Document Number: CTC-2003-40058.

Chlorine Chemistry Council (2005). "Background: September 13, 2005 Hazmat Transportation Protest." Retrieved December 1, 2005 from http://c3.org/news_center/media_kits/security/background.html.

Cook, T. (1999). *No Place to Run: The Canadian Corps and Gas Warfare in the First World War.* UBC Press: Vancouver, BC.

Croddy, E. (2001). *Chemical and Biological Warfare—A Comprehensive Survey for the Concerned Citizen*. Copernicus Books: New York, NY.

Cordas, S. (2003). Responding to the Threat of Weapons of Mass Destruction, Part III & IV. University of North Texas Health Science Center at Fort Worth. Retrieved December 1, 2005 from: http://www.hsc.unt.edu/education/pace/WMD3-4.pdf.

Council on Foreign Relations (2005). "Terrorism Q & A—VX." Retrieved December 1, 2005 from: http://cfrterrorism.org/weapons/vx.html.

Council on Foreign Relations (2005a). "Terrorism Q & A—Smallpox." Retrieved December 1, 2005 from: http://cfrterrorism.org/weapons/smallpox.html.

Federation of American Scientists (2005). Special Weapons Primer—Biological Warfare Agents. Retrieved December 1, 2005 from: http://www.fas.org/nuke/intro/bw/agent.htm.

General Accounting Office (1999). *Combating Terrorism: Need for Comprehensive Threat and Risk Assessments of Chemical and Biological Attacks.* United States General Accounting Office. GAO-NSIAD-99-13.

Kushner, H. (2004). *Encyclopedia of Terrorism.* Sage Publications: New York, NY.

Kortepeter, M. and G. Parker (1999). "Potential Biological Weapons Threats." *Emerging Infectious Diseases,* Vol. 5, No. 4, July-August 1999, pp. 523-527.

Lama, A. (1999, March 16). "HEALTH-PERU: PREVENTION KEEPS CHOLERA IN CHECK." IPS-Inter Press Service.

Langford, R.E. (2004). *Introduction to Weapons of Mass Destruction—Radiological, Chemical, and Biological.* Hoboken, NJ: Wiley-IEEE.

Levine, S. and S. Horwitz (2005, October 2). "Test Results Cited in Delay of Mall Alert." *Washington Post,* B01.

NATO (1996). *HANDBOOK ON THE MEDICAL ASPECTS OF NBC DEFENSIVE OPERATIONS.* FM 8-9/ AMedP-6(B).

Office of Technology Assessment (1993). *Technologies Underlying Weapons of Mass Destruction, OTA-BP-ISC-115.* U.S. Government Printing Office: Washington, DC.

Olson, K.B. (1999). "Aum Shinrikyo: Once and Future Threat?" Special Issue of *Emerging Infectious Diseases*, Vol 5, No. 4. Centers for Disease Control: Atlanta, GA.

Robertson, N. (2002). "Tapes Shed New Light on bin Laden's Network." CNN In-Depth. August, 19, 2002.

Shea, D. and F. Gottron (2004). Ricin: Technical Background and Potential Role in Terrorism. Congressional Research Service. Code #: RS21383.

Shea, D.A. and F. Gottron (2004). *Small-Scale Terrorist Attacks using Chemical and Biological Agents: An Assessment Framework and Preliminary Comparisons.* CRS Report for Congress. Congressional Research Service, The Library of Congress.

Sidell, F.R. (2005). "Chemical Agent Terrorism." Online Resources—NBC-MED. Retrieved December 1, 2005 from: http://www.nbc-med.org/SiteContent/MedRef/OnlineRef/Other/chagter.html

SITE Institute (2005).

State of North Dakota (2005). Department of Health—Emergency Preparedness and Response. Retrieved December 1, 2005 from: http://www.health.state.nd.us/EPR/public/viral/VEEFacts.htm.

Tucker, J.B. (2001). *Smallpox: From Eradicated Disease to Bioterrorist Threat.* Atlantic Monthly Press: New York, NY.

United States Army Institute of Infectious Disease (2005). "Biological Agent Information Papers—Brucellosis." Retrieved December 1, 2005 from the NBC Information Server at: http://www.nbc-med.org/SiteContent/MedRef/OnlineRef/GovDocs/BioAgents.html.

Weintraub, P. (2002). *Bio-Terrorism—How to Survive the 25 Most Dangerous Biological Weapons.* Citadel Press: New York, NY.

The Council on Foreign Relations.

U.S. Central Intelligence Agency (1998). Chemical/Biological/Radiological Incident Handbook.

Part IV

Homeland Security and Beyond

Although the 9/11 attacks were the impetus behind creating the Department of Homeland Security, the security of the continental United States goes beyond counterterrorism and counterproliferation. As the country saw in late August and September 2005, more traditional threats such as natural disasters can be just as devastating and costly as a major terrorist attack. The 2005 hurricane season was the costliest in U.S. history and the Department of Homeland Security quickly found that it was not adequately structured to manage or respond to a natural disaster incident on the scale of Hurricanes Katrina and Rita. Some speculated that the counterterrorism focus of DHS crippled its ability to respond to natural disasters and more traditional threats to critical infrastructure and homeland security. Officially, it is still too early to tell. Chapter 12 addresses the role of DHS in responding to natural disasters and presents the response to Hurricane Katrina in Louisiana and Mississippi and Hurricane Rita in Texas as case studies managing these events.

Chapter 13 surveys the various legislation passed or amended since the 9/11 attacks that directly impact U.S. Homeland Security. The issue of individual privacy and the balance of fighting a war on terrorism with the civil liberties of individuals is an issue that will remain in the public spotlight and in national debate. Great detail is paid to the USA PATRIOT Act, which was one of the first pieces of legislation passed in the wake of the 9/11 attacks. This is probably the most controversial but least understood pieces of homeland security legislation that has been passed by Congress. It remains to be seen whether the most controversial aspects of the legislation, the Surveillance Procedures detailed in Title II of the Act, will be cemented into law or whether they will not be renewed as the legislation comes up for review. In addition to the USA PATRIOT Act legislation, the Foreign Intelligence Surveillance Act (FISA), the Communications Assistance for Law Enforcement Act (CALEA), and the Terrorism Risk Insurance Act (TRIA) are reviewed because they directly affect the law enforcement, intelligence, and first responder communities charged with homeland Security.

This text concludes with a discussion of future critical issues that concern Homeland Security. Many of these issues have been covered in the book previously, but they are dynamic and will be changing in the future. The issue of intelligence reform is not complete and there will likely be several more iterations before the homeland security transformation is complete. The new Director of National Intelligence (DNI) is only beginning to impact the way the U.S. Intelligence Community is structured and there are several power struggles looming between the DNI, the Department of Defense, and the Department of Homeland Security. The terrorist threat is constantly changing as U.S. counterterrorism efforts are succeeding throughout the world. It is still too early to tell how the situation in Iraq will affect global terrorism in the next 5-10 years. Finally, the Department of Homeland Security still has a long way to go in its ability to manage and respond to natural disasters.

Chapter 12

Responding to Natural Disasters

FALL 2005 HURRICANE SEASON

As a result of the government's reorganization following 9/11 the Department of homeland Security was vested with responsibility for handling natural disasters and the threat of pandemic disease outbreaks. The Federal Emergency Management Agency (FEMA) came under DHS jurisdiction, and in one of its earliest actions was responsible for the 2005 hurricanes that struck Louisiana and Texas. The following case studies of Hurricanes Katrina and Rita illustrate some of the problems associated with mounting a response to major disasters.

Hurricane Katrina

Reorganization of the government following 9/11 and the establishment of the Department of Homeland Security brought with it responsibility for the Federal Emergency Management Agency (FEMA), which is the lead federal agency responsible for responding to natural disasters. It was not until August 29, 2005, when Hurricane Katrina struck land in Louisiana wreaking havoc on the City of New Orleans and adjoining towns and cities as far away as Mississippi, that shortfalls in emergency planning came to light. The result left tens of thousands of citizens, most of whom refused to leave their homes, awash in water that at times rose to extraordinarily high levels and destroyed houses and infrastructure throughout the region. It is estimated that Hurricane Katrina produced storm surges as high as 27 feet in Mississippi, and stretched up to 12 miles inland along bays and rivers and 6 miles inland in coastal portions of the state. In Louisiana, storm surges and breaks in levees resulted in approximately 80 percent of the city flooded up to depths of 20 feet.[1] Hurricane Katrina is considered the costliest hurricane and the fifth deadliest hurricane on record in the United States. As of December 2005, an estimated 1,336 fatalities were a result, either direct or indirect, of Hurricane Katrina. This figure includes 1,090 fatalities in Louisiana, 228 in Mississippi, 14 in Florida, 2 in Georgia, and 2 in Alabama. It is important to note that the exact number of fatalities caused by the storm will probably never be known and, as of press time, there are approximately 4,000 individuals still considered missing from the storm. Hurricane Katrina is responsible for approximately $75 billion in damages, with approximately $20-$60 billion of that total to be of insured losses.

Breaches in the levees protecting the city, which lies as much as ten feet below the water line, left thousands of people struggling for their lives. Just what went wrong in the response of local, state, and federal authorities continues to be a subject of much debate, but one thing is clear: the country was not prepared for a disaster of this magnitude, and the ensuing lack of planning, coordination, communication and response proved to be too little too late.

Hurricane Katrina—Crisis Leadership

Hurricane Katrina struck with all of the fury a severe hurricane would be expected to deliver. Katrina devastated the offices, equipment, fleet, communications, and homes of the emergency services community in the Greater New Orleans area. As soon as the winds died down, the levee system began to breach ultimately flooding over half of area homes and businesses. As emergency service personnel scrambled to assess and react, a portion of the cities residents who had not evacuated began looting and in some cases violently resisted police attempts to restore order, with two New Orleans Police officers shot in a single night, one fatally.

In the days that followed, law enforcement leadership worked to reestablish command and control over an area of devastation in the tens of thousands of square miles. Complicating the matter was the continual evolving of the emergency as one problem morphed into another. For the Louisiana State Police (LSP), substantial successes in adjusting and responding to the many challenges were realized due to many factors. Among these factors is planning.

Hurricanes are no new threat to Louisiana. Katrina was a matter of scale and magnitude over the ability and resources of the response community. However, planning a response for mass disasters of human or natural origin requires thinking through the process and exercising the plans. The state's evacuation plan was implemented flawlessly and removed over one million persons from the New Orleans area before Katrina made landfall. Foreseeable consequences were planned for and resources were checked and pre-staged for rapid and effective deployment. Planning continued throughout the response as new problems emerged and new capabilities were deployed.

Another important factor in the Katrina response was relationships. LSP was able to coordinate restoration of vital communications due to their standing relationships with service providers and state regulators. Moreover, strong partnerships with the Department of Defense (DoD) Advanced Concepts Technology Demonstration on cutting edge command and control technologies and practices resulted in the instant coordination with military and National Guard elements deployed to the area. Additionally, DoD Northern Command personnel and their prime contractors were sent to assist LSP and provided invaluable communications augmentation to LSP. These DoD offices were essential to restoring command and control. When Hurricane Rita struck in the midst of the Katrina response,

Hurricane Katrina—Crisis Leadership, *continued*

having the considerable assets of USNORTH-COM the ground was a key part of the LSP preparation and response to Rita's effects.

Adaptability in an emergent environment is the difference between success and failure. Further, subordinates desire their leaders to be in control and not stunned at an evolving situation. LSP leaders showed great adaptability in taking over tasks that were both foreseeable and not. LSP took over tasks for the entire affected area for which they had not been given the responsibility in prior planning. For instance, flooding caused telephone and power switches to fail, disabling area 911 systems. Almost instantly, 911 calls for most of the affected area began ringing at LSP Troop and Headquarters offices. A classroom at LSP headquarters was turned into a 911 center, untrained civilian employees volunteered to take the calls and compile the data onto a data base hastily constructed onto the new Homeland Security Information Network (HSIN). Distribution of 911 call lists were then distributed to proper agencies, sometimes by hand delivery.

Finally, the individual tenacity of the average responder was what held the line for LSP. With over sixty (60) of its officers homeless in the hours immediately following Katrina, not one Trooper or Department of Public Safety Police Officer failed to miss a single roll call, even though some of them reported to work not knowing where their families were. LSP leaders were able to instill and maintain a devotion to duty that is unsurpassed. Troopers poured in from across the state demanding to work in the ruins of a city where there was no power, clean water, or place to sleep, and no end to near death rescues. Depth of character is not situational. It is the result of a legacy of honorable and disciplined service.

Lt. Colonel Booth, Incident Commander,
Louisiana State Police

Although FEMA took the brunt of the criticism, resulting in the resignation of its Director, Michael Brown, following yet another catastrophe as a second hurricane, Rita, struck the coast of Texas and Louisiana three weeks later. In testimony before Congress, Brown heaped criticism on everyone from the Mayor of New Orleans, the Louisiana Governor, the media, and response of the federal government.

> My mistake was in recognizing that for whatever reason that we might want to discuss later, for whatever reason, Mayor Nagin and Governor Blanco were reticent to order a mandatory evacuation. If I, Mike Brown, individual, could have done something to convince them that this was the 'big one,' that they needed to order mandatory evacuation, I would have done it.[2]

To be sure, the results of Katrina and Rita displayed major weakness in the country's ability to respond to massive natural disasters. This brought into question overall planning efforts for mass evacuations, the role of the military and national guard, and the ability to cope with essential supply shortages—including water, food and gasoline—and the means of handling thousands of refugees. The problem was exacerbated by the collapse of the infrastructure in cities and towns affected by the hurricanes.

FEMA—An Organization In Disarray

The Federal Emergency Management Agency is responsible for responding to, planning for, and recovering from disasters. FEMA coordinates the work of federal, state, and local agencies in responding to floods, hurricanes, earthquakes, and other natural disasters. FEMA provides financial assistance to individuals and governments to rebuild homes, businesses, and public facilities; trains firefighters and emergency medical professionals; and funds emergency planning throughout the United States and its territories.Charged with charged with building and supporting the nation's emergency management system, FEMA is present at every stage of a disaster. It is important to note that FEMA is a not a first responder, but rather a coordinating agency.

The United States Federal Emergency Management Agency (FEMA) has existed in one form or another for more than 200 years. The Congressional Act of 1803 is largely hailed as the first piece of disaster legislation. This act provided assistance to a New Hampshire town following a devastating fire, and paved the way for national assistance agencies. Through the next century, ad hoc legislation was passed more than one hundred times in response to various natural disasters.

In 1932 President Hoover established the Reconstruction Finance Corporation, which, among other things, was given the authority to make disaster loans for repair and reconstruction of certain public facilities following an earthquake. Later, it was amended to include other types of natural disasters as well.

In 1934, the Bureau of Public Roads began to provide funding to highways and bridges damaged by natural disasters.

The Flood Control Act of 1944, as amended and supplemented by other flood control acts and river and harbor acts, authorizes various Corps of Engineers water development projects that have significant benefits for navigation and flood control and which could be operated consistent with other river uses.

The Federal Disaster Assistance Administration, part of Department of Housing and Urban Development (HUD) was created in the 1960s. The government added to its disaster-relief functions with the passage of the National Flood Insurance Act in 1968. This was followed by the 1974 Disaster Relief Act, which created the process of Presidential disaster declarations.

President Carter signed the 1979 Executive Order on July 20, 1979 which further consolidated federal disaster response, creating the Federal Emergency Management Agency (FEMA), which absorbed, among others, the Federal Insurance Administration, the National Fire Prevention and Control Administration, the National Weather Service Community Preparedness Program, the Federal Preparedness Agency of the General Services Administration and the Federal Disaster Assistance Administration activities from HUD. In addition FEMA took over civil defense responsibilities from the Defense Department's Defense Civil Preparedness Agency.

In 1993 President Bill Clinton elevated FEMA to a cabinet level position and named James Lee Witt as FEMA Director.

Following the Terrorist Attacks of 11 September 2001, President Bush created the Department of Homeland Security (DHS) to better coordinate between the different federal agencies that deal with law enforcement, disaster preparedness and recovery, border protection and civil defense. FEMA was absorbed into DHS as of 2003, and is now part of the Emergency Preparedness and Response Directorate of DHS. Prior to reorganization, the director of FEMA reported directly to the President, but this changed in March 2003 when the agency came under and reported to the Director of Homeland Security. Critics argued that this move, and the emphasis on counterterrorism, had a negative impact on FEMA's ability to respond to a natural disaster. FEMA currently employs more than 2,600 full time employees that are supplemented by more than 5,000 stand-by reservists.

Hurricane Rita

In September 2005 Hurricane Rita formed in the Atlantic Ocean and was projected to hit land just east of Galveston, Texas, bringing forth yet another problem as more than 2 million people from as far away as 100 miles from the coast took to the roads in the largest mass evacuation in the country's history. Media coverage of the first hurricane prompted an exodus that clogged highways and roads for days. To some degree the lessons of Katrina contributed to a much more effective government response at all levels, and despite extensive damage along the coast of Texas the loss of life was minimal. Unfortunately, Rita's path struck the coast of Louisiana, once again breaching the New Orleans levee that was being repaired by the Army Corps of Engineers. Once again the water level was rising.

A critical analysis of the nation's response to these natural disasters is beyond the scope of this book, but some understanding of the many organizations, groups, and agencies involved does provide an overview of what it takes to manage a major disaster, and the importance of prior planning, centralized communication, and the means of coping with large number of evacuees and their basic health and supply needs. The New Orleans situation also exposed the inadequacy of dealing with potential disease threats, repairing infrastructure, and bringing normalcy to a chaotic situation.

The following list is not all inclusive, but does illustrate the many entities involved in disaster relief:

- Federal Emergency Management Agency (Lead organization)
- Local police, fire, and emergency medical services (The front line first responders)[3]
- State authorities (Governor and state agencies, such as state police)
- National Guard (Under the authority of the governor to be activated)
- Civilian authorities at local level (Mayors, city managers, public service employees)
- Disaster response agencies (the Red Cross, Salvation Army and others)
- Private sector organizations (that supply power, communications, and supplies)
- Out of area and state responders (numerous private organizations and groups that respond to emergencies)[4]
- Out of area and state law enforcement agencies.[5]
- U.S. Military (Army, Navy, Air Force, Marines, Coast Guard)

- Federal law enforcement agencies (FBI, DEA, ATF, Customs)
- Other federal or local agencies and groups.

Consider the problems associated with coordinating and controlling the activities and assignments of such a large number of responders and individual leaders, each with some level of authority, and others with clear

First responders marked homes as cleared in New Orleans following Hurricane Katrina. *Photo Courtesy of FEMA.*

limitations as to their jurisdiction and organizational responsibilities.[6] Participants from numerous agencies described the days following the storm as one of chaos. Any number of command and control centers were established, frequently without crossover liaison, and much confusion as to what needed to be accomplished and when. Further, communications not only between groups, but at times within groups was frequently non-existent. Downed cell phone towers eliminated cell phone usage in many areas, downed power lines meant no electricity, and even when generators were present there was frequently no gas to operate them.

During the evacuation in Texas, hundreds of cars ran out of gas and were stranded alongside the highways and roads. Within a day stores and supermarkets were stripped of bottled water, bread and other consumables by local residents and the thousands of travelers. Thousands of people took refuge in hastily prepared refuge stations, many of which had only recently released evacuees from Louisiana.

In the aftermath of Hurricane Katrina the government, and particularly the legislative branch and President Bush came under increasing criticism for what was viewed initially as too little too late. Although criticism of the President following Rita was less, the massive traffic jam that stretched for almost 100 miles displayed the weaknesses associated with mass evacuation, and the inability of state and local government to manage an event of this size. Very quickly gas stations ran dry, stranding vehicles alongside the highways; grocery stores and supermarkets from as far away as 100 miles from the

Rescue personnel search for victims of Hurricane Katrina in flooded neighborhoods. *Courtesy of Department of Defense, photo by U.S. Navy Petty Officer 1st Class Robert McRill.*

coast ran out of bottled water, bread and other staples in less than 24 hours as people stocked up, some would say hoarded, basic food and other supplies. Health concerns developed due to the presence of certain bacteria, infections, and the large amount of sewage and waste in affected areas.

After action critiques and briefings identified as many as hundreds of minor and serious problems associated with disaster relief that occurred, including the lack of effective coordination and control, misinformation, the actions of crowds or displaced persons, the lack of adequate generators, looting, lines of authority, lack of proper training, inadequate supplies, and a lack of leadership or control from government authorities.

A major problem was the abandonment of posts by large numbers of police officers—who just "disappeared," and other key personnel, such as medical personnel, airport workers, and utility repair technicians. This was compounded by instances of sniping at helicopters and emergency personnel. Inadequate or uncertain policies on military rules of engagement frequently hampered their responses.

Despite procedures for searching and clearing widespread areas of destruction, the response resulted in many locations being searched many times on numerous occasions, duplicating relief efforts, and leaving other areas that were never searched because of confusion or misinformation. Some of the more egregious situations occurred when 34 bodies were later discovered in an elderly hospice, and the husband-wife owners of the facility were charged with negligent homicide after refusing offers to evacuate their patients, and then abandoning their patients during the storm; another case includes an investigation into the possibility of doctors and hospital staff euthanizing patients after 45 bodies were found in a hospital in New Orleans and reports were found that described these acts.

Ultimately, the Hurricanes Katrina and Rita exposed serious weaknesses in the country's ability to cope with a major relief operation. Critics pointed to the fear that, despite prior planning and training models, the country is not prepared to cope with a major terrorist attack

KEY CONCEPTS

- The Federal Emergency Management Agency (FEMA) is part of the Department of Homeland Security and is responsible for effectively managing federal response and recovery efforts following any national incident, including natural disasters.

- Hurricane Katrina, which struck the southern U.S. coast in September 2005, is considered the costliest and fifth deadliest hurricane in the history of the nation. The response to the disaster was uncoordinated and lacked preparation by local, state, and federal agencies.

- A few weeks after Hurricane Katrina, Hurricane Rita formed in the Atlantic Ocean and threatened the east Texas coast with another strong hurricane. More than two million began to leave the expected affected areas and became the part of the largest mass evacuation in the nation's history.

- There are numerous agencies involved in disaster relief situations, including FEMA; local police, fire, and emergency medical services; state authorities; National Guard; local civilian authorities; disaster response agencies; private sector organizations; out of area and state responders; military; and federal law enforcement agencies.

- Reports of chaos following Hurricane Katrina and during the mass evacuation of Hurricane Rita were reported, as well as a lack of communication between and among groups. FEMA took the brunt of the criticism for the response in both hurricanes, and special sessions of Congress were called to address the concerns.

ADDITIONAL READINGS

Brake, J. *Terrorism and the Military's Role in Domestic Crisis Management: Background and Issues for Congress.* (2001). CRS Report for Congress. Congressional Research Service, The Library of Congress.

RELATED WEBSITES

Federal Emergency Management Agency (FEMA) www.fema.gov

Department of Homeland Security (DHS) www.dhs.gov

REFERENCES

Tropical Cyclone Report compiled by the National Hurricane Center, December 20, 2005.

House Select Bipartisan Committee to Investigate the Preparation for and Response to Hurricane Katrina (2005). Statement of Michael D. Brown.

NOTES

[1]   From the *Tropical Cyclone Report* compiled by the National Hurricane Center, December 20, 2005.

[2]   FEMA Director Michael Brown, testifying before the Select Bipartisan Committee to Investigate the Preparation for and Response to Hurricane Katrina, September 27, 2005

[3] In New Orleans as many as 250 police officers in a force of almost 1,500 were investigated for abandoning their positions, as did many individuals in health care centers, hospitals, and other such facilities. In one case more than 34 elderly persons died after being abandoned in a nursing home facility.

[4] Some of these include teams that did animal search and rescue; tree removal; home and building "gutting"; and supplies replenishment.

[5] In New Orleans police personnel arrived from as far away as New York City and California to provide assistance.

[6] For example, police officers from various jurisdictions will frequently have different operating procedures and legal constraints. The military has specific rules of engagement, and limitations on their power and authority.

Chapter 13

Legal Issues in Homeland Security

INTRODUCTION

The Homeland Security Act of 2002, which created the Department of Homeland Security, was only one of several legislative actions passed in the wake of the 9/11 attacks. These legislative acts, covering everything from surveillance, technology acquisition, immigration, insurance, and environmental protection, have proven to be some of the most wide-ranging and controversial laws ever enacted. The Constitutionality of these laws has frequently been challenged by both partisan and non-partisan advocacy groups for their alleged intrusion into the private lives of American citizens. While the majority of judicial challenges to these acts have been upheld following judicial review, it is still too early to tell whether these legislative acts will stand up to judicial scrutiny over the long term.

The USA PATRIOT Act (an acronym for Uniting and Strengthening America by Providing the Appropriate Tools to Intercept and Obstruct Terrorism Act) is perhaps the most controversial and widely challenged of legislation passed following the 9/11 attacks. At more than 130 pages long and divided into 10 titles, the USA PATRIOT Act was the first significant homeland security legislation passed after the September 11, 2001 attacks.

Other legislative actions passed in the wake of the terrorist attacks on the World Trade Center and the Pentagon included the Terrorism Risk Insurance Act, which helped commercial property-casualty policyholders obtain terrorism insurance and give the insurance industry time to develop mechanisms to provide such insurance after the act expires on December 31, 2005, and the SAFETY Act (Support Anti-Terrorism by Fostering Effective Technologies Act of 2002), which was an attempt by Congress to encourage manufacturers or sellers of anti-terrorism technologies to continue to develop and deploy these technologies without fear of overwhelming civil liability.

Several laws that had been in place long before the September 11, 2001 attacks were amended and even expanded to assist the U.S. Government in its fight against terrorism. The Foreign Intelligence Surveillance Act (FISA), which was created in 1978 and described the procedures for requesting judicial authorization for electronic surveillance and physical search of persons engaged in espionage or international terrorism against the United States on behalf of a foreign power, was amended by the USA PATRIOT Act in 2002 and was a major political issue during the various congressional hearings into the September 11, 2001 attacks. The Communications Assistance for Law Enforcement Act (CALEA), which was enacted in 1994 to make it easier for law enforcement to wiretap digital telephone networks, has been amended to allow for emerging technologies not covered in the original legislative language, for instance Voice Over IP (VoIP) and Instant Messaging services. Even the Freedom of Information Act (FOIA), which was signed into law by President Lyndon B. Johnson in 1966, has been amended as a result of the September 11, 2001 attacks, largely through the creation of additional exemptions for homeland security.

Significant Legislative Legal Acts

USA PATRIOT Act

    a.   Overview

    b.   Title I—*Enhancing Domestic Security Against Terrorism*

    c.   Title II—*Enhanced Surveillance Procedures*

    d.   Title III—*International Money Laundering Abatement and Anti-Terrorist Financing Act of 2001*

    e.   Title IV—*Protecting the Border*

    f.   Title V—*Removing Obstacles to Investigating Terrorism*

    g.   Title VI—*Providing for Victims of Terrorism, Public Safety Officers, and Their Families*

    h.   Title VII—*Increased Information Sharing for Critical Infrastructure Protection*

    i.   Title VIII—*Strengthening the Criminal Laws Against Terrorism*

    j.   Title IX—*Improved Intelligence*

    k.   Title X—*Miscellaneous*

Foreign Intelligence Surveillance Act (FISA)

Terrorism Risk Insurance Act

Communications Assistance for Law Enforcement Act (CALEA)

This chapter will provide an overview of the major legislative acts related to homeland security and examine some of the legal issues that have arisen since the acts have been passed or amended. As the USA PATRIOT Act is by far the most sweeping and controversial of the post-9/11 legislation, the bulk of this chapter will be dedicated to exploring and understanding this piece of legislation and the concerns raised by its critics. Other legislative acts like the Terrorism Risk Insurance Act, and the SAFETY Act, as well as modifications to the Foreign Intelligence Surveillance Act, the Communications Assistance for Law Enforcement Act, and the Freedom of Information Act will be discussed in this chapter.

USA PATRIOT Act

Congress passed the USA PATRIOT Act (the Act) in response to the terrorists' attacks of September 11, 2001. The Act gives federal officials greater authority to track and intercept communications, both for law enforcement and foreign intelligence gathering purposes. It vests the Secretary of the Treasury with regulatory powers to combat corruption of U.S. financial institutions for foreign money laundering purposes. It seeks to further close our borders to foreign terrorists and to detain and remove those within our borders. It creates new crimes, new penalties, and new procedural efficiencies for use against domestic and international terrorists.

A portion of the Act addressed issues suggested originally in a Department of Justice proposal circulated in mid-September. The first of its suggestions called for amendments to federal surveillance laws, laws which govern the capture and tracking of suspected terrorists' communications within the United States. Federal law features a three tiered system, erected for the dual purpose of protecting the confidentiality of private telephone, face-to-face, and computer communications while enabling authorities to identify and intercept criminal communications.

The USA PATRIOT Act consists of 10 titles which, among other things:

- give federal law enforcement and intelligence officers increased short-term authority to gather and share evidence particularly with respect to wire and electronic communications;

- amend federal money laundering laws, with an emphasis on those involving overseas financial activities;

- incorporate acts of terrorism into new federal crimes, increase the penalties for existing federal crimes that relate to terrorism, and adjust existing federal criminal procedure to deal with the challenges of prosecuting terrorists

- modify immigration law to prevent foreign terrorists from entering the U.S., to detain foreign terrorist suspects at the borders, to deport foreign terrorists, and to provide immigration benefits to foreign victims of September 11; and

- authorize appropriations to enhance the capacity of immigration, law enforcement, and intelligence agencies to more effectively respond to the threats of terrorism.

Given the controversy surrounding this legislation and the sheer impact that it has on U.S. efforts against terrorism, espionage, and other threats to national security, it is useful to briefly examine each of the ten sections that make up the USA PATRIOT Act. What follows is a discussion of these ten titles and legislative developments relevant to the USA PATRIOT Act since its enactment in 2002.

Title I—Enhancing Domestic Security Against Terrorism

The first title of the USA PATRIOT Act expands the power of the U.S. government by amending prior legislative acts, increasing budgetary allocations to certain agencies responsible for counterterrorism, and made a commitment to social justice for all Americans in light of the September 11, 2001 terrorist attacks. The Posse Comitatus Act, originally enacted in 1878 to restrict military involvement in domestic law enforcement activities, was amended to allow an additional exception for circumstances where weapons of mass destruction beyond biological, chemical, or nuclear weapons are used against the United States. Clearly this exception would cover a scenario like the September 11, 2001 attacks where non-state actors turned a commercial airliner into a weapon of mass destruction by crashing it into a skyscraper.

The power of the President of the United States of America to confiscate property was also amended by in this section. Traditionally, the International Emergency Economic Powers Act, enacted in 1977 to prescribe what actions the President may take upon declaring a peace-time national emergency based on a foreign threat to the national security, foreign policy, or economy of the United States, gave the President the power to freeze or confiscate the assets of a foreign national or national responsible for the threat. The USA PATRIOT Act expanded these powers to allow the President to freeze or confiscate foreign property or assets in response to foreign aggression, regardless if the actors are state-sponsored. This essentially means that the President of the United States of America would have the power to freeze or confiscate the assets and/or property of any foreign person (such as Osama bin Laden), organization (such as al Qaeda), or nation (such as Taliban-ruled Afghanistan) which planned, authorized, aided or engaged in an attack against the U.S.

Title I amended the use of the Counterterrorism Fund, established by the United States after the 1995 terrorist attack on the Alfred P. Murrah Federal Building in Oklahoma City, to provide funding to rebuild facilities or capacities destroyed by terrorists, use financial rewards to capture or kill terrorists, and protect existing federal facilities from terrorism through risk assessments. The Federal Bureau of Investigation (FBI) received one of its first post-9/11 funding boosts with the approval of an additional $200 million for its Technical Support Center, which serves as a centralized technical resource for federal, state and local law enforcement in responding to the increased use of encryption in criminal cases. The U.S. Secret Service was mandated to implement the National Electronic Crime Task Force Initiative, which established a nationwide network of electronic crime task forces to protect against and investigate threats to critical infrastructure.

In the days following the September 11, 2001 terrorist attacks, there were widespread reports of violence, intimidation, and harassment against Muslim Americans, Arab Americans, and Americans from South Asia. The U.S. Congress recognized that these actions represented a major threat to the fabric of American society and used the first title of the USA PATRIOT Act to strongly condemn any violence or discrimination against Americans, regardless of color, creed, ethnicity, religion, or appearance.

Title II—Enhanced Surveillance Procedures

The United States has long afforded its law enforcement and intelligence agencies with powers of surveillance, although the scope of these powers have been curtailed since their enactment due to concerns about protecting the civil liberties of U.S. citizens. Surveillance techniques were initially prescribed for federal law enforcement agencies in Title III of the Omnibus Crime Control and Safe Streets Act of 1968 but has have been revised several times. Federal intelligence officials are afforded surveillance authority similar to federal law enforcement officials, but are authorized through the Foreign Intelligence Surveillance Act (FISA) enacted in 1978. It should be noted that the surveillance powers of federal law enforcement had been restricted since their enactment through either additional legislation or judicial review. These restrictions were eliminated and federal surveillance powers were expanded with the enactment of Title II of the USA PATRIOT Act.

It should not be surprising, then, that Title II is by far the most controversial section of the USA PATRIOT Act because it creates the potential for law enforcement and intelligence officials to make inroads into the private lives and daily activities of individuals. The surveillance powers created or expanded in Title II can be broken down into two categories, those that were to be renewed by Congress, and those that were not. Those to be renewed are known as *sunset provisions* because they expire after a designated period of time unless the U.S. Congress passes additional legislation to keep or reinstate those provisions. The sunset provisions in Title II were far more controversial and more intrusive into the privacy of individuals in the U.S. Of the 25 sections of Title II, 16 are sunset provisions that were scheduled to expire on December 31, 2005. These provisions were extended twice during negotiations in early 2006. In March 2006, the U.S. Congress passed, and President Bush signed, the USA PATRIOT Improvement and Reauthorization Act of 2005, which was modified by the USA PATRIOT Act Additional Reauthorization Act of 2006. This law made permanent 14 of the 16 sunset provisions, while extending provisions for sections 206 and 215 until 2009.

USA PATRIOT Act Provisions Subjected to Review and Expiration

- §201. Authority To Intercept Wire, Oral, And Electronic Communications Relating To Terrorism.
- §202. Authority To Intercept Wire, Oral, And Electronic Communications Relating To Computer Fraud And Abuse Offenses.
- §203(b), (d). Authority To Share Criminal Investigative Information.
- **§206. Roving Surveillance Authority Under The Foreign Intelligence Surveillance Act of 1978.**
- §207. Duration Of FISA Surveillance Of Non-United States Persons Who Are Agents Of A Foreign Power.
- §209. Seizure Of Voice-Mail Messages Pursuant To Warrants.
- §212. Emergency Disclosure Of Electronic Communications To Protect Life And Limb.
- §214. Pen Register And Trap And Trace Authority Under FISA.
- **§215. Access To Records And Other Items Under FISA.**
- §217. Interception Of Computer Trespasser Communications.
- §218. Foreign Intelligence Information. (Lowers standard of evidence for FISA warrants.)
- §220. Nationwide Service Of Search Warrants For Electronic Evidence.
- §223. Civil Liability For Certain Unauthorized Disclosures.
- §224. Sunset. (self-cancelling)
- §225. Immunity For Compliance With FISA Wiretap.

Sections in bold will be subjected to additional sunset provisions in 2009. All other provisions were made permanent in 2006.

Many of the sunset provisions in Title II were designed to improve the short-term efficiency and effectiveness of law enforcement and intelligence agencies charged with counterterrorism. The Omnibus Crime Control and Safe Streets Act of 1968, which was the legislation that prescribed the procedures for law enforcement to intercept wire, oral, or electronic communications, was modified by the USA PATRIOT Act to include terrorism, computer fraud, and abuse offenses. This does not mean that law enforcement and intelligence officers were not allowed to intercept wire, oral, or electronic communications, only that they had to go through a longer and often more difficult review process.

This section also eliminated the bureaucratic wall that had historically separated federal law enforcement officers from federal intelligence officers. Prior to the passage of Title II of the USA PATRIOT Act, there was a general prohibition on sharing information and intelligence on the actions and activities of terrorists or foreign agents. An exception was created that allowed for evidence collected through means of interception or through presentation to a grand jury to be shared with federal intelligence officers, provided that it was related to actions that pose a threat to national security (i.e., espionage, terrorism, hostile actions by foreign powers). This provision also applies to the evidence collected in investigations and operations against foreign intelligence that are governed by the Foreign Intelligence Surveillance Act (FISA).

Several protocols of FISA and intercept operations were extended in Title II of the USA PATRIOT Act. For instance, surveillance orders were extended from 90 days to 120 days, with an option to extend for up to one year, and physical search orders, these are the operations where federal officials search (often clandestinely), were extended from 45 to 90 days. Further, telephone and communications providers are compelled to provide credit card, subscriber information, and other payment details on terrorists or foreign agents when presented with a subpoena from a federal law enforcement official or when an emergency involving immediate danger of death or serious physical injury to any person exists.

The use of pen register and trap and trace devices, which are tools used by intelligence and law enforcement officials to secretly identify the source and destination of telephone calls on a particular phone, were expanded in Title II of the USA PATRIOT Act beyond the mere facilities of suspected terrorists or foreign agents. Ostensibly, this means that any potential phone, within reason, that a terrorist or foreign agent might use would qualify a pen register or trap and trace devise under the revised FISA and communication intercept rules. Electronic communications like e-mail and instant messaging now receive the same treatment as telephone conversations under this section of Title II.

Title II of the USA PATRIOT Act also changed the way that search warrants are secured and carried out. Historically, federal law enforcement officials were required to obtain a warrant within the district where the property was located. An investigator, for example, located in Boston who was investigating a suspected terrorist in that city, might have to seek a suspect's electronic e-mail from an Internet service provider (ISP) account located in California. The investigator would then need to coordinate with agents, prosecutors and judges in the district in California where the ISP is located to obtain a warrant to search. Under the revised rules, the court where the investigation originated can issue a search warrant without consulting the appropriate legal organ where the warrant will be served.

Title III—International Money Laundering Abatement and Anti-Terrorist Financing Act of 2001

Terrorist financing quickly became one of the key investigative areas for counterterrorism officials in the days and weeks after the September 11, 2001 attacks. The cliche "Follow the Money" quickly became the mantra of terrorism investigators as it became obvious that financial transactions were oftentimes the best leads that terrorism investigators had to work from. However, the methods used by al Qaeda and other terrorist organizations from the Middle East were different from the money laundering methods used by more traditional criminal organizations. For instance, the system of Islamic Banking and alternative remittance schemes like *hawala* presented substantial difficulties for American investigators, both procedurally and substantively. Title III was enacted to empower investigators in their hunt to trace terrorist financial transactions while hurting the terrorist organizations in their attempts to raise, save, and transfer funds.

Title III addresses several issues of jurisdiction and scope that present in most terrorism cases. First, federal jurisdiction is expanded to cover money laundering transactions related to terrorism regardless of the where or how the money was laundered. Reporting mechanisms were created to track suspicious transactions from private banks and foreign shell banks.

The forfeiture powers of the U.S. Government were strengthened by this section. This includes funds held in offshore offices of foreign banks as well as foreign bank agencies and branches operating in the United States. Forfeiture was also extended to property derived from or traceable to violations of felonious controlled substance laws of foreign nations. These provisions are specifically intended to give the U.S. Government the power to seize many of the fund-raising assets of foreign terrorist organizations.

Title III also imposed regulatory procedures on financial institutions operating in the United States. Chief among these regulations was the requirement that each institution develop an anti-money laundering program complete with an audit function to test institutional programs. Securities Brokers and Dealers received specific regulations requiring them to complete Suspicious Activity Reports (SARs) for any suspicious activities they observe related to money laundering or terrorist financing.

Alternative remittance systems were targeted by Title III, although it will be difficult to enforce regulations underground, trust-based interpersonal banking systems. Title III subjected to mandatory records and reports on monetary instruments transactions any licensed sender of money or any other person who engages as a business in the transmission of funds, including through an informal value transfer banking system or network (e.g., hawala) of people facilitating the transfer of money domestically or internationally outside of the conventional financial institutions system.

Title IV—Protecting the Border

The United States shares geographic borders with two nations, Mexico and Canada, that together represent one of the most daunting post-9/11 homeland security challenges. The land border with Mexico is 1,989 miles long with more than 40 official points of entry and is the thoroughfare for more than $650 million in cross-border trade per day. The U.S. Bureau of Transportation Statistics estimated that in 2002, 800,000 people arrive in the United States from Mexico. In 2001, there were more than 300 million two-way border crossing at 43 points of entry along the U.S./Mexico border.

The U.S. border with Canada spans more than 4,000 miles and is considered to be the longest undefended border in the world. Canada is the United States' largest trading partner with 2004 imports and exports totaling more than more than $445 billion. Migration across the U.S./Canada border is substantially less than the U.S./Mexico border; in 2004, nearly 94 million travelers were processed through the northern border.

Title IV of the USA PATRIOT Act addresses three principle areas related to protecting the U.S. borders:

- Expanding border security efforts along the northern border

- Enhancing provisions on immigration to cover terrorists

- Preserving immigration benefits for victims of the September 11, 2001 attacks

With more than 90 percent of immigration, customs, and border patrol resources being dedicated to the U.S. border with Mexico, the northern border was seen as the weakest link in border security. Title IV enabled federal agencies charged with border security to quickly address this weakness by hiring additional border security agents, reassigning existing agents, and paying overtime for agents already assigned to the northern border. The FBI and Attorney General were compelled to share criminal history information for use in the visa screening process. Title IV also addressed the technological malaise experienced by America's border security agencies. More than $50 million was appropriated to improve monitoring capabilities along the northern border and a mandate was passed to create electronic means of sharing information and intelligence among all agencies with responsibility for border security.

The September 11, 2001 attacks exposed some glaring inadequacies in the Immigration and Nationality Act for dealing with terrorists and suspected terrorists. Title IV of the USA PATRIOT Act revised this statute creating legislative authority to deny entry into the U.S. and deport any alien who is member of a terrorist organization or who is engaged in terrorist activities. Further, suspected terrorists are subject to mandatory detention until their deportation and have their habeas corpus rights limited. Entry and exit procedures for immigrants were revised and foreign passports were required to be machine readable within two years of passage of the Act.

For the families of those immigrants killed in the September 11, 2001 attacks, Title IV granted citizenship to immediate family members who had filed an application for citizenship prior to the terrorist attacks. This

Title V—Removing Obstacles to Investigating Terrorism

The U.S. Government recognized that the September 11, 2001 attacks, while not the first salvo from a new terrorist enemy, were indicative of the struggles against terrorism that the United States would face in the near future. With this in mind, Congress and the President wanted to remove any potential obstacles that law enforcement and intelligence officials might face in their counterterrorism investigations.

Title V authorized the Attorney General and the Department of State to pay rewards for assisting federal law enforcement agencies to combat terrorism and defend the Nation against terrorist acts. Domestic rewards are subjected to ceilings of either $100,000 or $250,000, depending on the circumstances, whereas rewards for assistance in international terrorism cases are not subject to any ceiling. International rewards are limited to information concerning the whereabouts of terrorist leaders and facilitating the dissolution of terrorist organizations.

The FISA is further amended in Title V to authorize consultation between intelligence officials and federal law enforcement officials in cases involving a foreign attack or act of sabotage or international terrorism by a foreign power or agent. This section specifically addresses the elimination of the "wall" that traditionally separated intelligence activities from law enforcement activities.

Title V also revises the National Security Letter procedures for securing confidential communication transaction records, financial reports, and credit information for counterterrorism purposes. Before the USA PATRIOT Act, the Director of the Federal Bureau of Investigation was required to request in writing (through a National Security Letter) subscriber information and toll billing records of a wire or electronic communication service provider. This process required federal investigators to battle a stiff bureaucracy and accumulate specific and articulable evidence of terrorism or espionage activities. Title V eliminated these burdensome standards and allows the FBI senior staff to write National Security Letters requiring only that the requested information be "relevant" to counterintelligence or counterterrorism operations.

Suspected terrorists also had their civil rights reduced in Title V. First, suspected terrorists can be compelled to have their DNA taken and exempted from falling under the DNA Analysis Backlog Elimination Act of 2000. Second, terrorists lose the right to have their educational records and individually identifiable educational survey responses withheld during a counterterrorism investigation or prosecution.

Title VI—Providing for Victims of Terrorism, Public Safety Officers, and Their Families

The first five titles of the USA PATRIOT Act were generally concerned with the powers and protections of federal law enforcement and intelligence officials and aiding the victims of terrorism. However, the September 11, 2001 attacks were most devastating on the public safety community (fire, medical, state and local police) because they were the first responders who gave their lives trying to save others. The Congress and the President recognized the importance of providing assistance to public safety officers and their families who were victimized by the terrorist attacks. Title VI enacted expedited processes for providing aid to public safety victims and their families and increased the overall benefit from $100,000 to $250,000.

Title VI also amended the Victims of Crime Act of 1984 to cover terrorism related crimes and established a $50 million antiterrorism emergency reserve fund within the Victims of Crime Fund.

Title VII—Increased Information Sharing for Critical Infrastructure Protection

Title VII amended the Omnibus Crime Control and Safe Streets Act of 1968 to extend Bureau of Justice Assistance regional information sharing system grants to state and local information sharing systems that enhance the investigation and prosecution abilities of participating Federal, State, and local law enforcement agencies in addressing multi-jurisdictional terrorist conspiracies and activities.

Title VIII—Strengthening the Criminal Laws Against Terrorism

Similar to the laws relevant to immigration, the September 11, 2001 attacks exposed substantial inadequacies in the Federal criminal law with regard to charging and prosecuting acts of terrorism. Congress and the President moved quickly to correct the Federal criminal law to allow for swift and certain adjudication, disposition, and punishment of terrorism suspects. Title VII amended the Federal criminal code to fully include acts of international terrorism, the actions of individuals conducting terrorist activities, and the activities of individuals who harbor terrorists, whether they have committed a terrorist act or are involved in the planning of terrorist attacks.

Terrorist organizations, operatives, and sympathizers materially involved with terrorist groups were made subject to the civil forfeiture of all assets, both foreign and domestic. Further jurisdiction for investigating and prosecuting terrorism cases was expanded beyond the territorial boundaries of the United States.

The statute of limitations was removed for certain types of terrorist acts that result in death or serious bodily injury, while all other terrorist actions are subject to an eight-year statute of limitations. Terrorist conspiracies are generally indistinguishable from the terrorist acts they are committing, and no distinction is made between attempted terrorist attacks and completed terrorist attacks. Acts of terrorism were also included in the predicate offense list for RICO (racketeering influenced and corrupt organizations) prosecutions.

Title VII also took up the issue of cyberterrorism revised existing prohibitions and penalties for fraud in connection with computers to include a wide range of cyberterrorism activities. Appropriations were designated to establish regional computer forensic laboratories, ostensibly to assist law enforcement and intelligence officials in counterterrorism investigations that involve computers or digital information

Title IX—Improved Intelligence

Title IX formally addresses several issues that have been partially covered in the preceding eight sections of the USA PATRIOT Act, namely the elimination of the "wall" between law enforcement and intelligence officials, and the need to share terrorism-related information between agencies. The Director of Central Intelligence (DCI) (and eventually the National Intelligence Director) was directed to establish requirements and priorities for foreign intelligence collected under the Foreign Intelligence Surveillance Act of 1978 and to provide assistance to the Attorney General (AG) to ensure that information derived from electronic surveillance or physical searches is disseminated for efficient and effective counterterrorism and counterintelligence purposes. Law enforcement officials were also mandated to share any foreign intelligence acquired during the course of a criminal investigation.

The controversial ruling by DCI Stansfield Turner that CIA agents not maintain intelligence relationships with individuals known to be involved in criminal activities like murder, narcotics trafficking, etc. was essentially repealed in Title IX. For the purposes of counterterrorism operations, intelligence officials were encouraged to develop the best possible sources without regard for a source's potentially criminal past actions.

Title X—Miscellaneous

This section of the USA PATRIOT Act is essentially a compendium of definitional issues, political statements, condolences, and assorted appropriations. Some of the more notable directives include:

- Defined critical infrastructure as systems and assets, whether physical or virtual, so vital to the United States that their incapacity or destruction would have a debilitating impact on security, national economic security, national public health or safety, or any combination of those matters

- Amended the Telemarketing and Consumer Fraud and Abuse Prevention Act to cover fraudulent charitable solicitations. Requires any person engaged in telemarketing for the solicitation of charitable contributions, donations, or gifts to disclose promptly and clearly the purpose of the telephone call

- Amended the Immigration and Nationality Act to make inadmissible into the United States any alien engaged in money laundering. Directed the Secretary of State to develop a money laundering watchlist which: (1) identifies individuals worldwide who are known or suspected of money laundering; and (2) is readily accessible to, and shall be checked by, a consular or other Federal official before the issuance of a visa or admission to the United States

THE FOREIGN INTELLIGENCE SURVEILLANCE ACT (FISA)

In 1978, Congress passed the Foreign Intelligence Surveillance Act (FISA), which establishes a separate legal regime for "foreign intelligence" surveillance. Title III (the "Wiretap Statute) outlines the strict guidelines regulating ordinary law enforcement surveillance, while FISA regulates the government's collection of "foreign intelligence" information in furtherance of U.S. counterintelligence. FISA was initially limited to electronic eavesdropping and wiretapping. In 1994 it was amended to permit covert physical entries in connection with "security" investigations, and in1998, it was amended to permit pen/trap orders. FISA can also be used to obtain some business records.

Under the Fourth Amendment, a search warrant must be based on probable cause to believe that a crime has been or is being committed. This is not the general rule under FISA: surveillance under FISA is permitted based on a finding of probable cause that the surveillance target is a foreign power or an agent of a foreign power, irrespective of whether the target is suspected of engaging in criminal activity. However, if the target is a "U.S. person," there must be probable cause to believe that the U.S. person's activities may involve espionage or other similar conduct in violation of the criminal statutes of the United States. Nor may a U.S. person be determined to be an agent of a foreign power "solely upon the basis of activities protected by the first amendment to the Constitution of the United States."

FISA established a special court—the Foreign Intelligence Surveillance Court (FISC)—composed of seven federal district court judges appointed by the Chief Justice for staggered terms and from different circuits. Individual judges of the FISC review the Attorney General's applications for authorization of electronic surveillance aimed at obtaining foreign intelligence information. The FISC meets two days monthly.

The proceedings are not adversarial: they are based entirely on the DOJ's presentations through its Office of Intelligence Policy and Review.

National Security Agency Domestic Spying Program

On December 16, 2005, the New York Times printed a story asserting that, under White House pressure and with an executive order from President George W. Bush, the National Security Agency, in an attempt to thwart terrorism, had been conducting warrantless phone-taps on individuals in the U.S. calling persons outside the country. Eventually it was revealed that the National Security Agency had been maintaining wiretaps on international communications, including some international communications to citizens located within the United States. Electronic surveillance on U.S persons without the approval of the United States Foreign Intelligence Surveillance Court is barred under the Foreign Intelligence Surveillance Act (FISA) unless additional congressional authorization is provided. There was no congressional authorization for these wiretaps, so there is some controversy over whether the National Security Agency was conducting wiretaps in violation of US laws. The Bush Administration, which authorized the warrantless wiretaps in 2002, maintained that such surveillance was authorized implicitly by the congressional Authorization for Use of Military Force of 2001. The White House has also argued that FISA does not apply during wartime because they believe Congress does not have authority to interfere in the "means and methods of engaging the enemy."

Under FISA, the Justice Department reviews applications for counterintelligence warrants by agencies before submitting them to the FISC. The Attorney General must personally approve each final FISA application. The application must contain, among other things:

- a statement of reasons to believe that the target of the surveillance is a foreign power or agent of a foreign power,

- a certification from a high-ranking executive branch official stating that the information sought is deemed to be foreign intelligence information, and that the information sought cannot reasonably be obtained by normal investigative techniques;

- statements regarding all previous applications involving the target;

- detailed description of the nature of the information sought and of the type of communication or activities to be subject to the surveillance;

- the length of time surveillance is required;

- whether physical entry into a premises is necessary, and

- proposed procedures to minimize the acquisition, use, and retention of information concerning nonconsenting U.S. persons.

For U.S. persons, the FISC judge must find probable cause that one of four conditions has been met:

1. the target knowingly engages in clandestine intelligence activities on behalf of a foreign power which "may involve" a criminal law violation;

2. the target knowingly engages in other secret intelligence activities on behalf of a foreign power under the direction of an intelligence network and his activities involve or are about to involve criminal violations;

3. the target knowingly engages in sabotage or international terrorism or is preparing for such activities; or

4. the target knowingly aids or abets another who acts in one of the above ways.

An order of the FISC may approve electronic surveillance of an agent of a foreign power for ninety days and of a foreign power for a year. Extensions may be granted on the same terms.

The records and files of the cases are sealed and may not be revealed even to persons whose prosecutions are based on evidence obtained under FISA warrants (except to a limited degree set by district judges' rulings on motions to suppress). There is no provision for the return of executed warrants to the FISC, for certification that the surveillance was conducted according to the warrant and its "minimization" requirements, or for inventory of items taken pursuant to a FISA warrant. As discussed previously, FISA has been substantially amended (and expanded) by the USA PATRIOT Act.

In sum, the USA PATRIOT act lowered the legal standard required for federal intelligence officials to conduct surveillance on suspected terrorists or foreign intelligence agents. The authority to grant a wiretap was significantly decentralized, allowing for so-called "roving" wiretaps which allows the interception of any communications made to or by an intelligence target without specifying the particular telephone line, computer or other facility to be monitored. Finally, the USA PATRIOT Act removed the pre-existing statutory requirement that the government prove the surveillance target is "an agent of a foreign power" before obtaining a pen register/trap and trace order under the FISA.

Communications Assistance for Law Enforcement Act (CALEA)

The U.S. Congress passed the Communications Assistance for Law Enforcement Act (CALEA) in 1994 to aid law enforcement in its effort to conduct surveillance of digital telephone networks. CALEA forced telephone companies to redesign their network architectures to make such surveillance easier. It expressly excluded the regulation of data traveling over the Internet.

Congress passed CALEA to force telecommunications carriers to design their networks so as not to impede authorized law enforcement surveillance requests. At the same time, CALEA's legislative history shows that Congress recognized the need to protect the privacy of communications "in the face of increasingly powerful and personally revealing technologies" (H.R. Rep. No. 103-827, 1994 U.S.C.C.A.N. 3489, 3493 (1994)) by mandating that carriers protect the privacy and security of communications and call-identifying information not authorized to be intercepted." (47 U.S.C. § 1002(a)(4)(A)). And Congress explicitly recognized the need to accomplish both of these goals without impeding innovation in the marketplace for new technologies, products, and services.

Under CALEA, a manufacturer of telecommunications transmission or switching equipment and a provider of telecommunications support services shall, on a reasonably timely basis and at a reasonable charge, make available to the telecommunications carriers using its equipment, facilities, or services such features or modifications as are necessary to permit such carriers to comply with the assistance capability requirements and the capacity requirements.

The FBI has implemented a reimbursement strategy that will allow many telecommunications carriers to receive CALEA software at no charge for certain high priority switching platforms. Under nationwide right-to-use (RTU) license agreements, the Government pays for the development of CALEA software solutions for certain high priority switching platforms. This allows carriers to receive CALEA software at a nominal charge for equipment, facilities, or services installed or deployed now and in the future.

Terrorism Risk Insurance Act

In November 2002, the federal government signed into law the Terrorism Risk Insurance Act (TRIA). In doing so, the government acknowledged the critical role insurers play in supporting the U.S. business infrastructure—the bedrock of America's economic strength and prosperity. That role consists of three primary functions:

- providing the security of instant liquidity to compensate victims, restore property and rebuild businesses in the wake of catastrophe;

- providing the capacity to continue paying existing and new claims;

- teaming up with governments and businesses to support safety, emergency preparedness and crisis management programs to prevent and manage loss.

TRIA established a financial partnership between the federal government and the insurance industry, stipulating that, in the event of future terrorist attacks, the government and the industry would share the losses according to a prescribed formula. TRIA is scheduled to expire on December 31, 2005.

Since 2002, this public-private partnership has worked precisely as intended. TRIA has stabilized insurance markets and improved the availability and affordability of insurance coverage. As a result, businesses of all kinds—and the American economy—have continued to prosper.

The solution to the terrorism threat should match the duration of the risk. Terrorism represents a continuing threat to American society. Congress has begun intense discussion about whether TRIA needs to be extended, and, if so, whether the extension should be temporary or TRIA should be transformed into a long-term program. Liberty Mutual has engaged policymakers and business leaders from a wide spectrum of public and private organizations in an effort to create an enduring solution.

The urgency of the TRIA discussions is highlighted in a recent report issued by the RAND Center for Terrorism Risk Management Policy. "Trends in Terrorism: Threats to the United States and the Future of the Terrorism Risk Insurance Act" presents a forceful argument that TRIA be both extended and reformed. The report specifically recommends that Congress "expand and improve the financial protections offered by TRIA, instead of allowing the law to expire as scheduled in December."

As summarized in a September 2004 report, "The Economic Effects of Federal Participation in Terrorism Risk," TRIA's expiration would have a profound and damaging effect on the nation with consequences rippling through the country's business infrastructure and economy. Because the need for terrorism protection exceeds the insurance industry's capacity, there may be affordability and availability problems as insurers restrict the promises they make to match their ability to deliver. Such restrictions fall into two categories:

- Insurers will adopt terrorism exclusions or other coverage limitations on the policies they offer to reduce potential losses to a level they can manage.

- Where coverage restrictions are not permitted [and especially for workers compensation insurance, where coverage is defined by state law and must be provided without exclusion or policy limit], insurers will limit the volume of policies they write to ensure that potential losses in a given geographic area, or for individual locations with unusually high exposures, will not exceed their ability to pay.

KEY CONCEPTS

- Several acts have been introduced to fight terrorism and further protect the U.S. from future attacks. Laws that have been in place for many years have also been repealed and modified to reflect the current situation and concentration on terrorism as a major national threat.

- The USA PATRIOT Act (Uniting and Strengthening America by Providing Appropriate Tools to Intercept and Obstruct Terrorism Act) gives federal officials greater authority to track and intercept communications, seeks to combat corruption of financial institutions for foreign money laundering purposes, seeks to close the borders and detain and remove foreign terrorists within the borders, and creates new crimes, penalties, and procedures against domestic and international terrorists.

- The Foreign Intelligence Surveillance Act of 1978 outlines guidelines for foreign intelligence surveillance and was originally intended for counterintelligence, although it was amended in 1994 to also include security investigations. It established a special court (the Foreign Intelligence Surveillance Court) to review applications for authorization of electronic surveillance for foreign intelligence investigations. FISA was additionally amended and its requirements for use were lowered in the USA PATRIOT Act.

- The Communications Assistance for Law Enforcement Act (CALEA) was passed in 1994 to force telephone companies to redesign their networks and regulated data traveling over the internet to make surveillance by for law enforcement much easier. Congress wanted to ensure that telecommunications carriers would not design their networks in a way that would impeded authorized law enforcement surveillance requests.

- The Terrorism Risk Insurance Act of 2002 provided a financial partnership between the federal government and the insurance industry, so that in case of future terror attacks, the government and insurance industry would share the losses. Since its passage, insurance markets have stabilized and there has been an improvement n the availability and affordability of insurance coverage.

ADDITIONAL READINGS

The Homeland Security Act of 2002

USA PATRIOT Act (Uniting and Strengthening America by Providing the Appropriate Tools to Intercept and Obstruct Terrorism Act)

SAFETY Act (Support Anti-Terrorism by Fostering Effective Technologies Act of 2002)

Communications Assistance for Law Enforcement Act (CALEA)

Freedom of Information Act (FOIA)

Terrorism Risk Insurance Act

International Emergency Economic Powers Act

Foreign Intelligence Surveillance Act (FISA)

Omnibus Crime Control and Safe Streets Act of 1968

Immigration and Nationality Act

DNA Analysis Backlog Elimination Act of 2000

Victims of Crime Act of 1984

Teitelbaum, L. (2005). *The Impact of the Information Revolution on Policymakers' Use of Intelligence Analysis.* Arlington, VA: Pardee Rand Graduate School.

RELATED WEBSITES

U.S. Secret Service www.secretservice.gov

Bureau of Transportation Statistics (BTS) www.bts.gov

Department of Justice (DOJ) www.usdoj.gov

Chapter 14

The Future: Critical Issues in Homeland Security

INTRODUCTION

In looking back at the warnings that preceded the 9/11 attacks perhaps it is difficult to understand how an organization like al Qaeda could plan and mount an attack that took years to implement and do so without raising significant concerns among intelligence agencies, government organizations and political leaders. There is ample evidence to indicate that there were those who saw and identified a threat, but their numbers were few and the lack of consensus among different groups certainly contributed to the surprise attacks.

The problem, of course, was compounded by interagency rivalries, incoherent threat analysis, an unsuspecting and ill-informed public, and the recognition that in American culture the country is generally more attuned to solving problems after they become problems.

In an open and democratic society operating under the rule of law there are also a great many restrictions on the ability of the intelligence and criminal justice community. Nevertheless, one should recognize that terrorism can also thrive in autocratic and despotic regimes, as well as in democracies.

The book has focused largely on international terrorist threats, particularly from the Middle East. One should recognize that domestic threats and local groups should not be overlooked. Single issue movements, hate groups, and religious extremists all represent significant threats.

Homeland security depends on a number of basic foundations, including public awareness, political support, effective intelligence, an effective legal system, and well trained and equipped personnel who serve on the front lines of America's defense. These include:

Law enforcement
The judiciary
The correctional system
Fire and bomb service

The health care system
The National Guard and military
The private sector
    The business and corporate sector
    Volunteer Groups

PREMPTIVE PLANNING

Prior to and following the 9/11 attacks, the government addressed terrorist threats from a disparate point of view. Despite reorganization and consolidation and the development of the National Counterterrorism Center (NCTC) in Virginia, which brings individuals from approximately 13 agencies under one roof, there continues to be factions that hamper a fully effective model for counterterrorism.

Having noted the deficiencies in our defensive measures it is also important to note that great progress has been made at federal and state levels, with local levels of the security apparatus still relatively far behind.

This should not be surprising given the recognition that target opportunities abound for those who would seek to commit violent acts designed to make a "statement."

Given the vulnerability of America how does one plan to prevent or protect targets. Among the targets of terrorism are:

Facilities
Infrastructure
Transportation
Vital Resources (Food and Water)
People
    Population Centers
    Individuals
    Target groups (police, military, politicians, judges, and individuals targeted by special interest groups)
Communications
Technology Systems (computers, telecommunications,

Planning needs to involve threat assessments, which means identifying those targets that have varying degrees of vulnerability, and the risk assessment (cost, involved facilities) associated with each one.

Further analysis will involve the costs associated with protecting targets, as well as analyzing various types of protective strategies.

Costs involve personnel, technology, and target hardening. The use of personnel is generally the most costly, wherein technology, such as intrusion devices and closed circuit TV monitoring is generally more efficient. Target hardening costs may vary considerably, but may also have long-term savings—these include barriers, entry protection, alarms, and design strategies.

Today, the private security industry has become a multi-billion dollar enterprise, and there are more private security guards in the country than police officers. Most are relatively low paid and poorly trained.

Planning should be an ongoing component of every organization and bureaucratic structure, in both the public and private sector. The National Response Plan (NRP) of the federal government is designed to provide a national level response to major crises, including natural disasters, terrorism and health care threats. Statewide efforts have been implanted to include more effective reporting capabilities, the incorporation of statewide plans, and provide a rapid response by governmental and private support agencies.

Among the key components of the plan are more broadly defined guidelines for defining any event that presents a severe hazard to people, the infrastructure, or security of the country. These include accidents (such as explosions, utility failures; civil or political incidents (such as riots), terrorist or criminal incidents (such as the Washington, DC sniper attacks; major events (such as sports or Olympic events or conferences). The NRP places great emphasis on public awareness, prevention, and preparedness. Response by government agencies includes the measures necessary for recovery. The responsibilities of the Department of Homeland Security and its relationship to other federal agencies in responding to an incident is an important part of the plan. Among the key operational components are: Information and intelligence; terrorism preparedness; counterterrorism, transportation and border security; infrastructure protection, weapons of mass destruction; and emergency management issues.

INTELLIGENCE

The backbone of any approach to combat terrorism is the intelligence function. Generally when one thinks of the intelligence function the Central Intelligence Agency (CIA) and other organs of the federal government come to mind. Certainly at the highest levels of government these agencies—as noted in Chapter 4—play a critical role.

But, the effectiveness of any intelligence function depends in large measure on the resources on the front lines that provide the information that becomes intelligence. At the local level police, and to some degree the citizenry, must be aware of their surroundings and what may be suspicious.

The human resources of other agencies serve as yet another level of collection. So-called three-letter agencies such as the FBI, DEA, ATF, and ICE also have access to potential sources of information.

On other levels electronic surveillance and other forms of technology have become important, as well as controversial, methods in the war on terrorism.

Presidential Power

Should the president have the right to use electronic surveillance to monitor communications of American citizens who may possibly be suspects in a terrorism investigation?

In 2005 and 2006 the New York Times revealed that President Bush had authorized the National Security Agency (NSA) to intercept international communications of U.S. citizens without following the protocol outlined in Foreign Intelligence Surveillance Act (FISA). The matter was the subject of Congressional hearings and, at the time of publication, there was no resolution to the issue.

In a poll conducted by USA Today/CNN/Gallup Poll that in January 2006, over half the sample did not agree with President Bush's use of wiretapping phone conversations of American citizens. The survey, which asked 506 participants if they thought the Bush administration was right or wrong in wiretapping telephone conversations between U.S. citizens and suspected terrorists in other countries without getting a court order, found that 51% of those polled thought the Bush administration actions were wrong, 46% thought the actions were right, and 3% had no opinion.*

Should a President have this power to electronically intercept communications that appear suspicious?

* USA Today/CNN/Gallup Poll conducted interviews with 1,006 adults aged 18 and older between January 20-22, 2006, and asked questions about a variety of political issues.

Figure 14.1 The Intelligence Cycle

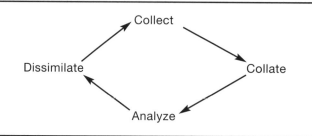

One of the major deficiencies in the intelligence community is a lack of trained analysts. The 9/11 Commission cited the need for intelligence analysts.

> The FBI had little appreciation for the role of analysis. Analysts continued to be used primarily in a tactical fashion- providing support for existing cases. Compounding the problem was the FBI's tradition of hiring analysts from within instead of recruiting individuals with the relevant educational background and expertise.[1]

The foundation of a counterterrorism strategy begins with intelligence, and the strides taken to consolidate and improve the intelligence function represent an important first step in the country's efforts top protect the citizenry. Because the threat of foreign influences and connections, whether they are from al Qaeda or other groups, will continue to be an important consideration. The diplomatic and intelligence communities must also strengthen the relationships with other nations. This effort will require a major effort to reintroduce the importance of language/instruction into college and university curricula. Diplomats and intelligence professionals who do not speak the language of the countries in which they operate is a major drawback to developing contacts and gathering information, but also in helping to better understand the cultures and legal systems of other nations.

In many ways the intelligence function of the United States has come to depend largely on various forms of technology, particularly satellite and photography imaging. These are extremely important, but the failure of such efforts in Iraq where numerous countries concluded that Saddam Hussein had a nuclear and WMD capability, clearly demonstrated the need for human intelligence, known as HUMINT. The intelligence community's reliance on information from dissidents proved to be weak at best.

As the techniques and technology available to future terrorist groups and rogue nations increases the threat will grow. This will also be true of domestic violent groups who have access to and knowledge of weapons of mass destruction. The anthrax attacks in 2001 are only one example of the chaos that can arise from such an attack.[2] The bombing of the federal building in Oklahoma City in 1995, and the World Trade Center bombing in 1993 are also examples of how relatively easy obtainable fertilizer (ammonium nitrate) could be used to inflict mass casualties. To assume that future terrorists will not utilize new methods, new forms of weapons, and new tactics is a mistake. With this in mind, the intelligence community must recognize the importance of research and surveillance (awareness) of new types of threats.

WEAPONS OF MASS DESTRUCTION

Nuclear, biological and chemical threats (NBC) have become important areas of concern to the government because of their capability to cause massive harm to large numbers of citizens and create chaos in a community. The threat of radiological terrorism, added to the WMD list represents yet another concern because small amounts of highly radioactive materials placed in a radiological explosive device (RDD) has the capacity kill or injure hundreds if not thousands of persons. In May, 2002, an al Qaeda suspect was arrested in an effort to detonate an RDD in an American city, and materials confiscated in Afghanistan from an al Qaeda site included a diagram if an RDD.

The use or threat by terrorist groups to employ weapons of mass destruction has gone beyond mere speculation, and there are numerous instances throughout the world of cases in which chemical, biological, radiological and nuclear attacks are on record. Although cases in the United States have been relatively rare, some experts believe that it is only a matter of time before the threat will become a reality.

Future efforts will increasingly focus on the importance of an informed public, the control and monitoring of plants and factories which produce materials, facilities protection, and a proactive intelligence capability. To some degree the privacy rights of individuals must be weighed against the ability of the intelligence community and law enforcement to conduct surveillance and open investigations of suspicious activities. This is no simple matter, and the debate over this issue will continue to be an important consideration in a free society.

Dr. David Carter, in *Law Enforcement Intelligence: A Guide for State, Local and Tribal Law Enforcement Agencies*, stresses the importance of new initiatives in the intelligence community. They include:

- Development of the FBI Intelligence program with a new emphasis on intelligence requirements and products.

- Development of new FBI counterterrorism initiatives and programs.

- New intelligence products from the Department of Homeland Security (DHS), as well as a substantive input role of raw information into the DHS intelligence cycle by state, local and tribal law enforcement agencies.

- Expansion and articulation of the Intelligence-Led Policing concept.

- Implementation of the National Criminal Intelligence Sharing Plan.

- Creation of a wide variety of initiatives and standards as a result of the Global Intelligence Working Group (GIWG) of the Global Justice Information Sharing Initiative.

- Renewed vigor toward the adoption 28 CFR Part 23, *Guidelines for Criminal Intelligence Records Systems*, by law enforcement agencies that are not required to adhere to the regulation.

- Secure connections for email exchange, acces to advisories, reports, reports, and information exchange, as well as integration and streamlining the use of Law Enforcement Online (LEO), Regional Information Sharing Systems' RISS.net, and creation of the Anti-Terrorism Information Exchange (ATIX).

- New operational expectations and training opportunities for intelligence analysts, law enforcement executives, managers and line officers.

WMD Threats

Chemical threats can range from individual poisonings to mass casualty attacks against chemical facilities or transports that contain industrial chemicals.

Biological terrorism threats can range from individual poisonings using well-known, potent toxins to mass casualty incidents involving aerosol dissemination of highly lethal bacteria or viruses.

Radiological terrorism threats can range from exposing individuals to small, highly radioactive materials to widely dispersing significant amounts of radioactive materials through an explosive radiological dispersal device (RDD).

Nuclear terrorism threats can range from attacks on nuclear power plants and associated facilities to the detonation of an improvised nuclear device (IND) or a nuclear weapon.

TERRORIST THREATS

A terrorist matrix of future threats involves both international and domestic groups, many of which are likely to emerge in a rapidly changing world. American supremacy and global involvement makes the country a likely target for those who see terrorism as an effective means to address political, religious, hate, and single-issue grievances. A rapidly emerging form of terrorist violence has become apparent in the area of organized crime, where drugs, human trafficking, and other forms of criminal activity are supported by using terrorist tactics (i.e., bombing, armed assault, arson, hijacking, weapons of mass destruction). Additionally, the growing number of conflicts in other countries, where terrorist groups are operating, has the capability to spill over into the United States, and American interests and global corporations continue to be targets overseas.

As America's global reach increases—through business, tourism, and deployment of military and economic aid to countries threatened with conflict—the likelihood of terrorist attacks on the country's interests will also expand. Attacks on international corporations, government officials, and citizens visiting and living abroad will increase. American embassies in many parts of the world have become nothing short of fortresses, and corporations considering or involved in international trade must consider the terrorist threat in their planning. Many large corporations have expanded their security operations, and security guidelines for executives are now an important aspect of travel briefings.

Today there are no fewer than 200 well-established terrorist groups operating in countries throughout the world. Although most focus on domestic issues within their countries American citizens have become the focus of kidnapping and other forms of violence, either to raise funds through ransom or to impact U.S. support of friendly nations. The problem is compounded by a growing number of "splinter" groups or emerging "cells" who target American interests.

The international threat is not limited to actions in other countries, and attacks within the United States, by international based groups, is not limited to al Qaeda and other radical Middle Eastern groups. Historically, the U.S. has been targeted by terrorist organizations with real or imagined grievances, such as the Puerto Rican independence movement, and South American revolutionaries wanting to discourage involvement in support of their country.

The United states is also a major source of funding for terrorism, through fund-raising and immigrant support of a cause. The Irish Republican Army (IRA), Hamas, and the Tamils of Sri Lanka are but a few of the groups that draw upon expatriate sympathizers for support. Conflict between immigrant groups living within the United States has also resulted in violence.

The war on al Qaeda and other like minded terrorist groups in the middle east has grown today into a global conflict in which attacks on other countries—some supporting the war in Iraq—has resulted in an international recognition that cooperation and the sharing of information and intelligence is critical. The global reach of violent groups has become a serious threat because internet and telecommunications innovations have made it easier for groups and individuals to communicate. The following acts of terrorism provide examples of the global reach of the terrorist movement:

- On October 12, 2002, 202 people were killed and more than 300 were injured on the island of Bali in Indonesia. Two bombs were detonated in the busy nightclub area in the Kuta district, which was popular among many foreign tourists.

- On February 6, 2004, 39 were killed and more than 100 injured when a bomb exploded on a train during morning rush hour in Moscow, Russia.

- On March 11, 2004, 192 people were killed and more than 1,400 injured when 10 bombs were detonated on four trains at three Madrid, Spain train stations during the morning rush hour.

- On September 1, 2004, more than 1,200 people were held hostage in a Russian middle school in the Caucasus republic of North Ossetia, close to the Chechnya border, by armed terrorists. After the hostage situation ended 52 hours later amidst an explosion and gunfire, approximately 340 were killed and more than 700 injured, with most of the victims children.

- On September 9, 2004, a bomb exploded outside the Australian embassy in Jakarta, Indonesia. Ten people were killed and more than 160 were injured.

- On July 7, 2005, four suicide bombers struck the London transit system and 52 people were killed and more than 700 injured. Three of the bombs were detonated simultaneously on separate underground trains, and the fourth exploded about an hour later on a double-decker bus.

Islamic Extremists

In many ways the al Qaeda movement has "morphed" into a new form of warfare that knows no boundaries, characterized by a loose network of radical fundamentalist terrorist groups operating independently with the common goals of converting all nations into Muslim nations and removing all non-Muslim influences from society. The modern "jihad," as described by Radical Islamists and media personnel as the "holy war" against all non-Muslims, has resulted in many violent attacks, including the attacks on September 11, 2001 and the numerous suicide bombings in the Middle East. Jihad, in its origins in the Quran, describes the spiritual struggle that Muslims must face both internally and externally to fulfill that Muslims must deal with at every aspect of their life, and does not mention a violent approach to attaining this goal. Instead, it has been compared to the inner spiritual journey and evangelization practiced by many Christians in the Western world. Much like some Christians take their beliefs to extreme levels (such as violent anti-abortion groups and white Aryan churches that base their beliefs on the Bible), some Islamists take their beliefs to the extreme and attribute their behavior to teachings of the Quran.

The radical extremist Moslem movement, that bears no real resemblance to the teachings of Islam, represents a relatively small number of followers in most countries where terrorism exists. In democratic countries, such as the United States and England, the cell structure of such groups has proven to be difficult to investigate. The international connections and communication among these cells have been hampered by more effective investigative methods, but it should be recognized that the vulnerability of democratic countries makes future attacks likely. Radical Islamists view Western countries that participate in democracy as threats to their Muslim ideologies.

The Domestic Threat

Within the borders of America, a broad range of so-called single-issue groups, as well as violent hate groups represent an ongoing area of concern.

Race and religious hatred will continue to spawn small groups of individuals bent on violence. The emerging threat by individuals protesting the global economic system; an increasing number of violent criminal groups who use terror to threaten communities; and disenchanted or disenfranchised individuals bent on reform through violence represent a continuing concern in the future.

The vulnerability of a free society is apparent to anyone who watches television or who has access to a variety of weapons. In the United States arson, bombings and shootings have become commonplace. Although most incidents do not involve political issues today they do serve as a blueprint for those bent on venting grievances, and as individuals become groups the likelihood of terrorism increases.

The risk of terrorist acts by domestic extremists is growing and U.S. citizens, particularly law enforcement officers, are much more likely to come into contact with a domestic terrorist than an international terrorist. In recent years, there has been a focus on domestic extremists by the law enforcement community. Additional training for responding to these groups and individuals has been implemented in many police departments; it is not known how many attempted attacks have been thwarted by this additional training.

RESPONSES TO TERRORIST ATTACKS AND OTHER DISASTERS

First Responders

Despite a major increase in domestic security few would disagree with the premise that terrorism will be a major area of concern well into this century. The United States will likely experience a continuing use of violence in a variety of forms, with bombings being the most prevalent tactic of extremists. Where intelligence and investigations fail the burden of responding to such attacks will fall largely upon first responders: police, medical, emergency, social service, and aid workers.

The role of Homeland Security in responding to natural disasters and other emergencies place an even greater burden on the new organization. Here again, first responders must be called upon to handle the bulk of the work during a disaster. In facing an uncertain future, the importance of combined training, interoperability of planning and communications, and the development of flexible responses to different types of emergencies must be a high priority. Much has been done to address mistakes of the past, but much also remains to be addressed.

First responders should be familiar with their responsibilities in terrorist attacks or other emergency situations. The Department of Homeland Security published the National Response Plan in December 2004 in an attempt to provide an effective resource for the coordination of all first responders. The broad area of first responders make up several sectors of the nation's industry: federal, state, local, tribal, nongovernmental, and the private sector.

In many respects most states are ill-equipped to cope with massive emergencies, particularly with regard to weapons of mass destruction, or multiple attacks such as those that occurred on 9/11. Oddly enough, the natural disasters resulting from hurricanes Katrina and Rita displayed what can happen as a result of massive panic by the public, and the inability of first responders to handle all of the emergency situations that are occurring simultaneously. Of particular importance is the need for command and control centers, staffed with well-trained personnel who are well equipped with interoperable communications systems and preplanned operations plans.

First responders may be tasked to handle difficult situations, and the success of their efforts will depend largely upon the availability of the equipment, tools, and protective equipment necessary to handle different types of emergencies. Realistically, it will be difficult or impossible to pre-plan or pre-position equipment for every type of potential emergency, but experience has shown that adequate training of first responders can help reduce loss of life. The heroic efforts of police, firefighters, medical personnel, and citizen volunteers during the 9/11 attacks in New York and Washington, DC are testimony to the dedication of the American people during a major crisis.

Of particular concern during a major emergency is the role that the media plays in informing the public, and command and control centers must recognize the importance of maintaining links with media outlets. Accurate and timely reporting is critical, and the media should be a part of planning efforts, which should include telecommunication and technology links with the media. Early and accurate reporting can help reduce panic, and serve to advise the public of actions that should be taken—such as evacuation routes, emergency medical locations, and individual protection.

One of the many lessons learned in past emergencies is the importance of providing assistance and information to the families of first responders. Experience has shown that families left alone during a crisis can have a devastating impact upon emergency service personnel, whose natural concern for their families, and the uncertainty of their safety adds to emotional and psychological stress. Planning and educational programs can help alleviate the problems associated with crises.

THE AFTERMATH OF DISASTER

In the aftermath of a terrorist attack or natural disaster confusion, disorientation and panic can also contribute to the failure of rescue efforts and efforts to the restore order. In addition to the importance of providing information through the media, planning should include the possible use of mutual aid assistance from surrounding communities. The 9/11 attacks in New York City saw a vigorous response from law enforcement and fire departments from as far away as California. Neighboring communities dispatched vehicles and personnel to assist, and an orderly restoration of security and personal safety took place over the several weeks following the attacks.

Unfortunately, this was not the case during Hurricane Katrina, and it was weeks before the crisis was brought under control. The deployment of National Guard and military assistance was delayed by confusion and uncertainty, resulting in many deaths that might have been prevented. A breakdown in law and order further complicated the situation, and it would be months before some semblance of order was restored. Nevertheless, the Herculean efforts of many of those who responded to the crisis should not be overlooked. Although too many lives were lost, a great many more people were saved by military, police, fire and medical personnel who responded from throughout the country.

In many ways Katrina and Rita were "wakeup" calls to the need for much more effective planning in the event of a major disaster. How the country will respond to future threats, be they natural or man-made, will depend largely on the lessons learned in Louisiana and New York.

Key components of actions in the aftermath of a disaster involve both the public and private sector. The emotional and psychological stress that accompanies a natural disaster, a terrorist attack or pandemic disease threat goes far beyond the geographic area of the occurrence—impacting the citizenry and the body politic. The 9/11 attacks resulted in a reorganization of government, the implantation of new laws, and the recognition that the country is still not prepared for major attacks on American soil, or to protect U.S. interests abroad. The natural disasters of 2005 provided further evidence of the importance of developing an effective, comprehensive plan for homeland security in the decades ahead.

FACING THE FUTURE

Few people would argue with the proposition that terrorism will continue to be a major threat in the future, or that natural disasters will occur. How the country prepares for such uncertainties will depend upon a great many factors, not the least of which is the spirit of Americans to overcome crises, and step up to the challenges of uncertainty. Throughout the history of the country America has met and withstood a great many challenges to security—from its founding, through wars, economic crises, civil rights issues, the abolition of slavery, and both internal and external strife. The storms of uncertainty have been met largely by the willingness of the citizenry to adapt to change.

The 21st century began with a great many new challenges, not the least of which has been the threat of terrorism. As the world's so-called greatest superpower, the United States must adapt to a global environment, in which homeland security will depend largely upon a willingness to work more closely with other countries in areas of mutual concern. An isolationist or "go-it-alone" model of democracy is a greater threat to homeland security than at any time in the country's history.

At the heart of security is an informed public, a willingness to adjust our educational, economic and corporate structure, and legislative process that adheres to democratic principles and human rights. Federal, state and local entities must adapt to a strategy that emphasizes an understanding of other cultures, languages, religions, and political and legal philosophies.

Homeland security will also necessitate a paradigm shift that prepares future generations to cope with future threats, as well as future opportunities. The organizations of government and the private sector must educate and train a new generation of young people to adapt to technological, economic, transportation and global changes. In a digital age reliance on technology must be accompanied by an adherence to the principles of a democracy and the rule of law.

KEY CONCEPTS

- Homeland security depends on several basic foundations, including public awareness, political support, effective intelligence, effective legal system, and well trained and equipped personnel. The numerous local, state, and federal agencies must be able to cooperate and work together in order for homeland security to work effectively.

- Planning for future terror attacks involves identifying the intended targets of the attacks, protecting the intended targets, and addressing the costs of identifying and protecting the intended targets. The targets can be protected by personnel, target hardening, and technology initiatives.

- The Intelligence Cycle includes collection, collation, analysis, and dissimilation. All stages of the cycle must be thorough and competent in order to retrieve useful intelligence.

- There is a constant threat of terrorism by international and domestic groups that have strikingly different methodologies and ideologies. It is vital to know the characteristics and methods of groups in both categories.

- First responders will be depended on in future terrorist attacks, natural disasters, and other emergencies. It is important that they are well trained, properly equipped, and that interoperable communications is available.

ADDITIONAL READINGS

National Response Plan published by the DHS in December 2004.

Bea, K. *The National Preparedness System: Issues in the 109th Congress.* (2005). CRS Report for Congress. Congressional Research Service, The Library of Congress.

RELATED WEBSITES

Carter, David L. *Law Enforcement Intelligence: A Guide for Satte, Local and Tribal Law Enforcement Agencies.* U.S. Department of Justice Office of Community Oriented Policing Services. Available online at www.cops.usdoj.gov

Department of Homeland Security, www.dhs.gov

REFERENCES

Carter, David L. *Law Enforcement Intelligence: A Guide for Satte, Local and Tribal Law Enforcement Agencies.* U.S. Department of Justice Office of Community Oriented Policing Services. (November, 2004)

NOTES

[1] 9/11 Commission Report Page 77.

[2] In October 2001, seven envelopes containing what has been termed "weapons grade anthrax" was mailed to ABC News, CBS News, NBC News, and the *New York Post* headquarters in New York City and senators Tom Daschle (D- South Dakota) and Patrick Leahy (D- Vermont). This incident resulted in the deaths of 5 persons and a major disruption in mail service throughout the country.

Appendices

Appendix 1

Selected Commission Recommendations

National Advisory Commission on Civil Disorders (Kerner Report – 1968)

- Community Response

    ○ Establish comprehensive grievance-response mechanisms in order to bring all public agencies under public scrutiny

    ○ State and federal financial assistance for mayors and city councils to support the research, consultants, staff, and other resources needed to respond effectively to federal program initiatives.

- Police and Community

    ○ Review police operations in the ghetto to ensure proper conduct by police officers, and eliminate abrasive practices.

    ○ Provide more adequate police protection to ghetto residents to eliminate their high sense of insecurity and the belief in the existence of a dual standard of law enforcement

    ○ Establish a "Community Service Officer" program to attract ghetto youths between the ages of 17 to 21 to police work

- Control of Disorder

    ○ Develop guidelines to the use of control equipment and provide alternatives to the use of lethal weapons.

  - ○ Establish an intelligence system to provide police and other public officials with reliable information that may help to prevent the outbreak of a disorder and to institute effective control measures in the event a riot erupts.

- Damages: Repair and Condition

  - ○ Amend the Federal Disaster Act—which now applies only to natural disasters- to permit federal emergency food and medical assistance to cities during major civil disorders, and provide long-term economic assistance afterwards.

- The News Media and the Disorders

  - ○ Expand coverage of the Negro community and of race problems through permanent assignment of reporters familiar with urban and racial affairs, and through establishment of more and better links with the Negro community.

Selected Recommendations from the President's Commission on Law Enforcement and Administration of Justice (1967)

- Crime in America

  - ○ Adopt centralized procedures in each city for handling crime reports from citizens with controls to make those procedures effective.

  - ○ Separate the present Index of reported crime into 2 wholly separate parts, 1 for crimes of violence and 1 for crimes against property.

- Juvenile Delinquency and Crime

  - ○ Develop methods to provide minimum income

- Police

  - ○ Establish community relations units in departments serving substantial minority population

  - ○ Establish citizen advisory committees in minority-group neighborhoods

  - ○ Increase police salaries, especially maximums to competitive levels

  - ○ Require minimum of 400 hours of training

  - ○ Establish strong internal investigation units in all departments to maintain police integrity

- Courts
  - Unify felony and misdemeanor courts
  - Abolish or overhaul State justice of the peace and U.S. commissioner systems
  - Insure fair and visible negotiated guilty pleas

- Corrections
  - Make parole and probation supervision available for all offenders
  - Provide mandatory supervision of released offenders not paroled
  - Develop more intensive community treatment program as alternative to institutionalization

- Science and Technology
  - Permit public access to police callboxes
  - Establish single, uniform police telephone number
  - Develop police radio networks
  - Consider allocating portions of TV spectrum to police use
  - Initiate research on new fingerprint recognition system
  - Establish National Criminal Justice Statistics Center

- Research
  - Establish a National Foundation for Criminal Research

- A National Strategy
  - Establish agency or officials in every state and city responsible for planning and encouraging improvements in criminal justice

Selected Recommendations of the United States Senate Select Committee to Study Governmental Operations with Respect to Intelligence Activities Report (Church Committee – 1975)

- There is no inherent constitutional authority for the President or any intelligence agency to violate the law.

- To supplement the prohibitions in the 1947 National Security Act against the CIA exercising "police, subpoena, law enforcement powers or internal security functions," the CIA should be prohibited from conducting domestic security activities within the United States, except as specifically permitted by these recommendations.

- The CIA should not conduct electronic surveillance, unauthorized entry, or mail opening within the United States for any purpose

- The CIA should not use in experimentation on human subjects, any drug, device or procedure which is designed or intended to harm, or is reasonably likely to harm, the physical or mental health of the human subject, except with the informed written consent, witnessed by a disinterested third party, of each human subject, and in accordance with the guidelines issued by the National Cornmission for the Protection of Human Subjects for Biomedical and Behavioral Research. The jurisdiction of the Commission should be amended to include the Central Intelligence Agency and other intelligence agencies of the United States Government.

- NSA should not engage in domestic security activities. Its functions should be limited in a precisely drawn legislative charter to the collection of foreign intelligence from foreign communications

a Except as specifically provided herein, the Department of Defense should not engage in domestic security activities. Its functions, as they relate to the activities of the foreign intelligence community, should be limited in a precisely drawn legislative charter to the conduct of foreign intelligence and foreign counterintelligence activities and tactical military intelligence activities abroad, and production, analysis, and dissemination of departmental intelligence.

- No agency of the Department of Defense should conduct investigations of violations of criminal law or otherwise perform any law enforcement or domestic security functions within the United States, except on military bases or concerning military personnel, to enforce the Uniform Code of Military Justice.

- Except as provided in Recommendation 27 (below), the Department of Defense should not direct any covert technique (e.g., electronic surveillance, informants, etc.) at American civilians.

- The IRS should not, on behalf of any intelligence agency or for its own use, collect any information about the activities of Americans except for the purposes of enforcing the tax laws.

- All domestic security investigative activity, including the use of covert techniques, should be centralized within the Federal Bureau of Investigation, except those investigations by the Secret Service designed to protect the life of the President or other Secret Service protectees. Such investigations and the use of covert techniques in those investigations should be centralized within the Secret Service.

- All domestic security activities of the federal government and all other intelligence agency activities covered by the Domestic Intelligence Recommendations should be subject to Justice Department oversight to assure compliance with the Constitution and laws of the United States.

- The FBI should be permitted to investigate an American or foreigner to obtain evidence of criminal activity where there is "reasonable suspicion" that the American or foreigner has committed, is committing, or is about to commit a specific act which violates a federal statute pertaining to the domestic security.

- All non-consensual electronic surveillance, mail-opening, and unauthorized entries should be conducted only upon authority of a judicial warrant.

- Covert human sources may not be directed at an American except:

  (1.) In the course of a criminal investigation if necessary to the investigation provided that covert human sources should not be directed at an American as a part of an investigation of a committed act unless there is reasonable suspicion to believe that the American is responsible for the act and then only for the purpose of identifying the perpetrators of the act.

  (2.) If the American is the target of a full preventive intelligence investigation and the Attorney General or his designee makes a written finding that (i) he has considered and rejected less intrusive techniques; and (ii) he believes that covert human sources are necessary to obtain information for the investigation.

- Except as limited elsewhere in these recommendations or in Title III of the Omnibus Crime Control and Safe Streets Act of 1968, information obtained incidentally through an authorized covert technique about an American or a foreigner who is not the target of the covert technique can be used as the basis for any authorized domestic security investigation.

- Information previously gained by the FBI or any other intelligence agency through illegal techniques should be sealed or purged as soon as practicable.

- The Attorney General should review the internal regulations of the FBI and other intelligence agencies engaging in domestic security activities to ensure that such internal regulations are proper and adequate to protect the constitutional rights of Americans.

- The Attorney General should have ultimate responsibility for the investigation of alleged violations of law relating to the Domestic Intelligence Recommendations.

- The heads of all intelligence agencies affected by these recommendations are responsible for the prevention and detection of alleged violations of the law by, or on behalf of, their respective agencies and for the reporting to the Attorney General of all such alleged violations. Each such agency head should also assure his agency's cooperation with the Attorney General in investigations of alleged violations

- The Office of Professional Responsibility created by Attorney General Levi should be recognized in statute. The director of the office, appointed by the Attorney General, should report directly to the Attorney General or the Deputy Attorney General. The functions of the office should include:

    (a.) Serving as a central repository of reports and notifications provided the Attorney General; and

    (b.) Investigation, if requested by the Attorney General of alleged violations by intelligence agencies of statutes enacted or regulations promulgated pursuant to these recommendations.

- The Committee believes that criminal penalties should apply, where appropriate, to willful and knowing violations of statutes enacted pursuant to the Domestic Intelligence Recommendations.

Appendix 2

9/11 Hijackers

Flight 11

Mohamed Atta al Sayed

Mohamed Atta was born on September 1, 1968 in Kafr El Sheikh, Egypt. He graduated with a degree in architecture from Cairo University. From 1993 to 1999, he was a student at the Technical University of Hamburg-Harburg located in Hamburg, Germany. He pledged allegiance to al Qaeda in 1995. In 2000, the CIA placed Atta under surveillance in Germany. He entered the United States on June 3, 2000. In July, he started attending Huffman Aviation International in Venice, FL. In preparation for the attacks, Atta made "surveillance flights" on two known occasions to Las Vegas. Mohamed Atta hijacked and piloted flight 11 into the North Tower of the World Trade Center. Many government officials believe that he was the leader of the September 11 attacks. In a video made by al Qaeda terrorists, Osama bin Laden points to Atta as the leader of the attacks.

Abdulaziz al Omari

Abdulaziz al Omari was from the Asir province in Saudi Arabia. In Saudia Arabia, he was highly active in his mosque, often serving as an imam. He obtained a degree from the Iman Muhammad Ibn Saud Islamic University. Al Omari was one of the only terrorists to have a close relationship at that time outside of the al Qaeda group; he was married and had a daughter. He first traveled to the United States on June 29, 2001 to New York City. He was able to enter the United States by using the Visa Express Program (a controversial program that has since been terminated).

Satam al Suqami

Satam al Suqami was born on June 28, 1976. He was from Riyadh, Saudi Arabia. He first arrived in the United States on April 23, 2001. Al Suqami was the only hijacker of the nineteen others who did not obtain a United States form of identification

Waleed al Shehri

Waleed al Sheri was from the 'Asir province of Saudi Arabia. His date of birth is unknown, he has used dates ranging from 1974 to 1979. He worked security at the Khandahar Airport, learning about the common procedures in airline security. He came to the United States between April and June of 2001. According to captured al Qaeda terrorists, al Sheri was to convey a message from Osama bin Laden to Mohamed Atta. The message was that bin Laden would rather attack the White House than the US Congress. Sheri, like many of the hijackers, conducted "surveillance flights" on various flights from Fort Lauderdale to Boston, Boston to San Francisco, San Francisco to Las Vegas, and Las Vegas back to Fort Lauderdale. Al Sheri never received any training in how to fly a plane.

Wail al Shehri

Wail al Sheri is believed to have been born on September 1, 1968, although this date is not confirmed. On June 8, 2001, he entered the United States at Miami, FL with fellow al Qaida member, Ahmed al Haznawi.

Flight 175

Marwan al Shehhi

Marwan al Shehhi was born on May 9, 1978 in Ras al Khaimah in the United Arab Emirates. In February of 1996, he began attending a language institute in Bonn, Germany. In 1999, he moved to Hamburg, Germany where he took part in the formation of the Hamburg Cell with Mohammed Atta and Ramzi Binalshibh. In late 1999, he, along with several other future terrorists, decided to go to Chechnya to aid the Muslims in the fight against Russia. However, instead they went to Afghanistan where they met with Osama bin Laden and began training to conduct terrorist attacks. On May 29, 2001 al Shehhi enter the United States. He and Mohammed Atta attended the Huffman Aviation pilot school in Venice, Florida. Shehhi and Atta are believed to have been related. He is also suspected of being in charge of most of the funds that paid for the preparation and execution of the terrorist attacks.

Hamza al Ghamdi

Hamza al Ghamdi was from the al Bahah province in Saudi Arabia. In 2000, he may have fought amongst fellow Muslims in Chechnya against Russia. He is believed to have first entered the United States in early 2001.

Fayez Banihammad

Fayez Banihammad was from the 'Asir province of Saudi Arabia. He arrived in the United States for the first time on June 27, 2001 using the Visa Express program. He was a licensed pilot and registered as having learned to fly at the Spartan Aeronautics School in Tulsa, Oklahoma.

Ahmed al Ghamdi

Ahmed Salah al Ghamdi was from the al Bahah province of Saudi Arabia. Al Ghamdi fought alongside other Chechen Muslims against Russia in 2000. He first came to the United States on May 2, 2000 using a student visa

Mohand al Shehri

Mohand al Sheri was from the 'Asir province of Saudi Arabia. He was deeply committed to Wahhabism, it allegedly even distracted him from completing his college degree. He is believed to have first come to the United States in May of 2001.

Flight 77

Hani Hanjour

Hani Hanjour was born on August 13, 1972 in Ta'if, Saudi Arabia. Hanjour arrived in the United States, for the first time, on October 3, 1991. He studied English at the University of Arizona and Holy Names College in Oakland, California. In April of 1999, he earned his pilot's license. He frequently visited Abdussattar Shaikh's house after going to San Diego, California in December of 2000. Shaikh's house was shared with Nawaf al Hazmi and Khalid al Mihdhar. In August of 2001, Hanjour began making cross-country "surveillance flights" to test airport security

Khalid al Mihdhar

Khalid al Mihdhar was born in Mecca, Saudi Arabia. In 1995, he fought with Nawaf al Hazmi in Bosnia with the Muslims against Serbs. In 1998, he fought with Chechen Muslims against Russia. On April 7, 1999, he obtained a United States visa from the US Consulate in Jeddah, Saudi Arabia. Mihdhar first entered the United States in 2000. He left in June and stayed in Yemen until July of the following year. His decision to leave the United States was not ordered or agreed upon by al Qaida. This enraged Khalid Sheikh Mohammed to the point of removing Mihdhar from the planned attacks on September 11. However, Osama bin Laden decided that he should still take part in the assault. His location at the time, raised suspicion that he was involved in the bombing of the USS Cole on October 12, 2000; knowingly conducted by al Qaida members. When he returned in July of 2001, he used the Visa Express program to gain entry. He was the first hijacker to show connections to Osama bin Laden. Mihdhar was also one of the organizers of the attacks on September 11.

Nawaf al Hazmi

Nawaf al Hazmi was born in Mecca, Saudi Arabia. In 1995, he aided his fellow Muslims in Bosnia against Serbs. And again in 1998, he fought with Chechnya against Russia. In April of 1999, he obtained a United States visa through the US Consulate in Jeddah, Saudi Arabia. He entered the United States for the first time in 2000. The INS placed al Hazmi and al Mihdhar on a watchlist in August of 2001 to hinder their entry into the United States, but they had been in the United States for more than a year at that time. And later that month, the FBI launched a search for them. Despite the fact that al Hazmi and al Mihdhar were on the terrorist watchlist, they were still able to buy their plane tickets for flight 77. Due to lack of inter-agency communication, the FAA had not been informed of their potential threat.

Salem al Hazmi
In April of 1999, al Hazmi obtained a United States visa through the US Consulate in Jeddah, Saudi Arabia. Much later, on June 29, 2001, using the Visa Express program, he entered the United States. Al Hazmi would be considered an al Qaida veteran at the time he was chosen to take part in the terrorist attacks of September 11.

Majed Moqed
Majed Moqed was born in Annakhil, Saudi Arabia. He was reportedly recruited into al Qaida in 1999. On May 2, 2001, he first arrived in the United States.

Flight 93

Ziad Jarrah
Ziad Jarrah was born on May 11, 1975 in Mazra, Lebanon. As a child, he attended a Catholic private school in Beirut, Lebanon. He later attended college in Greifswald and Hamburg, Germany from 1996 to 1999. Jarrah became part of the plot to attack the United States while in college. In late 1999, he planned to fight with the Chechen Muslims against Russia, but he went to Afghanistan instead. There, he met with Osama bin Laden and began training for terrorist attacks. On June 27, 2000, he arrived in the United States for the first time. Jarrah attended the Florida Flight Training Center in Venice, Florida from June of 2000 to January 15, 2000. He was one of the only hijackers whom had close ties with his family, he also had a German girlfriend. Ziad Jarrah is believed to have piloted flight 93. According to his family, ever sense he was a child he wanted to be a pilot. His family, however, did not approve of his choice. In an ironic statement from his father he said, "I stopped him from being a pilot, I only have one son and I was afraid that he would crash."

Ahmed al Nami
Ahmed al Nami was born in December of 1977 in Saudi Arabia. At King Khaled University in Saudi Arabia he studies Islamic law. In a mosque there he was known to be an imam (prayer leader). According to his family,

al Nami became very religious in early 1999. On May 28, 2001, he entered the United States for the first time. When obtaining a United States driver's license, he listed the Naval Air Station in Pensacola, Florida to be his permanent address.

Ahmad al Haznawi

Ahmed al Haznawi was born on October 11, 1981. He was from the al Bahah province of Saudi Arabia. He entered the United States for the first time on June 8, 2001 with Wail al Shehri, a hijacker on flight 11. Al Haznawi was treated at Holy Cross Hospital in Fort Lauderdale, Florida for a "skin lesion." Although not confirmed by the U.S. government, many people believe that he got the lesion from cutaneous anthrax.

Saeed al Ghamdi

Saeed al Ghamdi was from the al Bahah province of Saudi Arabia. He first arrived in the United States in June of 2001 by using the Visa Express program. While living in Delray Beach, Florida, he and Ahmed al Nami were roommates. He listed the Naval Air Station in Pensacola, Florida to be his permanent address on his driver's license.

Appendix 3

Organizational Charts and Mission Statements of Selected Agencies

Bureau of Alcohol, Tobacco, Firearms, and Explosives
October 2004

The mission of the Bureau of Alcohol, Tobacco, Firearms, and Explosives is to conduct criminal investigations, regulate the firearms and explosives industries, and assist other law enforcement agencies in order to suppress and reduce violent crime as well as protect the public in a manner that is faithful to the Constitution and laws of the United States.

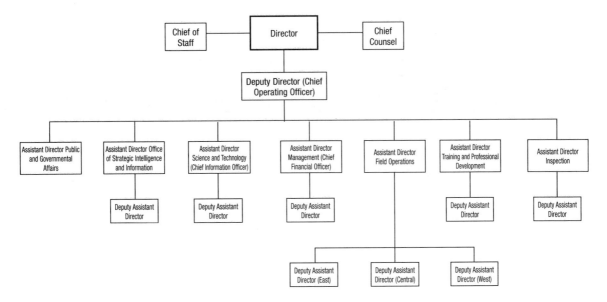

U.S. Customs and Border Protection
December 2005

The Mission Statement of Customs and Border Protection is as follows: We are the guardians of our Nation's border. We are America's frontline. We safeguard the American Homeland at and beyond our borders. We protect the American public against terrorists and the instruments of terror. We steadfastly enforce the laws of the United States while fostering our Nation's economic security through lawful international trade and travel. We serve the American public with vigilance, integrity, and professionalism.

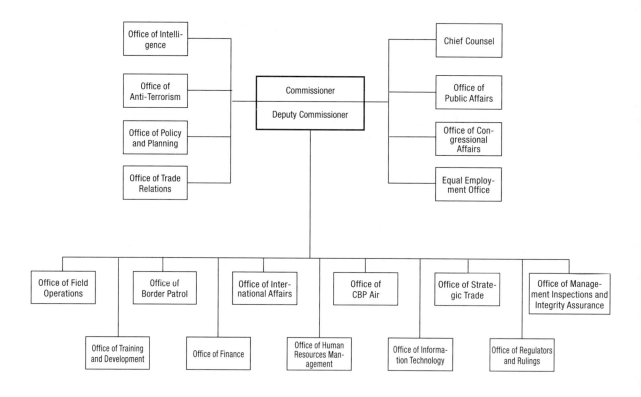

Central Intelligence Agency
November 2005

The mission of the Central Intelligence Agency is that it is the eyes and ears of the nation and at times its hidden hand. We accomplish this mission by collecting intelligence that matters; providing relevant, timely, and objective all-source analysis; and conducting covert action at the direction of the President to preempt threats or achieve United States policy objectives.

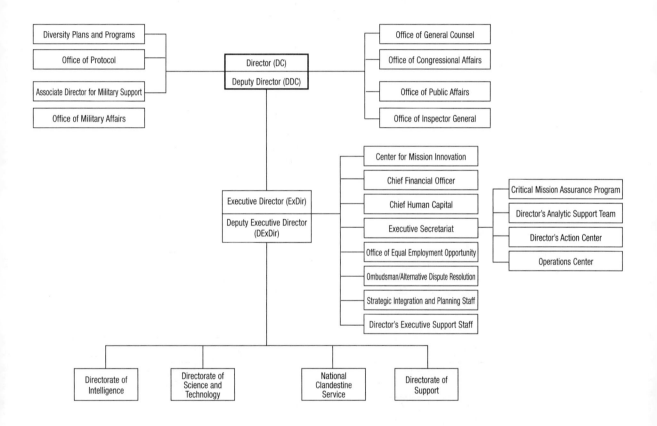

Drug Enforcement Administration
October 2004

The mission of the Drug Enforcement Administration is to enforce the controlled substance laws and regulations of the United States and bring to the criminal and civil justice system of the United States, or any other competent jurisdiction, those organizations and principal members of organizations, involved in the growing, manufacture, or distribution of controlled substances appearing in or destined for illicit traffic in the United States; and to recommend and support non-enforcement programs aimed at reducing the availability of illicit controlled substances on the domestic and international markets.

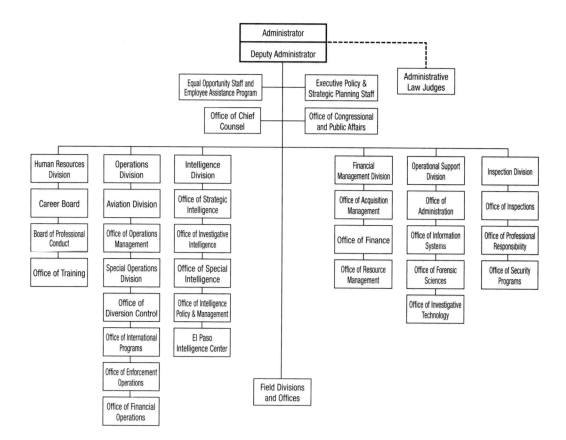

Defense Intelligence Agency
December 2005

The mission of the Defense Intelligence Agency is to provide timely, objective, and cogent military intelligence to war fighters, defense planner, and defense and national security policy makers.

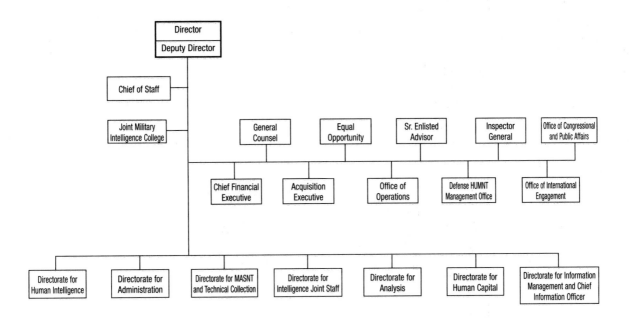

Office of Director of National Intelligence
2005

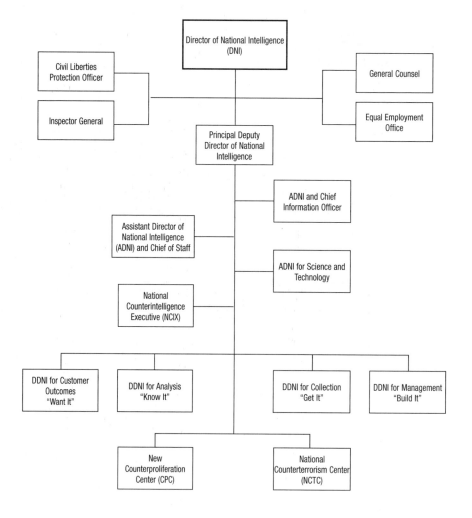

Department of Defense
March 2001

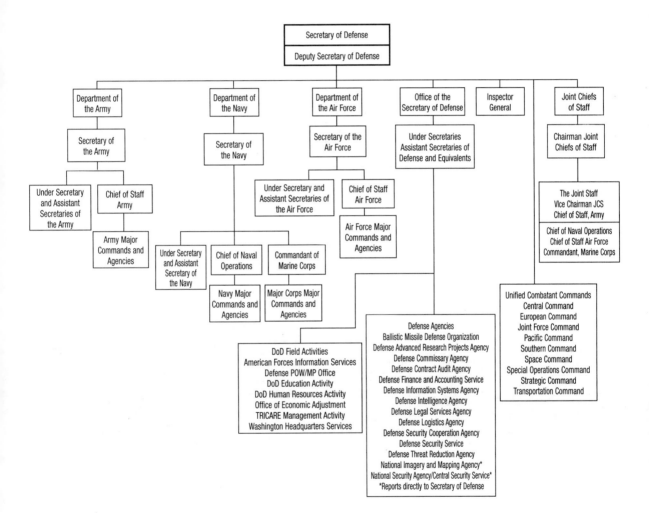

Department of Justice
August 2005

The mission of the Department of Justice is to enforce the law and defend the interests of the United States according to the law; to ensure public safety against threats foreign and domestic; to provide Federal leadership in preventing and controlling crime; to seek just punishment for those guilty of unlawful behavior; to administer and enforce the Nation's immigration laws fairly and effectively; and to ensure fair and impartial administration of justice for all Americans.

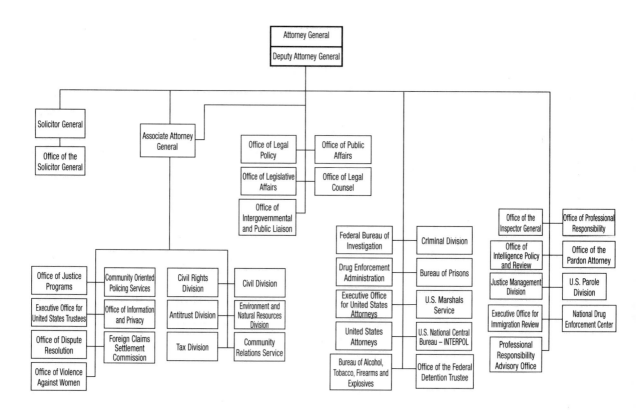

Department of Energy
October 2005

The Department of Energy's overarching mission is to advance the national, economic and energy security of the United States; to promote scientific and technological innovation is support of that mission; and to ensure the environmental cleanup of the national nuclear weapons complex.

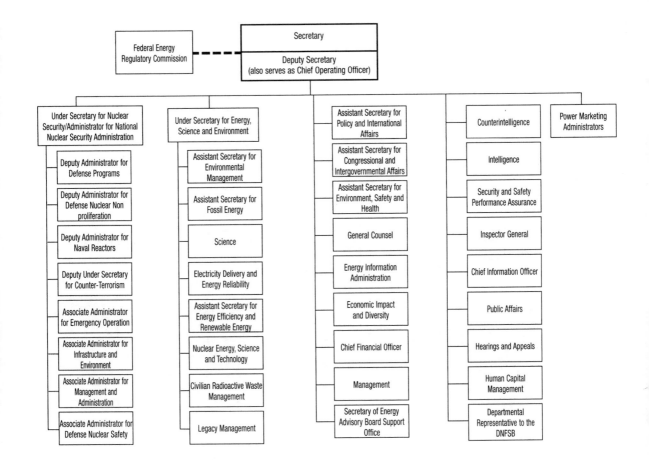

Federal Bureau of Investigation
June 2005

The mission of the Federal Bureau of Investigation is to protect and defend the United States against terrorist and foreign intelligence threats, to uphold and enforce the criminal laws of the United States, and to provide leadership and criminal justice services to federal, state, municipal, and international agencies and partners.

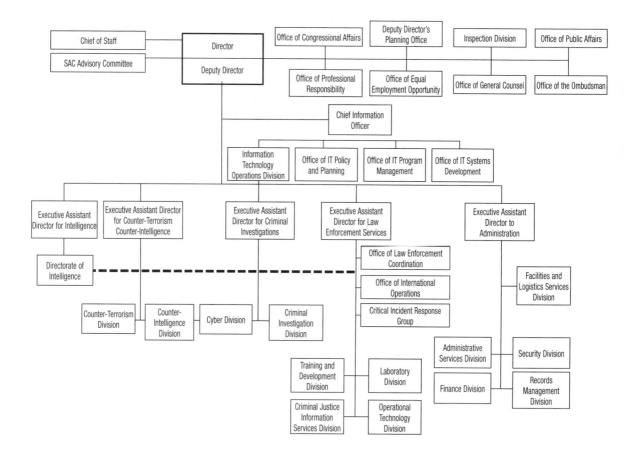

Department of Homeland Security
July 2006

The mission of the Department of Homeland Security is to lead the unified national effort to secure America. We will prevent and deter terrorist attacks and protect against and respond to threats and hazards to the nation. We will ensure safe and secure borders, welcome lawful immigrants and visitors, and promote the free-flow of commerce.

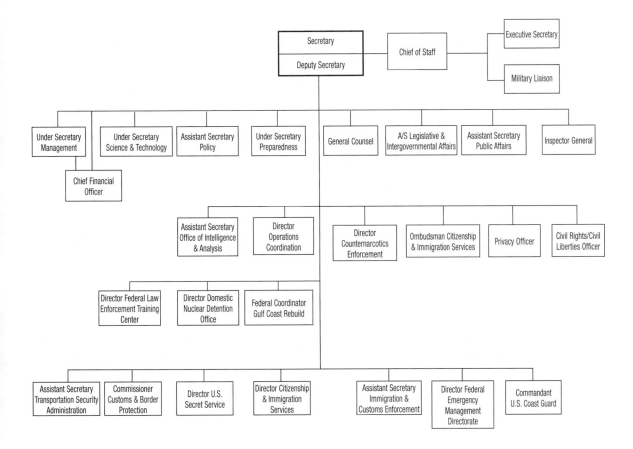

Immigration and Customs Enforcement
January 2006

The mission of Immigration and Customs Enforcement is to prevent acts of terrorism by targeting the people, money, and materials that support terrorist and criminal activities. The group is also responsible for identifying and shutting down vulnerabilities in the nation's border, economic, transportation and infrastructure security.

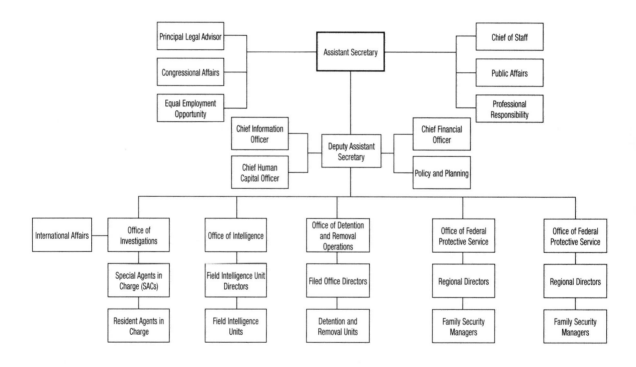

Military Departments
1999

The mission of the Navy is to maintain, train and equip combat-ready Naval forces capable of winning wars, deterring aggression and maintaining freedom of the seas.

The mission of the Air Force is to defend the United States and protect its interests through air and space power.

The mission of the Army is to fight and win our Nation's wars by providing prompt, sustained land dominance across the full range of military operations and spectrum of conflict in support of combatant commanders.

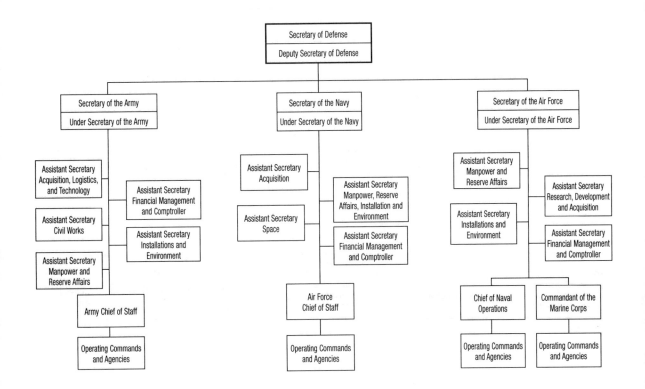

National Reconnaissance Office

The mission of the National Reconnaissance Office is to develop and operate unique and innovative space reconnaissance systems and to conduct intelligence-related activities essential for U.S. National Security.

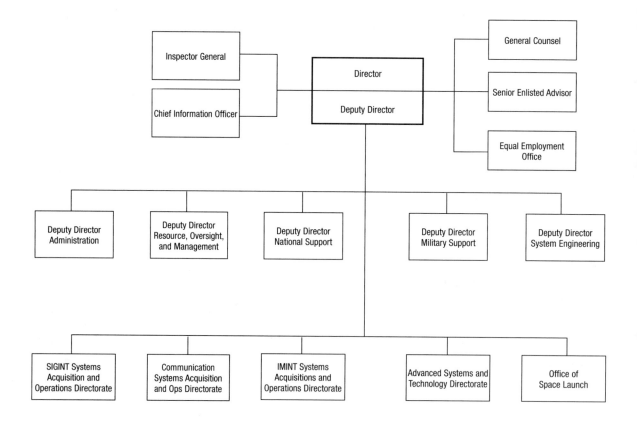

National Security Agency
1998

The mission of the National Security Agency is to provide the solutions, products, services and conducts defensive information operations to achieve information assurance for information infrastructures critical to U.S. national security interests and to provide effective, unified organization and control of all the foreign signals collection and processing activities of the United States.

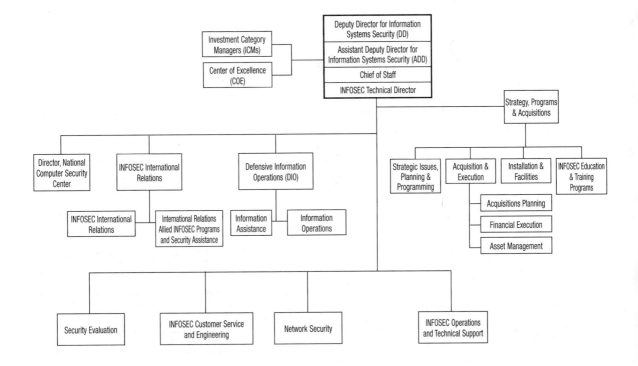

United States Postal Inspection Service

The mission of the United States Postal Inspection Service is to protect the U.S. Postal Service, its employees and its customers from criminal attack, and protect the nation's mail system from criminal misuse.

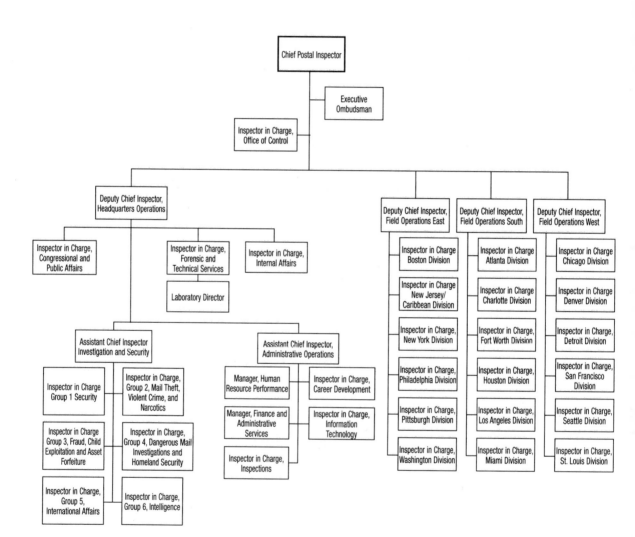

Department of State
October 2005

The mission of the Department of State is to create a more secure, democratic, and prosperous world for the benefit of the American people and the international community.

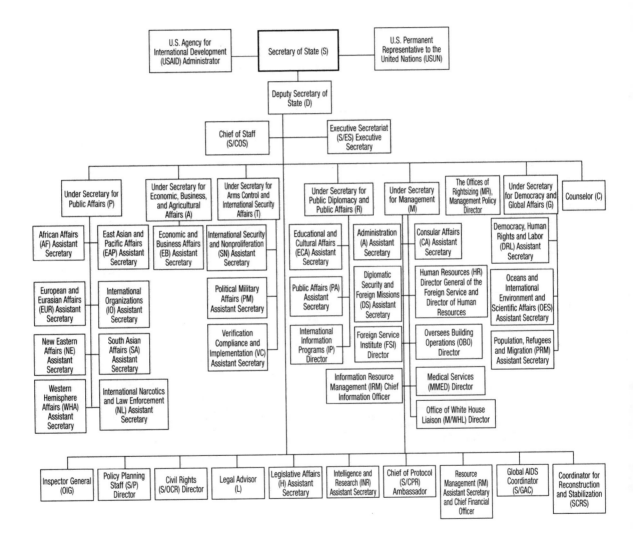

Treasury Department
December 2005

The mission of the Department of Treasury is to promote the conditions for prosperity and stability in the United States and encourage prosperity and stability in the rest of the world.

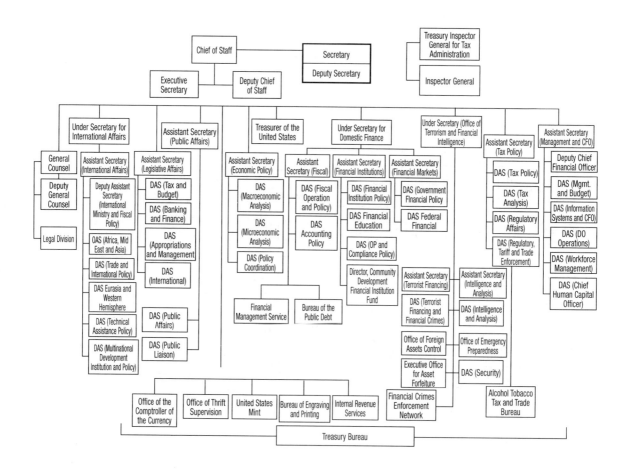

U.S. Marshals Service
September 2005

The mission of the USMS is to enforce federal laws and provide support to virtually all elements of the federal justice system by providing for the security of federal court facilities and the safety of judges and other court personnel; apprehending criminals; exercising custody of federal prisoners and providing for their security and transportation to correctional facilities; executing federal court orders; seizing assets gained by illegal means and providing for the custody, management and disposal of forfeited assets; assuring the safety of endangered government witnesses and their families; and collecting and disbursing funds.

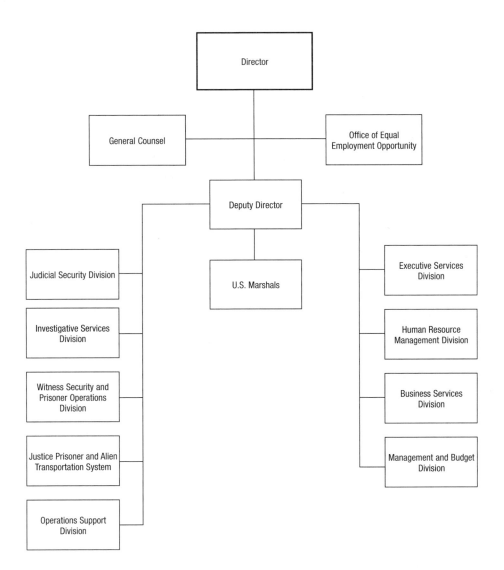

Name Index

Subject Index